EXPOSITORY THOUGHTS ON
JOHN

VOLUME 1

J. C. Ryle — a photograph taken when he was Vicar of Stradbroke, Suffolk.

EXPOSITORY THOUGHTS ON

JOHN

Volume 1

J. C. Ryle

THE BANNER OF TRUTH TRUST

THE BANNER OF TRUTH TRUST

Head Office
3 Murrayfield Road
Edinburgh, EH12 6EL
UK

North America Office
610 Alexander Spring Road
Carlisle, PA 17015
USA

banneroftruth.org

❦

First published 1869
First Banner of Truth Trust edition 1987
Reprinted 1997, 2005, 2009,
This retypeset edition (clothbound) 2012
Reprinted 2015 (clothbound), 2015 (paperback),
2020 (clothbound), 2023 (paperback), 2023 (clothbound)

© The Banner of Truth Trust 2012

❦

ISBN
Print (clothbound): 978 1 84871 132 7
Print (paperback): 978 1 84871 610 0
EPUB: 978 1 84871 213 3

Seven-volume set ISBN: 978 1 84871 136 5

❦

Typeset in 10/14 Berkeley Oldstyle Medium
at The Banner of Truth Trust, Edinburgh

Printed in the USA by
Versa Press Inc.,
East Peoria, IL.

PREFACE

I SEND forth the volume now in the reader's hands, with much diffidence, and a very deep sense of responsibility. It is no light matter to publish an exposition of any book in the Bible. It is a peculiarly serious undertaking to attempt a commentary on the Gospel of St John.

I do not forget that we are all apt to exaggerate the difficulties of our own particular department of literary labour. But I think every intelligent student of Scripture will bear me out when I say, that St John's Gospel is pre-eminently full of things 'hard to be understood' (2 *Pet.* 3:16). It contains a large portion of our Lord Jesus Christ's doctrinal teaching. It abounds in 'deep things of God,' and 'sayings of the King,' which we feel instinctively we have no line to fully fathom, no mind to fully comprehend, no words to fully explain. It must needs be that such a book of Scripture should be difficult. I can truly say that I have commented on many a verse in this Gospel with fear and trembling. I have often said to myself, 'Who is sufficient for these things?'—'The place whereon thou standest is holy ground' (2 *Cor.* 2:16; *Exod.* 3:5).

The nature of the work now published requires a few words of explanation. It is a continuation of the *Expository Thoughts on the Gospels*, of which four volumes, comprising the first three Gospels, have been already sent forth. Like the volumes on St Matthew, St Mark, and St Luke, the basis of the work is a continuous series of short expositions intended for family or private reading, or for the use of those who visit the sick and the poor. But, unlike the previous volumes, the work now in the reader's hands contains full explanatory notes on every verse of the portions expounded, forming, in fact, a complete commentary.

This 'commentary' is so extensive that it occupies far more space than the 'expository thoughts,' and is, I must honestly confess, the principal part of the work. To some it may appear far too long and full. But the circumstances of the times are my justification.[1] We live in a day of abounding vagueness and indistinctness on doctrinal subjects in religion. Now, if ever, it is the duty of all advocates of clear, well-defined, sharply-cut theology, to supply proof that their views are thoroughly borne out by Scripture. I have endeavoured to do so in this commentary. I hold that the Gospel of St John, rightly interpreted, is the best and simplest answer to those who profess to admire a vague and indistinct Christianity.

The theological standpoint which the writer of this commentary occupies will be obvious to any intelligent reader. Such a one will see at a glance that I belong to that school in the Church of England which, rightly or wrongly, is called 'Evangelical.' He will see that I have no sympathy whatever with either Romish or Neologian tendencies. He will see that I hold firmly the distinctive theological views of the Reformers and doctrinal Puritans, and that I totally disapprove the loose and broad theology of some modern schools of divines.—But while I say all this, I must be allowed to add, that in interpreting Scripture, I 'call no man master or father.' I abhor the idea of wresting and warping God's Word in order to make it support party views. Throughout this commentary I have endeavoured honestly and conscientiously to find out the real meaning of every sentence on which

[1] The expectations of Bengel, the German commentator, appear likely to be fulfilled with curious accuracy in the present day. He said, in the year A.D. 1740, 'Though Socinianism and popery at present appear mutually aloof, they will in process of time form a mighty confluence, that will burst all bounds and bring everything to a crisis. We may expect it in the following way.—The residue of heavenly influence on the professing church, as a body, will have utterly evaporated, its holy things having been already more and more prostituted to the spirit of this world. The Holy Spirit being thus withdrawn from the camp at large, the world will deem its own victory and triumph secured. Now, therefore, a spirit of liberal Latitudinarianism will prevail everywhere,—a notion that everyone may be right in his own way of thinking, and consequently that all is well with the Jew, the Turk, and the pagan. Ideas of this kind will wonderfully prepare men for embracing the false prophet.' (*Life of Bengel*, Walker's edition, page 322.) How painfully correct these prognostications, made 125 years ago, have proved, anyone who observes the state of religious feeling in England must know only too well!

I have commented. I have evaded no difficulty, and shrunk from no inference. I have simply followed Scripture wherever its words seemed to point, and accepted whatever they seemed to mean. I have never hesitated to express my disagreement from the views of other commentators if occasion required; but when I have done so I have tried to do it with courtesy and respect.

On one point of vast importance in the present day, the reader will see that I hold very decided opinions. That point is *inspiration.* I feel no hesitation in avowing, that I believe in the 'plenary inspiration' of every word of the original text of Holy Scripture. I hold not only that the Bible *contains* the Word of God, but that every jot of it was written, or brought together, by divine inspiration, and *is* the Word of God. I entirely disagree with those who maintain that the writers of the Bible were partially inspired, or inspired to such a limited extent that discrepancies, inaccuracies, and contradictions to the facts of science and history, must be expected and do exist in their writings. I utterly repudiate such a theory. I consider that it practically destroys the whole value of God's Word, puts a sword in the hand of infidels and sceptics, and raises far more serious difficulties than it pretends to solve.

I grant freely that the theory of 'plenary verbal inspiration' involves some difficulties. I do not pretend to answer all the objections brought against it, or to defend all that has been written by its supporters.[2] I am content to remember that all inspiration is a miraculous operation of the Holy Ghost, and, like every operation of the Holy Ghost, must needs be mysterious. It is an operation of which not forty men in the world have been made the subjects, and

[2] When I speak of 'plenary verbal inspiration,' I do not for a moment admit the absurd theory that all parts of the Bible are equally important. I should never dream of saying that the catalogues in Chronicles are of as much value to the church as the Gospel of St John. But I do maintain that all parts of the Bible are equally 'given by inspiration of God,' and that all are to be regarded as 'God's Word.' If we do not see the divine character of any particular part, it is because we have at present no eyes to see it. The humblest moss is as much the handiwork of God's creative power as the cedar of Lebanon. Yet it would be foolish to say it was an equally important part of creation. The least verse in the Bible is just as truly 'given by inspiration' as the greatest. But it does not follow that it is equally valuable.

the manner of which not one of the forty has described. It stands to reason that the whole question of inspiration, like everything else supernatural, must necessarily contain much that is mysterious, and much that we cannot explain.—But the difficulties of the 'plenary verbal' theory appear to me mere trifles, compared with those which surround the counter theory of 'partial inspiration.' Once admit the principle that the writers of the Bible could make mistakes, and were not in all things guided by the Spirit, and I know not where I am. I see nothing certain, nothing solid, nothing trustworthy in the foundations of my faith. A fog has descended on the Book of God, and enveloped every chapter in uncertainty! Who shall decide when the writers of Scripture made mistakes, and when they did not? How am I to know where inspiration ends, and where it begins? What I think inspired, another may think uninspired! The texts that I rest upon may possibly have been put in by a slip of the pen! The words and phrases that I love to feed upon may possibly be weak earthly expressions, in writing which the author was left to his own private uninspired mind!—The glory is departed from my Bible at this rate. A cold feeling of suspicion and doubt creeps over me as I read it. I am almost tempted to lay it down in flat despair. A partially inspired Bible is little better than no Bible at all. Give me the 'plenary verbal' theory, with all its difficulties, rather than this. I accept the difficulties of that theory, and humbly wait for their solution. But while I wait, I feel that I am standing on a rock.

I grant the existence of occasional difficulties, and apparent discrepancies, in Scripture. They are traceable, in some cases, I believe, to the errors of early transcribers; and in others to our ignorance of explanatory circumstances and minute links and details. To tell us that things *cannot* be explained, merely because *we* are not at present able to explain them, is childish and absurd! 'He that believeth shall not make haste' (*Isa.* 28:16). A true philosopher will never give up a sound theory, on account of a few difficulties. He will rather say,—'I can afford to wait. It will all be plain one day.' For my own part, I believe that the whole Bible, as it came originally from the hands of the inspired writers, was verbally perfect and without flaw. I believe that the inspired writers were infallibly guided by the Holy Ghost, both in their selection of matter and their choice of words. I believe that even now, when we cannot explain alleged difficulties in Holy Scripture, the wisest course is to blame the interpreter and not the text, to suspect our own ignorance to be in fault, and not any defect in God's Word. The theological system of modern days, which delights in magnifying the so-called mistakes of the Bible, in explaining away its miraculous narratives, and in making as little as possible of its divine character and supernatural element, is a system that I cannot away with. It seems to me to take a rock from beneath our feet, and plant us on a quicksand. It robs us of bread, and does not give us in its place so much as a stone.

Nothing to my mind, is so unutterably painful as the patronizing tone of compassion which the modern advocates of 'partial inspiration' adopt in speaking of the writers of the Bible. They write and talk as if St Paul and St John, and their companions, were nothing better than well-meaning pious men, who on some points were greatly mistaken, and far below our enlightened age! They speak with pity and contempt of that system of divinity which satisfied the master-builders and giants of the church in bygone days! They tell us complacently that a new theology is needed for our age, and that a 'freer handling' of the Bible, with pens untrammelled by the fetters which cumbered former interpreters, will produce, and is producing, wonderful results! I thoroughly distrust these new theologians, however learned and plausible they may be, and I expect the church will receive no new light from them. I see nothing solid in their arguments, and am utterly unmoved by them. I believe that the want of our age is not more 'free' handling of the Bible, but more 'reverent' handling, more humility, more patient study, and more prayer. I repeat my own firm conviction, that no theory of inspiration involves so few difficulties as that of 'plenary verbal inspiration.' To that theory I entirely adhere, and on that theory my readers will find this commentary is written.

In preparing this commentary I have made it a point of duty to look through every work on St John's Gospel, which I could meet with. I append a list of books, partly because it may be interesting and useful to some readers, and partly because I wish to show that when I differ from the authors, I have not written in ignorance of their opinions.

The commentaries and expository works on St John which I have looked through are the following:—

1. *Of Fathers.* Origen, Cyril of Alexandria, Chrysostom, Augustine, Theophylact, Euthymius, and the Catena Aurea.

2. *Of Foreign Reformers and their successors, to the close of the seventeenth century.* Melanchthon, Zwingle, Calvin, Ecolampadius, Brentius, Bucer, Bullinger, Gualter, Pellican, Flacius Illyricus, Musculus, Beza, Aretius, Chemnitius,[3] Diodati, Calovius, De Dieu, Cocceius, Gomarus, Nifanius, Heinsius, Glassius,[4] Critici Sacri.

3. *Of Roman Catholic Writers.* Rupertus, Ferus, Arias Montanus, Toletus, Barradius, Maldonatus, Cornelius à Lapide, Jansenius, Quesnel.

4. *Of Scotch and English Writers.* Rollock, Hutcheson, Poole's Synopsis and Annotations, Cartwright, Trapp, Mayer, Leigh, Lightfoot, Baxter, Hammond, Hall, Henry, Burkitt, Whitby, Pearce, Gill, Scott, Blomfield, Doddridge, A. Clarke, Barnes, Burgon, Alford, Webster, Wordsworth, J. Brown, D. Brown, Ford. To this list I may also add Arrowsmith, on John 1; Dyke, on John 2:3; Hildersam, on John 4; Trench on Miracles; and Schoettgen's *Horæ Hebraicæ.*

5. *Of German Writers, from the beginning of the eighteenth century to the present day.* Lampe, Bengel, Tittman, Tholuck, Olshausen, Stier, Besser, Hengstenberg.

---

[3] The work I here refer to is the commentary on the *Harmony of the Gospels,* begun by Chemnitius, and continued by Lyserus and Gerhard.

[4] The work of Glassius to which I here refer, is his *Expositions of the Gospels and Epistles Appointed for Sundays.* It is a collection of homilies.

Of course no man can spend years, as I have now done, in looking through this formidable mass of books, without forming some decided opinions about the comparative merits of their respective authors. Some of these opinions I have no hesitation in putting down, as they may be of use to some of my younger brethren in the ministry.

a. The Fathers appear to me greatly overrated, as commentators and expositors. Cyril and Chrysostom are far the most valuable of them, in my judgment, on St John.

b. The continental Reformers and their successors appear to me greatly underrated and neglected. Brentius and Musculus, for instance, abound in excellent thoughts and suggestions, but seem quite ignored by most modern commentators.

c. The Roman Catholic writers often contain much that is useful and little that is objectionable. Happy would it be for the Church of England if all her clergy knew their Bibles as well as such men as Ferus and Toletus!

d. The few German writers that I have consulted, appear to me to be far too highly esteemed, with the exception of Bengel and Lampe. Stier is always reverential, but tremendously diffuse. As to Olshausen, Tholuck, and Tittman, I have generally laid down their works with unmixed disappointment. What people can mean by telling us that we have much to learn from modern German writers on Scripture passes my comprehension!—I can only suppose, from my own acquaintance with them, that many say it without having read them, or without having read other expositors.

e. The Scotch and English commentators I shall pass over in silence, as most of them are well known. I must confess that I think we have little to show, in this department of theological literature. Of our old writers, Rollock, the Scotch divine, is incomparably the best. In fact, I do not know such a 'buried treasure' as his Latin commentary on St John.[5]—Of modern writers Burgon and Wordsworth strike me as two of the most valuable, though I differ widely from them on such points as the church and the sacraments. But I admire their reverential spirit.—Alford is almost always able and clear, but not always in my opinion a safe theological guide.—A thoroughly satisfactory critical commentary on the Greek Testament, in the English language, is a great *desideratum*.

I have only to add that on all points of philology, grammar, etc., I have consulted Flacius, Ravanel, Parkhurst, Leigh, Schleusner, Raphelius, Suicer, Glassius, and Winer.

The vexed question of 'various readings,' I have deliberately left alone. It is not because I have no opinion on the subject. But the real extent to which all the various readings would affect the meaning of Scripture, if they were admitted, is so much exaggerated, that it does not seem to me worthwhile to mix up the question with such a work as that which I have undertaken. The Greek text which I have been content to use throughout is that of the third edition of Stephens (1550), edited by Scholefield. I do not say for a moment that it is the best text. I only say I have used it.

The occasional shortcomings of our authorized English translation I have not hesitated to notice. I have frequently pointed out expressions which in my judgment are not rendered so literally or accurately as they might have been. There is nothing perfect on earth. Our excellent translators undoubtedly fail occasionally to give the full sense of Greek words, and are not always sufficiently careful about tenses and the article. But it is useless to expect perfection in any translation. Translators are not inspired, and are all liable to err. The 'plenary verbal inspiration' which I firmly maintain, is that of the original text of Scripture, and not of any translation.—I have no sympathy however with those who wish to have the new English version of the Bible authorized for public use in our churches. I concede

---

[5] Rollock was born A.D. 1555, and died A.D. 1598. He was Principal of the University of Edinburgh.

the shortcomings of the old version, but I doubt much whether we should gain much by throwing it aside. Taking it for all in all, the authorized English version is an admirable translation. I am quite content to 'let well alone.'

I now conclude this preface with an earnest prayer, that it may please God to pardon the many deficiencies of this work on St John's Gospel, and to use it for his own glory and the good of souls. It has cost me a large amount of time and thought and labour. But if the Holy Ghost shall make it useful to the church of Christ, I shall feel abundantly repaid.

Ignorance of Scripture is the root of every error in religion, and the source of every heresy. To be allowed to remove a few grains of ignorance, and to throw a few rays of light on God's precious Word is, in my opinion, the greatest honour that can be put on a Christian.

J. C. RYLE, M.A.,
CHRIST CHURCH, OXFORD.

P.S. I feel it due to many of my readers to offer some explanation of the long delay which has taken place since the publication of this work on St John began. An interval of almost five years has elapsed between the publication of the first four chapters and of the fifth and sixth. This delay, I am afraid, has caused inconvenience and annoyance in many quarters. For this I am unfeignedly sorry.

But the delay has been unavoidable, and has arisen from circumstances entirely beyond my own control. Deaths, domestic anxieties, illness, and change from one residence to another, have had much to do with it. The principal cause has been my removal to my present parish. The work was begun in a little quiet parish of 300 people. It has been resumed in a widely-scattered parish of 1400 people, requiring almost the whole of my attention.

Even now, in sending forth the first volume of the *Expository Thoughts on St John*, I dare not promise anything certain as to the time when the work will be completed. I have the will to finish it, but I find it almost impossible to secure the necessary leisure. What absolute need there is of entire freedom from distraction and interruption in writing a commentary, none know but those who have attempted it. What endless petty interruptions a clergyman must submit to in a poor rural parish of 1400 people, where there is no resident landlord, and no layman who has leisure, and where many things must necessarily hinge on the clergyman, no one can know unless he has filled the position.

If the great Head of the church intends me to finish this work, I believe that he will make my way plain, and remove all obstacles. But my readers must kindly make allowances for my altered position. There are but twelve hours in the day. I cannot create time. It is not one of the primary duties of a parochial clergyman's office to write commentaries. If therefore the work does not go on so fast as they could wish, they must have the goodness to consider my position, and to believe that there is a cause.

TABLE OF CONTENTS

CONTENTS

JOHN 1:1-5

1 In the beginning was the Word, and the Word was with God, and the Word was God.

2 The same was in the beginning with God.

3 All things were made by him; and without him was not any thing made that was made.

4 In him was life; and the life was the light of men.

5 And the light shineth in darkness; and the darkness comprehended it not.

THE Gospel of St John, which begins with these verses, is in many respects very unlike the other three Gospels. It contains many things which they omit. It omits many things which they contain. Good reason might easily be shown for this unlikeness. But it is enough to remember that Matthew, Mark, Luke, and John wrote under the direct inspiration of God. In the general plan of their respective Gospels, and in the particular details,—in everything that they record, and in everything that they do not record,—they were all four equally and entirely guided by the Holy Ghost.

About the matters which St John was specially inspired to relate in his Gospel, one general remark will suffice. The things which are peculiar to his Gospel are among the most precious possessions of the church of Christ. No one of the four Gospel writers has given us such full statements about the divinity of Christ,—about justification by faith,—about the offices of Christ,—about the work of the Holy Ghost,—and about the privileges of believers, as we read in the pages of St John. On none of these great subjects, undoubtedly, have Matthew, Mark, and Luke been silent. But in St John's Gospel, they stand out prominently on the surface, so that he who runs may read.

The five verses now before us contain a statement of matchless sublimity concerning the divine nature of our Lord Jesus Christ. He it is, beyond all question, whom St John means, when he speaks of 'the Word.' No doubt there are heights and depths in that statement which are far beyond man's understanding. And yet there are plain lessons in it, which every Christian would do well to treasure up in his mind.

1

We learn, firstly, that our Lord Jesus Christ is *eternal*. St John tells us that 'in the beginning was the Word.' He did not begin to exist when the heavens and the earth were made. Much less did he begin to exist when the gospel was brought into the world. He had glory with the Father 'before the world was' (*John* 17:5). He was existing when matter was first created, and before time began. He was 'before all things' (*Col.* 1:17). He was from all eternity.

We learn, secondly, that our Lord Jesus Christ is *a person distinct from God the Father, and yet one with him*. St John tells us that 'the Word was with God.' The Father and the Word, though two persons, are joined by an ineffable union. Where God the Father was from all eternity, there also was the Word, even God the Son,—their glory equal, their majesty co-eternal, and yet their Godhead one. This is a great mystery! Happy is he who can receive it as a little child, without attempting to explain it.

We learn, thirdly, that the Lord Jesus Christ is *very God*. St John tells us that 'the Word was God.' He is not merely a created angel, or a being inferior to God the Father, and invested by him with power to redeem sinners. He is nothing less than perfect God,—equal to the Father as touching his Godhead,—God of the substance of the Father, begotten before the worlds.

We learn, fourthly, that the Lord Jesus Christ is *the Creator of all things*. St John tells us that 'by him were all things made, and without him was not anything made that was made.' So far from being a creature of God, as some heretics have falsely asserted, he is the being who made the worlds and all that they contain. 'He commanded and they were created' (*Psa.* 148:5).

We learn, lastly, that the Lord Jesus Christ is *the source of all spiritual life and light*. St John tells us, that 'in him was life, and the life was the light of men.' He is the eternal fountain, from which alone the sons of men have ever derived life. Whatever spiritual life and light Adam and Eve possessed before the fall, was from Christ. Whatever deliverance from sin and spiritual death any child of Adam has ever enjoyed since the fall, whatever light of conscience or understanding anyone has obtained, all has flowed from Christ. The vast majority of mankind in every age have refused to know him, have forgotten the fall, and their own need of a Saviour. The light has been constantly shining 'in darkness.' The most have 'not comprehended the light.' But if any men and women out of the countless millions of mankind have ever had spiritual life and light, they have owed all to Christ.

Such is a brief summary of the leading lessons which these wonderful verses appear to contain. There is much in them, without controversy, which is above our reason; but there is nothing contrary to it. There is much that we cannot explain, and must be content humbly to believe. Let us however never forget that there are plain practical consequences flowing from the passage, which we can never grasp too firmly, or know too well.

Would we know, for one thing, the exceeding sinfulness of sin? Let us often read these first five verses of St John's Gospel. Let us mark what kind of being the Redeemer of mankind must needs be, in order to provide eternal redemption for sinners. If no one less than the eternal God, the Creator and Preserver of all things, could take away the sin of the world, sin must be a far more abominable thing in the sight of God than most men suppose. The right measure of sin's sinfulness is the dignity of him who came into the world to save sinners. If Christ is so great, then sin must indeed be sinful!

Would we know, for another thing, the strength of a true Christian's foundation for hope? Let us often read these first five verses of St John's Gospel. Let us mark that the Saviour in whom the believer is bid to trust is nothing less than the eternal God, One able to save to the uttermost all that come to the Father by him. He that was 'with God,' and 'was God,' is also 'Emmanuel, God with us.' Let us thank God that our help is laid on One that is mighty (*Psa.* 89:19). In ourselves we are great sinners. But in Jesus Christ we have a great Saviour. He is a strong foundation stone, able to bear the weight of a world's sin. He that believeth on him shall not be confounded (*1 Pet.* 2:6).

Notes—John 1:1-5

[*The Gospel according to St John.*] The following prefatory remarks on St John's Gospel may prove useful to some readers.

Firstly.—There is no doubt that this Gospel was written by John the Apostle, the son of Zebedee, and brother of James, once a fisherman on the Sea of Galilee, and afterwards called to be a disciple of the Lord Jesus, an eye-witness of all Christ's ministry, and a pillar of the church. John, be it remembered, is specially called 'the disciple whom Jesus loved.' He was one of the chosen three who alone saw the daughter of Jairus raised—were eye-witnesses of the transfiguration—and were by-standers during our Lord's agony in the garden. He was the one who leaned on Christ's breast at the last supper, and to whom our Lord committed the care of the Virgin Mary, when he was dying on the cross. It is an interesting fact, that he was the disciple who was specially inspired to write the deepest things concerning Christ.

Secondly.—There is little doubt that this Gospel was written at a much later date than the other three Gospels. How much later and at what precise time, we do not know. It is commonly supposed that it was written after the rise of heresies about the person and natures of Christ, such as those attributed to Ebion and Cerinthus. It is not likely that it was written at so late a period as the destruction of Jerusalem. If this had been the case, John would hardly have spoken of the 'sheep-market' at Jerusalem as still standing (*John* 5:2).

Thirdly.—The substance of this Gospel is, for the most part, peculiar to itself. With the exception of the crucifixion, and a few other matters, the things which St John was inspired to record concerning our Lord, are only found in his Gospel. He says nothing about our Lord's birth and infancy,—his temptation,—the Sermon on the Mount,—the transfiguration,—the prophecy about Jerusalem, and the appointment of the Lord's supper. He gives us very few miracles, and even fewer parables. But the things which John does relate are among the most precious treasures which Christians possess. The chapters about Nicodemus,—the woman of Samaria,—the raising of Lazarus, and our Lord's appearance to Peter after his resurrection at the Sea of Galilee,—the public discourses of the fifth, sixth, seventh, eighth, and tenth chapters,—the private discourses of the thirteenth, fourteenth, fifteenth, and sixteenth chapters,—and, above all, the prayer of the seventeenth chapter, are some of the most valuable portions of the Bible. All these chapters, be it remembered, we owe to St John.

Fourthly.—The style of this Gospel is no less peculiar than its substance. There appears extraordinary simplicity in many of its statements, and yet there is a depth about them which no man can entirely fathom.—It contains many expressions which are used in a profound and spiritual sense, such as 'light,' 'darkness,' 'world,' 'life,' 'truth,' 'to abide,' 'to know.'—It contains two names of the second and third persons of the Trinity, not found in the other Gospels. These are, 'the Word,' as a name of our Lord, and 'the Comforter,' as a name of the Holy Ghost.—It contains, from time to time, explanatory comments and remarks on our Lord's words.—Moreover, it contains frequent short explanations of Jewish customs and terms, which serve to show that it was not written so much for Jewish readers as for the whole church throughout the world. 'Matthew' (says Gregory Nazianzen, quoted by Ford), 'wrote for the Hebrews; Mark, for the Italians; Luke, for the Greeks; the great herald, John, for all.'

Lastly.—The preface of this Gospel is one of the most striking peculiarities about the whole book. Under the term preface, I include the first eighteen verses of the first chapter. This preface forms the quintessence of the whole book, and is composed of simple, short, condensed propositions. Nowhere in the Bible shall we find such clear and distinct statements about our Lord Jesus Christ's divine nature. Nowhere shall we find so many expressions, which for want of mental power, no mortal man can fully grasp or explain. In no portion of Scripture is it so deeply important to notice each word, and even each tense employed in each sentence. In no portion of Scripture do the perfect grammatical accuracy and verbal precision of an inspired composition shine out so brightly. It is not, perhaps, too much to say, that not a single word could be altered in the first five verses of St John's Gospel, without opening the door to some heresy.

The first verse of St John's Gospel, in particular, has always been allowed to be one of the sublimest verses in the Bible. The ancients used to say that it deserved to be written in golden letters in every Christian church. It has well been said to be an opening worthy of him whom Jesus called 'a sun of thunder.'

1.—[*In the beginning, etc.*] This wonderful verse contains three things. It tells us that our Lord Jesus Christ, here called the Word, is eternal,—that he is a distinct person from God the Father, and yet most intimately united to him,—and that he is God. The term 'God,' be it remembered, in the second clause, is to be taken personally for God the Father, and in the third to be taken essentially as signifying the divine being.

The expression, 'In the beginning,' means in the beginning of all creation. It is like the first verse of Genesis, 'In the beginning God created the heavens and the earth' (*Gen.* 1:1).

The expression, 'was,' means 'existed, was existing.' The whole sentence signifies that when the world was first called into being, however long ago that may be,—when matter was first formed, however many millions of ages ago that may be,—at that period the Lord Jesus Christ was existing. He had no beginning. He was before all things. There never was the time when he was not. In short, the Lord Jesus Christ is an eternal being.

Several of the Fathers dwell strongly on the immense importance of the word 'was' in this sentence, and on the fact that it is four times repeated in the two first verses of this Gospel. It is not said, 'the Word was made,' but 'the Word was.' Basil says, 'Those two terms, "beginning" and "was," are like two anchors,' which the ship of a man's soul may safely ride at, whatever storms of heresy may come.

The expression, 'the Word,' is a very difficult one, and is peculiar to St John. I see no clear proof that it is used by any other New Testament writer. The texts, Acts 20:32, and Hebrews 4:12, are, to say the least, doubtful proofs. That it here signifies a 'person,' and not a spoken word, and that it is applied to our Lord Jesus Christ, is clear from the after sentence, 'The Word was made flesh, and dwelt among us.' That it was a term familiar to the Jews is undeniable. But why this particular name is used by St John, both here and in his other writings, is a point on which commentators have differed greatly.

Some think, as Tertullian, Zwingle, Musculus, Bucer, and Calvin, that Christ is called 'the Word' because he is the wisdom of God, and the 'wisdom' of the book of Proverbs. These would have the expression translated, 'reason, wisdom, or counsel.'

Some think, as some of the Fathers, that Christ is called 'the Word,' because he is the image and offspring of the Father's mind, 'the express image of the Father's person,' just as our words, if honest and sincere, are the image and representation of our minds.

Some think, as Cartwright and Tittman, that Christ is called 'the Word,' because he is the person who is spoken of in all the Old Testament promises, and the subject of prophecy.

Some think, as Melanchthon, Rollock, Gomarus, and Scott, that Christ is called 'the Word,' because he is the speaker, utterer, and interpreter of God the Father's will. It is written in this very chapter, that 'the only begotten Son hath *declared* the Father.' It is also written, that 'God . . . hath in these last days *spoken* unto us by his Son' (*Heb.* 1:1, 2).

I think the last of these views the simplest and most satisfactory. All of them are at best only conjectures. There is probably something about the expression which has not yet been discovered.

It is thought by many that the expression 'the Word,' is used in several places of the Old Testament, concerning the second person in the Trinity. Such places are Psalm 33:6; Psalm 107:20; and 2 Samuel 7:21, compared with 1 Chronicles 17:19. The proof in all these cases is somewhat doubtful. Nevertheless the idea is strengthened by the fact that in rabbinical writings the Messiah is often spoken of as 'the Word.' In the third of Genesis, the Chaldee paraphrase says that Adam and Eve 'heard the Word of the Lord walking in the garden.'

Arrowsmith, in his admirable work on this chapter, suggests a probable reason why John did not say, 'In the beginning was the Son of God,' but 'the Word.'—'John would not at first alienate the hearts of his readers. He knew that neither Jews nor Gentiles would endure the term, the Son of God. They could not endure to hear of a sonship in the Deity and Godhead: but with this term "Word," applied to the Godhead, they were well acquainted.'—Poole observes that no term was so abhorred by the Jews as the term 'Son of God.'—Ferus remarks, that by calling our Lord 'the Word,' St John excludes all idea of a material, carnal relationship between the Father and the Son. This is also shown by Suicer to be the view of Chrysostom, Theodoret, Basil, Gregory Nyssen, and Theophylact.

Whatever difficulty we may feel about this expression, 'the Word,' in our times, there does not seem to have been the same difficulty felt about it, either by Jews or Gentiles, when St John wrote his Gospel. To say, as some have done, that he borrowed the expression from the philosophers of his time, is dishonouring to inspiration. But we may safely say that he used an expression, of which the meaning was quite familiar to the first readers of his Gospel, as a name of the second person of the Trinity. With this we may be content. Those who wish more information, should consult Witsius' Dissertation on the word Logos, Suicer's Thesaurus, and Adam Clarke's Commentary.

[*The Word was with God.*] This sentence means that from all eternity there was a most intimate and ineffable union between the first and second persons in the blessed Trinity,—between Christ the Word, and God the Father. And yet, though thus ineffably united, the Word and the Father were from all eternity two distinct persons. 'It was he,' says Pearson, 'to whom the Father

said, 'Let us make man in our image' (*Gen.* 1:26).

The truth contained in this sentence, is one of the deepest and most mysterious in the whole range of Christian theology. The nature of this union between the Father and the Son we have no mental capacity to explain. Augustine draws illustrations from the sun and its rays, and from fire and the light of fire, which, though two distinct things, are yet inseparably united, so that where the one is the other is. But all illustrations on such subjects halt and fail. Here, at any rate, it is better to believe than to attempt to explain. Our Lord says distinctly, 'I am in the Father and the Father in me.' 'I and my Father are one.' 'He that hath seen me hath seen the Father' (*John* 14:9-11; *John* 10:30). Let us be fully persuaded that the Father and the Son are two distinct persons in the Trinity, co-equal and co-eternal,— and yet that they are one in substance and inseparably united and undivided. Let us grasp firmly the words of the Athanasian Creed: 'Neither confounding the persons nor dividing the substance.' But here let us stop.

Musculus remarks on this sentence, how carefully St John writes that 'the Word was with God,' and not 'God was with God.' He would have us remember that there are not two Gods, but one. And yet 'the Word was with God, and was God.'

[*The Word was God.*] This sentence means that the Lord Jesus Christ, the eternal Word, was in nature, essence, and substance very God, and that 'as the Father is God, so also the Son is God.' It seems impossible to assert Christ's divinity more distinctly than it is here asserted. The sentence cannot possibly mean that the Father is God, since no one ever thought of disputing that. Nor yet can it possibly mean that the title of God was conferred on some being inferior to God and created, as the princes of this world are called 'gods.' He who is here called God, is the same who was uncreated and eternal. There is no inferiority in the Word to God the Father. The Godhead of the Father, of the Son, and of the Holy Ghost, is all one. To maintain in the face of such a text, as some so-called Christians do, that our Lord Jesus Christ was only a man, is a mournful proof of the perversity of the human heart.

The whole verse, honestly and impartially interpreted, is an unanswerable argument against three classes of heretics. It confutes the Arians, who regard Christ as a being inferior to God.—It confutes the Sabellians, who deny any distinction of persons in the Trinity, and say that God sometimes manifested himself as the Father, sometimes as the Son, and sometimes as the Spirit, and that the Father and the Spirit suffered on the cross!—Above all it confutes the Socinians and Unitarians who say that Jesus Christ was not God but man, a most holy and perfect man, but only a man.

In leaving this verse, it is useless to deny that there are deep mysteries in it which man has no mind to comprehend, and no language to express. How can there be a plurality in unity, and a unity in plurality, three persons in the Trinity and one God in essence,—how Christ can be at the same time *in* the Father, as regards the unity of the essence, and *with* the Father, as regards the distinction of his person,—these are matters far beyond our feeble understanding. Happy are we, if we can agree with Bernard's devout remark about the subject, 'It is rashness to search too far into it. It is piety to believe it. It is life eternal to know it. And we can never have a full comprehension of it, till we come to enjoy it.'

2.—[*The same was in the beginning, etc.*] This verse contains an emphatic repetition of the second clause of the preceding verse. St John anticipates the possible objection of some perverse mind, that perhaps there was a time when Christ, the Word, was not a distinct person in the Trinity. In reply to this objection, he declares that the same Word who was eternal, and was God, was also from all eternity a person in the Godhead distinct from God the Father, and yet with him by a most intimate and ineffable union. In short, there never was a time when Christ was not 'with God.'

There are two passages in the Old Testament which throw strong light on the doctrine of this verse. The one is in the book of Proverbs 8:22-31. The other is in Zechariah 13:7. The passage in Proverbs seems intended to explain the verse before us. The passage in Zechariah contains an expression which is almost a parallel to the expression 'with God.' 'Awake, O sword, against my shepherd, and against the man that is my fellow, saith the Lord.' 'The man that is my fellow,' according to the best commentators, means the Messiah, Jesus Christ; and a reference to Poole's Synopsis will show that the words signify 'the man that is near me, or joined to me.'

Arrowsmith says, 'Ask the sun, if ever it were without its beams. Ask the fountain, if ever it were without its streams. So God was never without his Son.'

We must not suppose that the repetition of this second verse is useless or unmeaning. Arrowsmith remarks that 'Repetitions have divers uses in Scripture. In *prayer* they argue affection. In *prophecy* they note celerity and certainty. In *threatenings* they note unavoidableness and suddenness. In *precepts* they note a necessity of performing them. In *truths*, like that before us, they serve to show the necessity of believing and knowing them.'

3.—[*All things ... made by him.*] This sentence means that creation was the work of our Lord Jesus Christ, no less than of God the Father. 'By him were all things created' (*Col.* 1:16). 'Thou, Lord, in the beginning hast laid the foundation of the earth' (*Heb.* 1:10). Now he that made all things must needs be God.

The expression, we must carefully remember, does not imply any inferiority of God the Son to God the Father, as if God the Son was only the agent and workman under another. Nor yet does it imply that creation was in no sense the work of God the Father, and that he is not the maker of heaven and earth. But it does imply that such is the dignity of the eternal Word, that in creation as well as in everything else, he co-operated with the Father. 'What things soever [the Father] doeth, these also doeth the Son likewise' (*John* 5:19). 'By whom also he made the worlds' (*Heb.* 1:2). When we read the expression 'by me kings reign' (*Prov.* 8:15), we do not for a moment suppose that kings are superior in dignity to him by whom they reign.

Jansenius remarks that this verse completely overthrows the heretical notion entertained by the Manichees, that the material world was formed by an evil spirit, as well as the notion of the Platonic school, that some part of creation was made by angels and demons.

[*Without him was not anything made, etc.*] This sentence appears added to show the utter impossibility of our Lord Jesus Christ being no more than a created being. If not even the slightest thing was created without him, it is plain that he cannot possibly be a creature himself.

The Fathers raised curious speculations about the origin of evil from the expression now before us. 'If nothing was made without Christ,' they argued, 'from whence came sin?' The simplest answer to this question is, that sin was not among the things which were originally created at the beginning. It came in afterwards, at the fall, 'By one man sin *entered* into the world' (*Rom.* 5:12). That it could not have entered without divine permission, and that its entrance has been overruled to the display of divine mercy in redemption, are undeniable truths. But we have no right to say that sin was among the 'all things,' which were 'made by Christ.'

4.—[*In him was life.*] This sentence means that in the eternal counsels of the Trinity, Christ was appointed to be the source, fountain, origin, and cause of life. From him all life was to flow. As to the kind of 'life' which is here meant, there is much difference of opinion among commentators.

Some think, as Cyril, Theophylact, Chemnitius, and Calvin, that the expression refers specially to the continued preservation of all created things by Christ's providence. Having created all things, he keeps all alive and in order.

Some think, as Zwingle, Cartwright, Arrowsmith, Poole, Alford, and most modern commentators, that the expression includes all sorts of life, both vegetable, animal, and spiritual. 'Thou sendest forth thy spirit, they are created' (*Psa.* 104:30). 'In him we live, and move, and have our being (*Acts* 17:28).

Some think, as Luther, Melanchthon, Brentius, Flacius, Lightfoot, Lampe, and Pearce, that the expression applies solely to spiritual life, and that it is meant to declare that Christ alone is the source of all life to the souls of men, whether in time or eternity. He was the Creator of all things, and he also was the author of the new creation. To this opinion I decidedly incline. For one thing, natural life seems already included in the preceding verse about creation. For another thing, it is the view which seems to agree best with the conclusion of the verse, and to be in harmony with the words 'With thee is the fountain of life: in thy light shall we see light.' 'God hath given to us eternal life, and this life is in his Son' (*Psa.* 36:9; *1 John* 5:11).

[*The life was the light of men.*] This sentence means that the life which was in Christ, was intended before the fall to be the guide of man's soul to heaven, and the supply of man's heart and conscience,—and that since the fall of man it has been the salvation and the comfort of all who have been saved. It is those and those only who have followed Christ as their light, who have lived before God and reached heaven. There has never been any spiritual life or light enjoyed by men, excepting from Christ.

5.—[*The light shineth in darkness.*] This sentence means that the spiritual light which Christ, the source of life, offers to man, has always been neglected since the fall, and is still neglected by unregenerate men. It has been like a candle shining in a dark place, a light in the middle of a world of darkness,—making the darkness more visible. Unregenerate men are darkness itself about spiritual things. 'Ye were sometimes darkness' (*Eph.* 5:8).

Arrowsmith remarks on this sentence, 'Christ hath shined in all ages in the works of creation and providence. He left not himself without witness. Every creature is a kind of professor that readeth man a lecture concerning God, of his wisdom, and power, and goodness.'

[*The darkness comprehended it not.*] This sentence means that the natural heart of man has always been so dark since the fall, that the great majority of mankind have neither understood, nor received, nor laid hold upon the light offered to them by Christ.

The difference in the tenses of the two verbs used in this verse is very remarkable. About the 'light' the present tense is used: 'It shineth now as it has always shone; it is still shining.'—About the 'darkness' the past tense is used: 'It has not comprehended the light; it never has comprehended it from the first, and does not comprehend it at the present day.'

The Greek word which we render 'comprehended,' is the same that is used in Ephesians 3:18. In Acts 4:13, it is translated 'perceived,'—in Romans 9:30 'attained,'—in Philippians 3:13, 'apprehended,'—in John 8:3, 'taken,'—and in 1 Thessalonians 5:4, 'overtake.'

At this point, the remark of Bengel upon the whole passage deserves attention. 'In the first and second verses of this chapter, mention is made of a state before the creation of the world; in the third verse, the world's creation; in the fourth, the time of man's uprightness; in the fifth, the time of man's decline and fall.'

I cannot close these notes on the opening verses of St John's Gospel without expressing my deep sense of the utter inability of any human commentator to enter fully into the vast and sublime truths which the passage contains. I have laboured to throw a little light on the passage, and have not hesitated to exceed the average length of these notes on account of the immense importance of this part of Scripture. But after saying all that I have said, I feel as if I had only faintly touched the surface of the passage. There is something here which nothing but the light of eternity will ever fully reveal.

JOHN 1:6-13

6 There was a man sent from God, whose name *was* John.

7 The same came for a witness, to bear witness of the Light, that all *men* through him might believe.

8 He was not that Light, but *was sent* to bear witness of that Light.

9 *That* was the true Light, which lighteth every man that cometh into the world.

10 He was in the world, and the world was made by him, and the world knew him not.

11 He came unto his own, and his own received him not.

12 But as many as received him, to them gave he power to become the sons of God, *even* to them that believe on his name:

13 Which were born, not of blood, nor of the will of the flesh, nor of the will of man, but of God.

ST JOHN, after beginning his Gospel with a statement of our Lord's nature as God, proceeds to speak of his forerunner, John the Baptist. The contrast between the language used about the Saviour, and that used about his forerunner, ought not to be overlooked. Of Christ we are told that he was the eternal God,—the Creator of all things,—the source of life and light. Of John the Baptist we are told simply, that 'there was a man sent from God, whose name was John.'

We see, firstly, in these verses, *the true nature of a Christian minister's office*. We have it in the description of John the Baptist: he 'came for a witness, to bear witness of the Light, that all men through him might believe.'

Christian ministers are not priests, nor mediators between God and man. They are not agents into whose hands men may commit their souls, and carry on their religion by deputy. They are witnesses. They are intended to bear testimony to God's truth, and specially to the great truth that Christ is the only Saviour and Light of the world. This was St Peter's ministry on the day of Pentecost: 'With many other words did he *testify*' (*Acts* 2:40). This was the whole tenor of St Paul's ministry: '*Testifying* both to the Jews, and also to the Greeks, repentance toward God, and faith toward our Lord Jesus Christ' (*Acts* 20:21). Unless a Christian minister bears a full testimony to Christ, he is not faithful to his office. So long as he does testify of Christ, he has done his part, and will receive his reward, although his hearers may not believe his testimony. Until a minister's hearers believe on that Christ of whom they are told, they receive no benefit from the ministry. They may be pleased and interested; but they are not profited until they believe. The great end of a minister's testimony is 'that through him, men may believe.'

We see, secondly, in these verses, *one principal position which our Lord Jesus Christ occupies towards mankind*. We have it in the words, he 'was the true Light, which lighteth every man that cometh into the world.'

Christ is to the souls of men what the sun is to the world. He is the centre and source of all spiritual light, warmth, life, health, growth, beauty, and fertility. Like the sun, he shines for the common benefit of all mankind,—for high and for low, for rich and for poor, for Jew and for Greek. Like the sun, he is free to all. All may look at him, and drink health out of his light. If millions of mankind were mad enough to dwell in caves underground, or to bandage their eyes, their darkness would be their own fault, and not the fault of the sun. So, likewise, if millions of men and women love spiritual 'darkness rather than light,' the blame must be laid on their blind hearts, and not on Christ. 'Their foolish heart was darkened' (*John* 3:19; *Rom.* 1:21). But whether men will see or not, Christ is the true sun, and the light of the world. There is no light for sinners except in the Lord Jesus.

We see, thirdly, in these verses, *the desperate wickedness of man's natural heart.* We have it in the words, Christ 'was in the world, and the world was made by him, and the world knew him not. He came unto his own, and his own received him not.'

Christ was in the world invisibly, long before he was born of the Virgin Mary. He was there from the very beginning, ruling, ordering, and governing the whole creation. By him all things consisted (*Col.* 1:17). He gave to all life and breath, rain from heaven, and fruitful seasons. By him kings reigned, and nations were increased or diminished. Yet men knew him not, and honoured him not. They 'worshipped and served the creature more than the Creator' (*Rom.* 1:25). Well may the natural heart be called 'wicked'!

But Christ came visibly into the world when he was born at Bethlehem, and fared no better. He came to the very people whom he had brought out from Egypt, and purchased for his own. He came to the Jews, whom he had separated from other nations, and to whom he had revealed himself by the prophets. He came to those very Jews who had read of him in the Old Testament Scriptures, seen him under types and figures in their temple services, and professed to be waiting for his coming. And yet, when he came, those very Jews received him not. They even rejected him, despised him, and slew him. Well may the natural heart be called 'desperately wicked'!

We see, lastly, in these verses, *the vast privileges of all who receive Christ, and believe on him.* We are told that 'as many as received him, to them gave he power to become the sons of God, even to them that believe on his name.'

Christ will never be without some servants. If the vast majority of the Jews did not receive him as the Messiah, there were, at any rate, a few who did. To them he gave the privilege of being God's children.

He adopted them as members of his Father's family. He reckoned them his own brethren and sisters, bone of his bone, and flesh of his flesh. He conferred on them a dignity which was ample recompense for the cross which they had to carry for his sake. He made them sons and daughters of the Lord Almighty.

Privileges like these, be it remembered, are the possession of all, in every age, who receive Christ by faith, and follow him as their Saviour. They are 'children of God by faith in Christ Jesus' (*Gal.* 3:26). They are born again by a new and heavenly birth, and adopted into the family of the King of kings. Few in number, and despised by the world as they are, they are cared for with infinite love by a Father in heaven, who, for his Son's sake, is well pleased with them. In time he provides them with everything that is for their good. In eternity he will give them a crown of glory that fadeth not away. These are great things! But faith in Christ gives men an ample title to them. Good masters care for their servants, and Christ cares for his.

Are we ourselves sons of God? Have we been born again? Have we the marks which always accompany the new birth,—sense of sin, faith in Jesus, love of others, righteous living, separation from the world? Let us never be content till we can give a satisfactory answer to these questions.

Do we desire to be sons of God? Then let us 'receive Christ' as our Saviour, and believe on him with the heart. To everyone that so receives him, he will give the privilege of becoming a son of God.

Notes—John 1:6-13

6.—[*There was a man sent from God, ... John.*] This is a short and striking description of John the Baptist. He was the messenger whom God promised to send before Messiah's face. He was born when his parents were aged, by God's miraculous interposition. He was filled with the Holy Ghost from his mother's womb. He received a special commission from God to preach the baptism of repentance, and to proclaim the immediate coming of Christ. In short, he was specially raised up by God to prepare the way for the Messiah. For all these reasons he is here called 'a man sent from God.' It is, in one sense, the common mark of all true ministers of the gospel. Ignorant, blind, and unconverted ministers may be ordained and sent by man. But they are not 'sent from God.'

7.—[*Came for a witness.*] This does not

mean, as it might at first sight appear, 'came to be a witness.' The Greek word which we translate 'witness,' does not mean 'a person,' but the testimony which a witness bears.

[*To bear witness of the Light.*] This means, to testify concerning Jesus Christ the Light of the world, that he was the promised Messiah, the Lamb of God, the Bridegroom, the almighty Saviour, to whom all dark souls ought to apply.

[*All men.*] This cannot of course signify 'all mankind.' It means all who heard John's testimony, and all Jews who were really looking for a Redeemer. One end of John the Baptist's testimony was, that all such should believe on Christ the true Light.

[*Through him.*] This does not mean 'through Christ' and Christ's grace, but through John the Baptist and John's testimony. It is one of those texts which show the immense importance of the ministerial office. It is a means and instrument through which the Holy Spirit is pleased to produce faith in man's heart. 'Faith cometh by hearing.' Through John the Baptist's testimony, Andrew was led to believe in Jesus and become a disciple. Just so now, through the preaching of ministers sinners learn to believe on Christ and are saved.

8.—[*He was not that Light.*] This expression would be more literally rendered, 'He was not *the* Light,' the promised light of sinners, the light of the world. The Greek article 'the' is used in a similar emphatic manner, to denote eminence and distinction, in the following passages. 'That bread' (*John* 6:32). 'That prophet' (*John* 1:21-25). 'That day' (*1 Thess.* 5:4). 'This way' (*Acts* 9:2).

Let it be noted that our Lord himself calls John the Baptist at a later period, 'A burning and a shining light' (*John* 5:35). But it is a curious fact that the Greek word there rendered 'light,' is not the one used here. It is a word which is frequently translated 'candle.' John the Baptist was a 'candle,' but not the Light itself. Believers are called 'the light of the world' (*Matt.* 5:14), but only as members of Christ the Light, and borrowing light from him. Christ alone is the great sun and fountain of all light, the Light itself.

9.—[*That was the true Light.*] The force of the expression 'true' in this sentence is well brought out by Arrowsmith in his commentary on this verse. He says that Christ is 'the true Light' in four respects. Firstly, he is undeceiving light, the true light in opposition to all the false lights of the Gentiles.—Secondly, he is real light, true in opposition to ceremonial types and shadows.—Thirdly, he is underived light, true in opposition to all light that is borrowed, communicated, or participated from another.—Fourthly, he is supereminent light, true in opposition to all that is ordinary and common.

[*Which lighteth every man ... cometh ... world.*] This sentence has caused much difference of opinion among commentators, in respect to two points.

a. In the first place, men differ as to the application of the words, 'that cometh into the world.' Some connect these words with 'the true Light,' and read the words, 'this is the true light that coming into the world lighteth every man.' In favour of this view, the words 'light is come into the world' (*John* 3:19), and 'I am come a light into the world' (*John* 12:46), deserve notice.—Others connect the words with 'every man,' and regard them as a sweeping description of everyone naturally born of the seed of Adam. That 'coming into the world' is a Hebrew phrase for being born, is shown by Nifanius. The construction of the whole verse in the original Greek, is such that either rendering is grammatical and correct.

Opinions are so nicely balanced on this point, and so much may be said on either side, that I venture my own judgment with much hesitation. But I am inclined to think on the whole, with Chemnitius and Glassius, that our translators are right, and that the clause 'that cometh into the world,' is better connected with 'every man' than with 'the true light.'—If the verse is rendered 'this is the true light that coming into the world lighteth every man,' it seems rather to narrow the blessing of the true light, and to confine his illumining benefits to the times after his incarnation. This, be it remembered, is precisely the view of the Socinian. And yet it is unquestionably true that Christ's incarnation increased greatly the spiritual light in the world. St John says, 'The darkness is past, and the true light now shineth' (1 John 2:8). If, on the other hand, the verse is rendered as our version has it, the words 'that cometh into the world,' seem very suitably joined to 'every man,' as expressing the universality of the blessings which Christ confers on man. He is not only the true light of the Jew, but of 'every man that is born into the world,' of every name, and people, and tongue. To suppose, as some have done, that this application of the words 'come into the world,' involves the pre-existence of souls, is, to say the least, a foolish thought.

The point is, happily, one on which men may agree to differ. Sound doctrine may be got out of either view.

b. The second difference of opinion respecting this verse arises from the words, 'lighteth every man.' This expression has received widely different interpretations. All, except heretics, are agreed that the words cannot mean that all are converted, and cannot signify the final, universal salvation of all mankind. What then do they mean?

Some think, as Cyril, that Christ 'the true light,' lighteth every man and woman on earth with the light of reason, intelligence, and consciousness of right and wrong. This view is partially true, and yet it seems weak and defective.

Some think, as the Quakers are reported to do, that Christ lighteth every man and woman on earth with an inward light of grace, sufficient to save them, if they will only use it. This view is a dangerous one, and beside contradicting many texts of Scripture, leads on to downright Pelagianism.

Some think, as Augustine, that Christ lighteth all that are lighted by his grace, and that 'every man' is practically the same as every believer. They quote in support of this view, the verse, 'The Lord upholdeth all that fall' (Psa. 145:14), where 'all' can only mean, 'all those that are upheld are upheld by the Lord.' A favourite illustration of this view is the saying, that a schoolmaster 'teaches all the boys in a town,' that is, 'all who are taught are taught by him.' This interpretation, however, is not thoroughly satisfactory, and has an appearance of quibbling and unfairness about it.

Some think, as Chrysostom, and Brentius in his Homilies, and Lightfoot, that Christ is really given to be the light of all mankind. They think that when it is said, he 'lighteth every man,' it means that he shines sufficiently for the salvation of all mankind, both Jews and Gentiles (like the sun shining upon all creation), though the majority of men are so blinded by sin that they do not see him. Yet Christ is for every man. 'He lighteth all,' says Chrysostom, 'as far as in him lies.'—'There is power and good will in the light,' says Chemnitius, 'to illumine all; but some love darkness rather than light.' Arrowsmith says, 'Christ doth dispense to everyone light sufficient to leave him without excuse. But Christ doth not dispense to everyone converting light sufficient to bring him to salvation.'

I believe this last view to be the most probable one, though I confess that it is not unattended by difficulties. But I rest in the conclusion that Christ is offered as a light to all the world, and that everyone born into the world will prove at last to have been in some way indebted to Christ, even though not saved.

Pearce says of the Greek word rendered 'lighteth,' that, 'in the Hebrew tongue that which is only intended to be done is often expressed as a thing actually done.' He regards this expression before us as a similar one. He gives, as parallel instances, 1 Corinthians 10:33, 'please,' for 'intend to please;' Galatians 5:4, 'justified,' for 'intend to be justified;' and 1 John 2:26, 'seduce,' for 'intend to seduce.'

The Greek word rendered 'lighteth' is used eleven times in the New Testament, and is translated 'to give light, to light, to bring to light, to enlighten, to illuminate.'

10.—[*He was in the world, etc ... knew him not.*] This verse describes the unbelief of the whole world before Christ's incarnation. He 'was in the world' invisibly, before he was born of the Virgin Mary, as in the days of Noah (1 Pet. 3:19, 20). He was to be seen in his works and in his providential government of all things, if men had only had eyes to see him. And yet the very world which he had made, the work of his hands, did not acknowledge, believe, or obey him. It knew him not. At Athens, Paul found an altar 'to the unknown God.'

That the expression applies to Christ before his incarnation, and not after, is said by Lampe to be the unanimous opinion of Origen, Chrysostom, Augustine, Cyril, Theodoret, Beda, Theophylact, and Euthymius.

There is a striking similarity between the declaration of this verse and the contents of the latter part of the first chapter of the Epistle to the Romans. In fact the line of argument by which St Paul shows the Gentiles to be guilty, in the first chapter of that epistle, and the Jews to be equally guilty and excuseless in the second chapter, is only a full exposition of what St John here states briefly in two verses.

11.—[*He came unto his own ... received him not.*] This verse describes the unbelief of the Jewish nation after the incarnation of Christ, and during his ministry among them. He came to a people who were peculiarly his own, by their redemption from Egypt, by their introduction into the land of Canaan, and by their possession of the law of Moses, and the covenants, and yet they did not believe on him, or receive him, but actually rejected and slew him.

There is a peculiarity about the Greek words rendered 'his own,' in this verse, which ought not to be overlooked. The first 'his own' is in the neuter gender, and means literally 'his own things.' The second 'his own' is in the masculine gender, and means 'his own men, servants, or subjects.' It is probably meant to show that our Lord came to a people whose land, territory, cities, temple, were all his own property, and had been originally granted by himself. The Jews, Palestine, Jerusalem, the temple, were all Christ's peculiar possession. Israel was 'his inheritance' (*Psa.* 78:71).—This made the sin of those who 'received him not,' even more sinful.

12.—[*As many as received him.*] This expression signifies, 'as many as believed on Christ, and acknowledged him as the Messiah.' It is only another form of the expression at the end of the verse, 'believed

on his name.' To receive Christ is to accept him with a willing heart, and to take him as our Saviour. It is one of many forms of speech, by which that justifying faith which unites the sinner's soul to Christ is expressed in the Bible. To believe on Christ with the heart, is to receive him, and to receive him is to believe on him.—St Paul says to the Colossians, 'As ye have ... received Christ ... so walk ye in him' (*Col.* 2:6).

The Greek word rendered, 'As many as,' is literally, 'whosoever,' 'whatsoever persons.' Glassius remarks that the expression denotes the universality of the benefits which Christ conferred. 'Whosoever' received him, Pharisees, Sadducees, learned or unlearned, male or female, Jews or Gentiles, to them he gave the privilege of sonship to God.

[*To them gave he power to become the sons of God.*] This expression means, 'He gave them the privilege of adoption into God's family.' They became 'the children of God by faith in Christ Jesus' (*Gal.* 3:26). 'Whosoever believeth that Jesus is the Christ is born of God' (*1 John* 5:1). There is no sonship to God without living faith in Christ. Let this never be forgotten. To talk of God being men's Father, and men being God's children, while they do not believe on the Son of God, is contrary to Scripture. Those are not children of God who have not faith in Jesus.

The word 'power' in this sentence requires careful guarding against misrepresentation. It means, as the marginal reading says, 'right or privilege.' It does not mean strength or ability. It does not mean that Christ confers on those who receive him a spiritual and moral strength, by which they convert themselves, change their own hearts, and make themselves God's children. No doubt Christ gives to all his people all needful grace to supply all the wants of their hearts, and the necessities of their position. No doubt he gives them strength to carry the cross, fight the good fight, and overcome the world. But that is not the truth taught in the words before us, and must be sought in other places. The words before us only mean that Christ confers the privilege of adoption on all believers, and did so especially on his first disciples. While their unbelieving fellow-countrymen were boasting of being children of Abraham, Christ gave his disciples the far higher privilege of being children of God.

The Greek word rendered 'power' is used 102 times in the New Testament, and never on one occasion in the sense of physical, moral, or spiritual strength to do a thing. It is generally translated, 'authority, right, power, liberty, jurisdiction.'

[*To them that believe on his name.*] These words are added to make clearer, if possible, the character of those who have the privilege of being sons of God. They are they who receive Christ and believe on his name. Arrowsmith remarks, 'The word "name," in the Scripture, is often put for person. The receivers of Christ are said to believe on his name, because the direct object of their faith is the person of Christ. It is not the believing that Christ died for all, or for me, or for the elect, or any such proposition, that saveth. It is believing on Christ. The person, or name of Christ, is the object of faith.'

The expression, 'believe on his name,' ought not to be overlooked. Arrowsmith remarks that there is a known distinction among divines, between believing God, that there is such a Being,—believing God, that what he says is true,—and believing on God in the way of faith and confidence as our God. And he observes, most truly, that precisely the same distinction exists between faith that there is such a Saviour as Christ,—faith that what Christ says is true,—and faith of reliance on Christ as our Saviour. Believing on Christ's name is exactly this faith of reliance, and is the faith that saves and justifies.

13.—[*Which were born, etc., etc ... of God.*] The birth here spoken of is the new birth, or regeneration, that complete change of heart and nature which takes place in a man when he becomes a real Christian. It is a change so great that no other figure but that of birth can fully express it. It is as when a new being, with new appetites, wants, and desires, is brought into the world. A person born of God is 'a new creature: old things are passed away; behold, all things are become new' (2 *Cor.* 5:17).

The persons who believe on Christ's name are said to be born 'not of blood, nor of the will of the flesh, nor of the will of man, but of God.' The interpretation of this expression which is usually given by commentators appears to me neither correct nor seemly. The true meaning of the words, I believe, is this. Believers did not become what they are 'by blood,'—that is by descent from Abraham or blood connection with godly people: grace does not descend from parent to child. Nor yet did believers become what they are by the will of the flesh,—that is by the efforts and exertions of their own natural hearts. Nature can never change itself: 'That which is born of the flesh is flesh.' Nor yet did believers become what they are by the will of man,—that is by the acts and deeds of others: neither ordained ministers, nor anyone else, can confer grace upon another. Man cannot regenerate hearts.—Believers become what they are solely and entirely by the grace of God. It is to God's free grace, preventing, calling, converting, renewing, and sanctifying, that they owe their new birth. They are born of God, or, as the third chapter says more distinctly, 'born of the Spirit.'

The word which we render 'blood,' in the singular number, is, in the Greek, plural, 'bloods.'—This peculiarity has made some conjecture that the expression refers to the blood shed in circumcision and sacrifice, and teaches the inability of these things to regenerate man. But this idea seems far-fetched and improbable. The use of the plural number appears to me intended to exclude all fleshly confidence in *any* descent, or relationship. It was neither the blood of Abraham, nor of David, nor of Aaron, nor of Judah, nor of Levi, which could give grace or make anyone a child of God.

This is the first time the new birth is spoken of by name in Scripture. Let us not fail to notice how carefully the doctrine is fenced against errors, and how emphatically we are told what this new birth does *not* come from, as well as what it *does* come from. It is a striking fact that when St Peter mentions the new birth, he fences it in like manner (1 *Pet.* 1:23), and when he speaks of baptism 'saving' us, he carefully adds that it is 'not the putting away of the filth of the flesh' (*1 Pet.* 3:21). In the face of all these cautions, it is curious to observe the pertinacity with which many overthrow the whole doctrine of the new birth by the assertion that all baptized persons are born again!

We must be careful that we do not interpret the words 'which were born' as if the new birth was a change which takes place in a man *after* he has believed in Christ, and is the next step *after* faith. Saving faith and regeneration are inseparable. The moment that a man really believes in Christ, however feebly, he is born of God. The weakness of his faith may make him unconscious of the change, just as a new-born infant knows little or nothing about itself. But where there is faith there is always new birth, and where there is no faith there is no regeneration.

JOHN 1:14

14 And the Word was made flesh, and dwelt among us, (and we beheld his glory, | the glory as of the only begotten of the Father,) full of grace and truth.

THE passage of Scripture now before us is very short, if we measure it by words. But it is very long, if we measure it by the nature of its contents. The substance of it is so immensely important that we shall do well to give it separate and distinct consideration. This single verse contains more than enough matter for a whole exposition.

The main truth which this verse teaches is *the reality of our Lord Jesus Christ's incarnation, or being made man.* St John tells us that 'the Word was made flesh, and dwelt among us.'

The plain meaning of these words is, that our divine Saviour really took human nature upon him, in order to save sinners. He really became a man like ourselves in all things, sin only excepted. Like ourselves, he was born of a woman, though born in a miraculous manner. Like ourselves, he grew from infancy to boyhood, and from boyhood to man's estate, both in wisdom and in stature (*Luke* 2:52). Like ourselves, he hungered, thirsted, ate, drank, slept, was wearied, felt pain, wept, rejoiced, marvelled, was moved to anger and to compassion. Having become flesh, and taken a body, he

17

prayed, read the Scriptures, suffered being tempted, and submitted his human will to the will of God the Father. And finally in the same body, he really suffered and shed his blood, really died, was really buried, really rose again, and really ascended up into heaven. And yet all this time he was God as well as man!

This union of two natures in Christ's one person is doubtless one of the greatest mysteries of the Christian religion. It needs to be carefully stated. It is just one of those great truths which are not meant to be curiously pried into, but to be reverently believed. Nowhere, perhaps, shall we find a more wise and judicious statement than in the Second Article of the Church of England. 'The Son, which is the Word of the Father, begotten from everlasting of the Father, the very and eternal God, and of one substance with the Father, took man's nature in the womb of the blessed Virgin of her substance: so that two whole and perfect natures, that is to say, the Godhead and the manhood, were joined together in one person, never to be divided, whereof is one Christ, very God and very man.' This is a most valuable declaration. This is 'sound speech, which cannot be condemned.'

But while we do not pretend to explain the union of two natures in our Lord Jesus Christ's person, we must not hesitate to fence the subject with well-defined cautions. While we state most carefully what we *do* believe, we must not shrink from declaring boldly what we do *not* believe. We must never forget, that though our Lord was God and man at the same time, the divine and human natures in him were never confounded. One nature did not swallow up the other. The two natures remained perfect and distinct. The divinity of Christ was never for a moment laid aside, although veiled. The manhood of Christ, during his lifetime, was never for a moment unlike our own, though by union with the Godhead, greatly dignified. Though perfect God, Christ has always been perfect man from the first moment of his incarnation. He that is gone into heaven, and is sitting at the Father's right hand to intercede for sinners, is man as well as God. Though perfect man, Christ never ceased to be perfect God. He that suffered for sin on the cross, and was made sin for us, was 'God manifest in the flesh.' The blood with which the church was purchased, is called the blood 'of God' (*Acts* 20:28). Though he became 'flesh' in the fullest sense, when he was born of the Virgin Mary, he never at any period ceased to be the eternal Word. To say that he constantly manifested his divine nature during his earthly ministry, would, of course, be contrary to plain facts. To attempt to explain why his Godhead was sometimes veiled and at other times unveiled, while he was on earth, would be venturing on ground which we had better leave alone. But to say that at any instant of his earthly ministry he was not fully and entirely God, is nothing less than heresy.

The cautions just given may seem at first sight needless, wearisome, and hair-splitting. It is precisely the neglect of such cautions which ruins many souls. This constant undivided union of two perfect natures in Christ's person is exactly that which gives infinite value to his mediation, and qualifies him to be the very Mediator that sinners need. Our Mediator is One who can sympathize with us, because he is very man. And yet, at the same time, he is One who can deal with the Father for us on equal terms, because he is very God.—It is the same union which gives infinite value to his righteousness, when imputed to believers. It is the righteousness of One who was God as well as man.—It is the same union which gives infinite value to the atoning blood which he shed for sinners on the cross. It is the blood of One who was God as well as man.—It is the same union which gives infinite value to his resurrection. When he rose again, as the Head of the body of believers, he rose not as a mere man, but as God.—Let these things sink deeply into our hearts. The second Adam is far greater than the first Adam was. The first Adam was only man, and so he fell. The second Adam was God as well as man, and so he completely conquered.

Let us leave the subject with feelings of deep gratitude and thankfulness. It is full of abounding consolation for all who know Christ by faith, and believe on him.

Did the Word become flesh? Then he is One who can be touched with the feeling of his people's infirmities, because he has suffered himself being tempted. He is almighty because he is God, and yet he can feel with us, because he is man.

Did the Word become flesh? Then he can supply us with a perfect pattern and example for our daily life. Had he walked among us as an angel or a spirit, we could never have copied him. But having dwelt among us as a man, we know that the true standard of holiness is to 'walk, even as he walked' (1 John 2:6). He is a perfect pattern because he is God. But he is also a pattern exactly suited to our wants, because he is man.

Finally, did the Word become flesh? Then let us see in our mortal bodies a real, true dignity, and not defile them by sin. Vile and weak as our body may seem, it is a body which the eternal Son of God was not ashamed to take upon himself, and to take up to heaven. That simple fact is a pledge that he will raise our bodies at the last day, and glorify them together with his own.

Notes—John 1:14

[*And the Word was made flesh.*] This sentence means that the eternal Word of God, the second person in the Trinity, became a man, like one of ourselves in all things, sin only excepted. This he accomplished, by being born of the Virgin Mary, after a miraculous manner, through the operation of the Holy Ghost. And the end for which he became flesh, was that he might live and die for sinners.

The expression 'the Word,' shows clearly that 'the Word' who 'was with God and was God,' must be a person. It could not reasonably be said of anyone but a person, that he became 'flesh and dwelt among us.' Whether St John could have found any other name for the second person of the Trinity equally proper, we need not trouble ourselves to inquire. It certainly would not have been accurately correct to say that 'Jesus was made flesh,' because the name Jesus was not given to our Lord till after his incarnation. Nor yet would it have been

correct to say, 'In the beginning was Christ,' because the name Christ belongs to the times after the fall of man.

This is the last time that John uses this expression, 'the Word,' about Christ in his Gospel. From the time of his incarnation he generally speaks of him as 'Jesus', or 'the Lord.'

[*Was made.*] This expression might perhaps have been better translated 'became.' At any rate we must carefully remember that it does not signify, 'was created.' The Athanasian Creed says truly, 'The Son is of the Father alone, neither made nor created, but begotten.'

[*Flesh.*] The use of this word, instead of 'man,' ought not to be overlooked. It is purposely used in order to show us that when our Lord became incarnate, he took upon him nothing less than our whole nature, consisting of a true body and a reasonable soul. As Arrowsmith says, 'That which was not taken could not be healed.

If Christ had not taken the whole man, he could not have saved the soul.'—It also implies that our Lord took upon him a body liable to those weaknesses, fatigues, and pains, which are inseparable from the idea of flesh. He did not become a man like Adam before the fall, with a nature free from all infirmity. He became a man like any one of Adam's children, with a nature liable to everything that fallen humanity is liable to, except sin. He was made 'flesh,' and 'all flesh is grass.'—Finally, it teaches that our Lord did not assume the human nature of any one family, or class, or people, but that nature which is common to all Adam's children, whether Jews or Gentiles. He came to be a Saviour for 'all flesh,' and so was made 'flesh.'

The subject of this sentence is a deeply mysterious one, but one about which it is most important to have clear views. Next to the doctrine of the Trinity, there is no doctrine on which fallen man has built so many deadly heresies as the incarnation of Christ. There is unquestionably much about this union of two natures in one person which we cannot explain, and must be content to believe. There is much that we cannot understand, be it remembered, in the union of body and soul in our own persons. But there are some points in the subject of Christ's incarnation which we must hold fast, and never let go.

a. In the first place, let us carefully remember, that when 'the Word became flesh,' he became so by the union of two perfect and distinct natures in one person. The manner of this union we cannot explain, but the fact we must firmly believe. 'Christ,' says the Athanasian Creed, 'is God and Man; God of the substance of the Father, begotten before the world, and man of the substance of his mother, born in the world; perfect God and perfect man. Who, although he be God and man, yet is he not two but one Christ; one not by conversion of the Godhead into flesh, but by taking of the manhood into God.' These words are very important. The Word was not made flesh by changing one nature into another, or by laying aside one nature and taking up another. In all our thoughts about Christ, let us take care that we do not divide his person, and that we maintain steadily that he has two distinct and perfect natures. The old Latin line on the subject, quoted by Gomarus, is worth remembering. It represents 'the Word made flesh,' as saying, 'I am what I was, that is God:—I was not what I am, that is man: I am now called both, that is both God and man.'

b. Secondly, when 'the Word became flesh,' he did not cease for a moment to be God. No doubt he was pleased to veil his divinity and to hide his power, and more especially so at some seasons. He emptied himself of external marks of glory and was called 'the carpenter.' But he never laid his divinity aside. God cannot cease to be God. It was as God-man that he lived, suffered, died, and rose again. It is written that God 'has purchased the church with his own blood.' It was the blood of one who was not man only, but God.

c. Thirdly, when 'the Word became flesh,' he was made a man in the truth of our nature like unto us in all things, and from that hour has never ceased to be man. His humanity was not a humanity different from our own, and though now glorified is our humanity still. It was perfect man no less than perfect God, who resisted temptation, fulfilled the law perfectly, endured the contradiction of sinners, spent nights in prayer, kept his will in subjection to the Father's will, suffered, died, and at length ascended up to heaven with flesh, bones, and all things appertaining to man's nature. It is written, that 'in all things it behoved him to be made like unto his brethren.' Moreover he did not lay aside his humanity, when he left the world. He that ascended up on the Mount of Olives, and is sitting at the right hand of God to intercede for believers, is one who is still man as well as God. Our High Priest in heaven is not God only, but man. Christ's humanity as well as divinity are both in heaven. One in our nature, our elder Brother has gone as our Forerunner to prepare a place for us.

d. Lastly, when 'the Word became flesh,' he did not take on him 'peccable flesh.' It is written that he was made in 'the likeness of sinful flesh' (*Rom.* 8:3). But we must not go beyond this. Christ was 'made . . . sin for us' (*2 Cor.* 5:21). But he 'knew no sin,' and was holy, harmless, undefiled, separate from sinners, and without taint of corruption. Satan found nothing in him. Christ's human nature was liable to weakness, but not to sin. The words of the Fifteenth Article must never be forgotten: Christ was 'void from sin, both in his flesh and in his Spirit.'

For want of a clear understanding of this union of two natures in Christ's person, the heresies which arose in the early church were many and great. And yet Arrowsmith points out that no less than four of these heresies are at once confuted by a right interpretation of the sentence now before us.

'The Arians hold that Jesus Christ was not true God. This text calleth him the Word, and maketh him a person in the Trinity.

'The Apollinarians acknowledge Christ to be God, yea, and man too; but they hold that he took only the body of a man, not the soul of a man, while his divinity supplied the room of a soul. We interpret the word "flesh" for the whole human nature, both soul and body.

'The Nestorians grant Christ to be both God and man; but then they say the Godhead made one person, and the manhood another person. We interpret the words "was made" as implying a union, in which Christ assumed not the person of man, but the nature of man.

'The Eutychians held but one person in Christ; but then they confounded the natures. They say the Godhead and manhood made such a mixture as to produce a third thing. Here they also are confuted by the right understanding of the union between the Word and flesh.'

He then goes on to show how the ancient church met all these heretics with four adverbs, which briefly and conveniently defined the union of two natures in Christ's person. They said that the divine and human natures when 'the Word was made flesh,' were united *truly*, to oppose the Arians,—*perfectly*, to oppose the Apollinarians,—*undividedly*, to oppose the Nestorians,—and *unmixedly*, to oppose the Eutychians.

Those who wish to examine this subject further, will do well to consult Pearson on the Creed, Dods on the Incarnation of the Eternal Word, and Hooker's *Ecclesiastical Polity*, B. v., chap. 51, 52, 53, 54.

[*Dwelt among us.*] The Greek word rendered dwelt, means literally 'tabernacled,' or 'dwelt in a tent.' The sentence does not mean that Christ dwelt in his human body as in a tabernacle, which he left when he ascended up to heaven. 'Christ,' says Arrowsmith, 'continueth now, and shall for ever, as true man as when he was born of the Virgin Mary.—He so took human nature as never to lay it down again.' The sentence only means that Christ dwelt among men on earth for thirty-three years. He was on earth so long conversing among men, that there could be no doubt of the reality of his incarnation. He did not appear for a few minutes like a phantom, or ghost. He did not come down for a brief visit of a few days, but was living among us in his human body for the duration of a whole generation of men. For thirty-three years he pitched his tent in Palestine, and was going to and fro among its inhabitants.

Arrowsmith remarks that three sorts of men are described in the Bible as living in tents: shepherds, sojourners, and soldiers. He thinks that the phrase here used has reference to the calling of all these three, and that it points to Christ's life on earth being that of a shepherd, a traveller, and a soldier. But it may be doubted whether this is not a somewhat fanciful idea, however pleasing and true. The Greek word rendered 'dwelt' is only used in four other places in the New Testament (*Rev.* 7:15; 12:12; 13:6; 21:3), and in each of them is applied to a permanent, and not a temporary dwelling.

[*We beheld his glory.*] St John here declares, that although 'the Word was made flesh,' he and others beheld from time to time his glory, and saw manifest proof that he was not man only, but the 'only begotten Son of God.'

There is a difference of opinion among commentators as to the right application of these words. Some think that they apply to Christ's ascension, which John witnessed, and to all his miraculous actions throughout his ministry, in all of which, as it is said of the miracle of Cana, he 'manifested forth his glory,' and his disciples saw it.—Others think that they apply especially to our Lord's transfiguration, when he put on for a little season his glory, in the presence of John, James, and Peter. I am on the whole inclined to think that this is the true view, and the more so, because of Peter's words in speaking of the transfiguration (2 *Pet.* 1:16, 18), and the words which immediately follow in the verse we are now considering.

[*The glory as of the only begotten of the Father.*] This sentence means 'such glory as became and was suitable to one who is the only begotten Son of God the Father.' These words will hardly apply to Christ's miracles. They seem to confine the glory which John says 'we beheld,' to the vision of glory which he and his two companions saw when Christ was transfigured, and they heard the Father saying, 'This is my beloved Son.'

Lightfoot's paraphrase of this expression is worth reading, though he does not apply the passage to the transfiguration, 'We saw his glory as what was worthy, as became, the only begotten Son of God. He did not glisten in any worldly pomp or grandeur, according to what the Jewish nation fondly dreamed their Messiah would do. But he was dressed with the glory of holiness, grace, truth, and the power of miracles.'

We must carefully remember that the adverb 'as' in this place does not imply comparison, or similitude, as if John only meant that the Word's glory was *like* that of the only begotten Son of God. Chrysostom says, 'The expression "as" in this place does not belong to similarity or comparison, but to confirmation and unquestionable definition, as though he said, we beheld glory such as it was becoming and likely that he should possess, who is the only begotten and true Son of God and King of all.' He also remarks that it is a common manner of speaking, when people are describing the appearance of a king in state, to say that 'he was like a king,' meaning only that he was a real king.

Glassius, in his *Philologia*, makes the same comment on the expression, and quotes as parallel cases of the use of the adverb 'as', 2 Peter 1:3; 1 Peter 1:19; Philemon 9; Romans 9:32; Matthew 14:5;

2 Corinthians 3:18. He thinks it a Hebraism, denoting not the similitude, but the reality and truth of a thing, and quotes Psalm 122:3, and Hosea 4:4, as Old Testament instances.

[*The only begotten of the Father.*] This remarkable expression describes our Lord's eternal generation, or Sonship. He is that person who alone has been begotten of the Father from all eternity, and from all eternity has been his beloved Son.

The phrase is only used five times in the New Testament, and only in St John's writings. That God always had a Son appears in the Old Testament. 'What is his son's name?' says Agur (*Prov.* 30:4). So also the Father says to Messiah, 'Thou art my Son; this day have I begotten thee' (*Psa.* 2:7). But the Sonship now before us, we must carefully remember, is not to be dated from any 'day'. It is the everlasting Sonship of which John speaks.

The subject is one of those which we must be content to believe and reverence, but must not attempt to define too narrowly. We are taught distinctly in Scripture that in the unity of the Godhead there are three persons of one substance, power, and eternity,—the Father, the Son, and the Holy Ghost. We are taught, with equal distinctness, that 'Sonship' describes the everlasting relation which exists between the first and second persons in the Trinity, and that Christ is the only begotten and eternal Son of God. We are taught, with equal distinctness, that the Father loveth the Son, and loved him before the foundation of the world (*John* 17:24). But here we must be content to pause. Our feeble faculties could not comprehend more if more were told us.

Let us however remember carefully, when we think of Christ as the only begotten Son of the Father, that we must not attach the least idea of inferiority to the idea of his Sonship. As the Athanasian Creed says, 'The Godhead of the Father, of the Son, and of the Holy Ghost is all one, the glory equal, the majesty co-eternal. Such as the Father is, such is the Son.' And yet the Father is not the Son, and the Son is not the Father. The argument of the ancient Arians, that if Christ is the Son of God, he must necessarily be inferior in dignity to

God, and subsequent in existence to God, is one that will not stand for a moment. The reply is simple. We are not talking of the relationship of mortal beings, but of the relationship between the persons of the Trinity, who are eternal. All analogies and illustrations drawn from human parents and children are necessarily defective. As Augustine said, so must we say, 'Show me and explain to me an eternal Father, and I will show you and explain to you an eternal Son.' We must believe and not try to explain. Christ's generation, as God, is eternal,—who shall declare it? He was begotten from everlasting of the Father. He was always the beloved Son. And yet 'he is equal to the Father as touching his Godhead, though inferior to him as touching his manhood.'

[*Full of grace and truth.*] These words do not belong to the Father, though they follow his name so closely. They belong to 'the Word.' The meaning of them is differently explained.

Some think that they describe our Lord Jesus Christ's character, during the time that he was upon the earth, in general terms. Full of grace were his lips, and full of grace was his life. He was full of the grace of God, the Spirit dwelling in him without measure; full of kindness, love, and favour to man; full of truth in his deeds and words, for in his lips was no guile; full of truth in his preaching concerning God the Father's love to sinners, and the way of salvation, for he was ever unfolding in rich abundance all truths that man can need to know for his soul's good.

Some think that the words describe especially the spiritual riches that Christ brought into the world, when he became incarnate, and set up his kingdom. He came full of the gospel of grace, in contradistinction to the burdensome requirements of the ceremonial law. He came full of truth, of real, true, solid comfort, in contradistinction to the types, and figures, and shadows of the law of Moses. In short the full grace of God, and the full truth about the way of acceptance, were never clearly seen until the Word became flesh, dwelt among us on earth, opened the treasure-house, and revealed grace and truth in his own person.

I decidedly prefer the second of these two views. The first is truth, but not the truth of the passage. The second appears to me to harmonize with the seventeenth verse, which follows almost immediately, where the law and the gospel are contrasted, and we are told that 'grace and truth came by Jesus Christ.'

JOHN 1:15-18

15 John bare witness of him, and cried, saying, This was he of whom I spake, He that cometh after me is preferred before me: for he was before me.

16 And of his fulness have all we received, and grace for grace.

17 For the law was given by Moses, *but* grace and truth came by Jesus Christ.

18 No man hath seen God at any time; the only begotten Son, which is in the bosom of the Father, he hath declared *him*.

THE passage before us contains three great declarations about our Lord Jesus Christ. Each of the three is among the foundation principles of Christianity.

We are taught, firstly, that *it is Christ alone who supplies all the spiritual wants of all believers*. It is written that 'of his fulness have we all received, and grace for grace.'

There is an infinite fulness in Jesus Christ. As St Paul says, 'It pleased the Father that in him should all fulness dwell.'—In him 'are hid all the treasures of wisdom and knowledge' (*Col.* 1:19; 2:3). There is laid up in him, as in a treasury, a boundless supply of all that any sinner can need, either in time or eternity. The Spirit of Life is his special gift to the church, and conveys from him, as from a great root, sap and vigour to all the believing branches. He is rich in mercy, grace, wisdom, righteousness, sanctification, and redemption. Out of Christ's fulness, all believers in every age of the world, have been supplied. They did not clearly understand the fountain from which their supplies flowed, in Old Testament times. The Old Testament saints only saw Christ afar off, and not face to face. But from Abel downwards, all saved souls have received all they have had from Jesus Christ alone. Every saint in glory will at last acknowledge that he is Christ's debtor for all he is. Jesus will prove to have been all in all.

We are taught, secondly, the *vast superiority of Christ to Moses, and of the gospel to the law*. It is written that 'the law was given by Moses, but grace and truth came by Jesus Christ.'

Moses was employed by God 'as a servant,' to convey to Israel the moral and ceremonial law (*Heb.* 3:5). As a servant, he was faithful to him who appointed him, but he was only a servant. The moral law, which he brought down from Mount Sinai, was holy, and just, and good. But it could not justify. It had no healing power. It could wound, but it could not bind up. It 'worked wrath' (*Rom.* 4:15). It pronounced a curse against any imperfect obedience.—The ceremonial law, which he was commanded to impose on Israel, was full of deep meaning and typical instruction. Its ordinances and ceremonies made it an excellent schoolmaster to guide men toward Christ (*Gal.* 3:24). But the ceremonial law was only a schoolmaster. It could not make him that kept it perfect, as pertaining to the conscience

(*Heb.* 9:9). It laid a grievous yoke on men's hearts, which they were not able to bear. It was a ministration of death and condemnation (*2 Cor.* 3:7-9). The light which men got from Moses and the law was at best only starlight compared to noonday.

Christ, on the other hand, came into the world 'as a Son,' with the keys of God's treasury of grace and truth entirely in his hands (*Heb.* 3:6). Grace came by him, when he made fully known God's gracious plan of salvation, by faith in his own blood, and opened the fountain of mercy to all the world.—Truth came by him, when he fulfilled in his own person the types of the Old Testament, and revealed himself as the true Sacrifice, the true mercy-seat, and the true Priest. No doubt there was much of 'grace and truth' under the law of Moses. But the whole of God's grace, and the whole truth about redemption, were never known until Jesus came into the world, and died for sinners.

We are taught, thirdly, that *it is Christ alone who has revealed God the Father to man*. It is written that 'No man hath seen God at any time: the only begotten Son, which is in the bosom of the Father, he hath declared him.'

The eye of mortal man has never beheld God the Father. No man could bear the sight. Even to Moses it was said, 'Thou canst not see my face: for there shall no man see me, and live' (*Exod.* 33:20). Yet all that mortal man is capable of knowing about God the Father is fully revealed to us by God the Son. He, who was in the bosom of the Father from all eternity, has been pleased to take our nature upon him, and to exhibit to us in the form of man, all that our minds can comprehend of the Father's perfections. In Christ's words, and deeds, and life, and death, we learn as much concerning God the Father as our feeble minds can at present bear. His perfect wisdom,—his almighty power,—his unspeak-able love to sinners,—his incomparable holiness,—his hatred of sin,—could never be represented to our eyes more clearly than we see them in Christ's life and death. In truth, 'God was manifest in the flesh,' when the Word took on him a body (*1 Tim.* 3:16). He was the brightness of the Father's glory, and 'the express image of his person' (*Heb.* 1:3). He says himself, 'I and my Father are one' (*John* 10:30). 'He that hath seen me, hath seen the Father' (*John* 14:9). 'In him dwelleth all the fulness of the Godhead bodily' (*Col.* 2:9). These are deep and mysterious things. But they are true.

And now, after reading this passage, can we ever give too much honour to Christ? Can we ever think too highly of him? Let us banish the unworthy thought from our minds for ever. Let us learn to exalt him more in our hearts, and to rest more confidingly the whole weight of our souls in his hands. Men may easily fall into error about the three persons in the holy Trinity, if they do not carefully adhere to the teaching of Scripture. But no man ever errs on the side of giving too much honour to God the Son. Christ is the meeting point between the Trinity and the sinner's soul. 'He that honoureth not the Son honoureth not the Father which hath sent him' (*John* 5:23).

Notes—John 1:15-18

15.—[*John bare witness ... cried.*] The time at which John the Baptist bore this testimony is not specified. We have not yet come to the historic part of John's Gospel, properly speaking. We are still in the introductory preface. It seems therefore probable, as Lightfoot says, that the sentence before us describes the habitual character of John's testimony to Christ. He was, throughout his ministry, continually proclaiming Christ's greatness and superiority to himself, both in nature and dignity.

[*Cried.*] The Greek word so rendered, implies a very loud cry, like that of one making a proclamation. Parkhurst defines it in this place as 'speaking out very openly.'

[*He that cometh after me ... preferred before ... was before me.*] This sentence has caused much discussion and some difference of opinion. The Greek words literally translated would be, 'He that cometh after me has become, or been made, in front of me,—for he was first of me.' I feel no doubt

that our English version gives the correct meaning of the sentence.—Hammond's note on the text is very good.

The first 'before,' signifies before in place, position, or dignity. The Greek adverb so rendered, is used forty-nine times in the New Testament, but never once in the sense of 'before in point of time or age.'

The second 'before,' signifies before in point of time or existence. 'He was existing before me, at the time when I was not.' The expression is certainly remarkable and uncommon, but there is another exactly like it in this Gospel, 'It hated me before it hated you,' where the literal rendering would be 'it hated me first of you.'

The sentence 'He was before me,' is a distinct statement of Christ's pre-existence. He was born at least six months after John the Baptist, and was therefore younger in age than John. Yet John says, 'He was before me. He was existing when I was born.' If he had meant only that our Lord was a more honourable person than himself, he would surely have said, 'He is before me.'

The greatness of John the Baptist's spiritual knowledge appears in this expression. He understood the doctrine of Christ's pre-existence. Christians are apt to think far too slightingly of John the Baptist's attainments, and the depths of his teaching.

16.—[*Of his fulness have all we received.*] This sentence means, 'all we who believe on Jesus, have received an abundant supply of all that our souls need, out of the full store that resides in him for his people. It is from Christ and Christ alone, that all our spiritual wants have been supplied.'

Waterland, in his book on the Trinity, calls particular attention to this expression. He thinks that it was specially used with a view to the strange doctrines of the Gnostics in general, and the Corinthians in particular, whose heresies arose before St John's Gospel was written. They seem to have held that there was a certain fulness or plenitude of the Deity, into which only certain spiritual men, including themselves, were to be received, and from which others who were less spiritual, though they had grace, were to be excluded. 'St John,' says Waterland, 'here asserts, that all Christians, equally and indifferently, all believers at large, have received of the plenitude or fulness of the divine Word, and that not sparingly, but in the largest measure, even grace upon grace.'

Melanchthon on this verse, calls particular attention to the word 'all.' He observes that it embraces the whole church of God, from Adam downwards. All who have been saved have received out of Christ's fulness, and all other sources of fulness are distinctly excluded.

[*Grace for grace.*] This expression is very peculiar, and has caused much difference of opinion among commentators.

1. Some think it means 'the new grace of the gospel in place of, or instead of, the old grace of the law.' This is the view of Cyril, Chrysostom, Theophylact, Euthymius, Rupertus, Lyranus, Bucer, Beza, Scaliger, De Dieu, Calovius, Jansenius, Lampe, and Quesnel.

2. Some think that it means 'grace, on account of God's grace or favour, and specially his favour towards his Son.' This is the view of Zwingle, Melanchthon, Chemnitius, Flacius, Rollock, Grotius, Camerarius, Tornovius, Toletus, Barradius, Cartwright, and Cornelius à Lapide.

3. Some think that it means 'grace on account of, or in return for, the grace of faith that is in us.' This is the view of Augustine, Gomarus, and Beda.

4. Some think that it means 'grace answering to, or proportioned to, the grace that is in Christ.' This is the view of Calvin, Leigh, and Bridge.

5. Some think that it means 'grace for the propagation of grace.' This is the view of Lightfoot.

6. Some think that it means 'accumulated grace, abundant grace, grace upon grace.' This is the view of Schleusner, Winer, Bucer, Pellican, Musculus, Gualter, Poole, Nifanius, Pearce, Burkitt, Doddridge, Bengel, A. Clarke, Tittman, Olshausen, Barnes, and Alford.

Brentius, Bullinger, Aretius, Jansenius, Hutcheson, Gill, Scott, and Henry, give several views, but signify their adhesion to no one in particular.

On the whole, I am inclined to think that the sixth and last is the correct view. I admit fully that the Greek preposition, here rendered 'for,' is only found in three senses in the Greek Testament: viz., 'In the room or place of' (*Matt.* 2:22), 'In return for' (*Rom.* 12:17), and 'On account of' (*Acts* 12:23; *Eph.* 5:31). In composition it also signifies 'opposition;' but with that we have nothing to do here. In the present case I think the meaning is 'grace in the place of grace; constant, fresh abundant supplies of new grace, to take the place of old grace; and therefore unfailing, abundant grace, continually filling up and supplying all our need.'

17.—[*For the law was given, etc.*] This verse seems intended to show the inferiority of the law to the gospel. It does so by putting in strong contrast the leading characteristics of the old and new dispensations,—the religion which began with Moses, and the religion which began with Christ.

By Moses was given the law,—the moral law, full of high and holy demands, and of

28

stern threatenings against disobedience;—the ceremonial law, full of burdensome sacrifices, ordinances, and ceremonies, which never healed the worshipper's conscience, and at best were only shadows of good things to come.

By Christ, on the other hand, came grace and truth,—grace by the full manifestation of God's plan of salvation, and the offer of complete pardon to every soul that believes on Jesus,—and truth, by the unveiled exhibition of Christ himself, as the true sacrifice, the true Priest, and the true atonement for sin.

Augustine, on this verse, says, 'The law threatened, not helped; commanded, not healed; showed, not took away, our feebleness. But it made ready for the Physician, who was to come with grace and truth.'

18.—[*No man hath seen God, etc.*] This verse seems intended to show the infinite personal superiority of Christ to Moses, or to any other saint that ever lived.

No man hath ever seen God the Father; neither Abraham nor Moses, nor Joshua, nor David, nor Isaiah, nor Daniel. All these, however holy and good men, were still only men, and quite incapable of beholding God face to face, from very weakness. What they knew of God the Father, they knew only by report, or by special revelation, vouchsafed to them from time to time. They were but servants, and 'The servant knoweth not what his lord doeth' (*John* 15:15).

Christ, on the other hand, is the only begotten Son, which is in the bosom of the Father. He is one who is most intimately united from all eternity to God the Father, and is equal to him in all things. He, during the time of his earthly ministry here, fully showed to man all that man can bear to know concerning his Father. He has revealed his Father's wisdom, and holiness, and compassion, and power, and hatred of sin, and love of sinners, in the fullest possible way. He has brought into clear light the great mystery how God the Father can be just, and yet justify the ungodly. The knowledge of the Father which a man derived from the teaching of Moses, is as different from that derived from the teaching of Christ as twilight is different from noonday.

We must carefully remember that none of the appearances of God to man, described in the Old Testament, were the appearances of God the Father. He whom Abraham, and Jacob, and Moses, and Joshua, and Isaiah, and Daniel saw, was not the first person in the Trinity, but the second.

The speculations of some commentators on the sentence now before us, as to whether any created being, angel or spirit, has ever seen God the Father, are, to say the least, unprofitable. The sentence before us speaks of man, being written for man's use.

The expression, 'which is in the bosom of the Father,' is doubtless a figurative one, mercifully accommodated to man's capacity. As one who lies in the bosom of another is fairly supposed to be most intimate with him, to know all his secrets, and possess all his affections, so is it, we are to understand, in the union of the Father and the Son. It is more close than man's mind can conceive.

The Greek word rendered 'declared,' means literally, 'hath expounded.' It is the root of the words, which are well known among literary students of the Bible, 'exegesis and exegetical.' The idea is that of giving a full and particular explanation (*Acts* 15:14). Whether the 'declaring of God the Father,' here described, is to be confined to Christ's oral teaching about the Father, or whether it means also that Christ has in his person given a visible representation of many of the Father's attributes, is a doubtful point. Perhaps both ideas are included in the expression.

In leaving this passage, I must say something about the disputed question,—To whom do the three verses beginning, 'and of his fulness,' belong? Are they the words of John the Baptist, and a part of his testimony? Or are they the words of John the Gospel writer, and an explanatory comment of his, such as we occasionally find in his Gospel?—There is something to be said on both sides.

a. Some think that these three verses were spoken by John the Baptist, because of the awkwardness and abruptness with which his testimony ends upon the other

29

theory,—because they run on harmoniously with the fifteenth verse,—and because there is nothing in them which we might not reasonably expect John the Baptist to say.

This is the opinion of Origen, Athanasius, Basil, Cyprian, Augustine, Theophylact, Rupertus, Melanchthon, Calvin, Zwingle, Erasmus, Chemnitius, Gualter, Musculus, Bucer, Flacius, Bullinger, Pellican, Toletus, Gomarus, Nifanius, Rollock, Poole, Burkitt, Hutcheson, Bengel, and Cartwright.

b. Others think that the three verses are the comment of John the Gospel writer, arising out of John's testimony about Christ's pre-existence, and out of the expression, 'grace and truth,' in the fourteenth verse.—They regard the verses as an exposition of the expression, 'full of grace and truth.'—They question whether the language is such as would have been used by John the Baptist,—whether he would have said 'all we,' after just saying 'me,'—whether he would have used the word 'fulness,'—whether he would, at so early a period, have contrasted the religion of Moses and of Christ,—and whether he would have so openly declared Christ to be the only begotten Son, which is in the bosom of the Father.—Finally, they think that if these were John the Baptist's words, the Gospel would not have begun again in the nineteenth verse, 'This is the record of John'.

This is the opinion of Cyril, Chrysostom, Euthymius, Beda, Lyranus, Brentius, Beza, Ferus, Grotius, Aretius, Barradius, Maldonatus, Cornelius à Lapide, Jansenius, Lightfoot, Arrowsmith, Gill, Doddridge, Lampe, Pearce, Henry, Tittman, A. Clarke, Barnes, Olshausen, Alford, and Wordsworth.—Baxter and Scott decline any decided opinion on the point, and Whitby says nothing about it.

The arguments on either side are so nicely balanced, and the names on either side are so weighty, that I venture an opinion with much diffidence. But on the whole, I am inclined to think that the three verses are not the words of John the Baptist, but of John the Evangelist.—The remarkable style of the first eighteen verses of this chapter makes the abruptness and brevity of the testimony which John the Baptist bears, upon this theory, appear to me not strange.—And the connection between the three verses, and the words 'full of grace and truth' in the fourteenth verse, appears to me much more marked and distinct, than the connection between John's testimony, and the words 'of his fulness all we have received.'

Happily the point is one which involves no serious question, and is therefore one on which Christians may be content to differ, if they cannot convince one another.

JOHN 1:19-28

19 And this is the record of John, when the Jews sent priests and Levites from Jerusalem to ask him, Who art thou?

20 And he confessed, and denied not; but confessed, I am not the Christ.

21 And they asked him, What then? Art thou Elias? And he saith, I am not. Art thou that prophet? And he answered, No.

22 Then said they unto him, Who art thou? that we may give an answer to them that sent us. What sayest thou of thyself?

23 He said, 'I *am* the voice of one crying in the wilderness, Make straight the way of the Lord, as said the prophet Esaias.

24 And they which were sent were of the Pharisees.

25 And they asked him, and said unto him, Why baptizest thou then, if thou be not that Christ, nor Elias, neither that prophet?

26 John answered them, saying, I baptize with water: but there standeth one among you, whom ye know not;

27 He it is, who coming after me is preferred before me, whose shoe's latchet I am not worthy to unloose.

28 These things were done in Bethabara beyond Jordan, where John was baptizing.

THE verses we have now read begin the properly historical part of St John's Gospel. Hitherto we have been reading deep and weighty statements about Christ's divine nature, incarnation, and dignity. Now we come to the plain narrative of the days of Christ's earthly ministry, and the plain story of Christ's doings and sayings among men. And here, like the other Gospel writers, St John begins at once with 'the record' or testimony of John the Baptist (*Matt.* 3:1; *Mark* 1:2; *Luke* 3:2).

We have, for one thing, in these verses, *an instructive example of true humility*. That example is supplied by John the Baptist himself.

John the Baptist was an eminent saint of God. There are few names which stand higher than his in the Bible calendar of great and good men. The Lord Jesus himself declared that 'Among them that are born of women there hath not risen a greater than John the Baptist' (*Matt.* 11:11). The Lord Jesus himself declared that he was 'a burning and a shining light' (*John* 5:35). Yet here in this passage we see this eminent saint lowly, self-abased, and full of humility. He puts away from himself the honour which the Jews from Jerusalem were ready to pay him. He declines all flattering titles. He speaks of himself as nothing more than the 'voice of one crying in the wilderness,' and as one who 'baptized with water.' He proclaims loudly that there is One standing among the Jews far greater than himself, One whose shoe-latchet he is not worthy to unloose. He claims honour not for himself but for Christ. To exalt Christ was his mission and to that mission he steadfastly adheres.

The greatest saints of God in every age of the church have always been men of John the Baptist's spirit. In gifts, and knowledge, and general character they have often differed widely. But in one respect they have always been alike: they have been 'clothed with humility'

(*1 Pet.* 5:5). They have not sought their own honour. They have thought little of themselves. They have been ever willing to decrease if Christ might only increase, to be nothing if Christ might be all. And here has been the secret of the honour God has put upon them. 'He that humbleth himself shall be exalted' (*Luke* 14:11).

If we profess to have any real Christianity, let us strive to be of John the Baptist's spirit. Let us study humility. This is the grace with which all must begin, who would be saved. We have no true religion about us, until we cast away our high thoughts, and feel ourselves sinners.—This is the grace which all saints may follow after, and which none have any excuse for neglecting. All God's children have not gifts, or money, or time to work, or a wide sphere of usefulness; but all may be humble.—This is the grace, above all, which will appear most beautiful in our latter end. Never shall we feel the need of humility so deeply, as when we lie on our death-beds, and stand before the judgment seat of Christ. Our whole lives will then appear a long catalogue of imperfections, ourselves nothing, and Christ all.

We have, for another thing, in these verses, *a mournful example of the blindness of unconverted men.* That example is supplied by the state of the Jews who came to question John the Baptist.

These Jews professed to be waiting for the appearance of Messiah. Like all the Pharisees they prided themselves on being children of Abraham, and possessors of the covenants. They rested in the law, and made their boast of God. They professed to know God's will, and to believe God's promises. They were confident that they themselves were guides of the blind, and lights of them that sat in darkness (*Rom.* 2:17-19). And yet at this very moment their souls were utterly in the dark. There was standing among them, as John the Baptist told them, One whom they knew not. Christ himself, the promised Messiah, was in the midst of them, and yet they neither knew him, nor saw him, nor received him, nor acknowledged him, nor believed him. And worse than this, the vast majority of them never would know him! The words of John the Baptist are a prophetic description of a state of things which lasted during the whole of our Lord's earthly ministry. Christ 'stood among the Jews,' and yet the Jews knew him not, and the greater part of them died in their sins.

It is a solemn thought that John the Baptist's words in this place apply strictly to thousands in the present day. Christ is still standing among many who neither see, nor know, nor believe. Christ is passing by in many a parish and many a congregation, and the vast majority have neither an eye to see him, nor an ear to hear him. The spirit of slumber seems poured out upon them. Money, and pleasure, and the world they know; but they know not Christ. The kingdom of God is close to them; but they sleep. Salvation is within their reach; but they sleep. Mercy, grace, peace, heaven, eternal life, are so nigh that they might touch them; and yet they sleep. 'Christ standeth among them and they know him not.' These are sorrowful things to write down. But every faithful minister of Christ can testify, like John the Baptist, that they are true.

What are we doing ourselves? This, after all, is the great question that concerns us. Do we know the extent of our religious privileges in this country, and in these times? Are we aware that Christ is going to and fro in our land, inviting souls to join him and to be his disciples? Do we know that the time is short and that the door of mercy will soon be closed for evermore? Do we know that Christ rejected will soon be Christ withdrawn?—Happy are they who can give a good account of these inquiries, and who 'know the day of their visitation!' (*Luke* 19:44). It will be better at the last day never to have been born, than to have had Christ 'standing among us' and not to have known him.

Notes—John 1:19-28

19.—[*This is the record.*] The Greek word translated 'record,' is the same that is rendered 'witness' in the seventh verse. The sentence means, 'This is the testimony that John bore.'

[*When.*] This word raises the question, 'At what time was this testimony of John borne?' It appears to have been after our Lord Jesus Christ's baptism, and at the end of his forty days' temptation in the wilderness. The twenty-ninth verse tells us, that 'the next day John seeth Jesus coming unto him.' It is worthy of notice, that nowhere in the Gospels do we find 'days' so carefully marked as in that portion of the first chapter of St John which we have now begun.

[*The Jews.*] This expression is remarkable, as peculiar to St John's Gospel. He generally speaks of our Lord's enemies and questioners, as 'the Jews.' It seems to indicate that St John did not write his Gospel in Palestine or at Jerusalem, and that it was written especially for the Gentile Christians scattered over the world, and much later than the other three Gospels.

[*Sent priests and Levites ... Jerusalem.*] These words show that those who questioned John the Baptist on this occasion, were a formal deputation sent with authority from the Sanhedrim, or ecclesiastical council of the Jews, to inquire about John's proceedings, and to report what he taught, and whom he gave himself out to be.

Wordsworth remarks, that 'More honour was paid by the Jews to John than to Christ, both in the persons sent, and in the place from which they were sent. They esteemed John for his sacerdotal lineage.' When Christ appeared, they called him the carpenter's son. Our Lord refers to this great respect at first shown to John, when he says, 'Ye were willing for a season to rejoice in his light' (*John* 5:35).

[*To ask him, Who art thou?*] We can hardly suppose that these priests and Levites were ignorant that John was the son of a priest, Zacharias, and therefore a Levite himself. Their inquiry seems to refer to John's office. 'What did he profess to be? Did he assume to be the Messiah? Did he claim to be a prophet? What reason could he assign for his having taken up his remarkable position as a preacher and a baptizer at a distance from Jerusalem? What account could he give of himself and his ministry?'

Two things are plainly taught in this verse. One is, the great sensation which John the Baptist's ministry caused throughout Palestine. He attracted so much notice, and such crowds followed him, that the Sanhedrim felt it necessary to inquire about him.—The other is, the state of expectation in which the minds of the Jews were at this particular season. Partly from the seventy weeks of Daniel having expired, partly from the sceptre having practically departed from Judah, there was evidently an expectation that some remarkable person was about to appear.—As to the sort of person the Jews expected, it is plain that they only looked for a temporal King, who would make them once more an independent nation. They had no idea of a spiritual Saviour from sin. But as to the fact that this vague expectation existed throughout the East at this particular time, we have the direct testimony of Latin historians. The extraordinary ministry of John the Baptist at once suggested the idea to the Jews at Jerusalem that he might possibly be the expected Redeemer. Therefore they sent to ask, 'Who art thou? Art thou the long-expected King?'

20.—[*He confessed ... denied not ... confessed, etc.*] This is a peculiar form of speech, implying a very positive, unmistakable, emphatic asseveration. It gives the idea of a man shrinking with holy indignation from the very thought of being regarded as the Christ: 'Pain me not by suggesting that such a one as I can be the Christ of God. I am one far inferior to him.'

Bengel says on this verse, 'Whilst John denied himself, he did not deny Christ.'—Luther makes some excellent remarks on the strong temptation which was here put in John's way, to take honour to himself, and the humility and faith which he showed in overcoming it.

21.—[*Art thou Elias?*] This question was not an absurd and unnatural one, as some commentators have thought fit to say. It was based upon that prophecy of Malachi, which speaks of God 'sending Elijah the prophet before . . . the great and dreadful day of the Lord' (*Mal.* 4:5). The manner, dress, and ministry of John the Baptist, as well as his appearing in the wilderness, constituted a great similarity between him and Elijah, and suggested the idea that John might possibly be Elijah. 'If this man,' thought the priests and Levites, 'is not the Christ, perhaps he is his forerunner, the prophet Elijah.'

[*And he saith, I am not.*] This answer of John deserves particular notice, and involves a grave difficulty. How could John say, 'I am not Elias,' when Christ says distinctly in another place, 'This is Elias'? How shall we reconcile these two statements?—To me it seems impossible to explain John's words, except on the simple theory that there are two comings of Elijah the prophet. The first was only a coming in spirit and in power, but not a literal coming. The second will be a literal and real appearance on earth, of him whom Elisha saw taken up into heaven. The first coming took place at Christ's first advent, and was fulfilled by John the Baptist going before Messiah's face in the spirit and power of Elijah. The second coming of Elijah will take place at the second advent of Jesus Christ, and will be fulfilled by Elijah himself once more coming as a prophet to the tribes of Israel.

It is of this second, future, literal coming of Elias, that John speaks in this place. When he says, 'I am not Elias,' he means, 'I am not that Elijah you mean, who was taken up to heaven 900 years ago. The coming of that Elijah is yet a future thing. I am the forerunner of the first advent in humiliation, not of the second advent in glory. I am not the herald of Christ coming to reign, as Elijah will be one day, but the herald of Christ coming to suffer on the cross. I am not come to prepare the way for a conquering King, such as you fondly expect, but for a meek and lowly Saviour, whose great work is to bear our sins and to die. I am not the Elias you expect.

In confirmation of this view, our Lord's remarkable words in another Gospel ought to be carefully studied. He says distinctly, 'Elias truly shall first come, and restore all things' (*Matt.* 17:11). And yet he adds in the same breath, 'I say unto you that Elias is come already:' that is, 'He is come, in a certain sense, by John the Baptist going before my face in the spirit and power of Elias.' In short, our Lord says at the same time, 'Elias shall come,' and 'Elias is come!'—To me his words seem a plain proof of the theory I am here maintaining,—that there are two comings of Elias. In *spirit* Elias came when John the Baptist came, a man like to Elias in mind and habits. But in the *flesh* Elias has not yet come, and is yet to appear. And it was in the view of this future, literal coming, that John the Baptist said, 'I am not Elias.'—He knew that the Jews were thinking of the times of Messiah's glory, and of the literal coming of Elijah, which would usher in those times. Therefore he says, 'I am not the Elias you mean. I belong to a different dispensation.'

The other view, which is undoubtedly maintained by the vast majority of commentators, appears to me surrounded with insuperable difficulties. According to them, there never was to be more than one fulfilment of Malachi's prophecy about Elias. It was to be fulfilled by John the Baptist; and when he appeared, it had received its full accomplishment. How John the Baptist's answer in this place can be satisfactorily explained, according to this theory, I am quite unable to see. The Jews ask him plainly, whether he is Elias; that is, whether he is the person who is to fulfil Malachi's prophecy. This, at any rate, was evidently the idea in their minds. He answers distinctly that he is not. And yet according to the theory against which I contend, he *was* Elias, and he ought to have replied, 'I am.' In short, he appears to say that which is not true!—There never was to be anyone after him, who was to fulfil Malachi's prophecy, and yet he declares in effect that he does not fulfil it, by saying that he is not Elias!

About the future literal coming of Elijah the prophet, when the Jews will at last see a living person, who will say, 'I am Elias,' this is not the place to speak. Whether or not he will minister to any but the Jews,—whether or not he will prove one of the two witnesses spoken of in Revelation (*Rev.* 11:3), are interesting and disputed questions. I will only remark, that the subject deserves far more attention than it ordinarily receives.

The following quotations from the Fathers will show that the opinion I have expressed is not a modern one.

Chrysostom, on Matthew 17:10, says, 'As there are two comings of Christ,—first, to suffer,—secondly, to judge; so there are two comings of Elias; first of John before Christ's first coming, who is called Elias because he came in the manner and spirit of Elias; secondly, of the person of Elijah, the Tishbite, before Christ's second coming.'—Jerome and Theophylact say just the same.

Gregory, quoted by Mayer, says, 'Whereas John denieth himself to be Elias, and Christ after affirmeth it, there is no contradiction. There is a double coming of Elias. The one is in spirit, before Christ's coming to redeem; the other in person, before Christ's coming to judgment. According to the first, Christ's saying is true, "This is Elias." According to the second, John's speech is true, "I am not." This was the fittest answer to men asking in a carnal sense.'

Augustine says, 'What John was to the first advent, Elias will be to the second advent. As there are two advents, so there are two heralds.'

[*Art thou that prophet?*] There are two views of this question. Some think, as Augustine and Gregory, that the words should be as our marginal reading has them, 'Art thou a prophet?' Others think, as Cyril and Chrysostom, that the question referred to 'the prophet' of whom Moses foretold that he would come (*Deut.* 18:15). I decidedly prefer the latter view. It seems very improbable that John the Baptist would entirely deny that he was a prophet.— Besides this, it seems not unreasonable that the Jews would ask whether he was 'the great prophet foretold by Moses.' And to this question, John answers most truly, that he was not.—It admits of doubt whether the Jews who questioned him clearly saw that the 'prophet like unto Moses,' and the 'Messiah,' were to be one and the same. It rather looks as if they thought 'Christ' and 'the prophet' were two different persons.

Lightfoot thinks that the question refers to a common expectation among the Jews, that the prophets were to rise again at the coming of Messiah, and that John's questioners meant, 'Art thou one of the prophets raised from the dead?' This superstitious notion explains the words of the disciples in Luke: 'Others say, that one of the old prophets is risen again' (*Luke* 9:19). But the Greek article in the words before us, seems to me too strong to be rendered 'a prophet.'

22.—[*An answer to them that sent us.*] This expression confirms the opinion already given, about the character of those who questioned John. They were not idle inquirers, but a formal deputation sent down from the Sanhedrim at Jerusalem, with a commission to find out who John was, and to make a report of what they discovered.

23.—[*He said, I am the voice, etc.*] John the Baptist's account of himself in this verse, consists of a reference to Scripture. He reminds the priests and Levites who wanted to know who he was, of Isaiah's prophecy concerning the times of the Messiah (*Isa.* 40:3). They would there find Isaiah saying, with the abruptness of an inspired prophet, and speaking as if he saw what he was describing, 'The voice of him that crieth in the wilderness'! That means, 'I hear in spirit, as I look forward to Messiah's time, a man crying in a wilderness, Prepare ye the way of the Lord.'—'That prophecy,' says John the Baptist, 'is this day fulfilled in me. I am the person whom Isaiah saw and heard in vision. I am come to prepare the way for Messiah, like a man going before a king in a desert country, to prepare a road for his master. I am come to make ready the barren hearts of the Jewish nation for Christ's first advent, and the kingdom of God. I am only a voice. I do not come to work miracles. I do not want disciples to follow me, but my Master. The object of my mission is to be a herald, a crier, a warning voice to my fellow-countrymen, so that when my Master begins his ministry they may not be found unprepared.'

[*The wilderness.*] The common view of this expression is, that it refers to John the Baptist's ministry having begun in the wilderness of Judæa. I rather doubt the correctness of this idea. The whole quotation is undeniably figurative. The prophet compares Messiah's forerunner to one preparing a road for a king through a desert or uninhabited country. The 'way' or road, is unquestionably figurative, and the straightness of the way too. No one supposes that Isaiah meant that John the Baptist was literally to make a road. But if the 'way' is figurative, the country through which it is made must surely be figurative too. I therefore think that the wilderness is a prophetical and figurative description of the spiritual barrenness of Israel when the Messiah's forerunner began his ministry. At the same time, I fully admit that John's retired and ascetic habits, and his residence in the wilderness, form a remarkable co-incidence with the text.

The expression 'voice,' has often been remarked as a beautiful illustration of the general character of John's ministry. He was eminently a humble man. He was one who desired to be *heard*, and to awaken attention by the sound of his testimony, but not to be *seen* or visibly honoured.

24.—[*And they ... sent ... Pharisees.*] The object of this verse is somewhat doubtful. Some think that it refers to the verse preceding, which contains a quotation from Isaiah. They which were sent, being Pharisees, and not Sadducees or Herodians, should have seen and admitted the scriptural character of John's mission.—Some think, as Bengel, that it refers to the following verse, in which a question was raised about baptism. They which were sent, being Pharisees, were specially strict about ceremonies, ordinances, and forms. Therefore they were not satisfied with a reference to Scripture. They asked John's authority for baptizing.—Some think that it refers generally to the notorious enmity and dislike with which the Pharisees regarded John the Baptist all through his ministry. Our Lord says in another place that they 'rejected the counsel of God ... being not baptized of him' (*Luke* 7:30). The text before us would then mean, that they which asked all these questions, asked them with a thoroughly unfriendly spirit, and with no real desire to learn God's truth, because they were Pharisees.

25.—[*Why baptizest thou ... if thou be not, etc.*] This verse evidently implies that John's questioners expected the Messiah, or his forerunner, to baptize whenever he appeared. It is not unlikely, as Lightfoot says, that the idea arose from the text in Ezekiel, describing Messiah's time, 'Then will I sprinkle clean water upon you, and ye shall be clean,' etc. (*Ezek.* 36:25).

Luther thinks that this verse shows that the questioners who came to John now changed their tone. Hitherto they had flattered. Now they began to threaten.

One thing is very clear from this verse. The Jews were not unacquainted with baptism as a religious ordinance. It was one of the ceremonies, according to Lightfoot, by which proselytes were admitted into the Jewish church. Moreover it is worthy of notice, that when proselytes were so admitted, their children were baptized together with them. It was not therefore the fact of John baptizing, which the Pharisees here called in question, but his authority for administering baptism.

26.—[*I baptize with water; but, etc.*] The answer of John the Baptist here reported is very elliptical, and the full meaning of what he said must be supplied from other places. He seems to say, 'I do not baptize by my own authority, but by a commission from One far higher than either you or I. I only baptize with water; and I do not do it to make disciples for myself, but for my Master. I form no party. I ask no man to follow me. I tell all whom I baptize to believe on that Mighty One who is coming after me. I am only the servant of One far greater than myself, who is even now standing among you, if you had eyes to see him. He is one so much above me in nature and dignity, that I am not worthy to be his humblest servant. He can baptize hearts, and will fulfil the promises about Messiah to which you are vaguely referring. In the meantime, I only baptize with water all those who profess repentance and willingness to receive my Master.—I baptize for another and not for myself.'

[*There standeth one among you.*] I doubt whether these words literally mean, 'There is standing in the crowd of you my hearers.' I prefer the sense, 'There is already *living* and abiding among you, in this land of Judæa, One greater than I.' I think this the sense, because of the words in the twenty-ninth verse, 'John seeth Jesus coming to him,' which seem to imply that he was not with him the previous day.—The thought seems parallel to that contained in the words, 'The kingdom of God cometh not with observation.'—The messenger of God shall suddenly come to his temple' (*Luke* 17:20; *Mal.* 3:1). All serve to point to the same truth: viz., that when Messiah came the first time, he came quietly, without noise, without display, without the nation of the Jews knowing it; so that he 'stood among them,' and yet they were not aware of his presence.

The Greek word rendered 'standeth,' is in the perfect tense, and would be literally rendered, 'there hath stood;' that is, 'hath stood for some little time, and is still standing.' The Messiah has come and is present. Bengel renders it, 'hath taken his stand.'

The view I have maintained of the meaning of the word 'standeth,' is held by Parkhurst, who defines it as 'being or living,' and quotes John 6:22 as a parallel instance. Pearce takes the same view, and quotes Acts 26:22. Jansenius renders it, 'has conversed among you, as when he sat among the doctors' in the temple. Aretius renders it, 'He is present in the flesh, and walking in Judæa.'

[*Ye know not.*] This seems to mean, not only that the Jews knew not Jesus the Messiah by sight, but that they had no spiritual knowledge of him, and of the true nature of his office, as the Saviour of sinners.—'Ye look for a conquering, reigning, Messiah. Ye know not the suffering Messiah, who came to be cut off, and to be crucified for sinners.'

Bengel remarks that John is here specially 'addressing inhabitants of Jerusalem who had not been present at the baptism of Jesus. And he whets their desires, that they may be anxious to become acquainted with him.'

27.—[*Coming after ... preferred before.*] The remarks made on the fifteenth verse apply fully to this expression. John declares that though his Master, in point of time, began his ministry after him, in point of dignity he was far above him. To exalt Christ, and abase himself, seem ideas never long out of John's mind.

[*Shoe's latchet ... worthy to unloose.*] This is evidently a proverbial expression. 'I am so inferior to him that came after me, that in comparison with him, I am like the humblest servant compared to his master.' To be not fit to carry a person's shoes, in our times, is a well-known proverb, describing inferiority.

28.—[*These things ... done ... in Bethabara.*] In hot countries like Palestine, it was evidently important for John the Baptist to be near a supply of water, suited to the baptism of the multitudes who came to him. If Beth-barah, spoken of in Gideon's history, is the same place, it is worthy of notice that it is specially mentioned as near 'waters' (*Judg.* 7:24).

The name of the place ought always to be dear to the hearts of Christians. It is the place where the first disciples of Jesus were made, and the foundation of the Christian church was laid. It was here, 'the next day,' that Jesus was publicly proclaimed as the 'Lamb of God.' It was here, 'the day after,' that Andrew and another disciple followed Jesus. Here then the church of Christ, properly so called, began.

In leaving this passage, let us remember that John the Baptist's ministry left the Jews entirely without excuse, when afterwards they refused to believe on Christ. They could never plead that our Lord's ministry came on them unawares and took them by surprise. The whole nation dwelling in Palestine, from the great ecclesiastical council down to the humblest classes, were evidently aroused to a state of attention by John's doings.

JOHN 1:29-34

29 The next day John seeth Jesus coming unto him, and saith, Behold the Lamb of God, which taketh away the sin of the world.

30 This is he of whom I said, After me cometh a man which is preferred before me: for he was before me.

31 And I knew him not: but that he should be made manifest to Israel, therefore am I come baptizing with water.

32 And John bare record, saying, I saw the Spirit descending from heaven like a dove, and it abode upon him.

33 And I knew him not: but he that sent me to baptize with water, the same said unto me, Upon whom thou shalt see the Spirit descending, and remaining on him, the same is he which baptizeth with the Holy Ghost.

34 And I saw, and bare record that this is the Son of God.

THIS passage contains a verse which ought to be printed in great letters in the memory of every reader of the Bible. All the stars in heaven are bright and beautiful, and yet one star exceedeth another star in glory. So also all texts of Scripture are inspired and profitable, and yet some texts are richer than others. Of such texts the first verse before us is pre-eminently one. Never was there a fuller testimony borne to Christ upon earth, than that which is here borne by John the Baptist.

Let us notice, firstly, in this passage, *the peculiar name which John the Baptist gives to Christ.* He calls him 'the Lamb of God.'

This name did not merely mean, as some have supposed, that Christ was meek and gentle as a lamb. This would be truth no doubt, but only a very small portion of the truth. There are greater things here than this! It meant that Christ was the great Sacrifice for sin, who was come to make atonement for transgression by his own death upon the cross. He was the true Lamb which Abraham told Isaac at Moriah God would provide (*Gen.* 22:8). He was the true Lamb to which every morning and evening sacrifice in the temple had daily pointed. He was the Lamb of which Isaiah had prophesied, that he would be brought 'to the slaughter' (*Isa.* 53:7). He was the true Lamb of which the passover lamb in Egypt had been a vivid type. In short, he was the great propitiation for sin which God had covenanted from all eternity to send into the world. He was God's Lamb.

39

Let us take heed that in all our thoughts of Christ, we first think of him as John the Baptist here represents him. Let us serve him faithfully as our Master. Let us obey him loyally as our King. Let us study his teaching as our Prophet. Let us walk diligently after him as our Example. Let us look anxiously for him as our coming Redeemer of body as well as soul. But above all, let us prize him as our Sacrifice, and rest our whole weight on his death as an atonement for sin. Let his blood be more precious in our eyes every year we live. Whatever else we glory in about Christ, let us glory above all things in his cross. This is the cornerstone, this is the citadel, this is the root of true Christian theology. We know nothing rightly about Christ, until we see him with John the Baptist's eyes, and can rejoice in him as 'the Lamb that was slain.'

Let us notice, secondly, in this passage, *the peculiar work which John the Baptist describes Christ as doing.* He says that he 'taketh away the sin of the world.'

Christ is a Saviour. He did not come on earth to be a conqueror, or a philosopher, or a mere teacher of morality. He came to save sinners. He came to do that which man could never do for himself,—to do that which money and learning can never obtain,—to do that which is essential to man's real happiness: he came to 'take away sin.'

Christ is a complete Saviour. He 'taketh away sin.' He did not merely make vague proclamations of pardon, mercy, and forgiveness. He 'took' our sins upon himself, and carried them away. He allowed them to be laid upon himself, and bore them 'in his own body on the tree' (*1 Pet.* 2:24). The sins of everyone that believes on Jesus are made as though they had never been sinned at all. The Lamb of God has taken them clean away.

Christ is an almighty Saviour, and a Saviour for all mankind. He 'taketh away the sin of the world.' He did not die for the Jews only, but for the Gentile as well as the Jew. He did not suffer for a few persons only, but for all mankind. The payment that he made on the cross was more than enough to make satisfaction for the debts of all.

The blood that he shed was precious enough to wash away the sins of all. His atonement on the cross was sufficient for all mankind, though efficient only to them that believe. The sin that he took up and bore on the cross was the sin of the whole world.

Last, but not least, Christ is a perpetual and unwearied Saviour. He 'taketh away' sin. He is daily taking it away from everyone that believes on him,—daily purging, daily cleansing, daily washing the souls of his people, daily granting and applying fresh supplies of mercy. He did not cease to work for his saints, when he died for them on the cross. He lives in heaven as a Priest, to present his sacrifice continually before God. In grace as well as in providence, Christ worketh still. He is ever taking away sin.

These are golden truths indeed. Well would it be for the church of Christ, if they were used by all who know them! Our very familiarity with texts like these is one of our greatest dangers. Blessed are they who not only keep this text in their memories, but feed upon it in their hearts!

Let us notice, lastly, in this passage, *the peculiar office which John the Baptist attributes to Christ.* He speaks of him as him 'which baptizeth with the Holy Ghost.'

The baptism here spoken of is not the baptism of water. It does not consist either of dipping or sprinkling. It does not belong exclusively either to infants or to grown-up people. It is not a baptism which any man can give, Episcopalian or Presbyterian, Independent or Methodist, layman or minister. It is a baptism which the great Head of the church keeps exclusively in his own hands. It consists of the implanting of grace into the inward man. It is the same thing with the new birth. It is a baptism, not of the body, but of the heart. It is a baptism which the penitent thief received, though neither dipped nor sprinkled by the hand of man. It is a baptism which Ananias and Sapphira did not receive, though admitted into church communion by apostolic men.

Let it be a settled principle in our religion that the baptism of which John the Baptist speaks here, is the baptism which is absolutely necessary to salvation. It is well to be baptized into the visible church; but it is far better to be baptized into that church which is made up of true believers. The baptism of water is a most blessed and profitable ordinance, and cannot be neglected without great sin. But the baptism of the Holy Ghost is of far greater importance. The man who dies with his heart not baptized by Christ can never be saved.

Let us ask ourselves, as we leave this passage, whether we are baptized with the Holy Ghost, and whether we have any real interest in the Lamb of God? Thousands, unhappily, are wasting their time in controversy about water baptism, and neglecting the baptism of the heart. Thousands more are content with a head-knowledge of the Lamb of God, or have never sought him by faith, that their own sins may be actually taken away. Let us take heed that we ourselves have new hearts, and believe to the saving of our souls.

Notes—John 1:29-34

29.—[*The next day.*] This means the day after the conversation between John the Baptist and the deputation of priests and Levites. The careful marking of days by St John at this stage of his Gospel deserves particular notice.

[*Seeth Jesus coming unto him.*] These words seem to prove that Jesus was not present on the preceding day, during the conversation with the priests and Levites, and that John's words, 'standeth among you,' cannot be literally taken.

It seems probable, as before observed, that our Lord came back to John after his temptation in the wilderness. The Spirit took him into the wilderness 'immediately' after his baptism (*Mark* 1:12), and it was upon his return, at the end of forty days, that John the Baptist saw him again.

[*And saith, Behold.*] This appears to have been a public, open proclamation made by John to his disciples and the multitude who surrounded him. 'Behold that person who is coming towards us. He is the Lamb of God, the Messiah of whom I have been preaching to you, and on whom I have told you to believe.'

[*The Lamb of God.*] There can be no reasonable doubt that John gave this name to our Lord because he was the true sacrifice for sin, the true antitype of the passover lamb, and the lamb prophesied of by Isaiah (*Isa.* 53:7). The idea that he only refers to the quietness and meekness of our Lord's personal character is utterly unsatisfactory. He is describing our Lord's official character as the great propitiation for sin.

The expression, 'Lamb of God,' according to some, signifies 'that eminent, great, divine, and most excellent Lamb.' It is a well-known Hebraism to describe anything very great as a thing 'of God.' Thus we read of 'thunderings of God,' and 'trembling of God' (*Exod.* 9:28; *1 Sam.* 14:15).— According to others it signifies the Lamb which God has provided from all eternity, and which God has long covenanted and promised to send into the world to be slain for sinners. Both views make good doctrine, but the second seems the preferable one.

Bengel thinks that John called our Lord 'the Lamb of God,' with a special reference to the passover, which was then near (*John* 2:13). He also sees a parallel between the expression 'Lamb of God,' and the phrase, 'sacrifice of God' (*Psa.* 51:17), which means 'the sacrifice which God acknowledges as pleasing to him.'

Chemnitius thinks, in addition to other reasons why John calls our Lord 'the Lamb,' that he desired to show that Christ's kingdom was not political. He was neither the ram nor the he-goat described in Daniel (*Dan.* 8:20, 21).

[*Taketh away.*] The Greek word so rendered, is given in the marginal reading, 'beareth.' Both ideas are included. It means 'taketh away by his expiatory death.' The Lamb of God 'beareth' the sin of the world by taking it upon himself. He allowed our guilt to be laid upon him, and carried it away like the scapegoat, so that there was none left. It is one of the many expressions which describe the great Scripture truth that Christ's death was a vicarious sacrifice for sin. He became our substitute. He took upon him our sin. He was made sin for us. Our sins were imputed to him. He was made a curse for us.

The word here rendered 'taketh away' is found at least one hundred times in the New Testament. In eighty-two places it is rendered, 'take,'—'take up,'—or 'take away.' In five places it is, 'bear.' In four it is, 'lift up.' In two it is, 'remove.' In most of the other places it is the imperative expression, 'away with!' All point to the same view of the text before us: viz., 'a complete atonement for sin.'

The use of the present tense, 'taketh away,' is remarked by all the best commentators, ancient and modern. It is intended to show the completeness of Christ's satisfaction for sin, and the continual application of his once-made sacrifice. He is always taking sin away. Rollock observes, 'The influence of Christ's sacrifice is perpetual, and his blood never dries up.'

The idea maintained by some, that 'taking away sin,' in this place, includes sanctification as well as justification, seems to me quite untenable. That Christ 'takes away' the power of a believer's sins, when he applies his redemption to his soul, is no doubt true. But it is not the truth of this text.

[*The sin.*] Let it be noted that the singular number is used here. It is 'the sin,' not 'the sins.' The expression seems to me purposely intended to show that what Christ took away, and bore on the cross, was not the sin of certain people only, but the whole accumulated mass of all the sins of all the children of Adam. He bore the weight of all, and made an atonement sufficient to make satisfaction for all.

The idea propounded by some, that 'the sin' which Christ is said here to take away, is only man's original sin,—and that for man's actual sins each man must make satisfaction himself, is destitute of the slightest foundation in Scripture, contradicts scores of plain texts, and utterly overthrows the whole gospel.

[*Of the world.*] It is almost needless to say that there are two views of this expression. Some say that it only means that Christ takes away the sin of Gentiles as well as Jews, and that it does not mean the sin of any but the elect.—Others say that it really means that Christ 'taketh away' the sin of all mankind; that is, that he made an atonement sufficient for all, and that all are *salvable*, though not all saved, in consequence of his death.

I decidedly prefer the latter of these two views. I hold as strongly as anyone, that Christ's death is profitable to none but to the elect who believe in his name. But I dare not limit and pare down such expressions as the one before us. I dare not say that no atonement has been made, in any sense, except for the elect. I believe it is possible to be more systematic than the Bible in our statements. When I read that the wicked who are lost, 'deny the Lord that bought them' (2 *Pet.* 2:1), and that 'God was in Christ, reconciling the world unto himself' (2 *Cor.* 5:19), I dare not confine the intention of redemption to the saints alone. Christ is for every man.

I am aware the objection is often made, that 'if Christ taketh away the sin of the world, and yet the vast majority of men die in their sins and are lost, Christ's work for many was wrought in vain.' I see no force in this objection. I think we might as well argue, that because sin came into the world and marred creation, creation was in vain. We are not talking of the works of men, but of the eternal Word, and we must be content to see much in his works that we do not entirely understand. Though multitudes are lost, I have no doubt the last day will prove that nothing that Christ did for them was in vain.

I rest in the view of the text, that in some ineffable and inscrutable way, the whole world's sin was borne and atoned for by Christ. 'He taketh away, or makes atonement for the sin of all the men and women in the world.' I have no doubt, from Scripture, that the vast majority of 'the world's' inhabitants will be found at last to have received no benefit from Christ, and to have died in their sins. I repudiate the idea of universal salvation, as a dangerous heresy, and utterly contrary to Scripture.—But the lost will not prove to be lost because Christ did nothing for them. He bore their sins, he carried their transgressions, he provided payment; but they would not put in their claim to any interest in it. He set the prison door open to all; but the majority would not come out and be free.—In the work of the Father in election, and of the Spirit in conversion, I see limitation in the Bible most clearly. But in the work of Christ in atonement I see no limitation. The atonement was made for all the world, though it is applied to and enjoyed by none but believers.—Christ's intercession is the peculiar privilege of his people. But Christ's atonement is a benefit which is offered freely and honestly to all mankind.

In saying all this I am fully aware that the word 'world' is sometimes used in a qualified sense, and must be interpreted with some limitation. When it is said, 'the world knew him not' (*John* 1:10), it cannot mean that not a single person in the world knew him. But in the text before us I see no necessity for limitation. I see the whole mass of mankind's guilt brought together in one singular word, 'the sin of the world,' and that sin, I am told, Christ 'taketh away.' And I believe the true meaning to be, that the Lamb of God has made atonement sufficient for all mankind, though efficient unquestionably to none but believers.

Augustine remarks, 'How weighty must be the blood of the Lamb, by whom the world was made, to turn the scale when weighed against the world!'

Calvin, in his commentary on this verse, says, 'John uses the word sin in the singular number for any kind of iniquity; as if he had said that every kind of unrighteousness which alienates men from God is taken away by Christ. And when he says "The sin of the world," he extends this favour indiscriminately to the whole human race, that the Jews might not think that he had been sent to them alone. Hence we infer that the whole world is involved in the same condemnation; and that as all men, without exception, are guilty of unrighteousness before God, they need to be reconciled to him. John the Baptist, by speaking generally of the sin of the world, intended to impress upon us the conviction of our own misery, and to exhort us to seek the remedy. Now our duty is to embrace the benefit which is offered to all, that each of us may be convinced that *there is nothing to hinder him* from obtaining reconciliation in Christ, provided that he comes to him by the guidance of faith.'

Brentius says, 'Although all the men in the world do not receive the benefit of Christ's passion, because all do not believe on Christ, yet that benefit is so offered to the whole world, that whosoever, whether circumcised or uncircumcised, king or peasant, high or low, rich or poor, sick or well, old or young, receives Christ by faith, is justified before God, and saved with an eternal salvation.'

Musculus says, 'John places before us no one particular person whose sins the Lamb has come to take away; but under the expression "the world," he comprehends the whole race of mortals from the very beginning of the world to the end of it.'

Melanchthon says, 'He taketh away the sin, that is the universal condemnation, of the human race.'

Chemnitius says, 'John affirms that the benefits of Christ belong not to the Jews only, but to the whole world, and that no one who is in the world is excluded from them, if he is only willing to receive them by faith.'

The deep spiritual knowledge exhibited by John the Baptist in this verse, ought not to be overlooked. Such a sentence as the one before us never fell from the lips of any other disciple of Christ before the day of Pentecost. Others could say that our Lord was the Christ, the Son of God, the Messiah, the Son of David, the King of Israel, the Son of the Blessed, who was to come into the world. But none seem to have seen so clearly as John that Christ was the sacrifice for sin, the Lamb that was to be slain. Well would it be for the church of Christ in the nineteenth century, if all its ministers possessed as much knowledge of Christ's atonement as is here shown by John the Baptist! John saw the vicarious sacrifice of Christ, before he died on the cross. Many so-called Christians cannot see Christ's vicarious sacrifice even at this day!

30.—[*This is he of whom I said.*] These words appear to have been spoken in our Lord's presence, and to have been specially intended to point the multitude to him. 'This person before you is he of whom I have repeatedly spoken in my ministry, as the coming One who is far greater than myself. You see him now before you.'

[*A man ... he was before me.*] The human and divine natures of our Lord are here brought together by John in one sentence. 'He of whom I spake to you is a man, and yet at the same time he is One who was before me, because he has existed from all eternity.'

31.—[*I knew him not.*] This means, 'I was not acquainted with him in time past. There has been no private collusion or arrangement between him and me. I did not even know him by sight until the day when he came to be baptized.' The difficulty connected with these words of John will be considered fully at verse 33.

[*That he should be made manifest to Israel, etc.*] John here declares that the great end of his ministry was, that this wonderful person, whom he had just pointed out, should be manifested and made known to the Jews. He did not come to form a party of his own, or to baptize in his own name. The whole object of his preaching and baptizing was now before his hearers. It was simply to make known to Israel the Mighty One, the Lamb of God, whom they now saw.

32.—[*And John bare record.*] These words seem to denote a public and solemn testimony borne by John to the fact, that our Lord had been visibly acknowledged by God the Father as the Messiah. If his hearers would have further proof that this person, to whom he was pointing them, was really the Christ, he would tell them what he had seen with his own eyes. He would bear witness that he had seen visible proofs that this person was really the Messiah.

[*I saw.*] This means, 'At the time when our Lord was baptized, I saw this heavenly vision.' Whether any beside John saw this vision, and heard the voice of the Father which accompanied it, may well be doubted. At any rate, if they did, they did not understand either what they saw or heard.

[*The Spirit descending, etc.*] This means that John saw something coming down from heaven after the manner of a dove flying downwards, and that what he saw was the Holy Spirit, graciously revealing himself in a visible manner.

[*It abode upon him.*] This means that the heavenly vision of the Holy Spirit rested upon Christ at the time of his baptism. It lighted down upon him as a dove would settle down, and did not leave him.

I cannot satisfy myself that the expression 'like a dove,' in this verse, means that any dove was really seen by John, when our Lord was baptized. All the four Gospel writers describe an appearance 'like a dove.' St Luke distinctly speaks of 'a bodily shape.' That something visible was seen by John is plain, and that its appearance descending on our Lord, resembled the downward flight of a dove, is also plain. But I am unable to see that the Holy Ghost took upon him the actual form of a dove.

Some think, as Augustine, that the likeness to a dove was especially employed at this time, to answer the figure of Noah's flood. He says, 'As a dove did at that time bring tidings of the abating of the water, so doth it now of the abating of the wrath of God upon the preaching of the gospel.'

We must beware of supposing for a moment that this vision of the Spirit descending was meant to imply that our Lord first received the grace of the Holy Ghost at that particular time, or that he had not received it before in the same degree. We must not doubt that the Holy Ghost dwelt in Jesus 'without measure' from the very time of his incarnation. The vision was meant to show the church, that when Christ's ministry began, a fuller revelation of all three persons in the Trinity was made at once to mankind. It was meant at the same time to be a formal testimony to John the Baptist that the Messiah was before him,—that this was the promised Saviour whom God had anointed with the Holy Ghost and sent into the world,—that the time of Christ's ministry had begun,—that he who had the Spirit to bestow on men was before him,—and that his entrance on his public work was attested by the presence both of the Father and the Holy Ghost, in short, by a manifestation of all three persons in the Trinity at one time.

As a Levite, John doubtless was familiar with all the ceremonies by which the Jewish high priests and kings were solemnly inducted into their office. For his satisfaction, therefore, our Lord received visible attestation from heaven, and was publicly recognized as the Messiah, the anointed Priest, and King, and Prophet, before his forerunner's eyes.

Musculus on this verse remarks, 'The Spirit did not descend on Christ's account, who was never separate, either from the Holy Spirit or from the Father,—but on our account, that he who came to redeem the world, might be made manifest through John's declaration of him.'

33.—[*I knew him not.*] The Greek word so rendered, both here and in verse 31, is literally, 'I had not known him.' There is a difficulty connected with the expression which demands explanation. St Matthew tells us, that when our Lord came to John to be baptized, John said to him, 'I have need to be baptized of thee, and comest thou to me?' (*Matt.* 3:14), showing plainly by these words that he knew he was before him. And yet here we find John saying,

'I knew him not.' How can this apparent inconsistency be reconciled?

Some think, as Chrysostom, that 'John is speaking of former times, and not of the times near to his baptism.'

Some think, as Augustine, that it means, 'I had not known till that day that Jesus would baptize with the Holy Ghost, although I had long known him personally, and had recognized him as the Christ of God. But when he came to be baptized, it was also revealed to me that he would confer on men the great gift of the Holy Ghost.'

Some think, as Brentius and Beza, that it means, 'I had not known Jesus by sight until the day when he came to be baptized. I knew that he had been born of the Virgin Mary, but was not personally acquainted with him, having been myself brought up in the desert' (*Luke* 1:80). 'I had only been told by him who sent me to baptize, that whenever the Messiah came to be baptized, I should recognize him by the descent of the Holy Ghost. When he did come, I received a secret revelation from God that Messiah stood before me, and under the power of that feeling I confessed my unworthiness to baptize him. But when at last I did baptize him, I received a full confirmation of my faith, by beholding the promised sign of the descent of the Holy Ghost.' Those who hold this view, think the case of Samuel receiving a secret revelation about Saul, an illustration of the matter (*1 Sam.* 9:15).

Some think, as Poole, that it means, 'I knew him not perfectly and distinctly, though I had an impression when I first saw him coming to be baptized, that he was one far greater than myself, and under that impression demurred to baptizing him. After his baptism I saw clearly who he was.'

The last explanation is perhaps the simplest, and most probable. That John at one time did not know our Lord by sight at all, that he afterwards knew him imperfectly, and that his perfect knowledge of him, his nature, office, and work, was not attained till the time when the Spirit descended at his baptism, are points that seem clear. The time when he said, 'I have need to be baptized of thee,' would seem to be the time of imperfect knowledge, when the fact that Jesus was the Messiah began to dawn upon him, and made him cry out, 'Comest thou to me?'

Chrysostom observes, that the expression is a proof 'that the miracles which they say belong to Christ's childhood are false, and the invention of those who bring them to notice. For if he had begun from his early age to work miracles, neither could John have been ignorant of him, nor would the multitude have needed a teacher to make him known.'

[*He that sent me ... same said.*] This expression indicates that John the Baptist had many special revelations of God concerning his work, of which we have no record given to us. He seems to have been taught and instructed like one of the old prophets.

[*He which baptizeth with the Holy Ghost.*] The remarkable description of our Lord, here given by John the Baptist, has received three very different interpretations.

Some think that it means, 'This is he who shall institute Christian baptism, with which the gift of the Holy Ghost shall be connected. His baptism shall be like mine, a baptism of water. But it shall not be a baptism of water only, as mine is, but a baptism accompanied by the regenerating grace of the Spirit.'

Some think that it means, 'This is he who shall baptize with the Holy Ghost on the day of Pentecost, and confer miraculous gifts on the church.'

Some think it means, 'This is he who shall baptize the hearts of men, which neither thou canst do nor any other human minister. He has the prerogative of giving spiritual life. He is the giver of the Holy Spirit to all who believe on him.'

I am decidedly of the opinion that this third view is the correct one. It is the only one which seems at all answerable to the majesty of the person spoken of, the dignity of the speaker, and the solemnity of the occasion.—To say, 'This is he who shall institute Christian baptism' seems a very lame and impotent account of the expression.—To say, 'This is he who shall bestow miraculous gifts at the day of Pentecost,' is a degree better, but gives a picture of our Lord's office confined to a single generation.—But to say, 'This is he who, in every age of the church, will baptize the hearts of his people by the Holy Ghost, and by this baptism continually replenish the ranks of his mystical body,' is saying that which exactly suits the occasion, and describes our Lord's work in the world in a worthy manner.

Musculus, on this verse, remarks, 'What is it to baptize with the Holy Ghost? It is to regenerate the hearts of the elect, and consecrate them into the fellowship of the sons of God.' Again, he says, 'It is Christ alone who baptizes with the Holy Ghost; a power which, as divine, he keeps in his own hands and never communicates to any minister.'

The view I have maintained is ably set forth in Bucer's commentary on this place. He says, 'By the baptism of water we are received into the outward church of God; by the baptism of the Spirit into the inward church.' The opinion of one who was Regius Professor of Divinity at Cambridge, in the reign of Edward the Sixth, and the personal friend and adviser of Cranmer and the other English Reformers, deserves much consideration. It proves, at any rate, that the doctrine of inward baptism of the Spirit, which Christ alone gives to every believer, and the identity of this baptism with conversion or new birth, are not such modern and contemptible notions as some persons are pleased to think.

The untenableness of the view, held by many, that John's baptism was not the same as Christian baptism, to all intents and purposes, is ably shown by Lightfoot, in his *Harmony of the Four Evangelists*. If it was not Christian baptism, it would be hard to prove that some of the disciples ever received Christian baptism at all. There is not the slightest evidence that Andrew, Peter, and Philip were baptized by Jesus.

The familiarity which John displays with the Holy Ghost and his work, deserves particular attention. To say, as many do, that the Holy Ghost was not known until the day of Pentecost, is saying what cannot be proved. The Holy Ghost has always been in the hearts of believers in every age of the world. His abundant outpouring is undoubtedly a leading mark of the days since Christ came into the world. But the Holy Ghost was ever in God's elect, and without him there never was a soul saved.

34.—[*I saw and bare record, etc.*] This means, 'I saw perfectly, and from that time have distinctly and unhesitatingly testified that the person whom you now see before you is the Christ, the Son of the living God. From the day of his baptism I have been fully convinced that this is the Messiah.'

John here declares his own firm conviction of our Lord's divinity and eternal generation. He was satisfied that our Lord was not the Son of Mary only, but the Son of God.

JOHN 1:35-42

35 Again the next day after John stood, and two of his disciples;

36 And looking upon Jesus as he walked, he saith, Behold the Lamb of God!

37 And the two disciples heard him speak, and they followed Jesus.

38 Then Jesus turned, and saw them following, and saith unto them, What seek ye? They said unto him, Rabbi, (which is to say, being interpreted, Master,) where dwellest thou?

39 He saith unto them, Come and see. They came and saw where he dwelt, and abode with him that day: for it was about the tenth hour.

40 One of the two which heard John *speak*, and followed him, was Andrew, Simon Peter's brother.

41 He first findeth his own brother Simon, and saith unto him, We have found the Messias, which is, being interpreted, the Christ.

42 And he brought him to Jesus. And when Jesus beheld him, he said, Thou art Simon the son of Jona: thou shalt be called Cephas, which is by interpretation, A stone.

THESE verses ought always to be interesting to every true Christian. They describe the first beginnings of the Christian church. Vast as that church is now, there was a time when it consisted of only two weak members. The calling of those two members is described in the passage which is now before our eyes.

We see, for one thing, in these verses, *what good is done by continually testifying of Christ.*

The first time that John the Baptist cried, 'Behold the Lamb of God,' no result appears to have followed. We are not told of any who heard, inquired, and believed. But when he repeated the same words the next day, we read that two of his disciples 'heard him speak, and followed Jesus.' They were received most graciously by him whom they followed. 'They came and saw where he dwelt, and abode with him that day.' Truly it was a day in their lives most eventful, and most blessed! From that day they became fast and firm disciples of the new-found Messiah. They took up the cross. They continued with him in his temptations. They followed him whithersoever he went. One of them at least, if not both, became a chosen apostle, and a master builder in the Christian temple. And all was owing to John the Baptist's testimony: 'Behold the Lamb of God.' That testimony was a little seed. But it bore mighty fruits.

This simple story is a pattern of the way in which good has been done to souls in every age of the Christian church. By such testimony as that before us, and by none else, men and women are converted and saved. It is by exalting Christ, not the church,—Christ, not the sacraments,—Christ, not the ministry;—it is by this means that hearts are moved, and sinners are turned to God. To the world such testimony may seem weakness and foolishness. Yet, like the rams' horns before whose blast the walls of Jericho fell down, this testimony is mighty to the pulling down of strongholds. The story of the crucified Lamb of God has proved, in every age, the power of God unto salvation. Those who have done most for Christ's cause in every part of the world, have been men like John the Baptist. They have not cried, Behold me, or, Behold the church, or, Behold the ordinances, but 'Behold the Lamb.' If souls are to be saved, men must be pointed directly to Christ.

One thing, however, must never be forgotten. There must be patient continuance in preaching and teaching the truth, if we want good to be done. Christ must be set forth again and again, as the 'Lamb of God which taketh away the sin of the world.' The story of grace must be told repeatedly,—line upon line, and precept upon precept. It is the constant dropping which wears away the stone. The promise shall never be broken, that 'God's word shall not return unto him void' (*Isa.* 55:11). But it is nowhere said that it shall do good the very first time that it is preached. It was not the first proclamation of John the Baptist, but the second, which made Andrew and his companion follow Jesus.

We see, for another thing, *what good a believer may do to others, by speaking to them about Christ.*

No sooner does Andrew become a disciple, than he tells his brother Simon what a discovery he has made. Like one who has unexpectedly heard good tidings, he hastens to impart it to the one nearest and dearest to him. He says to his brother, 'We have found the Messias,' and he 'brings him to Jesus.' Who can tell what might have happened if Andrew had been of a silent, reserved, and uncommunicative spirit, like many a Christian in the present day? Who can tell but his brother might have lived and died a fisherman on the Galilean lake? But happily for Simon, Andrew was not a man of this sort. He was one whose heart was so full that he must speak. And to Andrew's outspoken testimony, under God, the great Apostle Peter owed the first beginning of light in his soul.

The fact before us is most striking and instructive. Out of the three first members of the Christian church, one at least was brought to Jesus by the private, quiet word of a relative. He seems to have heard no public preaching. He saw no mighty miracle wrought. He was not convinced by any powerful reasoning. He only heard his brother telling him that he had found a Saviour himself, and at once the work began in his soul. The simple testimony of a warm-hearted brother was the first link in the chain by which Peter was drawn out of the world and joined to Christ. The first blow in that mighty work by which Peter was made a pillar of the church, was struck by Andrew's words: 'We have found the Christ.'

Well would it be for the church of Christ if all believers were more like Andrew! Well would it be for souls if all men and women who have been converted themselves, would speak to their friends and relatives on spiritual subjects, and tell them what they have found! How much good might be done! How many might be led to Jesus, who now live and die in unbelief! The work of testifying the gospel of the grace of God ought not to be left to ministers alone. All who have received mercy ought to find a tongue, and to declare what God has done for their souls. All who have been delivered from the power of the devil, ought to go home and tell their friends what great things God has done for them (*Mark* 5:19). Thousands, humanly speaking, would listen to a word from a friend, who will not listen to a sermon. Every believer ought to be a home-missionary,—a missionary to his family, children, servants, neighbours, and friends. Surely, if we can find nothing to say to others about Jesus, we may well doubt whether we are savingly acquainted with him ourselves.

Let us take heed that we are among those who really follow Christ, and abide with him. It is not enough to hear him preached from the pulpit, and to read of him as described in books. We must actually follow him, pour out our hearts before him, and hold personal communion with him. Then, and not till then, we shall feel constrained to speak of him to others. The man who only knows Christ by the hearing of the ear, will never do much for the spread of Christ's cause in the earth.

Notes—John 1:35-42

35.—[*The next day.*] Let St John's particularity in noting days at this period of our Lord's history, be observed again in this verse. If, as many suppose, St John was one of the two who this day followed Jesus and became his disciples, we can well understand that it was a memorable day to him.

[*John stood.*] This expression seems to imply that there was some particular spot near Bethabara where John the Baptist was in the habit of standing, to preach, and to receive those who came to be baptized. While he 'stood' here, the event which follows took place.

36.—[*Looking ... Jesus, as he walked.*] This probably means that he saw Jesus walking among the crowd of persons who were attracted to Bethabara, alone, without followers, and as yet not recognized by anyone as the Messiah.

Stier remarks, 'John saw Jesus walking in silent meditation, waiting for his hour and his Father's commands; in full preparation for the world and its sin: equipped, for the testimony to the truth, with that armour which has been tested and approved in his first great spiritual conflict, and for the utterance of the new words of God which the Father has given him.'

[*He saith, Behold, etc.*] This seems to have been a second public proclamation of our Lord's office and character, a partial repetition of what had been said the day before; and yet, as the event shows, a more effective proclamation. The same truth may do good the second time that it is preached, which does nothing the first time.

37.—[*Heard ... speak ... followed.*] The three steps described in this verse are very noteworthy. John the Baptist 'speaks:' the disciples 'hear.' After hearing they 'follow Jesus.' This is a succinct summary of God's way of saving myriads of souls.

Rollock, on this verse, remarks, 'We

learn by this example, how powerful is the preaching of Christ,—yea, one or two words about Christ and the cross, how powerful are they in changing the hearts of men! Preach, if you like, about the great deeds of kings and generals, and their courage and glory;—these things will please men for a little time, but they will not convert them. But preach concerning him that was crucified, a subject apparently ignominious and foolish,—and then the story of the cross, which is foolishness to them that perish, will be the power and wisdom of God to them that believe.'

38.—[*What seek ye?*] We cannot doubt that our Lord knew perfectly well the hearts and motives of these two disciples. In asking this question therefore, he spoke partly for their encouragement, and partly to stir them up to self-inquiry. 'What seek ye? Is there anything that I can do for you, any truth that I can teach you, any burden that I can take away? If so, speak, and be not afraid.'—'What seek ye? Are you sure that you are following me with right motives? Are you sure that you are not regarding me as a temporal ruler? Are you sure that you are not, like other Jews, seeking riches, honour, greatness, in this world? Prove your own selves, and be sure that you are seeking the right object.'

[*Which is to say, being interpreted.*] This is one of a class of expressions which shows that John wrote for Gentile readers rather than Jews. A Jew would not have needed this parenthetical comment. This same remark applies to verse 41.

[*Where dwellest thou?*] This question seems to imply a desire for conversation and private communion. 'We would fain know more of thee. We are drawn to thee by John the Baptist's proclamation. We would like to go aside with thee from the crowd, and inquire of thee more privately and quietly, at thy dwelling, about the things which are upon our hearts.'

To apply the text, as many do, to our Lord's spiritual dwelling in 'contrite hearts,' etc. (*Isa.* 57:15), may produce good doctrinal and practical theology. But it is not the point of the text.

39.—[*Come and see.*] The great affability, and condescension of these first words of our Lord's after his public appearance as Messiah, ought not to be overlooked. The very first thing that we hear him saying, after he has been publicly proclaimed as the 'Lamb of God,' is, 'Come and see.' It is a pleasant type of what he has been ever saying to the sons of men from that day down to this. 'Come and see who I am, and what I am. Come and be acquainted with me.'

Schoettgen and Lightfoot both remark that the expression 'Come and see,' is a very common one in rabbinical writings, and would be very familiar to the Jews.

[*Where he dwelt.*] We can only suppose that the place where our Lord was dwelling at this time, was some temporary residence in or near Bethabara. At the best, it was probably some humble lodging. It is not impossible that it was nothing more than a cave. He often 'had not where to lay his head.' If the two disciples had the least relic of Jewish expectation that Messiah would appear in royal dignity and glory, our Lord's dwelling would go far to disabuse their minds of the idea.

[*Abode with him that day ... tenth hour.*] The Jewish day began at six o'clock in the evening. The tenth hour therefore means four o'clock in the afternoon. At this late hour of the day his disciples found it impossible to conclude their conversation with Jesus, and therefore remained in the same lodging with him all night.

Many commentators, from Augustine downwards, make the natural remark that this evening must have been a blessed evening for these two disciples; and that it would have been pleasant if the conversation had been given to us! Yet if it had been good for us to know the conversation, it would doubtless have been recorded. There are no deficiencies in Scripture.

40.—[*One of the two ... was Andrew.*] The priority of Andrew to Peter ought not to be overlooked. Peter, to whom the Church of Rome boastfully attributes a primacy among the apostles, was neither converted nor made acquainted with Christ so soon as his brother.

Who the other of these two disciples was, we are not told. It is highly probable, as Chrysostom and Theophylact conjecture, that it was St John himself. On seven other occasions in this Gospel he humbly withholds his name (*John* 13:23; 19:26, 35; 20:2; 21:7, 20, 24). It is therefore very likely that he withheld it here.—The supposition of Musculus, and others, that the other disciple was a person of less zeal and sincerity than Andrew, and is therefore not named, appears to me improbable.

41.—[*He first.*] This expression must either mean that Andrew was the first of the two disciples who brought a brother to Jesus,—or that he was the first disciple, speaking generally, who spoke to others of the Messiah, when he had found him,—or that he was the first to tell his brother Peter, and Peter was not the first to tell him about Christ.

[*We have found.*] This expression implies an unexpected and joyful discovery. The evening's conversation which Andrew had held with Jesus had convinced him that he was indeed the Christ.

[*The Messias … interpreted … Christ.*] It is almost needless to remark that these names mean 'the anointed one.' The first is Hebrew, and the second is Greek. Kings, prophets, and priests, in the Old Testament, were anointed; and our Lord as the Prophet, Priest, and King of the church, was called the Anointed One, not because he was really anointed with oil, but because he was 'anointed with the Holy Ghost' (*Acts* 10:38).

The extent of Andrew's religious knowledge ought not to be overlooked. Poor and humble in station as he was, he seems, like all the Jews, to have known what the Old Testament prophets had foretold about Messiah, and to have been prepared to hear of a person appearing in the character of Messiah. It is one of many expressions in the Gospels which show that the lower orders among the Jews were far better acquainted with the letter of the Old Testament Scriptures, than the poor in our own day generally are with the letter of the New Testament, or indeed of any part of the Bible.

Calvin remarks on Andrew's conduct, 'Woe to our indolence, if we do not, after having been fully enlightened, endeavour to make others partakers of the same grace.'

42.—[*When Jesus beheld … said, Thou art Simon.*] Our Lord here displayed his perfect knowledge of all persons, names, and things. He needed not that any should tell him who and what a person was. This knowledge was supposed by the Jews to be a peculiar attribute of Messiah, whenever he came. He was to be one of 'quick understanding' (*Isa.* 11:3). Enough for us to know that it is a peculiar attribute of God. He alone knows the hearts of men. Our Lord's perfect knowledge of all hearts, was one among many proofs of his divinity. The same knowledge appears again in his address to Nathanael, in this chapter, verse 47, and in his conversation with the Samaritan woman (*John* 4:18, etc.).—The effect produced in both cases, is very worthy of notice.

[*Cephas.*] This is a Syriac word, and is equivalent to the Greek word Petros, which we render Peter. Both mean a stone, a portion of a rock. 'Petra' means a rock, 'Petros' a piece of a rock. Peter was the latter, but not the former.

[*A stone.*] The marginal reading here, as Lightfoot remarks, would have been much better than that which the translators have put in our version. If the words were 'Cephas, which is by interpretation Peter,' it would have conveyed our Lord's meaning far more clearly.

The custom of having two names appears to have been common in New Testament times. The Apostle Peter seems to have been only known as 'Cephas' in the Corinthian church. Out of the five other places in the New Testament where the name Cephas is found, four are in the Epistle to the Corinthians, while the name Peter is not used in that epistle at all.

Nifanius gives the names of three popes who have so grossly mistaken the origin of the word Cephas as to suppose that it is derived from the Greek word which signifies 'a head,' and that it indicated Peter's headship in the church! Such a palpable blunder is one of a thousand proofs that popes are no more infallible than other men. Calovius makes the same charge against no less a person than Cardinal Bellarmine.

If it be asked why our Lord gave Simon

this new name, the best answer appears to be that it was given with a special reference to the change which grace was to work in Simon's heart. Naturally impulsive, unstable, and unsteady, he was finally to become a firm, solid stone in the church of Christ, and to testify his unshaken adherence to Christ by suffering martyrdom.

Chrysostom thinks that our Lord altered Simon's name 'to show that it was he who gave the old covenant, that it was he who called Abram Abraham, and Sarai Sarah, and Jacob Israel.'

Lightfoot, on these verses, after noticing the error which Roman Catholic writers attempt to found upon it, about Peter being the rock on which the church is built, makes the following curious observation: 'If they will so pertinaciously adhere to it, let us apprehend our Lord speaking *prophetically*, and foretelling the grand error that would spring up in the church, namely, that Peter is a rock, than which the Christian church has known nothing more sad and destructive.'

Let it be noted, in leaving this passage, that the selection of such humble unlearned men as those here described, to be the first apostles and preachers of the gospel, is a strong evidence of the truth of Christianity. A religion which was propagated by such weak instruments, in the face of persecution and opposition from the great and learned, must be a religion from God. Such results from such instrumentality cannot possibly be accounted for on natural principles.

JOHN 1:43-51

43 The day following Jesus would go forth into Galilee, and findeth Philip, and saith unto him, Follow me.

44 Now Philip was of Bethsaida, the city of Andrew and Peter.

45. Philip findeth Nathanael, and saith unto him, We have found him, of whom Moses in the law, and the prophets, did write, Jesus of Nazareth, the son of Joseph.

46 And Nathanael said unto him, Can there any good thing come out of Nazareth? Philip saith unto him, Come and see.

47 Jesus saw Nathanael coming to him, and saith of him, Behold an Israelite indeed, in whom is no guile!

48 Nathanael saith unto him, Whence knowest thou me? Jesus answered and said unto him, Before that Philip called thee, when thou wast under the fig tree, I saw thee.

49 Nathanael answered and saith unto him, Rabbi, thou art the Son of God; thou art the King of Israel.

50 Jesus answered and said unto him, Because I said unto thee, I saw thee under the fig tree, believest thou? thou shalt see greater things than these.

51 And he saith unto him, Verily, verily, I say unto you, Hereafter ye shall see heaven open, and the angels of God ascending and descending upon the Son of man.

L ET us observe, as we read these verses, *how various are the paths by which souls are led into the narrow way of life.*

We are told of a man, named Philip, being added to the little company of Christ's disciples. He does not appear to have been moved, like Andrew and his companions, by the testimony of John the Baptist. He was not drawn, like Simon Peter, by the outspoken declaration of a brother. He seems to have been called directly by Christ himself, and the agency of man seems not to have been used in his calling. Yet in faith and life he became one with those who were disciples before him. Though led by different paths, they all entered the same road, embraced the same truths, served the same Master, and at length reached the same home.

The fact before us is a deeply important one. It throws light on the history of all God's people in every age, and of every tongue. There are diversities of operations in the saving of souls. All true Christians are led by one Spirit, washed in one blood, serve one Lord, lean on one Saviour, believe one truth, and walk by one general rule. But all are not converted in one and the same manner. All do not pass through the same experience. In conversion, the Holy Ghost acts as a sovereign. He calleth everyone severally as he will.

A careful recollection of this point may save us much trouble. We must beware of making the experience of other believers the measure of our own. We must beware of denying another's grace, because he has not been led by the same way as ourselves. Has a man got the real grace of God? This is the only question that concerns us.—Is he a penitent man? Is he a believer? Does he live a holy life?—Provided these inquiries can be answered satisfactorily, we may well be content. It matters nothing by what path a man has been led, if he has only been led at last into the right way.

Let us observe, secondly, in these verses, *how much of Christ there is in the Old Testament Scriptures*. We read that when Philip described Christ to Nathanael, he says, 'We have found him of whom Moses in the law and the prophets did write.'

Christ is the sum and substance of the Old Testament. To him the earliest promises pointed in the days of Adam, and Enoch, and Noah, and Abraham, and Isaac, and Jacob. To him every sacrifice pointed in the ceremonial worship appointed at Mount Sinai. Of him every high priest was a type, and every part of the tabernacle was a shadow, and every judge and deliverer of Israel was a figure. He was the Prophet like unto Moses, whom the Lord God promised to send, and the King of the house of David, who came to be David's Lord as well as son. He was the Son of the virgin, and the Lamb foretold by Isaiah,—the righteous Branch mentioned by Jeremiah,—the true Shepherd foreseen by Ezekiel,—the Messenger of the covenant promised by Malachi,—and the Messiah, who, according to Daniel, was to be cut off, though not for himself. The further we read in the volume of the Old Testament, the clearer do we find the testimony about Christ. The light which the inspired writers enjoyed in ancient days was, at best, but dim, compared to that of the gospel. But the coming person they all saw afar off, and on whom they all fixed their eyes, was one and the same. The Spirit, which was in them, testified of Christ (*1 Pet.* 1:11).

Do we stumble at this saying? Do we find it hard to see Christ in the Old Testament, because we do not see his name? Let us be sure that the fault is all our own. It is our spiritual vision which is to blame, and not the book. The eyes of our understanding need to be enlightened. The veil has yet to be taken away. Let us pray for a more humble, childlike, and teachable spirit, and let us take up 'Moses and the prophets' again. Christ is there, though our eyes may not yet have seen him. May we never rest till we can subscribe to our Lord's words about the Old Testament Scriptures: 'They are they which testify of me' (*John* 5:39).

Let us observe, thirdly, in these verses, *the good advice which Philip gave to Nathanael*. The mind of Nathanael was full of doubts about the Saviour of whom Philip told him. 'Can there any good thing,' he said, 'come out of Nazareth?' And what did Philip reply? He said, 'Come and see.'

Wiser counsel than this it would be impossible to conceive! If Philip had reproved Nathanael's unbelief, he might have driven him back for many a day, and given offence. If he had reasoned with him, he might have failed to convince him, or might have confirmed him in his doubts. But by inviting him to prove the matter for himself, he showed his entire confidence in the truth of his own assertion, and his willingness to have it tested and proved. And the result shows the wisdom of Philip's words. Nathanael owed his early acquaintance with Christ to that frank invitation: 'Come and see.'

If we call ourselves true Christians, let us never be afraid to deal with people about their souls as Philip dealt with Nathanael. Let us invite them boldly to make proof of our religion. Let us tell them confidently that they cannot know its real value until they have tried it. Let us assure them that vital Christianity courts every possible inquiry. It has no secrets. It has nothing to conceal. Its faith and practice are spoken against, just because they are not known. Its enemies speak evil of things with which they are not acquainted. They understand neither what they say nor whereof they affirm. Philip's mode of dealing, we may be sure, is one principal way to do good. Few are ever moved by reasoning and argument. Still fewer are frightened into repentance. The man who does most good to souls, is often the simple believer who says to his friends, 'I have found a Saviour; come and see him.'

Let us observe, lastly, in these verses, *the high character which Jesus gives of Nathanael*. He calls him 'an Israelite indeed, in whom is no guile.'

Nathanael, there can be no doubt, was a true child of God, and a child of God in difficult times. He was one of a very little flock. Like Simeon and Anna, and other pious Jews, he was living by faith, and waiting prayerfully for the promised Redeemer, when our Lord's ministry began. He had that which grace alone can give,—an honest heart, a heart without guile. His knowledge was probably small. His spiritual eyesight was dim. But he was one who had lived carefully up to his light. He had diligently used such knowledge as he possessed. His eye had been single, though his vision had not been strong. His spiritual judgment had been honest, though it had not been powerful. What he saw in Scripture he had held firmly, in spite of Pharisees and Sadducees, and all the fashionable religion of the day. He was an honest Old Testament believer, who had stood alone. And here was the secret of our Lord's peculiar commendation! He declared Nathanael to be a true son of Abraham,—a Jew inwardly, possessing circumcision in the spirit, as well as in the letter,—an Israelite in heart, as well as a son of Jacob in the flesh.

Let us pray that we may be of the same spirit as Nathanael. An honest, unprejudiced mind,—a childlike willingness to follow the truth, wherever the truth may lead us,—a simple, hearty desire to be guided, taught, and led by the Spirit,—a thorough determination to use every spark of light which we have,—are possessions of priceless value. A man of this spirit may live in the midst of much darkness, and be surrounded by every possible disadvantage to his soul. But the Lord Jesus will take care that such a man does not miss the way to heaven. 'The meek will he guide in judgment: and the meek will he teach his way' (*Psa.* 25:9).

Notes—John 1:43-51

43.—[*The day following.*] This is the fourth successive day which is specially named by St John, and its events described. The first contained John the Baptist's reply to the priests and Levites,—the second, his public announcement of our Lord as the Lamb of God,—the third, the calling of Andrew and his companion, and Peter,—the fourth describes the calling of Philip and Nathanael.

[*Would go forth.*] The Greek word rendered 'would,' signifies that our Lord 'willed,' or had a will.

[*Findeth Philip.*] It does not appear where Philip was when Jesus called him. He must either have been at Bethabara, among John's hearers,—or at some place on the road from Bethabara to Galilee,—or at his own native place, Bethsaida. The last is perhaps the most probable idea.

[*Follow me.*] This simple sentence describes the direct quickening voice of an almighty Saviour. It is evident that the power of the Holy Ghost accompanied our Lord's words, and that as soon as they were spoken, Philip, like Matthew the publican, arose, left all, and became a disciple. In conversion God acts as a sovereign. One is called in one way, and another in another. Rollock observes on this verse, 'This teaches us that Christ is able to call any one whom he pleases into the kingdom of heaven, without the ministry either of angel or man.'

44.—[*Philip ... of Bethsaida ... city ... Andrew ... Peter.*] This verse seems to make it probable that Philip's conversion and calling took place at Bethsaida. Andrew and Peter having been converted and become companions of Jesus on his way to Galilee, would appear to have taken him to their own native place, Bethsaida.

45.—[*We have found him.*] Philip, like his fellow-citizen, Andrew, seems to have expected the appearance of Messiah.

Chrysostom remarks, 'Seest thou what a thoughtful mind he had, how assiduously he meditates on the writings of Moses, and expected the advent? The expression, "We have found," belongs always to those who are in some way seeking.'

[*Him ... Moses ... prophets did write.*] Here, as in the case of Andrew, we should notice the familiarity with the general contents of Scripture which a poor Jew like Philip possessed. He thoroughly understood that 'Moses and the prophets' held forth the promise of a coming Redeemer, and that a better Priest, Prophet, and King were foretold in their writings. 'The Old Testament,' as the Church of England Article wisely declares, 'is not contrary to the New; for both in the Old Testament and New, everlasting life is offered to mankind by Christ.' We must beware in these latter days, of despising the Old Testament. It is one by-path to infidelity.

[*Jesus of Nazareth ... son of Joseph.*] Philip here describes our Lord according to the common report about him, and in all probability according to his own present knowledge. His heart was at present better than his head. The miraculous conception of Christ was hidden from him. Yet it is not unworthy of remark, that this ignorant account of our Lord was very likely the cause of Nathanael's doubt and prejudice, exhibited in the next verse. The mistakes of young converts are often mighty stumbling-blocks in the way of other people's souls. We must not, however, despise Philip because of his mistake. Rollock remarks, 'I had rather a man should stammer and babble about Christ, providing he does it sincerely and from his heart, and has before him as an object the glory of God and salvation of men, than say many things eloquently about Christ, for ostentation and vainglory.'

46.—[*Can ... any good thing come ... Nazareth?*] This question shows the low estimate in which Nazareth, where our Lord had been brought up, was held. It was an obscure town in a corner of Galilee, not far from the borders of the province, and its reputation seems to have been very bad. Nathanael could not remember any prophecy about Messiah coming out of Nazareth, and at once stumbled at the idea of him whom 'Moses and the prophets' had described, belonging to such a contemptible place.

The condescension of our Lord in living thirty years in such a place as Nazareth, is strongly brought out by Nathanael's question.

Augustine, Cyril, Origen, and others thought that the sentence before us ought not to be interpreted as a question, but as a simple affirmation: 'Some good thing may come out of Nazareth.' Wycliffe's version also takes this view. The sentence would then be the expression of a calm and unprejudiced mind, acknowledging the possibility of good coming from Nazareth. Musculus thinks it possible, in this view of the expression, that Nathanael might have had in his mind the remarkable prophetical saying quoted in St Matthew, 'He shall be called a Nazarene'! The judgment of the great majority of interpreters agrees with our own translation, that it is a question, and not an assertion; and it is by far the more probable view of the text.

[*Come and see.*] How common this expression was among the Jewish religious teachers has been already noticed. Philip's wisdom in not arguing and reasoning with Nathanael, should be observed. Ford gives a good quotation from Adam, 'Little good comes by disputing. Pride is generally at the bottom of it, and not charity or love of truth; and it is seldom managed with decency or candour enough to produce any good effect. Let fall a word in season, and wait in patience till the rain drops on it from heaven.'

47.—[*In whom is no guile.*] It is very likely that in using this expression our Lord referred to Psalm 32, where the character of the godly man is described. He is not only one whose iniquities are forgiven, but one 'in whose spirit there is no guile.' The expression implies a true heart, a really converted man, a genuine son of Abraham by faith, as well as a son according to the flesh.

Hutcheson observes, 'The true mark of a true Israelite in spirit, is not sinlessness or perfection, but sincerity.'

48.—[*Whence knowest thou me?*] This question implies Nathanael's surprise that Jesus should exhibit any knowledge of his character.

[*When ... under the fig tree, I saw thee.*] The common opinion about this expression is, that Nathanael was praying or holding communion with God under the fig-tree. It may be so. We are told nothing about it, and are entirely left to conjecture. If it had been good for us to know, it would have been told us. Sufficient for us to understand that when Nathanael thought he was alone and no eye upon him, the Lord Jesus, by his divine power of seeing and knowing all things, was perfectly acquainted with all that Nathanael said, thought, and did. His 'eyes are in every place' (*Prov.* 15:3).

Chrysostom and Theophylact think that the expression only refers to the conversation between Philip and Nathanael about Jesus, which had taken place under a fig-tree. Grotius takes the same view.

Gill mentions a tradition in the Syriac dictionary, 'that Nathanael's mother had laid him under a fig-tree when the infants were slain at Bethlehem by Herod' (*Matt.* 2:16), and that our Lord showed his perfect knowledge by referring to this fact.

Heinsius thinks there is a reference to the prophecy of Zechariah: 'In that day . . . shall ye call every man his neighbour under the vine and under the fig-tree' (*Zech.* 3:10), and that hence Nathanael drew the inference that Messiah's days were come, and Messiah before him.

Augustine sees an allegory in the fig-tree, and gravely says, that 'as Adam and Eve, when they had sinned, made themselves aprons of fig-leaves, fig-leaves must signify sins. Nathanael therefore being under the fig-tree signifies being under the shadow of death!'

49.—[*Thou art the Son of God ... King of Israel.*] These words are the outburst of a heart convinced at once that Jesus was the Messiah. They are a noble confession that our Lord was that divine person who was promised to come into the world to redeem sinners, and that King who was prophesied of as the future Gatherer and Ruler of the tribes of Israel. Whether Nathanael clearly understood the nature of our Lord's kingdom at this time, may be reasonably doubted. But that he saw, like Peter, that he was the Christ, the Son of the Blessed, we cannot doubt. The restoring of the kingdom to Israel was a subject which we know, from other passages of Scripture, was one of the last which the first disciples were able to understand aright (*Acts* 1:6).

The history of Nathanael's calling at this point should be compared with that of the woman of Samaria, in the fourth chapter of this Gospel. It is striking to observe that a discovery and conviction of our Lord's perfect knowledge of the most secret things, was in both cases the turning point.

It should not be forgotten, that the title 'King of Israel,' was one which our Lord never refused during his ministry, though he never took to himself his great power and actually reigned. The angel Gabriel foretold that the Lord God would 'give unto him the throne of his father David,' and that he would 'reign over the house of Jacob,' and that of his kingdom there would 'be no end' (*Luke* 1:32, 33). When the wise men came from the East, they inquired for him who was born 'King of the Jews' (*Matt.* 2:2). When our Lord was crucified, the title over his head was, 'King of the Jews.' All this shall yet be literally true. Christ shall yet be King in Zion, and reign over the gathered and restored tribes of Israel at his second coming. And then the words of Nathanael shall be seen completely fulfilled. He shall be acknowledged by all as the 'Son of God, and King of Israel.'

50.—[*Believest thou?*] It admits of a question whether this expression would not be better rendered, as it might be with perfect grammatical correctness, 'thou believest.' It would then be very like our Lord's words to Thomas, 'Because thou hast seen me, thou hast believed' (*John* 20:29). The sense would be, 'Because I said I saw thee under the fig-tree, thou believest. It is well. Great is thy faith. But I tell thee for thy comfort and encouragement, that thou shalt one day see far greater proofs of my divinity and Messiahship than these.' Wycliffe's, Tyndale's, and Cranmer's versions, all render the expression as an affirmation, and not as a question. Aretius maintains the same view.

51.—[*Verily, verily, I say.*] This expression is peculiar to St John's Gospel, and very remarkable. It is the word which is familiar to all Christians: 'Amen,' twice repeated. It is found twenty-five times in this Gospel, always at the beginning of a sentence, and always used by Christ. In every place it implies a very solemn, emphatic assertion of some great truth, or heart-searching fact. No other writer in the New Testament, except St John, ever gives the double 'Amen.'

[*Hereafter ye shall see heaven ... angels ... Son of man.*] This prediction is very remarkable. It should be carefully observed that it is not addressed to Nathanael alone. The preceding verse says, 'thou shalt see.' The present verse says, 'ye shall see,'—that is, 'thou and all my other disciples.'

About the true meaning of the prediction, commentators differ exceedingly. Arguing, as nearly all do, that the words plainly refer to Jacob's vision of the ladder reaching from heaven to earth (*Gen.* 28:12), they disagree about the way in which the prediction is fulfilled.

Some think, as Stier, that the prediction must be interpreted figuratively, and that it was fulfilled when our Lord was upon earth. They think it only means that Nathanael and the other disciples would see a still fuller revelation of Christ and the gospel by and by. They would see a figurative fulfilment of Jacob's vision, and a way opened from earth to heaven for all true Israelites, or believers. They would see still greater proofs, in the shape of miracles and signs, that Jesus was the Son of God. Heaven, in a spiritual sense shut by the sin of the first Adam, would be opened by the obedience of the second Adam. 'The heavenly ladder,' says Bonaventura, quoted by Calovius, 'was broken in Adam and repaired in Christ.'—According to this view, 'the angels of God' in the text mean nothing in particular, which, to say the least, seems a very loose and unsatisfactory explanation.

Others think, as Rollock, that the prediction must be interpreted literally, and that it was fulfilled while our Lord was on earth. They think it was accomplished when our Lord was transfigured,—when an angel appeared in the garden of Gethsemane,— and when our Lord ascended on the Mount of Olives. This view also seems very unsatisfactory. The transfiguration, and the agony in the garden, were not seen by Nathanael at all. There is nothing whatever said about angels appearing, either at the transfiguration or the ascension. And as to

'angels ascending and descending,' there is nothing at any period of the gospel history at all answering to the expression.

The only true and satisfactory view, I believe, is that which makes the whole prediction apply to events which are still future. Our Lord spoke of his second coming and kingdom. When he comes the second time to take his great power and reign, the words of this text shall be literally fulfilled. His believing people shall see heaven open, and a constant communication kept up between heaven and earth,—the tabernacle of God with men, and the angels visibly ministering to the King of Israel, and King of all the earth.

The context confirms me in this view of the text. Nathanael believed Jesus to be the Messiah, when he was lowly and poor. Jesus rewards his faith by assuring him that, lowly as he now seems, he shall one day come in the clouds of heaven and reign as a King.

I am further confirmed by the striking likeness between our Lord's words here, and those he addressed to the chief priests, in the day that he was arraigned as a prisoner before them. 'Hereafter shall ye see the Son of man sitting on the right hand of power, and coming in the clouds of heaven' (*Matt.* 26:64). This view of the prediction is maintained by Gomarus.

I am aware that some maintain, in opposition to the view I support, that the Greek word rendered 'hereafter,' must mean 'from henceforth: i.e., immediately after the present time, and ever hereafter,' and does not imply a distant event. In reply, I would have it specially noted, that the Greek word here translated 'hereafter,' is the very same that is used by our Lord in the solemn words, just quoted, which he addressed to the chief priests when he was arraigned (*Matt.* 26:64). In that case there cannot be any reasonable doubt that he spoke of a far distant event and time. I believe, that in like manner, he speaks of a far distant event and time in this place.

As to the nature of Christ's future kingdom, and the intercourse which shall then be kept up by angels between earth and heaven, this is not the place to speak. I only remark, that the words before us will probably receive a far more real and literal accomplishment than many of us are expecting.

It is worthy of remark that Nathanael calls our Lord 'the Son of God.' Jesus in his prediction tells him he shall see angels ascending and descending on the 'Son of man.' He whom Nathanael now saw as a man, would yet appear as man glorified in the heavenly kingdom. He would even then be God-man. The expression 'Son of man,' here first used by St John, seems derived, as Chemnitius says, from Daniel's words in a prophecy about Messiah (*Dan.* 7:13, 14). It is never applied to our Lord by any but himself, except by Stephen (*Acts* 7:56). Lightfoot thinks that 'it is used so often by our Saviour about himself, as intimating that he is the second Adam, the true seed of the woman.'

In leaving this passage, the question naturally arises, Who was Nathanael? How is it that we hear so little afterwards of so good a man and so clear-sighted a believer?

Some think, as Augustine and others, that Nathanael was purposely not placed among our Lord's immediate companions and apostles, because he was a man of learning and knowledge, lest any should say that our Lord chose learned men to be his first ministers. I can see nothing in this argument. There is no evidence to my own mind that Nathanael was more learned than other Jews of humble birth, in our Lord's time. Moreover he was a friend of Philip, one of our Lord's apostles, and most probably a man of similar position and attainments.—In fact we are told elsewhere that he lived at 'Cana of Galilee' (*John* 21:2).

Some think, because Nathanael lived at Cana, that he was the same person as the apostle Simon the Canaanite (*Matt.* 10:4; *Mark* 3:18).

Some think that he was Stephen the martyr, because Stephen saw the heavens opened in vision (*Acts* 7:56).

The most probable opinion to my own mind is, that Nathanael was the apostle who is called elsewhere Bartholomew, and who, like others of the apostles, had two names. In favour of this opinion there are three remarkable facts. The first is, that in three lists of the twelve apostles out of four, the names of Philip and Bartholomew are always found together (*Matt.* 10:3; *Mark* 3:18; *Luke* 6:14).—The second is, that Nathanael is specially mentioned after our Lord's ascension as a companion of Peter, Thomas, James, John, and two other disciples.—The third is, that St John never once mentions the name of Bartholomew in his Gospel.—The objection that Nathanael's name is never mentioned by Matthew, Mark, or Luke, is of no weight. No one of the three, it may be replied, tells us that Peter was called Cephas. Only Matthew gives Jude, the brother of James, the name of Lebbæus.

The point happily is not one of any particular importance. I only say that the conjectural probability that Nathanael was an apostle, and was the same as Bartholomew, seems to me very strong and well founded.

In leaving this chapter the observation of Aretius is worth quoting. He remarks that the chapter is singularly rich in names or epithets applied to the Lord Jesus Christ. He numbers up the following twenty-one. 1. The Word. 2. God. 3. Life. 4. Light. 5. The true light. 6. The only begotten of the Father. 7. Full of grace and truth. 8. Jesus Christ. 9. The only begotten Son. 10. The Lord. 11. The Lamb of God. 12. Jesus. 13. A Man. 14. The Son of God. 15. Rabbi. 16. Teacher. 17. Messiah. 18. Christ. 19. The Son of Joseph. 20. The King of Israel. 21. The Son of man.

JOHN 2:1-11

1 And the third day there was a marriage in Cana of Galilee; and the mother of Jesus was there:

2 And both Jesus was called, and his disciples, to the marriage.

3 And when they wanted wine, the mother of Jesus saith unto him, They have no wine.

4 Jesus saith unto her, Woman, what have I to do with thee? mine hour is not yet come.

5 His mother saith unto the servants, Whatsoever he saith unto you, do *it*.

6 And there were set there six waterpots of stone, after the manner of the purifying of the Jews, containing two or three firkins apiece.

7 Jesus saith unto them, Fill the water-pots with water. And they filled them up to the brim.

8 And he saith unto them, Draw out now, and bear unto the governor of the feast. And they bare *it*.

9 When the ruler of the feast had tasted the water that was made wine, and knew not whence it was: (but the servants which drew the water knew;) the governor of the feast called the bridegroom,

10 And saith unto him, Every man at the beginning doth set forth good wine; and when men have well drunk, then that which is worse: *but* thou hast kept the good wine until now.

11 This beginning of miracles did Jesus in Cana of Galilee, and manifested forth his glory; and his disciples believed on him.

THESE verses describe a miracle which should always possess a special interest in the eyes of a true Christian. It is the first, in order of time, of the many mighty works which Jesus did, when he was upon earth. We are distinctly told, 'This beginning of miracles did Jesus in Cana of Galilee.'—Like every other miracle which St John was inspired to record, it is related with great minuteness and particularity. And, like every other miracle in St John's Gospel, it is rich in spiritual lessons.

We learn, firstly, from these verses, *how honourable in the sight of Christ is the estate of matrimony*. To be present at 'a marriage' was almost the first public act of our Lord's earthly ministry.

Marriage is not a sacrament, as the Church of Rome asserts. It is simply a state of life ordained by God for man's benefit. But it is a state which ought never to be spoken of with levity, or regarded with disrespect. The Prayer Book service has well described it, as 'an honourable estate, instituted of God in the time of man's innocency, and signifying unto us the mystical union that is betwixt Christ and his church.' Society is never in a healthy condition, and true religion never flourishes in that land where the marriage tie is lightly esteemed. They who lightly esteem it have not the mind of Christ. He who 'beautified and adorned the estate of matrimony by his presence and first miracle that he wrought in Cana of Galilee,' is One who is always of one mind. 'Marriage,' says the Holy Ghost by St Paul, 'is honourable in all' (*Heb.* 13:4).

One thing, however, ought not to be forgotten. Marriage is a step which so seriously affects the temporal happiness and spiritual welfare of two immortal souls, that it ought never to be taken in hand 'unadvisedly, lightly, wantonly, and without due consideration.' To be truly happy, it should be undertaken 'reverently, discreetly, soberly, and in the fear of God.' Christ's blessing and presence are essential to a happy wedding. The marriage at which there is no place for Christ and his disciples, is not one that can justly be expected to prosper.

We learn, secondly, from these verses, that *there are times when it is lawful to be merry and rejoice.* Our Lord himself sanctioned a wedding feast by his own presence. He did not refuse to be a guest at 'a marriage in Cana of Galilee.' 'A feast,' it is written, 'is made for laughter, and wine maketh merry' (*Eccles.* 10:19). Our Lord, in the passage before us, countenances both the feast and the use of wine.

True religion was never meant to make men melancholy. On the contrary, it was intended to increase real joy and happiness among men. The servant of Christ unquestionably ought to have nothing to do with races, balls, theatres, and such-like amusements, which tend to frivolity and dissipation, if not to sin. But he has no right to hand over innocent recreation, and family gatherings to the devil and the world. The Christian who withdraws entirely from the society of his fellow-men, and walks the earth with a face as melancholy as if he was always attending a funeral, does injury to the cause of the gospel. A cheerful, kindly spirit is a great recommendation to a believer. It is a positive misfortune to Christianity when a Christian cannot smile. A merry heart, and a readiness to take part in all innocent mirth, are gifts of inestimable value. They go far to soften prejudices, to take up stumbling-blocks out of the way, and to make way for Christ and the gospel.

The subject no doubt is a difficult and delicate one. On no point of Christian practice is it so hard to hit the mean between that which is lawful and that which is unlawful, between that which is right and that which is wrong. It is very hard indeed to be both merry and wise. High spirits soon degenerate into levity. Acceptance of many invitations to feasts soon leads to waste of time, and begets leanness of soul. Frequent eating and drinking at other men's tables, soon lowers a Christian's tone of religion. Going often into company is a heavy strain on spirituality of heart. Here, if anywhere, God's children have need to be on their guard. Each must know his own strength and natural temperament, and act accordingly. One believer can go without risk where another cannot. Happy is he who can use his Christian liberty without abusing it! It is possible to be sorely wounded in soul at marriage feasts and the tables of friends.

One golden rule on the subject may be laid down, the use of which will save us much trouble. Let us take care that we always go to feasts in the spirit of our divine Master, and that we never go where he would not have gone. Like him, let us endeavour to be always 'about our Father's business' (*Luke* 2:49). Like him, let us willingly promote joy and gladness, but let us strive that it may be sinless joy, if not joy in the Lord. Let us endeavour to bring the salt of grace into every company, and to drop the word in season in every ear we address. Much good may be done in society by giving a healthy tone to conversation. Let us never be ashamed to show our colours, and to make men see whose we are and whom we serve. We may well say, 'Who is sufficient for these things?' But if Christ went to a marriage feast in Cana there is surely something that Christians can do on similar occasions. Let them only remember that if they go where their Master went, they must go in their Master's spirit.

We learn, lastly, from these verses, *the almighty power of our Lord Jesus Christ*. We are told of a miracle which he wrought at the marriage feast, when the wine failed. By a mere act of will he changed water into wine, and so supplied the need of all the guests.

The manner in which the miracle was worked deserves especial notice. We are not told of any outward visible action which preceded or accompanied it. It is not said that he touched the waterpots containing the water that was made wine. It is not said that he commanded the water to change its qualities, or that he prayed to his Father in heaven. He simply willed the change, and it took place. We read of no prophet or apostle in the Bible who ever worked a miracle after this fashion. He who could do such a mighty work, in such a manner, was nothing less than very God.

It is a comfortable thought that the same almighty power of will which our Lord here displayed is still exercised on behalf of his believing people. They have no need of his bodily presence to maintain their cause. They have no reason to be cast down because they cannot see him with their eyes interceding for them, or touch him with their hands, that they may cling to him for safety. If he 'wills' their salvation and the daily supply of all their spiritual need, they are as safe and well provided for as if they saw him standing by them. Christ's *will* is as mighty and effectual as Christ's *deed*. The will of him who could say to the Father, 'I will that they also, whom thou hast given me, be with me where I am,' is a will that has all power in heaven and earth, and must prevail (*John* 17:24).

Happy are those who, like the disciples, believe on him by whom this miracle was wrought. A greater marriage feast than that of Cana will one day be held, when Christ himself will be the bridegroom and believers will be the bride. A greater glory will one day be manifested, when Jesus shall take to himself his great power and reign. Blessed will they be in that day who are called to the marriage supper of the Lamb! (*Rev.* 19:9).

Notes—John 2:1-11

1.—[*The third day.*] The question naturally arises, 'What day was this? From what day was it the third?' The most probable answer is, that it was the third day after the last event described in the preceding chapter; the third day after Nathanael was brought to Jesus and became a disciple. The meaning therefore is, 'The third day after the conversation between Jesus and Nathanael.'

[*A marriage in Cana.*] Let it be remembered that we are told elsewhere that Nathanael was an inhabitant of Cana (*John* 21:2). This makes it far from improbable, that Nathanael, after he became a disciple, invited our Lord to visit the place where he lived. Cana is a place not mentioned in the Old Testament. Robinson, in his *Biblical Researches*, says it was a village about three hours' journey from Nazareth.

[*The mother of Jesus was there.*] We must suppose that the Virgin Mary was in some way connected with the bride or bridegroom, and was therefore present at the marriage and assisting in the arrangements of the feast. Without some such supposition it is difficult to understand her speaking to the servants, as she afterwards does.

The absence of Joseph's name, both here and in other places where the mother of our Lord is mentioned in the Gospels and Acts, has induced most commentators to think that Joseph was dead when our Lord began his public ministry. The point is one of which we know nothing except by conjecture. It deserves notice, however, that the Jews of Capernaum speak of Jesus as 'the son of Joseph, whose *father* and mother we *know*' (*John* 6:42). If it had been profitable to us to know more about Joseph, we should have been told more. The Roman Catholic Church has already given him a superstitious reverence, upon the authority of tradition, and without the slightest warrant of Scripture. What would have not been said about Joseph by the Romish Church, if he had been more prominently mentioned in God's Word?

Lightfoot points out that a comparison of Mark 3:18, Mark 6:3, and John 19:25, makes it exceedingly probable that the Virgin Mary's sister, called elsewhere Mary, the wife of Cleopas or Alphæus, and all her family, lived at Cana. He observes that in the list of our Lord's 'brethren' or cousins we find the following names,—James, Joses, Juda, and Simon. Of these he thinks that James, Juda, and Simon were apostles. James the apostle is expressly called 'the brother of our Lord,' and the son of Alphæus, and Jude is expressly called brother of this James (*Gal.* 1:19; *Jude* 1).

The remaining brother, Simon, he thinks was the apostle who is called Simon the Canaanite. This, Lightfoot argues, is a proof that his father and mother lived at Cana; and hence he concludes that this marriage feast was in the house of Alphæus. That Alphaeus and Cleopas were the same person is a general and well-founded opinion.

2.—[*Jesus was called . . . disciples.*] Our Lord was doubtless invited as the Virgin Mary's son. His disciples were invited as his friends and companions. We cannot, of course, suppose, at so early a period of our Lord's ministry, that he was recognized as a religious teacher, or those with him as disciples of a new faith. The disciples here spoken of must be the five mentioned in the last chapter, viz., Andrew and his companion (probably John), Simon Peter, Philip, and Nathanael.

[*To the marriage.*] We know nothing about the names of the bride and bridegroom. There is a legend among Romish writers that the bridegroom was John the apostle, and that though married, John left wife and home at once, in order to become Christ's disciple! The whole story is utterly destitute of scriptural foundation, and a tissue of improbabilities. Baronius conjectures that the bridegroom was Simon the Canaanite, but without any proof worth mentioning.

Let it be noted, that the presence of Jesus, and his disciples, and the Virgin Mary at a marriage, is a significant fact, which stands out in strong contrast to the patristic and Roman Catholic doctrine, of the imperfection of the state of marriage compared to that of celibacy. 'Forbidding to marry' is a doctrine of Antichrist, not of Christ (*1 Tim.* 4:3).

The Roman Catholic argument, that Christ, by his presence, made marriage a sacrament, is utterly worthless. Dyke remarks that we might as well call feasts and burials sacraments, because Christ was present at them. He says, 'There is required a word of institution to make a sacrament. Let the Papists show any such word here used. And if Christ did make marriage a sacrament, why do they call it a work of the flesh? Are sacraments works of the flesh?'

The suggestion of some modern writers, that our Lord's presence at a marriage feast condemns those Christians who decline to go to such amusements as balls, and routs, and dancing-parties, has no weight in it at all. The objects for which people meet together at a marriage feast and at a ball are widely different. The one is a mere irreligious assembly for pleasure and recreation of a very questionable tendency, entailing late hours, and ministering to worldliness, levity, and the love of display. The other is a gathering of friends to witness the most important step in life that two persons can take, and a gathering closely connected with a religious ceremony.

3.—[*When they wanted wine.*] The Greek words so rendered mean literally, 'Wine having failed.' This circumstance probably shows the poor and humble condition of those to whose marriage Jesus was invited. His acquaintances and those of his mother were not wealthy persons.

It throws light on this expression, and indeed on the whole story, to remember that a marriage feast among the Jews was often an affair of several days' duration, and an occasion when many were invited. Consequently it entailed not only much expense, but a considerable consumption of food and wine. Thus Samson's marriage feast lasted seven days (*Judg.* 14:10-18). Thus the marriage feast described in the parable of the king's Son, was a feast which large numbers were invited to attend (*Matt.* 22:2, etc.). This being the case, we may well understand that in the feasts of those who were not wealthy the wine might soon run short, without there having been any excess of drinking. So it seems to have happened in the case before us.

[*The mother of Jesus saith ... no wine.*] This little sentence has given rise to various and strange interpretations.

Some have thought, as Bengel, that Mary suggested to our Lord that it was time for him and his disciples to depart and leave the feast, in order to spare the feelings of the bride and bridegroom, and to avoid exposing their poverty.

Some have thought, as Calvin, that she wished our Lord to occupy the minds of the guests by profitable discourse, and so to take off their attention from the deficiency of wine.

By far the most reasonable and probable idea is, that Mary conjectured that our Lord might in some way supply the deficiency of wine. How it would be done she could not tell. There is not the slightest ground for supposing that our Lord had ever worked a miracle up to this time. But it would be foolish to suppose that Mary did not remember well all the miraculous circumstances of our Lord's birth, and all the words spoken before by the angel Gabriel concerning him.—We cannot doubt, that although our Lord had lived a quiet life at Nazareth for thirty years, and done no miracles, his mother must have observed in him a perfection of word and deed utterly unlike the behaviour of common men.—We cannot doubt that she was aware of all the events of the last few weeks,—our Lord's baptism by John, John's public proclamation of him as the Messiah, and the gathering around Jesus of a small knot of disciples.—Remembering all these things, we surely need not wonder that Mary's expectations were greatly raised. She looked for her Son speedily doing some great miracle. She was in daily expectation that he would prove himself the Messiah by some mighty act. And it was under these feelings that she turned to him, saying, 'They have no wine.' It is as though she said, 'Surely the time is come for declaring thyself. Manifest thy power, as I have long expected thee to do, by providing a supply of wine.'

The argument which the Roman Catholics draw from this expression in favour of the Virgin Mary's intercession in heaven for sinners, and the consequent lawfulness of praying to her, is utterly worthless, and most unhappy. For one thing, it does not follow, because the petitions of living saints are heard upon earth, that the petitions of dead saints in heaven are effectual. For another thing, it is an unfortunate fact, that this petition, the only one that we ever find addressed to our Lord by the Virgin Mary, brought from him an immediate rebuke! Men must be in great straits for an argument when they can reason in this way in defence of the invocation of saints!

Melanchthon, Chemnitius, and others, think that this want of wine at the marriage feast is purposely mentioned in order to remind married persons, or those who intend marriage, that matrimony brings with it cares as well as comforts, and specially cares from poverty. They that marry do well, and with Christ's blessing will have happiness. But they must not expect to escape 'trouble in the flesh' from the very day of marriage (*1 Cor.* 7:28).

4.—[*Jesus saith, Woman, what, etc.*] This remarkable verse has naturally attracted great attention. In interpreting it, it is very important to avoid the extremes into which some Protestants, and nearly all Roman Catholic writers have fallen, in their interpretations.

On the one side, we must not lay too much stress on the expression 'Woman.' It is surely a mistake to suppose, as Calvin and others suggest, that it conveys any reproof, or is anywise inconsistent with reverence and respect. The very same expression was used by our Lord, when he addressed his mother for the last time on the cross, and affectionately commended her to John's care. He said, 'Woman, behold thy son' (*John* 19:26). The Virgin Mary was an erring woman, like all other believing women, but we must not lay more blame on her than Scripture warrants.

On the other side, it is useless to deny that our Lord's words were intended, as Chrysostom, Theophylact, and Euthymius say, to be a rebuke to Mary. She erred here, perhaps from affectionate desire to bring honour to her Son, as she erred on other occasions. The words before us were meant to remind her that she must henceforth leave our Lord to choose his own times and modes of acting. The season of subjection to her and Joseph was over. The season of his public ministry had at length begun. In carrying on that ministry, she must not presume to suggest to him. The utter contrariety of this verse to the teaching of the Roman Catholic Church about the Virgin Mary, is too palpable to be explained away. She was not without error and sin, as Romish writers have dared to assert, and was not meant to be prayed to and adored. If our Lord would not allow his

mother even to suggest to him the working of a miracle, we may well suppose that all Roman Catholic prayers to the Virgin Mary, and especially prayers entreating her to 'command her Son,' are most offensive and blasphemous in his eyes.

The Greek expression, rendered 'What have I to do with thee?' would be translated literally, 'What to me and thee?' It is an elliptical expression, of which the full meaning probably is, 'What is there in common to me and thee?' 'My thoughts,' as Bengel says, 'are one thing, and thine another.'—It is the same phrase that is used in an interrogative form in Matthew 8:29; Mark 1:24; 5:7; Luke 8:28; and in an imperative form in Matthew 27:19.

[*Mine hour is not yet come.*] The simplest and most reasonable view of these words is to refer them to Christ's 'hour,' or time for working a miracle. It is like the expression, 'My time is not yet full come' (*John* 7:8). Our Lord did not tell Mary that he would not work a miracle; but he would have her know that she must not expect him to do mighty works to please his relatives after the flesh. He would only work a miracle, upon this or any other occasion, when the fitting season for it, the time appointed in God's counsel, had arrived.

There is a curious idea maintained by Augustine, Wordsworth, and others, that our Lord here referred to the hour of his crucifixion, and that he meant, 'My hour is not yet come for recognizing thee and honouring thee publicly as my mother, but I shall do it one day on the cross.' This however seems a very far-fetched and improbable application of the words.

5.—[*His mother saith ... do it.*] Two things are very noteworthy in this verse. One is the meekness with which the Virgin Mary submitted to the gentle rebuke which came from our Lord's mouth in the last verse; the other is the firm faith which she still exhibited in our Lord's power to work a miracle in order to supply the lack of wine, and in the probability of his working it.

Dyke observes, 'The direction which Mary gives to the servants belongs to us all. We must perform simple obedience to Christ in all things; his sayings must be our doings.

69

No reasoning of the matter must there be, no inquiry, as into men's commandments and speeches; but this must suffice, "Christ hath said it." This is the blind obedience which Jesuits yield to their superiors, but it is the obedience that belongs to Christ. Many will do *something* that Christ says, but not *whatsoever* he says.'

It is not, perhaps, going too far to say, that after observing her Son's perfect life and perfect wisdom during thirty years at Nazareth, Mary spoke the words before us with special confidence, and with a greater depth of meaning than appears on the surface of the sentence.—'Whatsoever he says deserves attention. Whatsoever he says, do it.'—At any rate the verse contains a deep practical lesson for the whole church of Christ. Whatsoever Christ says, let us obey and do.

6.—[*Six waterpots ... after the manner ... Jews.*] St John mentions these details in describing the miracle, with a special reference to Gentile readers. He meant them to understand that there was nothing remarkable in the circumstance that there were six large waterpots of stone in the place where the feast was held. The peculiar customs of the Jews about ceremonial washings and purifyings, made it necessary to have a large supply of water at hand. The words of St Mark throw light on the verse before us: 'The Pharisees, and all the Jews, except they wash their hands oft, eat not, holding the tradition of the elders,' etc. (*Mark* 7:3, etc.). The presence of the six waterpots, therefore, could not arise from collusion or pre-arrangement. It was a natural consequence of Jewish habits in our Lord's times.

[*Two or three firkins apiece.*] Many foolish and unprofitable remarks have been built on this expression, as to the very large quantity of wine which our Lord must have created when the miracle we are considering was wrought. It might suffice to reply that there is much uncertainty about the precise quantity of liquid which the ancient measure, which we here render 'firkins,' contained. But the best and safest answer is, that we must not measure the demands of a Jewish marriage feast, which perhaps lasted several days, and included a large number of guests, by the feasts of our own times.

7.—[*Jesus saith ... Fill the waterpots, etc.*] The remark is frequently made by commentators on this verse, with much propriety, that these simple words describe the duty of all who work for Christ, and especially of ministers and teachers. They are to hear Christ's voice, and do as he tells them, and then leave the result to him. Duties are ours. Events are God's. It is ours to fill the waterpots. It is Christ's to make the water wine.

[*Up to the brim.*] This circumstance is no doubt mentioned in order to show that there was no room left for trick, jugglery, or imposture. What was put into the waterpots was water, and only water, and they were so filled that nothing could be infused, or mingled with their contents.

8.—[*And he saith ... Draw out now.*] It was at this moment, no doubt, that the miracle took place. By an act of will our Lord changed the contents of the waterpots. That which was poured in was water. That which was drawn out was wine. To him who created the vine, and made it bear grapes at the first, the change was perfectly easy. He who could create matter out of nothing, could much more easily change one kind of matter into another.

[*The governor of the feast.*] This person appears to have been one who presided at large entertainments like that before us, and superintended all the proceedings. The Greek word so rendered is precisely the same as that translated 'ruler of the feast,' in the following verse. The presence of such a person at feasts, was a well-known custom among the Greeks and Romans.

9.—[*Tasted ... wine ... knew not whence it was.*] The testimony of the ruler of the feast is specially adduced, in order to show the reality of the miracle. He knew nothing of what had been done to the waterpots. He had not seen the water poured in by our Lord's command. There was no collusion or conspiracy between him and the servants, much less between him and our Lord. Hence the value of his testimony. He not only testifies that the liquid which a few minutes before was water was now wine, but that it was also wine of more than common goodness and strength,—not wine mixed with water, but pure, good wine.

Let the word 'tasted' be carefully noticed in this place. It supplies a strong incidental argument against the Romish doctrine of transubstantiation. The occasion before us is the only known occasion on which our Lord changed one liquid into another. When he did so change it, the reality of the change was at once proved by the 'taste.' Why is it then that in the pretended change of the sacramental wine in the Lord's supper into Christ's blood the change cannot be detected by the senses? Why does the wine after consecration taste like wine, just as it did before?—These are questions which the Roman Catholics cannot satisfactorily answer. The pretended change of the bread and wine in the Lord's supper is a complete delusion. It is contradicted by the senses of every communicant. The bread after consecration is still bread, and the wine is still wine. That which contradicts our senses we are nowhere required in God's Word to believe.

10.—[*Every man at the beginning, etc.*] The words in this sentence must not be pressed too closely, in order to bring out of them a spiritual meaning. The ruler of the feast makes a general remark about the way in which banquets were usually managed. The ordinary custom was to bring the best wine first, and the inferior wine last. But the wine before him, drawn from the waterpots, was so singularly good, that the custom on this day seemed reversed. The verse is a strong incidental testimony to the reality and greatness of our Lord's miracle. Not only did he change water into wine, but into wine so singularly good as to excite remark and attention.

[*When men have well drunk.*] Foolish remarks have sometimes been made on this expression, as if our Lord had countenanced excessive drinking on this occasion. For one thing, it may be remarked that the Greek word rendered 'have well drunk,' does not necessarily imply intoxication. It may be justly interpreted, as Schleusner and Parkhurst observe, 'have drunk sufficiently, or drunk freely.'—Men who have had enough, are indifferent as to the quality of the wine set before them. For another thing, we must remember that the ruler of the feast was only making a general remark about men's ordinary customs in supplying wine to their guests. There is nothing whatever to show that he was alluding to the guests actually before him.

[*Thou hast kept the good wine until now.*] A good practical remark has often been raised from these words of the ruler of the feast. The world gives its best things, like the best wine, first, and its worst things last. The longer we serve the world, the more disappointing, unsatisfactory, and unsavoury will its gifts prove. Christ, on the other hand, gives his servants their best things last. They have first the cross, the race, and the battle, and then the rest, the glory, and the crown. Specially will it be found true at his second advent. Then will believers say emphatically, 'Thou hast kept the good wine until now.' These are pious and useful thoughts. But it may be doubted whether they are more than accommodations.

This is perhaps the proper place to remark, that it seems utterly impossible, on any fair and honest interpretation, to reconcile the passage before us with the leading principles of what is commonly called 'Teetotalism.' If our Lord Jesus Christ actually worked a miracle in order to supply wine at a marriage feast, it seems to me impossible, by any ingenuity, to prove that drinking wine is sinful. Temperance in all things is one of the fruits of the Spirit. An intemperate man is an unconverted man. Total abstinence from fermented liquors is in many cases most useful and desirable. But to say, as many do say, that to drink any fermented liquor at all is 'a sin,' is taking up ground that cannot be maintained in the face of the passage before us, without wresting the plain meaning of Scripture, and charging Christ with abetting sin.

11.—[*This beginning of miracles, etc.*] The plain meaning of this sentence seems to be that this was the first miracle which our Lord Jesus Christ ever worked. The miracles which some have reported that he worked in his infancy and childhood, are destitute of the slightest foundation in Scripture, and utterly unworthy of credit.

Those who wish to see their absurdity will find specimens of them in the preliminary Essay to Trench's *Notes on Miracles*.

Lightfoot suggests the five following reasons why the miracle now before us was purposely the first that Christ worked. 1. As marriage was the first institution ordained by God, so at a marriage was Christ's first miracle. 2. As Christ had showed himself miraculous a little while ago by a fast, so he doth now by an extraordinary provision at a feast. When he would not make stones bread, it was not because he could not. 3. He would not make stones into bread to satisfy Satan, but he was willing to turn water into wine to show forth his own glory. 4. The first miracle wrought in the world by man was transformation (*Exod.* 7:9), and the first miracle wrought by the Son of man was of the same nature. 5. The first time you hear of John the Baptist, you hear of his strict diet, and so the first time you hear of Christ in his public ministry, you hear of him at a marriage feast.

[*Manifested forth his glory.*] I am unable to see that these words refer to the expression used in the first chapter, 'We beheld his glory' (*John* 1:14). I believe the meaning to be that 'by this miracle Jesus now for the first time opened or revealed his glorious and divine power, and his commission to be the Messiah.' After thirty years' seclusion at Nazareth, he now for the first time lifted up the veil which he had thrown over his divinity in becoming flesh, and revealed something of his almighty power and Godhead.

[*His disciples believed on him.*] These words cannot of course mean that Andrew, and John, and Peter, and Philip, and Nathanael now believed on Jesus for the first time. The probable meaning is, that from this time forth they believed more confidently, more implicitly, and more unhesitatingly. From this time they felt thoroughly convinced, in spite of much remaining ignorance, that he whom they were following was the Messiah.

I cannot close the note on this wonderful miracle without saying something about the allegorical and typical meanings assigned to it by the Fathers and many other commentators. Many see in the miracle an allegorical history of the introduction of the gospel into the world. Like the marriage feast, the gospel was an occasion of joy. As at the marriage feast, the personal presence of Jesus was the great feature of the gospel. The times of the Jewish dispensation were times of deficiency and dim light. The coming of Christ supplied all that was lacking. Revealed religion before Christ was like water. Christ coming into the world turned the water of the old dispensation into wine. The good wine was reserved until the time of Christ. The first miracle wrought by Moses was turning water into blood. The first wrought by Christ was turning water into wine.

These are undoubtedly pious thoughts, and full of truth. I should be sorry to speak harshly of them, or to pronounce decidedly that they may not be legitimately deduced from the miracle. I only venture the remark, that it is far wiser to abstain from allegorical interpretations as a general rule, and to be content with the plain meaning which appears on the surface of Scripture. Once begin allegorizing Scripture, and you never know where you are to stop. You may prove anything, and find anything in the Bible upon the allegorical system, and at last throw open the floodgate to a torrent of wild fanaticism.

The allegorical lessons drawn from this miracle by Augustine, Bernard, and Alcuin, are striking examples of the extremes into which allegory may run. When such a man as Augustine, for instance, tells us that the two or three firkins mean the two races of men, Jews and Greeks, or the three sons of Noah,—or when he says that the six waterpots in the miracle before us denote six successive prophetical periods in the days between Adam and Christ, one cannot but feel that there is something wrong. These are his words, 'The six waterpots, containing two or three firkins apiece, are six ages, containing the prophecy belonging to all nations, whether as referred to two kinds of men, Jews and Gentiles, as the apostle often says, or to three, on account of the three sons of Noah.' The system of interpreting Scripture which can lead a good man into such assertions as this, must surely be a dangerous two-edged weapon, and likely to do more harm than good.

That all our Lord's miracles were deeply significant, I do not deny. That all were intended to convey deep spiritual lessons, beside supplying proofs of his divinity, I make no question. All I maintain is that they require reverent and delicate handling, and that to rush hastily into allegorical interpretations of them, and invest every minute portion of them with a figurative meaning, is an unwise mode of handling Scripture, and eminently calculated to bring the Bible into contempt.

Hardly any commentator has drawn more useful practical lessons from this miracle than Melanchthon. Those who think lightly of Protestant divinity would do well to compare his commentary on the whole passage with that of Augustine.

JOHN 2:12-25

12 After this he went down to Capernaum, he, and his mother, and his brethren, and his disciples: and they continued there not many days.

13 And the Jews' passover was at hand, and Jesus went up to Jerusalem,

14 And found in the temple those that sold oxen and sheep and doves, and the changers of money sitting:

15 And when he had made a scourge of small cords, he drove them all out of the temple, and the sheep, and the oxen; and poured out the changers' money, and overthrew the tables;

16 And said unto them that sold doves, Take these things hence; make not my Father's house an house of merchandise.

17 And his disciples remembered that it was written, The zeal of thine house hath eaten me up.

18 Then answered the Jews and said unto him, What sign showest thou unto us, seeing that thou doest these things?

19 Jesus answered and said unto them, Destroy this temple, and in three days I will raise it up.

20 Then said the Jews, Forty and six years was this temple in building, and wilt thou rear it up in three days?

21 But he spake of the temple of his body.

22 When therefore he was risen from the dead, his disciples remembered that he had said this unto them; and they believed the scripture, and the word which Jesus had said.

23 Now when he was in Jerusalem at the passover, in the feast *day*, many believed in his name, when they saw the miracles which he did.

24 But Jesus did not commit himself unto them, because he knew all *men*,

25 And needed not that any should testify of man: for he knew what was in man.

THE second miracle which our Lord is recorded to have wrought demands our attention in these verses. Like the first miracle at Cana, it is eminently typical and significant of things yet to come. To attend a marriage feast, and cleanse the temple from profanation were among the first acts of our Lord's ministry at his first coming. To purify the whole visible church, and hold a marriage supper, will be among his first acts, when he comes again.

We see, for one thing, in this passage, *how much Christ disapproves all irreverent behaviour in the house of God.*

We are told that he drove out of the temple those whom he found selling oxen and sheep and doves within its walls,—that he poured out the changers' money and overthrew their tables,—and that he said to them that sold doves, 'Take these things hence; make not my Father's house a house of merchandise.' On no occasion in our Lord's earthly ministry do we find him acting so energetically, and exhibiting such righteous indignation, as on the occasion now before us. Nothing seems to have called from him such a marked display of holy wrath as the gross irreverence which the priests permitted in the temple, notwithstanding all their boasted zeal for God's law. Twice, it will be remembered, he discovered the same profanation of his Father's house going on, within three years, once at the beginning of his ministry and once at the end. Twice we see him expressing his displeasure in the strongest terms. 'The thing is doubled' in order to impress a lesson more strongly on our minds.

The passage is one that ought to raise deep searchings of heart in many quarters. Are there none who profess and call themselves Christians, behaving every Sunday just as badly as these Jews? Are there none who secretly bring into the house of God their money, their lands, their houses, their cattle, and a whole train of worldly affairs? Are there none who bring their bodies only into the place of worship, and allow their hearts to wander into the ends of the earth? Are there none who are 'almost in all evil, in the midst of the congregation?' (*Prov.* 5:14). These are serious questions! Multitudes, it may be feared, could not give them a satisfactory answer. Christian churches and chapels, no doubt, are very unlike the Jewish temple. They are not built after a divine pattern. They have no altars or holy places. Their furniture has no typical meaning. But they are places where God's Word is read, and where Christ is specially present. The man who professes to worship in them should surely behave with reverence and respect. The man who brings his worldly matters with him when he professes to worship, is doing that which is evidently most offensive to Christ. The words which Solomon wrote by the Holy Ghost are applicable to all times: 'Keep thy foot when thou goest to the house of God' (*Eccles.* 5:1).

We see, for another thing, in this passage, *how men may remember words of religious truth long after they are spoken, and may one day see a meaning in them which at first they did not see.*

We are told that our Lord said to the Jews, 'Destroy this temple, and in three days I will raise it up.' St John informs us distinctly that 'he spake of the temple of his body,' that he referred to his own resurrection. Yet the meaning of the sentence was not understood by our Lord's disciples at the time that it was spoken. It was not till 'he was risen from the dead,' three years after the events here described, that the full significance of the sentence flashed on their hearts. For three years it was a dark and useless saying to them. For three years it lay sleeping in their minds, like a seed in a tomb, and bore no fruit. But at the end of that time the darkness passed away. They saw the application of their Master's words, and as they saw it were confirmed in their faith. 'They remembered that he had said this,' and as they remembered 'they believed.'

It is a comfortable and cheering thought, that the same kind of thing that happened to the disciples is often going on at the present day. The sermons that are preached to apparently heedless ears in churches, are not all lost and thrown away. The instruction that is given in schools and pastoral visits, is not all wasted and forgotten. The texts that are taught by parents to children are not all taught in vain. There is often a resurrection of sermons, and texts, and instruction, after an interval of many years. The good seed sometimes springs up after he that sowed it has been long dead and gone. Let preachers go on preaching, and teachers go on teaching, and parents go on training up children in the way they should go. Let them sow the good seed of Bible truth in faith and patience. Their labour is not in vain in the Lord. Their words are remembered far

75

more than they think, and will yet spring up 'after many days' (*1 Cor.* 15:58; *Eccles.* 11:1).

We see, lastly, in this passage, *how perfect is our Lord Jesus Christ's knowledge of the human heart.*

We are told that when our Lord was at Jerusalem, the first time, he 'did not commit himself' to those who professed belief in him. He knew that they were not to be depended on. They were astonished at the miracles which they saw him work. They were even intellectually convinced that he was the Messiah, whom they had long expected. But they were not 'disciples indeed' (*John* 8:31). They were not converted, and true believers. Their hearts were not right in the sight of God, though their feelings were excited. Their inward man was not renewed, whatever they might profess with their lips. Our Lord knew that nearly all of them were stony-ground hearers (*Luke* 8:13). As soon as tribulation or persecution arose because of the Word, their so-called faith would probably wither away and come to an end. All this our Lord saw clearly, if others around him did not. Andrew, and Peter, and John, and Philip, and Nathanael, perhaps wondered that their Master did not receive these seeming believers with open arms. But they could only judge things by the outward appearance. Their Master could read hearts. 'He knew what was in man.'

The truth now before us, is one which ought to make hypocrites and false professors tremble. They may deceive men, but they cannot deceive Christ. They may wear a cloak of religion, and appear, like whited sepulchres, beautiful in the eyes of men. But the eyes of Christ see their inward rottenness, and the judgment of Christ will surely overtake them, except they repent. Christ is already reading their hearts, and as he reads, he is displeased. They are known in heaven, if they are not known on earth, and they will be known at length to their shame, before assembled worlds, if they die unchanged. It is written, 'I know thy works, that thou hast a name that thou livest, and art dead' (*Rev.* 3:1).

But the truth before us has two sides, like the pillar of cloud and fire at the Red Sea (*Exod.* 14:20). If it looks darkly on hypocrites, it looks brightly on true believers. If it threatens wrath to false professors, it speaks peace to all who love the Lord Jesus Christ in sincerity. A real Christian may be weak, but he is true. One thing, at any rate, the servant of Christ can say, when cast down by a sense of his own infirmity, or pained by the slander of a lying world. He can say, 'Lord, I am a poor sinner, but I am in earnest, I am true. Thou knowest all things: thou knowest that I love thee. Thou knowest all hearts, and thou knowest that, weak as my heart is, it is a heart that cleaves to thee.' The false Christian shrinks from the eye of an all-seeing Saviour. The true Christian desires his Lord's eye to be on him morning, noon, and night. He has nothing to hide.

Notes—John 2:12-25

12.—[*He went down to Capernaum.*] The strict accuracy of John's writing is noteworthy here. Cana was a village in the hill country. Capernaum was a town on the shore of the Lake of Galilee, at a very much lower level than Cana. It is therefore said that Jesus 'went *down*.'

Capernaum appears to have been our Lord's principal residence in Galilee during his earthly ministry. 'Leaving Nazareth, he ... dwelt in Capernaum' (*Matt.* 4:13). At no place does he seem to have worked so many miracles; and on no place does he denounce so severe a judgment for its impenitence and neglect of privileges: 'Thou, Capernaum, which art exalted unto heaven, shalt be brought down to hell' (*Matt.* 11:23). It is a striking fact that though Capernaum was a wealthy and important place in our Lord's time, it has so entirely passed away and been 'brought down,' that even its situation has never been clearly ascertained.

[*His mother.*] Here again we see no mention of Joseph. Whether the Virgin Mary was a constant companion of our Lord throughout his earthly ministry, may be doubted. We see her here. We see her again at the crucifixion. But we see her in another place 'standing without and desiring to speak with him' when he was talking to the people, and giving occasion to the solemn saying, 'Who is my mother?' (*Matt.* 12:46-48). Indeed there is no proof that Mary ever saw more clearly than the rest of our Lord's disciples the whole purpose of Christ's advent, or was at all more prepared than the rest for his crucifixion and sufferings.

[*His brethren.*] There is no good ground for supposing that these were our Lord's brethren according to the flesh, and that Mary ever had any other son after our Lord's miraculous birth.—For one thing, it is well known to every careful reader, that the word 'brethren' is applied in the Bible to many relatives besides those whom we call 'brethren.' Abraham says to Lot, 'We be *brethren*' (*Gen.* 13:8), though Lot was his nephew. Mishael and Elzaphan were called the 'brethren' of Nadab and Abihu, though they were only cousins (*Lev.* 10:4).—Jacob said 'unto his *brethren*,' gather stones (*Gen.* 31:46); yet they were his sons and servants. For another thing, it is quite possible that Joseph might have had children by a former marriage, before he was espoused to the Virgin Mary; and these children, we can well understand, would be called our Lord's 'brethren.'—In the last place, we know that the Apostle James was called our 'Lord's brother' (*Gal.* 1:19), and yet we are distinctly told that he was the son of Alphæus or Cleopas, the

77

husband of the Virgin Mary's sister. It is therefore most probable that 'brethren' in the verse before us means 'cousins,' some of whom believed on our Lord, though others did not (*John* 7:5).

It is an interesting fact, that two at least of our Lord's apostles were his kinsmen according to the flesh: viz., James and Jude, the sons of Alphæus. To them we may probably add Simon, on the strength of Mark 6:3, and perhaps Matthew also, on the strength of Mark 2:14 and Matthew 9:9.

[*And his disciples.*] This expression, being used after the words, 'his brethren,' may raise a doubt whether any of our Lord's relatives as yet believed on him, except the Virgin Mary. It is possible that they only followed him now out of curiosity, in consequence of the miracle he had just wrought.

13.—[*The Jews' passover was at hand.*] This expression is another proof that St John wrote his Gospel for Gentile believers rather than for Jews.

Our Lord's regular attendance on the feasts and ordinances of the Law of Moses, deserves notice. So long as the dispensation of the Old Testament lasted, he gave it all due honour, however unworthy the hands which administered it. The unworthiness of ministers will not justify us in neglecting God's ordinances.

The exact number of passovers which our Lord kept, and consequently the exact length of his ministry from his baptism to his crucifixion, are points on which there is much difference of opinion. For myself I can see no better view than the old one, that our Lord's ministry lasted three years. It evidently began shortly before a passover, and ended with a passover. But whether it included only three passovers, and in that case lasted between two and three years,— or four passovers, and in that case lasted between three and four years,—I think we have no materials for deciding positively. If I must venture an opinion, I think it most likely that our Lord only kept three passovers.—But it is an open question, and one happily not of deep moment.—Three passovers are distinctly named by John: viz., the one before us, the one in the sixth chapter (*John* 6:3), and the one at which our Lord was crucified. If the 'feast' mentioned in the fifth chapter (*John* 5:1) was the passover, our Lord kept four passovers. But this last point cannot be settled.

Sir Isaac Newton thought that our Lord kept no fewer than five passovers. Some few writers have maintained that he kept only two. Those who wish to see the subject discussed will find it in Doddridge's notes on this place.

[*Jesus went up to Jerusalem.*] Let it be noted, that this journey, and all the circumstances which attended this visit to Jerusalem, are only related by St John. For some wise reason the other three Gospel writers were inspired to leave out this part of our Lord's history.

14.—[*Found in the temple those that sold, etc.*] The presence of oxen, sheep, doves, and money-changers, within the temple courts is easily accounted for. The animals were intended to supply the wants of Jews who came to the passover and other feasts, from distant places, and required sacrifices. For them the dealers in oxen, sheep, and doves, were ready, within a few yards of the altar. The changers of money came naturally enough where buying and selling went on, to meet the convenience of Jews who had nothing but foreign money, which they wished to exchange for the current coin of Jerusalem. The tendency of the whole custom was evidently most profane. It was no doubt connived at by the priests from covetous motives. They were either connected with those who sold animals and changed money, and shared in their profits; or else they received a rent for the privilege of carrying on business within the sacred walls. No doubt they would have pleaded that all was done with a good intention! Their end was to provide facilities for worshipping God! But good intentions cannot sanctify unscriptural actions. As Dyke says on the passage, 'No pretence of good ends can justify that which is forbidden by God.'

When we are told that our Lord found all this going on 'in the temple,' we must of course understand that it means 'in the courtyards surrounding the temple,— within the precincts of the temple.' But these courtyards, we must remember, were regarded as part of the temple, and therefore holy ground.

I am inclined to see in this visit of our Lord to the temple at his first appearance in Jerusalem after beginning his ministry, a partial though very imperfect fulfilment of Malachi's prophecy: 'The Lord, whom ye seek, shall suddenly come to his temple' (*Mal.* 3:1). While the Jewish nation was expecting the appearance of a conquering Messiah with power and great glory, the true Messiah suddenly appeared in the temple, and declared his presence, not by exhibiting temporal power, but by insisting on greater purity in the temple worship, as the first thing which the nation needed.

That a fuller and more complete accomplishment of Malachi's words remains yet to come, I feel no doubt. But like many Old Testament prophecies about Messiah, the words were purposely intended to have a double fulfilment,—a partial one at Messiah's first coming to suffer, a complete one at Messiah's second coming to reign.

The great majority of the best commentators hold that our Lord cast out the buyers and sellers from the temple twice; once at the beginning of his ministry and once at the end. It is fair to say that Bishop Pearce and a few other writers think that it only happened once,—at the end of his ministry, just before his crucifixion. But the arguments in favour of this view do not appear to me at all weighty or satisfactory.

15.—[*Made a scourge of small cords.*] The Greek word translated 'small cords,' means literally a 'cord made of rushes.' Some have thought that these rushes were used as litter for the sheep and oxen. Others have thought that such small cords as these might very likely have been lying about, after having been used for tying up the oxen. Whether the scourge was applied to those persons who brought the animals into the temple, as a sort of chastisement, as some old painters have represented the scene, we do not know. The more probable view seems to be, that the scourge was simply meant to assist our Lord in speedily ejecting the sheep and oxen.

The whole transaction is a remarkable one, as exhibiting our Lord using more physical exertion, and energetic bodily action, than we see him using at any other period of his ministry. A word, a touch, or the reaching forth of a hand, are the ordinary limits of his actions. Here we see him doing no fewer than four things;—1. Making the scourge;—2. Driving out the animals;—3. Pouring out on the ground the changers' money;—4. Overthrowing the tables. On no occasion do we find him showing such strong outward marks of indignation, as at the sight of the profanation of the temple. Remembering that the whole transaction is a striking type of what Christ will do to his visible church at his second coming, we may get some idea of the deep meaning of that remarkable expression, 'The wrath of the Lamb' (*Rev.* 6:16).

A remark of Dyke on our Lord's conduct in this place, is worth noticing. 'This act of Christ is not to be drawn into imitation, because he did it as Lord of the temple by virtue of his Sonship. Therefore the Papists grossly abuse this place that hence gather the power of the pope to punish offenders even with corporal punishments, or to deprive princes of their kingdoms. As for ministers, the only whip they may use is their tongue, in powerful preaching against abuses.—As for private persons, God hath not tied their tongues, though he hath their hands. As occasion is offered, they may show their detestation and dislike of corruption.'

16.—[*Said ... sold doves, Take these things hence.*] The distinction between our Lord's mode of dealing with each of the objects of his displeasure deserves notice. The oxen and sheep he *drove out.* There was no danger of their being lost by such treatment. The money he *threw on the ground.* It might be soon picked up and carried away.—The doves he simply ordered to be *taken away.* Had he done more, they might have flown away, and been completely lost to their owners.—It would have been well for the church, if all church-reformers had blended like wisdom with a like zeal in their proceedings. In the present instance all were rebuked and all instructed. But no one was really injured, and nothing was lost.

[*My Father's house.*] This expression is noteworthy. Whether the Jews observed it, in the hurry and confusion of the whole transaction, may be questioned. It was evidently an assertion by our Lord of his divine Sonship, and consequently of his right to vindicate the purity of his Father's place of worship. On another occasion when our Lord called God his Father, the Jews at once said that he made imself 'equal with God' (*John* 5:18). Some have thought that the expression is parallel to that used in the description of Christ among the doctors (*Luke* 2:49), and that the words used there, 'I must be about my Father's business,' would have been better rendered, 'I must be in my Father's house.'

The fact that the profane custom which our Lord here reproved was resumed by the Jews, and that two or three years afterward our Lord found the same things going on again in the temple, and again cast out the buyers and sellers, ought not to be overlooked. It is a striking proof of the desperate wickedness and fallen condition of the priests and rulers of the temple. They were deaf to all counsel and reproof, and given over to a reprobate mind.—The difference between our Lord's language at the second visit and that used at the first, ought also to be noticed. At the first visit he only says, 'Make not my Father's house a house of merchandise:' a place of buying and selling. At the second visit he says, 'Ye have made it a den of thieves' (*Matt.* 21:13). The more wicked and hardened men are, the louder must be our protest, and the sharper our rebuke.

[*An house of merchandise.*] Musculus remarks on this expression, that if the sale of animals for sacrifices called forth Christ's displeasure, much more must he be displeased at what goes on continually in Roman Catholic churches. The sale of masses, indulgences, etc., must be far more offensive to Christ than the sale of oxen and sheep.

The complete success of our Lord on this occasion, and the absence of the slightest opposition on the part of the Jews, deserve notice. It is a fact that induced some of the Fathers to call this the greatest miracle Christ ever worked. There are, however, three things to be remembered in considering this matter. For one thing, the conscience of the Jews was on our Lord's side. They knew that he was right and they were wrong.—For another thing, as a nation familiar with the history of the Old Testament prophets, they would not be surprised at an individual apparently under a divine impulse suddenly doing what our Lord did.—Above all there can be little doubt that a divine influence was brought to bear on all present, as it was when our Lord rode into Jerusalem on an ass, and when he caused his enemies in the garden to 'go backward and fall to the ground' (*Matt.* 21:9, 10; *John* 18:6). Here, as on other occasions, our Lord showed his disciples that he had complete power over all wills and minds, when he thought fit to exercise it; and that when he was rejected and disobeyed by the Jews, it was not because he had no power to compel obedience. They had no power against him except when he permitted.

The allegorical meanings assigned to the sheep, oxen, and doves, by Augustine, Origen, and Bede, are too absurd to be quoted. They may be seen in the Catena of Aquinas. Origen sees in the casting out of the animals, a type of the dissolution of the Jewish dispensation with its offerings and sacrifices.

Beza sees a peculiar fitness in our Lord's action of purifying the temple. It became him who was to be our Prophet, Priest, and King, to exhibit the same zeal for the purity of God's house that was formerly exhibited by such men as the prophet Isaiah, the priest Jehoiada (2 *Chron.* 24:16), and the kings Hezekiah and Josiah.

17.—[*His disciples remembered, etc.*] These words certainly appear to mean that our Lord's disciples 'remembered' the text which is here quoted, at the very time when our Lord was casting out the buyers and sellers. It occurred to their minds as a striking illustration of the spirit which their divine Master was exhibiting. He was completely absorbed for the moment in zeal for the purity of God's house. It is one among many proofs of the familiarity of the poor and unlearned Jews with the Old Testament Scriptures. Whether, however, the disciples regarded the Psalm, of which they remembered this verse, as applicable to the Messiah, may be reasonably doubted.

[*The zeal of thine house ... eaten me.*] Psalm 69, from which this text is taken, is quoted no fewer than seven times in the New Testament, as the utterance of Messiah. In the first twenty-one verses of the Psalm the Messiah's sufferings are related by himself. The fifth verse is undoubtedly very remarkable as coming from Messiah's lips, when he speaks of 'my foolishness' and 'my sins.' Ainsworth says it means, 'false imputation of sins.' 'Thou knowest if there be any such as my foes charge me with.' Bonar says much the same.

The text before us shows that it is sometimes justifiable to be entirely absorbed and eaten up, so to speak, by zeal for some object in which God's glory is concerned. Moses, Phineas, and Paul at Athens, are examples of such zeal (*Exod.* 32:19; *Num.* 25:11; *Acts* 17:16).

Augustine remarks on this text, 'Let the zeal of the house of God ever eat thee.—For example: seest thou a brother running to the theatre? Stop him, warn him, be grieved for him, if the zeal of God's house hath now eaten thee.—Seest thou others running and wanting to drink themselves drunk? Stop whom thou canst, hold whom thou canst, frighten whom thou canst; whom thou canst, win in gentleness: do not in any wise sit still and do nothing.'

18.—[*Then answered the Jews, and said.*] Doddridge remarks here that these Jews were probably the rulers, because the Great Assembly, or Sanhedrim, sat in the temple, and our Lord's actions would undoubtedly come to their knowledge without delay. This makes the question and answer which follow the more important.

[*What sign showest thou ... doest these things?*] This question of the Jews shows us that they admitted the lawfulness of a man doing such things as our Lord had done, if he could prove that he had a divine commission. He had suddenly taken upon himself a great and independent authority. Though neither a priest nor a Levite, he had virtually interfered with the management of the temple courts. Let him now show that

he was a prophet, like Elijah or Amos, and they would concede he had a warrant for his conduct.

19.—[*Jesus answered ... Destroy this temple.*] The meaning of this remarkable expression is either hypothetical or prophetical. It must either be rendered, 'Supposing you destroy this temple,' or 'Ye will destroy this temple,'—'If ye kill my body,' or 'When ye shall kill my body.'—It is of course absurd to suppose that our Lord literally commanded the Jews to destroy him. The use of the imperative instead of the future, must surely be familiar to every Bible-reader. See especially Psalm 109. In the present case it is truly astonishing that anyone can see difficulty in our Lord's expression. He only used a mode of speaking which is in common use among ourselves. If a lawyer said to his client in a consultation, 'Take such a step, and you will be ruined,' we all know that he would not be commanding his client to take the step. He would only mean, 'If you do take such a step.'—A similar form of language may be seen in our Lord's words, 'Fill ye up then the measure of your fathers,' addressed to the Pharisees (*Matt.* 23:32). No one would say that our Lord commanded the Pharisees to do this. It is a prophecy.—See also, 'Make the tree good' (*Matt.* 12:33), is not so much a command as a hypothesis (see also *Isa.* 8:9, 10).

[*In three days I will raise it up.*] This is a prophecy of our Lord's resurrection. But it is a very remarkable one, from the fact that our Lord distinctly asserts his own power to raise himself up. It is like the expression, 'I have power to lay [down my life], and I have power to take it again' (*John* 10:18). Both the expressions deserve particular notice, because many nowadays assert that our Lord's resurrection was owing to the operation of God the Father and of God the Holy Ghost, and that he did not rise by his own power. This is a dangerous heresy. That the Father and the Holy Ghost cooperated in the resurrection of our Lord's body there can be no doubt. It is clearly taught in many places. But to say that our Lord did not raise his own body, is to contradict the text before us, and the other which has been already quoted.

81

Hurrion, quoted by Ford, observes, 'The efficient cause of Christ's resurrection was the infinite power of God, which being common to all the persons in the blessed Trinity, the resurrection is sometimes ascribed to the Father, sometimes to the Son, and sometimes to the Holy Ghost. Christ's being raised by the Father and the Spirit is not inconsistent with his raising himself; for "what things soever the Father doeth, these also doeth the Son" (*John* 5:19), for being one in nature, they are also one in operation.'

The questions naturally arise in many minds, Why did Jesus not work some miracle at once, as a sign, to convince the Jews? Why did he not at once proclaim himself the Messiah? Why did he give the Jews so dark and mysterious a reply as the one before us?—The answer to these questions is this. For one thing, we must remark, it was a leading principle in our Lord's dealings with men not to force conviction on them, but to speak to them according to what he saw was the state of their hearts. He answered fools according to their folly (*Prov.* 26:5). If he had given the Jews a more direct reply, he knew that it would have brought his ministry to an abrupt end, and would have led to his being cut off before the time.—For another thing, we must remember, that however dark our Lord's saying seemed when it was spoken, it did in effect tell the Jews of the greatest and most important sign which could be given them as a proof of his Messiahship. It told them of his future resurrection. It was equivalent to saying, 'You ask me for a sign, and I will give you one. I will rise again from the dead the third day after my crucifixion. If I do not so rise from the dead, you need not believe that I am the Messiah. But if I do so rise, you will be without excuse if you do not believe on me.' In effect our Lord staked the truth of his mission on his resurrection. He did the same when he said that he would give the Jewish nation no sign but that of the prophet Jonas (*Matt.* 12:39). When the apostles began to preach, they continually referred the Jews to Christ's resurrection, as the proof of his Messiahship. And why did they do so? One main reason was,

because their Master had told the Jews, the first time he appeared in the temple, that the great sign they must look to was his own rising again from the dead.

20.—[*Then said ... Jews, Forty and six years, etc.*] This expression has given rise to some difference of opinion. The temple to which the Jews refer cannot of course be the temple built by Solomon. That temple was completely destroyed by Nebuchadnezzar.—Nor yet does it seem likely to have been the temple built by Zerubbabel and his companions, after the return from Babylon. There is no sufficiently clear proof that this temple was forty and six years building.—By far the most probable view is, that the temple spoken of is the one repaired, or rather rebuilt, by Herod, and that the forty-six years here mentioned mean the time during which these repairs were going on, and that the entire completion of them had not been effected up to our Lord's time. These repairs, according to Josephus, had been going on exactly forty-six years when our Lord visited the temple. They were so extensive and costly, that eighteen thousand workmen were employed about them, and they amounted to a rebuilding. Moreover, the minds of the Jews would probably be full of them at this particular time, because they were of recent date, if not going on at that very time. The Greek words might fairly be rendered, 'Forty and six years has this temple been building.'— They denote a time, as Whitby remarks, not perfectly past.

If anyone desires to see an instance of the extravagant lengths into which a good man may be led, in following the allegorical system of interpreting Scripture, he will do well to read Augustine's allegorical explanation of the forty and six years. It is far too absurd to be worth inserting here.

[*Wilt thou rear it up in three days?*] This question implies three things,—a sneer, astonishment, and incredulity. There is probably an emphasis meant to be laid on the word 'thou.' Such a one as thou! Wilt thou do it?

That this saying of our Lord, nevertheless, was not thrown away and forgotten, but stuck in the minds of the Jews, though they did not understand it, is strikingly proved by two facts.—One is, that the false witnesses brought it forward, though in a garbled form, when our Lord was arraigned before the high priests.—The other is, that the Jews taunted him with it when he hung on the cross (*Matt.* 26:61; 27:40).

21.—[*But he spake ... temple ... body.*] This verse is an instance of St John's habit of making explanatory comments in his Gospel, as he goes on, in order to make things clear to his Gentile readers.

Let it be noted, that as our Lord calls his own body a 'temple,' so also the bodies of his believing people are called 'the temple of the Holy Ghost' (*1 Cor.* 6:19). If it was wrong to defile and profane the temple made of stone and wood, how much more is it wrong to defile by sin the temple of our bodies! St Paul and St Peter both call our bodies our 'tabernacle' (*2 Cor.* 5:1; *2 Pet.* 1:13).

22.—[*When ... risen ... dead ... disciples remembered.*] This sentence is an interesting proof of two things. For one thing, it shows how much light was brought to the minds of the disciples by our Lord's resurrection, and how many hard sayings of his were at once unravelled and made plain.—For another thing, it shows how long truth may lie dormant in men's minds without being understood, or doing them any service. It is one of the special offices of the Holy Ghost to bring things to remembrance (*John* 14:26). We must not suppose religious teaching does no good because it is not understood immediately. It may do good long after the teacher is dead.

[*They believed the scripture.*] What Scripture does this mean? It cannot of course be our Lord's saying. What our Lord said is specially added, as something beside the Scripture which the disciples 'believed.'—Nor yet does it seem likely that it means any particular text in the Old Testament about the resurrection. I incline to the opinion that it means generally the whole testimony of Scripture to our Lord's claim to be received as the Messiah. When Jesus rose from the dead, the disciples were fully convinced that the Scripture about the Messiah was fulfilled in their Master.

The expression 'believed' cannot mean that the disciples then believed for the first time. As in other places, it signifies that they believed fully, and without any more doubt and hesitation. The same may be said of John 14:1.

23.—[*Many believed.*] These persons do not appear to have really believed with the heart, but to have been only convinced in their understandings. The distinction between intellectual belief and saving belief, and between one degree of saving belief and another, ought to be carefully noticed in Scripture. There is a faith which devils have, and a faith which is the gift of God. The persons mentioned in this verse had the former, but not the latter. So also we are told that Simon Magus 'believed' (*Acts* 8:13). Again, there is a real heart-belief which a man may have, that admits of great increase. This is the belief spoken of in the preceding verse.

[*When they saw the miracles.*] This expression shows us that there were many miracles worked by our Lord which are nowhere recorded in Scripture. St John himself tells us so twice over (*John* 20:30; 21:25). Nicodemus refers to these miracles in the beginning of the following chapter (*John* 3:2). If it had been good for us to know anything about these miracles, they would no doubt have been recorded. But it is well to remember that there were such miracles, in order that we may rightly understand the unbelief and hardness of the Jews at Jerusalem. The miracles which are related as having been worked in or near Jerusalem, we must remember, are by no means all that our Lord worked there.

24.—[*Did not commit himself.*] The Greek word so rendered means literally, 'did not trust himself.' It is the same verb that is generally rendered 'believe.'

[*He knew all men.*] This is a direct assertion of our Lord's divine omniscience. As God he knew all mankind, and these seeming believers among others. As God, he knew that their hearts were like the stony ground in the parable, and their faith only temporary.

83

Melanchthon makes some very wise remarks on this verse, as to the example which our Lord sets us here of caution in dealing with strangers. It is a melancholy fact, which the experience of years always confirms, that we must not trust implicitly to appearances of kindness, or be ready to open our hearts to everyone as a friend, upon short acquaintance. The man who does not hastily contract intimacies, may be thought cold and distant by some; but in the long run of life he will escape many sorrows. It is a wise saying, that a man ought to be friendly with all, but intimate with few.

25.—[*Needed not ... testify of man.*] These words mean that our Lord had no need of anyone's testimony 'about man.' He required no information from others about the real character of those who professed faith in him.

[*He knew what was in man.*] This means that our Lord, as God, possessed a perfect knowledge of man's inner nature, and was a discerner of the thoughts and intents of the heart. We should remember Solomon's words in his prayer, 'Thou only knowest the hearts of all the children of men' (*1 Kings* 8:39).

The immense difference between our Lord and all ministers of his gospel appears strikingly in this verse. Ministers are constantly deceived in their estimate of people. Christ never was, and never could be. When he allowed Judas Iscariot to be a disciple, he was perfectly acquainted with his character.

Wordsworth observes that the two last verses of this chapter 'afford an instance of the peculiar manner in which the Holy Spirit, in St John's Gospel, pronounces judgment on things and persons. Compare 6:64, 71; 7:39; 8:27; 12:33, 37; 13:11; 21:17.'

In leaving the whole passage, I cannot help remarking what a faithful picture of human nature it exhibits, and how many are the ways in which human corruption and infirmity show themselves. Within the space of a few verses we find some openly profaning God's temple for the sake of gain,—some angrily demanding a sign of him who shows zeal for purity,—some professing a false faith,—and some few only believing, but even these believing with a weak, unintelligent faith. It is the state of things which exists everywhere and always.

JOHN 3:1-8

1 There was a man of the Pharisees, named Nicodemus, a ruler of the Jews:

2 The same came to Jesus by night, and said unto him, Rabbi, we know that thou art a teacher come from God: for no man can do these miracles that thou doest, except God be with him.

3 Jesus answered and said unto him, Verily, verily, I say unto thee, Except a man be born again, he cannot see the kingdom of God.

4 Nicodemus saith unto him, How can a man be born when he is old? can he enter the second time into his mother's womb, and be born?

5 Jesus answered, Verily, verily, I say unto thee, Except a man be born of water and *of* the Spirit, he cannot enter into the kingdom of God.

6 That which is born of the flesh is flesh; and that which is born of the Spirit is spirit.

7 Marvel not that I said unto thee, Ye must be born again.

8 The wind bloweth where it listeth, and thou hearest the sound thereof, but canst not tell whence it cometh, and whither it goeth: so is every one that is born of the Spirit.

THE conversation between Christ and Nicodemus, which begins with these verses, is one of the most important passages in the whole Bible. Nowhere else do we find stronger statements about those two mighty subjects, the new birth, and salvation by faith in the Son of God. The servant of Christ will do well to make himself thoroughly acquainted with this chapter. A man may be ignorant of many things in religion, and yet be saved. But to be ignorant of the matters handled in this chapter, is to be in the broad way which leadeth to destruction.

We should notice, firstly, in these verses, *what a weak and feeble beginning a man may make in religion, and yet finally prove a strong Christian.* We are told of a certain Pharisee, named Nicodemus, who, feeling concerned about his soul, 'came to Jesus by night.'

There can be little doubt that Nicodemus acted as he did on this occasion from the fear of man. He was afraid of what man would think, or say, or do, if his visit to Jesus was known. He came 'by night' because he had not faith and courage enough to come by day. And yet there was a time afterwards when this very Nicodemus took our Lord's part in open day in the council of the Jews. 'Doth our law judge any man,' he said, 'before it hear him, and know what he doeth?' (*John* 7:51).—Nor was this all. There came a time when this very Nicodemus was one of the only two men who did honour to our Lord's dead body. He helped Joseph of Arimathæa to bury Jesus, when even the apostles had forsaken their Master and fled. His last things were more than his first. Though he began ill, he ended well.

The history of Nicodemus is meant to teach us that we should never 'despise the day of small things' in religion (*Zech.* 4:10). We must not set down a man as having no grace, because his first steps towards God are timid and wavering, and the first movements of his soul are uncertain, hesitating, and stamped with much imperfection. We must remember our Lord's reception of Nicodemus. He did not break the bruised reed, or quench the smoking flax, which he saw before him (*Matt.* 12:20). Like him, let us take inquirers by the hand, and deal with them gently and lovingly. In everything there must be a beginning. It is not those who make the most flaming profession of religion at first, who endure the longest and prove the most steadfast. Judas Iscariot was an apostle when Nicodemus was just groping his way slowly into full light. Yet afterwards, when Nicodemus was boldly helping to bury his crucified Saviour, Judas Iscariot had betrayed him, and hanged himself! This is a fact which ought not to be forgotten.

We should notice, secondly, in these verses, *what a mighty change our Lord declares to be needful to salvation, and what a remarkable expression he uses in describing it.* He speaks of a new birth. He says to Nicodemus, 'Except a man be born again, he cannot see the kingdom of God.' He announces the same truth in other words, in order to make it more plain to his hearer's mind: 'Except a man be born of water and of the Spirit, he cannot enter into the kingdom of God.' By this expression he meant Nicodemus to understand that 'no one could become his disciple, unless his inward man was as thoroughly cleansed and renewed by the Spirit, as the outward man is cleansed by water.' To possess the privileges of Judaism a man only needed to be born of the seed of Abraham after the flesh. To possess the privileges of Christ's kingdom, a man must be born again of the Holy Ghost.

The change which our Lord here declares needful to salvation is evidently no slight or superficial one. It is not merely reformation, or amendment, or moral change, or outward alteration of life. It is a thorough change of heart, will, and character. It is a resurrection. It is a new creation. It is a passing from death to life. It is the implanting in our dead hearts of a new principle from above. It is the calling into existence of a new creature, with a new nature, new habits of life, new tastes, new desires, new appetites, new judgments, new opinions, new hopes, and new fears. All this, and nothing less than this is implied, when our Lord declares that we all need a 'new birth.'

This change of heart is rendered absolutely necessary to salvation by the corrupt condition in which we are all, without exception, born. 'That which is born of the flesh is flesh.' Our nature is thoroughly fallen. The carnal mind is enmity against God (*Rom.* 8:7). We come into the world without faith, or love, or fear toward God. We have no natural inclination to serve him or obey him, and no natural pleasure in doing his will. Left to himself, no child of Adam would ever turn to God. The truest description of the change which we all need in order to make us real Christians, is the expression, 'new birth.'

This mighty change, it must never be forgotten, we cannot give to ourselves. The very name which our Lord gives to it is a convincing proof of this. He calls it 'a birth.' No man is the author of his own existence, and no man can quicken his own soul. We might as well expect a dead man to give himself life, as expect a natural man to make himself spiritual. A power from above must be put in exercise, even that same power which created the world (*2 Cor.* 4:6). Man can do many things; but he cannot give life either to himself or to others. To give life is the peculiar prerogative of God. Well may our Lord declare that we need to be 'born again!'

This mighty change, we must, above all, remember, is a thing without which we cannot go to heaven, and could not enjoy heaven if we went there. Our Lord's words on this point are distinct and express. 'Except a man be born again, he can neither *see* nor *enter* the kingdom of God.' Heaven may be reached without money, or rank, or learning. But it is clear as daylight, if words have any meaning, that nobody can enter heaven without a 'new birth.'

We should notice, lastly, in these verses, *the instructive comparison which our Lord uses in explaining the new birth.* He saw Nicodemus perplexed and astonished by the things he had just heard. He graciously helped his wondering mind by an illustration drawn from 'the wind.' A more beautiful and fitting illustration of the work of the Spirit it is impossible to conceive.

There is much about the wind that is mysterious and inexplicable. 'Thou canst not tell,' says our Lord, 'whence it cometh and whither it goeth.' We cannot handle it with our hands, or see it with our eyes. When the wind blows, we cannot point out the exact spot where its breath first began to be felt, and the exact distance to which its influence shall extend. But we do not on that account deny its presence.—It is just the same with the operations of the Spirit in the new birth of man. They may be mysterious, sovereign, and incomprehensible to us in many ways. But it is foolish to stumble at them because there is much about them that we cannot explain.

But whatever mystery there may be about the wind, its presence may always be known by its sound and effects. 'Thou hearest the sound thereof,' says our Lord. When our ears hear it whistling in the windows, and our eyes see the clouds driving before it, we do not hesitate to say, 'There is wind.'—It is just the same with the operations of the Holy Spirit in the new birth of man. Marvellous and incomprehensible as his work may be, it is work that can always be seen and known. The new birth is a thing that 'cannot be hid.' There will always be visible 'fruits of the Spirit' in everyone that is born of the Spirit.

Would we know what the marks of the new birth are?—We shall find them already written for our learning in the First Epistle of St John. The man born of God 'believeth that Jesus is the Christ,'—'doth not commit sin,'—'doeth righteousness,'—loves 'the brethren,'—'overcometh the world,'—'keepeth himself' from the 'wicked one.'—This is the man born of the Spirit! Where these fruits are to be seen, there is the new birth of which our Lord is speaking. He that lacks these marks, is yet dead in trespasses and sins (1 John 5:1; 3:9; 2:29; 3:14; 5:4; 5:18).

And now let us solemnly ask ourselves whether we know anything of the mighty change of which we have been reading? Have we been born again? Can any marks of the new birth be seen in us? Can the sound of the Spirit be heard in our daily conversation? Is the image and superscription of the Spirit to be discerned in our lives?—Happy is the man who can give satisfactory answers to these questions! A day will come when those who are not born again will wish that they had never been born at all.

Notes—John 3:1-8

1.—[*There was a man, etc.*] The close connection of the conversation between Christ and Nicodemus with the end of the preceding chapter ought to be carefully noted. In fact the original Greek contains a connecting particle, which our translators have omitted to express in our version. The chapter should begin, 'And there was a man,' or, 'Now there was a man.'—The conversation took place when our Lord 'was in Jerusalem,' at the time of the passover. Nicodemus was one of those who 'saw the miracles which Jesus did,' and was so much struck by what he saw, that he sought out our Lord in order to converse with him.

[*Of the Pharisees.*] The striking variety of character in those who were brought to believe on Christ while he was on earth, ought not to be overlooked. His disciples were not drawn exclusively from any one class. As a general rule, none were more bitterly opposed to him and his doctrines than the Pharisees. Yet here we see that nothing is impossible with grace. Even a Pharisee became an inquirer, and ultimately a disciple! Nicodemus and St Paul are standing proofs that no heart is too hard to be converted. The third chapter shows us Jesus teaching a proud, moral Pharisee. The fourth will show him teaching an ignorant, immoral Samaritan woman. None are too bad to be taught by Christ.

[*A ruler of the Jews.*] The civil government of the Jews at this time, we must remember, was in the hands of the Romans. When Nicodemus is called 'a ruler,' it means that he was a chief person among the Jews, probably in high ecclesiastical position, and certainly a famous religious teacher. See verse 10.

2.—[*The same came ... by night.*] The fact here recorded appears to me to show that Nicodemus was influenced by the fear of man, and was afraid or ashamed to visit Jesus by day.—The view maintained by some, that we ought not to blame him for coming by night, because it was the quietest time for conversation, and the time when an interview was least liable to be interrupted, or because the Jewish teachers were in the habit of receiving inquirers by night, appears to me undeserving of attention. I am confirmed in this opinion by the fact, that on the only other occasions where Nicodemus is mentioned he is specially described as the man who 'came to Jesus by night.' This repeated expression appears to me to imply blame (*John* 7:50; 19:39).

How anyone can waste time, as some famous commentators do, in speculating how the conversation between Christ and Nicodemus was reported, is to my mind perfectly astonishing. To hint, as one has done, that Jesus must have told St John about the conversation afterwards, or that St John must have been present, appears to me to strike a blow at the very root of inspiration. Both here and elsewhere, frequently, St John describes things which he only knew by the direct inspiration of the Holy Ghost.

[*Rabbi.*] This expression was a name of dignity among the Hebrews, signifying Doctor or Master. Cruden says that the name came originally from the Chaldees, and that it was not used before the time of captivity, except in describing the officers of the kings of Assyria and Babylon. Thus we find the names of Rabsaris and Rab-shakeh (2 *Kings* 18:17). The use of the word here by Nicodemus, was intended to mark his respect for our Lord.

[*We know.*] Different reasons have been assigned for Nicodemus' use of the plural number in this place. Whom did he mean when he said 'we'? Some say that he meant himself and many of his brethren among the Pharisees.—Some say that he meant himself and the secret believers of all classes mentioned at the end of the last chapter.—Some say, as Lightfoot, that he meant no one in particular, but used the plural for the singular, according to an idiom common in all languages. He only meant 'It is commonly known.'—I venture the suggestion, that Nicodemus probably used the plural number intentionally, on account of its vagueness, and avoided the singular number from motives of caution, that he might not commit himself too much. Even at the present day people will talk of 'we' in religion, long before they will talk of 'I.'—Weak faith strives to be hid in a crowd.

[*Thou art a teacher come from God.*] This cautious sentence is an instructive indication of the state of Nicodemus' mind. He was naturally a timid, hesitating, slow-moving man. That Jesus was somebody remarkable, he was convinced by his miracles. That he might possibly be the Messiah, had probably crossed his mind, and the more so because he doubtless knew of the ministry of John the Baptist, and had heard that John spake of one greater than himself who was yet to come. But until he can make out more about Jesus, by private conversation, he declines to commit himself to any stronger statement than that before us. The Greek words would be more literally rendered, 'From God thou hast come a teacher.'

Lightfoot thinks that Nicodemus here refers to the long cessation of prophecy, which had now lasted for four hundred years. During this long period no one had appeared from God to teach the once-favoured Jewish nation, as the prophets did of old. But now, he seems to say, 'Thou hast appeared, as the prophets did in former times, to teach us.'

[*No man can do these miracles … with him.*] This sentence has been justly called an illustration of one great purpose of our Lord's miracles. They arrested men's attention. They were evidences of a divine mission. They showed that he who wrought them was no ordinary person, and ought to be listened to.

I am aware that some have thought that Nicodemus attached too much weight to our Lord's miracles, and have boldly asserted that miracles are no necessary proof of a divine mission, seeing that Antichrist will appear with signs and lying wonders (2 *Thess.* 2:9; *Rev.* 13:14). In reply it might be sufficient to remark that our Lord himself declared that his works bore witness that the Father had sent him (*John* 5:36; 10:25; 15:24). But I also think that sufficient stress is not laid on the expression, 'These miracles that thou doest.' The character and quality of our Lord's miracles were such as to prove his divine commission. False teachers and antichrists may

be permitted to work *some* miracles, like the magicians who withstood Moses. But there is a point beyond which Antichrist and his servants cannot go. Such miracles as our Lord worked could only be wrought by the finger of God. I therefore think that Nicodemus' argument was just and correct.—It is moreover worthy of note that the expression he uses is precisely the same as that used by St Peter when describing our Lord's ministry and miracles. He says, 'God was with him' (*Acts* 10:38).

The expression, 'God being with a man,' is a common phrase in the Scriptures, denoting the possession of certain special gifts or graces from God, beyond those ordinarily given to men. Thus 1 Samuel 16:18; 3:19; and 18:12-14.

3.—[*Jesus answered.*] The question has often been asked, 'To what did our Lord answer?' No question was put to him. What is the connecting link between the words of Nicodemus, and the solemn statement contained in the first words which our Lord addressed to him?

I believe the true reply to these questions is, that our Lord, as on many other occasions, made answer according to what he saw going on in Nicodemus' heart. He knew that the inquirer before him, like all the Jews, was expecting the appearance of Messiah, and was even suspecting that he had found him. He therefore begins, by telling him at once what was absolutely needful if he would belong to Messiah's kingdom. It was not a temporal kingdom, as he vainly supposed, but a spiritual one. It was not a kingdom, in which all persons born of the seed of Abraham, would, as a matter of course, have a place because of their birth. It was a kingdom in which grace, not blood, was the indispensable condition of admission. The first thing needful in order to belong to Messiah's kingdom, was to be 'born again.' Men must renounce all idea of privileges by reason of their natural birth. All men, whether Jews or Gentiles, must be born again, born anew, born from above by a spiritual birth.—'Nicodemus,' our Lord seems to say, 'If you want to know how a man is to become a member of Messiah's kingdom, understand this day, that the first step is to be born again. Think not because

Abraham is your father that Messiah will acknowledge you as one of his subjects. I tell you at once, that the first thing you and all other men need is a new birth.'

I am quite aware that several other explanations have been given of the link between Nicodemus' remark and our Lord's opening assertion. I will only say, that the one I have given appears to me by far the simplest and most satisfactory.

[*Verily, verily, I say unto thee.*] This expression, which is peculiar to St John's Gospel, has been already commented on (*John* 1:51). But it is useful to remark, in considering the verse before us, that the phrase is never used except in connection with some statement of great importance and solemnity.

[*Except a man.*] The Greek word which our version has rendered 'a man,' would be more literally translated, 'anyone,' or 'any person.' The change called the 'new birth,' our Lord would have us know, is of universal necessity. Nobody can be saved without it.

[*Born again.*] The Greek word here rendered 'again,' might be translated with equal correctness, 'from above:' i.e., from heaven, or from God. It is so translated in this chapter (v. 31), and in four other places in the New Testament (*John* 19:11; *James* 1:17; 3:15, 17). In one other place (*Gal.* 4:9), it is 'again.' Many commentators in every age, as Origen, Cyril, Theophylact, Bullinger, Lightfoot, Erasmus, Bengel, have maintained strongly, that 'born from above,' and not 'born again,' is the true and better translation of the phrase. Cranmer's version renders it 'born from above,' and our own translators have allowed it in a marginal reading. My own impression agrees with that of most commentators, that 'born again' is the right translation.—For one thing, it seems most probable that Nicodemus understood our Lord to mean 'born again,' or else he would hardly have asked the question, Can a man 'enter the *second time* into his mother's womb, and be born?'— For another thing, the Greek words used in four other places where regeneration is spoken of in the New Testament, admit of no other meaning than being 'born again,' and could not possibly be rendered 'born from above.' See 1 Peter 1:3, 23; Matthew

19:28; Titus 3:5.

The point is happily not one of importance, and men may agree to differ about it, if they cannot convince one another. Every true Christian is undoubtedly 'born from above' by the quickening power of God in heaven, as well as 'born again' by a second spiritual birth.

The meaning of our Lord when he said, 'Except a man be born again,' is unhappily a subject on which there is a wide difference of opinion in the church of Christ.—The expression at any rate cannot be said to stand alone. It is used six times in the Gospel of St John, once in the First Epistle of St Peter, and six times in the First Epistle of St John (*John* 1:13; 3:3, 5, 6, 7, 8; *1 Pet.* 1:23; *1 John* 2:29; 3:9; 4:7; 5:1, 4, 18). Common sense and fair interpretation of language point out that 'born again,' 'born of the Spirit,' and 'born of God,' are expressions so intimately connected with one another, that they mean one and the same thing. The only question is, 'What do they mean?'

Some think that to be 'born again,' means nothing more than 'an outward reformation, or such outward conformity as a proselyte might yield to a new set of rules of life.'—This is an almost obsolete and utterly unsatisfactory interpretation. It makes our Lord tell Nicodemus nothing more than he might have learned from heathen philosophers,—such as Socrates, Plato, or Aristotle; or than he might have heard from any rabbi about the duties of a proselyte from heathenism to Judaism.

Some think that to be 'born again,' means to be admitted into the church of Christ by baptism, and to receive a spiritual change of heart inseparably connected with baptism.—This again is an unsatisfactory interpretation. For one thing, it seems improbable, that the first truth which our Lord would propound to an inquiring Pharisee, would be the necessity of baptism. He certainly never did so on any other occasion.—For another thing, if our Lord only meant baptism, it is difficult to account for the astonishment and perplexity which Nicodemus expressed on hearing our Lord's words. Baptism was not a thing with which a Pharisee was unacquainted. In the Jewish church proselytes were baptized.—Last, but not least, it is clear from St John's First Epistle, that to be 'born again, born of the Spirit, or born of God,' means something much greater than baptism. The picture which the apostle there gives of the man who is 'born of God,' could certainly not be given of the man who is baptized.

The true view of the expression I believe to be this. Being 'born again,' means that complete change of heart and character which is produced in a man by the Holy Ghost, when he repents, believes on Christ, and becomes a true Christian. It is a change which is frequently spoken of in the Bible. In Ezekiel it is called taking away 'the stony heart' and giving 'a heart of flesh,'—giving 'a new heart,' and putting within 'a new spirit' (*Ezek.* 11:19; 36:26). In Acts it is called 'repentance and conversion' (*Acts* 3:19). In Romans it is called being 'alive from the dead' (*Rom.* 6:13). In Corinthians it is called being 'a new creature' (2 *Cor.* 5:17). In Ephesians it is called being 'quickened' (*Eph.* 2:1). In Colossians it is called 'putting off the old man and putting on the new' (*Col.* 3:9, 10). In Titus it is called the 'washing of regeneration' (*Titus* 3:5). In Peter it is called being 'called out of darkness into light,' and being made 'partakers of the divine nature' (*1 Pet.* 2:9; 2 *Pet.* 1:4). In John it is called 'passing from death to life' (*1 John* 3:14). I believe that all these expressions come to the same thing in the end. They are all the same truth, only viewed from different sides. They all mean that mighty inward change of heart which our Lord here calls a 'new birth,' and which John the Baptist foretold would specially characterize Messiah's kingdom. He was to baptize not with water, but with the Holy Ghost. Our Lord begins his address to Nicodemus by taking up his forerunner's prediction: he tells him that he must be 'born again' or baptized with the Spirit.—Human nature is so entirely corrupt, diseased, and ruined by the fall, that all who would be saved must be born again. No lesser change will suffice. They need nothing less than a new birth.

[*He cannot see.*] This expression has received two interpretations. Some think that it means, 'He cannot understand, or comprehend.' Others think that it means, 'He cannot enter, enjoy, partake of, or possess.' The latter I believe to be the true meaning of the expression. The first is truth, but not the truth of the text. The second is confirmed by the language used in the fifth verse, and is a common form of speech of which there are many instances in the Bible. Thus we find to 'see life' (*John* 3:36),—to 'see corruption' (*Psa.* 16:10),—to 'see death' (*John* 8:51),—to 'see evil' (*Psa.* 90:15),—to 'see sorrow' (*Rev.* 18:7).

[*The kingdom of God.*] This expression means that spiritual kingdom which Messiah came into the world to set up, and of which all believers are the subjects,—the kingdom which is now small, and weak, and despised, but which shall be great and glorious at the second advent. Our Lord declares that no man can belong to that kingdom and be one of its subjects, without a new birth. To belong to the covenant of Israel with all its temporal privileges, a man need only be born of Jewish parents. To belong to Messiah's kingdom, a man must be 'born again' of the Spirit, and have a new heart.

Luther's remark on this verse, quoted by Stier, is worth reading. He supposes our Lord to say, 'My doctrine is not of doing and of leaving undone, but of being and becoming; so that it is not a new work to be done, but the being new created;—not the living otherwise, but the being new born.'

The unvarying suitableness of our Lord's teaching to the special state of mind of those whom he taught deserves observation. To the young ruler fond of his money, he says, 'Sell all that thou hast, and distribute unto the poor.'—To the multitude craving food, he says, 'Labour not for the meat which perisheth.'—To the Samaritan woman coming to draw water, he commends 'living water.' To the Pharisee proud of his *birth*, as a son of Abraham, he says, 'Ye must be born again' (*Luke* 18:22; *John* 6:27; 4:10).

4.—[*Nicodemus saith ... How.*] The question of Nicodemus is precisely one of those which the natural ignorance of man in spiritual things prompts a person to ask. Just as the Samaritan woman, in the fourth chapter, put a carnal meaning on our Lord's words about 'living water,' and the Jews, in the sixth chapter, put a carnal meaning on the 'bread of God,' so Nicodemus puts a carnal meaning on the expression 'born again.'—There is nothing which the heart of man in every part and every age of the world is so slow to understand as the work of the Holy Ghost. Our minds are so gross and sensuous, that we cannot take in the idea of an inward and spiritual operation. Unless we can see things and touch things in religion we are slow to believe them.

[*When he is old.*] This expression seems to indicate that Nicodemus himself was an old man when this conversation took place. If this be so, it is only fair, in judging his case, to make some allowance for the slowness with which old age receives new opinions, and specially in the things of religion. At the same time it supplies an encouraging proof that no man is too old to be converted. One of our Lord's first converts was an old man!

5.—[*Except ... born of water and of the Spirit.*] This famous text has unhappily given rise to widely different interpretations. On one thing only respecting it nearly all commentators are agreed. It is the same truth that is laid down in the third verse, only laid down with greater fulness, in compassion to Nicodemus' weakness of understanding. But what does it mean? The expression 'born of water' is peculiar to this place, and occurs nowhere else in the Bible. It cannot be literally interpreted. No one can be literally 'born of water.' What then does the phrase signify? When can it be said of anyone, that he is 'born of water and of the Spirit'?

The first and commonest interpretation is to refer the text entirely to baptism, and to draw from it the inseparable connection of baptism and spiritual regeneration.—According to this view of the text, our Lord tells Nicodemus that baptism is absolutely necessary to salvation, and is the appointed means of giving new birth to the heart of man. 'If you wish to belong to my kingdom, you must be born again, as I have already said; and if you wish to be born again, the only way to obtain this mighty blessing is to be baptized. Except a man be regenerated or born again by baptism, he cannot enter my kingdom.' This is the

view of the text which is maintained by the Fathers, by the Roman Catholic writers, by the Lutheran commentators, and by many English divines down to the present day. It is a view which is supported by much learning, and by many strange and far-fetched arguments, such as Genesis 1:2. It is, however, a view which to my own mind is utterly unsatisfactory.

The second, and less common interpretation, is to refer the text partly to baptism and partly to that real regeneration of heart, which a man may receive, like the penitent thief, without having been baptized.—According to this view, our Lord tells Nicodemus that a new birth is absolutely necessary to salvation, and that to be baptized, or 'born of water,' is one of the appointed ways by which regeneration is effected. Those who hold this view deny as stoutly as any that there is any inseparable connection between baptism and regeneration. They hold that multitudes are 'born of water' who are never born of the Spirit. But they maintain that the word 'water' must be intended to point us to baptism, and that by the use of the expression, 'born of water,' our Lord meant to defend both John's baptism and his own, and to show their value. This is the view of the text which is maintained by some few of the best Roman Catholic writers, such as Rupertus and Ferus,—by almost all the English Reformers, and by many excellent commentators down to the present day. It is a view, which to my own mind seems not much more satisfactory than the former one, already described, on account of the strange consequences which it involves.

The third, and much the least common interpretation, is to refer the text entirely to the regeneration of man's heart, and to exclude baptism altogether from any place in it.—According to this view, our Lord explains to Nicodemus, by the use of a figure, what he had meant when he spoke of being 'born again.' He would have Nicodemus know that a man must have his heart as thoroughly cleansed and renewed by the Spirit as the body is cleansed and purified by water. He must be born of the Spirit working on his inward nature, as water works on the material body. In short, he must have a 'clean heart' created in him, if he would belong to Messiah's kingdom. Most of those who take this view, consider that baptism was certainly meant to point to the change of heart described in the text, but that this text was meant to point out something distinct from baptism, and even more important than baptism. This is the view which I believe to be the true one, and to which I unhesitatingly adhere.

Those who hold that baptism is not referred to in this text, are undoubtedly a small minority among theologians, but their names are weighty. Among them will be found Calvin, Zwingle, Bullinger, Gualter, Archbishop Whitgift, Bishop Prideaux, Whitaker, Fulke, Poole, Hutcheson, Charnock, Gill, Cartwright, Grotius, Cocceius, Gomarus, Piscator, Rivetus, Chamier, Witsius, Mastricht, Turretin, Lampe, Burkitt, A. Clarke, and, according to Lampe, Wycliffe, Daillé, and Paræus.—I do not assert this on second-hand information. I have verified the assertion by examining with my own eyes the works of all the authors above-named, excepting the three referred to by Lampe. On the precise meaning of the word 'water' they are not agreed. But they all hold that our Lord did not mean baptism when he spoke of being 'born of water and the Spirit.'—Dean Alford, I observe, says that the expression 'refers to the token, or outward sign of baptism, on any *honest* interpretation.' How far it is justifiable to use such language about an opinion supported by so many great names, I leave to the reader to decide! Those who wish to see the view of the text which I advocate more fully defended, will find what they want in Lampe's *Dissertations* and Chamier's *Panstratia*.

In adhering to a view of this text which is adopted by so few commentators, I feel a natural desire to give the reasons of my opinion at full length, and I think that the importance of the subject in the present day justifies me in doing so. In giving these reasons I must decline entering into questions which are not directly before me. The value of the sacrament of baptism,—the right of infants to baptism,—the true meaning of the Church of England Baptismal Service, are matters which I shall not touch. The meaning of our Lord's words, 'Except a man be born of water and the Spirit,' is the only point to which I shall confine myself. I believe that in using these words our Lord did *not* refer to baptism, and I think so for the following reasons.

a. Firstly, there is nothing in the words of the text which necessarily requires to be referred to baptism. 'Water,'—'washing,'—and 'cleansing' are figurative expressions, frequently used in Scripture, in order to denote a spiritual operation on man's heart (see *Psa.* 51:7-10; *Isa.* 44:3; *Jer.* 4:14; *Ezek.* 36:25; *John* 4:10; 7:38, 39). The expression, 'born of water and of the Spirit,' is doubtless very peculiar. But it is not more peculiar than the parallel expression, 'He shall baptize you with the Holy Ghost, and with fire' (*Matt.* 3:11). To explain this last text by the tongues of fire on the day of Pentecost, is an utterly unsatisfactory interpretation, and confines the fulfilment of a mighty general promise to one single act and one single day. I believe that in each case an element is mentioned in connection with the Spirit, in order to show the nature of the Spirit's operation. Men must be 'baptized with the Holy Ghost,' purifying their hearts from corruption, as *fire* purifies metal, and must be 'born of the Spirit,' cleansing their hearts as *water* cleanses the body. The use of fire and water as the great instruments of purification, was well known to the Jews. See Numbers 31:23, where both are mentioned together. Chrysostom well remarks that 'Scripture sometimes connects the grace of the Spirit with fire, and sometimes with water.'

b. Secondly, the assertion that 'water' must mean baptism, because baptism is the ordinary means of regeneration, is an assertion utterly destitute of scriptural proof. It is no doubt written of professing saints and believers, that they have been buried with Christ in baptism (*Rom.* 6:4), and that 'as many . . . as have been baptized into Christ have put on Christ' (*Gal.* 3:27).—But there is not a single text which declares that baptism is the *only* way by which people are born again. On the contrary, we find two plain texts in which regeneration is distinctly ascribed, not to baptism, but to the Word (*1 Pet.* 1:23; *James*

1:18). Moreover, the case of Simon Magus clearly proves that in apostolic times all persons did not receive grace when they were baptized. St Peter tells him a very few days after his baptism, 'Thou hast neither part nor lot in this matter . . . thy heart is not right in the sight of God . . . thou art in the gall of bitterness, and in the bond of iniquity' (*Acts* 8:21-23). The assertion, therefore, that 'water' *must* mean baptism, is a mere gratuitous assumption, and must fall to the ground.

c. Thirdly, if 'water' in the text before us means baptism, it follows as a logical consequence that baptism is absolutely necessary to salvation, and that all who have died unbaptized since these words were spoken, have been lost. The penitent thief was lost on this theory, for he was never baptized! All infants who have died unbaptized have been lost! The whole body of the Quakers, who die in their own communion, are lost! There is no evading this conclusion, unless we adopt the absurd and untenable hypothesis that the kingdom of God in this solemn passage means nothing more than the visible church. Where our Lord, in declaring a great general truth, makes no exceptions, we have no right to make them. If words mean anything, to refer 'water' to baptism excludes unbaptized persons from heaven! And yet there is not another instance in Scripture of an outward ordinance being made absolutely necessary to salvation, and specially an ordinance which a man cannot confer on himself. A new, regenerate heart is undoubtedly necessary to the salvation of everyone, without exception, and it is of this only, I believe, that the text before us speaks.

d. Fourthly, if we accept the theory that baptism is the ordinary means of conveying the grace of regeneration, that all baptized persons are necessarily regenerated, and that all who are 'born of water' are at the same time born of the Spirit, we are irresistibly involved in the most dangerous and pernicious consequences.—We pour contempt on the whole work of the Spirit, and on the blessed doctrine of regeneration. We bring into the church a new and unscriptural kind of new birth, a new birth that cannot be seen by its fruits. We make

out that people are 'born of God' when they have not one of the marks of regeneration laid down by St John.—We encourage the rankest antinomianism. We lead people to suppose that they have grace in their hearts while they are servants of sin, and that they have the Holy Spirit within them while they are obeying the lusts of the flesh.—Last, but not least, we pour contempt on the holy sacrament of baptism. We turn it into a mere form, in which faith and prayer have no place at all. We lead people to suppose that it matters nothing in what spirit they bring their children to baptism, and that if water is sprinkled, and certain words are used, an infant is, as a matter of course, born again. Worst of all, we induce people secretly to despise baptism, because we teach them that it always conveys a mighty spiritual blessing, while their own eyes tell them that in a multitude of cases it does no good at all.—I see no possibility of avoiding these consequences, however little some persons who hold the inseparability of baptism and regeneration may intend them. Happily I have the comfort of thinking that there is an utter want of logic in some hearts which have much grace.

e. Fifthly, if 'born of water and of the Spirit' was meant to teach Nicodemus that baptism is the ordinary means of conveying spiritual regeneration, it is very difficult to understand why our Lord rebuked him for not knowing it. 'Knowest thou not these things?' How could he know them? That there was such a thing as baptism, he knew as a Pharisee. But that baptism was the appointed means of conveying 'new birth,' he could not know. It was a doctrine nowhere taught in the old Testament. It is a doctrine, on the showing of its own advocates, peculiar to Christianity. And yet Nicodemus is rebuked for not knowing it! To my mind this is inexplicable. The necessity of a thorough change of heart, on the contrary, Nicodemus might have known from the Old Testament Scriptures. And it was for ignorance of this, not for ignorance of baptismal regeneration, that he was rebuked.

f. Sixthly and lastly, if it be true that 'to be born of water' means baptism, and that baptism is the ordinary means of conveying the grace of regeneration, it is most extraordinary that there is so little about baptism in the Epistles of the New Testament. In Romans it is only twice mentioned,—and in 1 Corinthians, seven times.—In Galatians, Ephesians, Colossians, Hebrews, and 1 Peter we find it named once in each epistle. In thirteen of the remaining epistles it is neither named nor referred to. In the two Pastoral Epistles to Timothy, where we might expect something about baptism, if anywhere, there is not a word about it! In the Epistle to Titus the only text that can possibly be applied to baptism is by no means clearly applicable (*Titus* 3:5). Nor is this all. In the one epistle which mentions baptism seven times, we find the writer saying that 'Christ sent [him] not to baptize, but to preach the gospel,' and actually 'thanking God,' that he had 'baptized none of [the Corinthians], but Crispus and Gaius' (*1 Cor.* 1:14, 17). He would surely never have said this, if all whom he baptized were at once born again. Imagine St Paul saying, 'I thank God I regenerated none of you'! Moreover, it is a startling fact, that this very same apostle, in the very same epistle, says to these same Corinthians, 'I have begotten you through the gospel' (*1 Cor.* 4:15). My deliberate conviction is, that St Paul would never have written these sentences if he had believed that the only way to be born of the Spirit was to be baptized.

I give these reasons with a sorrowful feeling that to many they are given in vain. But I have felt it due to myself, in maintaining an opinion about a most important text which is not commonly held, to state fully my reasons, and to show that my opinion is not lightly maintained.

Before leaving this subject, I think it right, in self-defence, to say something about the fact, that the view I maintain is not held by the great majority of commentators. This fact undoubtedly calls for some explanation.

With regard to the Fathers, no one can read their writings without seeing that they were fallible men. On no point does their weakness appear so strongly as in their language about the sacraments. The man who intends to abide by all the opinions of the Fathers about the sacraments, will have to swallow a great deal. After all, the very earliest Father, whose commentary on St John's Gospel is extant is Origen, who died in A.D. 253. The true view of the text before us, might easily be lost in the period of at least 150 years between Origen's day and the days of St John. Tertullian incidentally applies the text before us to baptism, in one of his writings. But even he was not born till A.D. 160, at least two generations after St John's time.

With regard to the Lutheran writers, their avowed opinions upon the sacraments make their interpretations of the text before us of little weight. They have a peculiar sacramental theory to maintain when they expound Scripture, and to that theory they steadfastly adhere. Yet even Brentius on this text confesses that the baptism here signified by 'water,' means something much more than the sacrament of baptism, and includes the whole doctrine of the gospel.—The Roman Catholic commentators are of course even more fettered in their views of the sacraments than the Lutherans, and hardly call for any remark. Their constant endeavour in expounding Scripture, is to maintain the sacramental system of their own Church, and a text like that before us is unhesitatingly applied to baptism.

With regard to our own English Reformers and their immediate successors, their opinions about a text like this are perhaps less valuable than upon any subject. They always display an excessive anxiety to agree with the Fathers. They were anxious in every way to conciliate opponents, and to support their own Protestantism by appeals to primitive antiquity. When, therefore, they saw that the Fathers referred the text before us to baptism, and that at best the point was doubtful, we cannot wonder that they held that to be 'born of water' was to be baptized. Yet even they seem not unanimous on the point; and Latimer's well-known assertion, that 'to be christened with water is not regeneration,' must not be forgotten.—The famous remarks of Hooker, which are so frequently thrown in the teeth of those who take the view of 'water and the Spirit,' which I do, are a curious instance of the coolness with which a great man can sometimes draw an illogical conclusion in his own favour, from some broad general premise. He lays down the general principle, that 'when a literal construction of a text will stand, that furthest from the letter is commonly the worst.' He then proceeds to take it for granted, that to interpret 'born of water' of baptism is the *literal* construction of the text now before us. Unfortunately this is precisely the point that I for one do not concede; and his conclusion is consequently, to my mind, worthless. Moreover when we talk of a 'literal' sense, there must evidently be some limit to it. If not, we cannot answer the Roman Catholic when he proves transubstantiation from the words, 'This is my body.'

I believe that for a true and sound exposition of the text before us we must look to the Puritans and Dutch divines of the seventeenth century. It was necessary for men to be a generation further off from Romanism before they were able to give a dispassionate opinion about such a text as this. The early Protestants did not see the consequences of the language they sometimes used about baptism with sufficient clearness. Otherwise, I believe they would not have written about it as they did. To anyone who asks for a specimen of the seventeenth-century divinity, I would say that one of the simplest and best statements of the true meaning of the text before us will be found in Poole's *Annotations*.

In leaving the whole subject, there is one fact which I think deserves very serious consideration. Those churches of Christendom at the present day which distinctly maintain that all baptized persons are born of the Spirit, are, as a general rule, the most corrupt churches in the world. Those bodies of Christians on the other hand, which deny the inseparable connection of baptism and the new birth, are precisely those bodies which are most pure in faith and practice, and do most for the extension of the gospel in the world. This is a great fact which ought not to be forgotten.

6.—[*That which is born ... flesh ... spirit.*] In this verse, our Lord gives Nicodemus the reason why the change of heart called 'new birth,' is a thing of such absolute necessity, and why no slight moral change will suffice. Nicodemus had spoken of 'entering a second time into his mother's womb.' Our Lord tells him that even if such a thing was possible it would not make him fit for the kingdom of God. The child of human parents would always be like the parents from which it sprung, if it was born a hundred times over. 'That which is born of the flesh is flesh.' All men and women are by nature corrupt, sinful, fleshly, and alienated from God. 'They that are in the flesh cannot please God' (*Rom.* 8:8). Their children will always be born with a nature like that of their parents. To bring a clean thing out of an unclean is proverbially impossible. A bramble will never bear grapes, however much it may be cultivated, and a natural man will never be a godly man without the Spirit. In order to be really spiritual and fit for the kingdom of God, a new power from without must enter into a man's nature. 'That which is born of the Spirit is spirit.'

The sentence is undoubtedly very elliptical, and expressed in abstract terms. It is like St Paul's words, 'The carnal mind is enmity against God' (*Rom.* 8:7). But the general meaning is unmistakable. Human nature is so utterly fallen, corrupt, and carnal, that nothing can come from it by natural generation, but a fallen, corrupt, and carnal offspring. There is no self-curative power in man. He will always go on reproducing himself. To become spiritual and fit for communion with God, nothing less is required than the entrance of the Spirit of God into our hearts. In one word, we must have that new birth of the Spirit which our Lord twice described to Nicodemus.

The word 'flesh,' I am inclined to think, with Poole and Dyke, is taken in two senses in this verse. In the first case, it means the natural body of man, as in John 1:14. In the second case, it means the corrupt carnal nature of man, as in Galatians 5:17.—The same remark applies to the word Spirit. In the first instance it means the Holy Spirit, and in the second, the spiritual nature which the Spirit produces. The offspring of all children of Adam is fleshly. The offspring of the Spirit is spiritual. Neither the grace, nor rank, nor money, nor learning of parents will prevent a child having a corrupt heart, if it is naturally born of the flesh. Nothing will make anyone spiritual but being born again of the Spirit.

It must be carefully remembered, in considering this verse, that it cannot be applied to the human nature of our Lord Jesus Christ. Though he had a true body like our own, he was not 'born of the flesh' as we are, by natural generation, but conceived by the miraculous operation of the Holy Ghost.

7.—[*Marvel not ... must be born again.*] In reading this verse, the stress ought to be laid on the two last words, 'born again.' It is evident that the thing which stumbled Nicodemus was the idea of any 'new birth' at all being necessary. He felt unable to understand what this 'new birth' was. Our Lord forbids him to marvel, and proceeds to explain the new birth by a familiar illustration.

It is a noteworthy and striking fact, that no doctrine has excited such surprise in every age of the church, and has called forth so much opposition from the great and learned, as this very doctrine of new birth. The men of the present day who sneer at conversions and revivals, as fanaticism and enthusiasm, are nowise better than Nicodemus. Like him, they expose their own entire ignorance of the work of the Holy Ghost.

8.—[*The wind bloweth, etc.*] The object of this verse appears to be to explain the work of the Holy Ghost in the regeneration of man, by a familiar illustration drawn from the wind. Mysterious as the Spirit's work was, Nicodemus must allow that there was much of mystery about the wind. 'The wind bloweth where it listeth.' We cannot account for the direction in which it blows, or for the beginning or extent of its influence. But when we hear the sound of the wind, we do not for a moment question that it is blowing. Our Lord tells Nicodemus that it is just the same with the operations of the Spirit. There is doubtless much about them that is mysterious and incomprehensible. But when we see fruit brought forth, in a manifest change of heart and life, we have no right to question the reality of the Spirit's operations.

The last clause of the verse is undeniably somewhat difficult.—'So is every one that is born of the Spirit.' We should rather have expected, 'So does the Spirit operate on everyone that is born again.' And this was, no doubt, our Lord's meaning. Yet the form of speech which our Lord uses is not altogether without parallel in the New Testament. For instance, we read, 'The kingdom of heaven is likened unto a man which sowed good seed' (*Matt.* 13:24). The likeness in this case is clearly not between the man and the kingdom. The meaning is that the whole story is an illustration of the kingdom of heaven. So also we read that 'the kingdom of heaven is like unto a merchant man, seeking goodly pearls,' and might make a similar remark (*Matt.* 13:45).

The Greek word translated 'wind,' at the beginning of this verse, might be rendered with equal correctness, 'the Spirit.' Many think, as Origen, Augustine, Rupertus, Bengel, Schoettgen, Ambrose, Jansenius, Wycliffe's Version, Bucer, and Bede, that it ought to be so rendered. They deny that our Lord brought in the idea of 'the wind' at all. They object to it being said of the wind that 'it listeth,' and say that the expression cannot be applied to any but a person.

This notion seems to me, as it does to the great majority of commentators, entirely untenable. For one thing, it creates great awkwardness to make a comparison between the Spirit and the work of the Spirit, which we must do if this theory is correct. 'The Spirit bloweth,—and so is everyone born of the Spirit!'—For another thing, it seems to me very strange to speak of the Holy Ghost as 'blowing,' and to speak of the 'sound,' of the Holy Ghost, or of that 'sound' being heard by Nicodemus.

I can see no difficulty whatever in the expression, 'The wind bloweth where it listeth.' It is common in the Bible to personify unintelligent things, and to speak of them as having mind and will. Thus our Lord speaks of the stones crying out (*Luke* 19:40). And the Psalmist says, 'The sun knoweth his going down' (*Psa.* 104:19). See also Job 38:7, 35.—In addition to this, I see a peculiar beauty in the selection of the wind as an illustration of the work of the Spirit. Not only is the illustration most apt and striking, but it is one which is used in other places in Scripture. See for instance, in the vision of the dry bones, how Ezekiel cries to the 'wind' to breathe on the slain (*Ezek.* 37:9). See also Song of Solomon 4:16, and Acts 2:2.—Last, but not least, it seems to me, that Nicodemus' state of perplexity makes it highly probable that our Lord would graciously help his ignorance by the use of a familiar illustration, like that of the wind. If no illustration at all was used in this verse, it is not quite easy to see how its language would help Nicodemus to understand the doctrine of the new birth.—But if the verse contains a familiar illustration, the whole purpose of our Lord in saying what he did becomes clear and plain.

JOHN 3:9-21

9 Nicodemus answered and said unto him, How can these things be?

10 Jesus answered and said unto him, Art thou a master of Israel, and knowest not these things?

11 Verily, verily, I say unto thee, We speak that we do know, and testify that we have seen; and ye receive not our witness.

12 If I have told you earthly things, and ye believe not, how shall ye believe, if I tell you *of* heavenly things?

13 And no man hath ascended up to heaven, but he that came down from heaven, *even* the Son of man which is in heaven.

14 And as Moses lifted up the serpent in the wilderness, even so must the Son of man be lifted up:

15 That whosoever believeth in him should not perish, but have eternal life.

16 For God so loved the world, that he gave his only begotten Son, that whosoever believeth in him should not perish, but have everlasting life.

17 For God sent not his Son into the world to condemn the world; but that the world through him might be saved.

18 He that believeth on him is not condemned: but he that believeth not is condemned already, because he hath not believed in the name of the only begotten Son of God.

19 And this is the condemnation, that light is come into the world, and men loved darkness rather than light, because their deeds were evil.

20 For every one that doeth evil hateth the light, neither cometh to the light, lest his deeds should be reproved.

21 But he that doeth truth cometh to the light, that his deeds may be made manifest, that they are wrought in God.

WE have in these verses the second part of the conversation between our Lord Jesus Christ and Nicodemus. A lesson about regeneration is closely followed by a lesson about justification! The whole passage ought always to be read with affectionate reverence. It contains words which have brought eternal life to myriads of souls.

These verses show us, firstly, *what gross spiritual ignorance there may be in the mind of a great and learned man*. We see a 'master of Israel' unacquainted with the first elements of saving religion. Nicodemus is told about the new birth, and at once exclaims, 'How can these things be?' When such was the darkness of a Jewish teacher, what must have been the state of the Jewish people? It was indeed due time for Christ to appear! The pastors of Israel had ceased to feed the people with knowledge. The blind were leading the blind, and both were falling into the ditch (*Matt.* 15:14).

Ignorance like that of Nicodemus is unhappily far too common in the church of Christ. We must never be surprised if we find it in quarters where we might reasonably expect knowledge. Learning, and rank, and high ecclesiastical office are no proof that a minister is taught by the Spirit. The successors of Nicodemus, in every age, are far more numerous than the successors of St Peter. On no point is religious ignorance so common as on the work of the Holy Ghost. That old stumbling-block, at which Nicodemus stumbled, is as much an offence to thousands in the present day as it was in the days of Christ. 'The natural man receiveth not the things of the Spirit of God' (*1 Cor.* 2:14). Happy is he who has been taught to 'prove all things' by Scripture (*1 Thess.* 5:21), and to call no man master upon earth (*Matt.* 23:9, 10).

These verses show us, secondly, *the original source from which man's salvation springs*. That source is the love of God the Father. Our Lord says to Nicodemus, 'God so loved the world, that he gave his only begotten Son, that whosoever believeth in him should not perish, but have everlasting life.'

This wonderful verse has been justly called by Luther, 'The Bible in miniature.' No part of it, perhaps, is so deeply important as the first five words, 'God so loved the world.' The love here spoken of is not that special love with which the Father regards his own elect, but that mighty pity and compassion with which he regards the whole race of mankind. Its object is not merely the little flock which he has given to Christ from all eternity, but the whole 'world' of sinners, without any exception. There is a deep sense in which God *loves* that world. All whom he has created he regards with pity and compassion. Their sins he cannot love;—but he loves their souls. 'His tender mercies are over all his works' (*Psa.* 145:9). Christ is God's gracious gift to the whole world.

Let us take heed that our views of the love of God are scriptural and well defined. The subject is one on which error abounds on either side.—On the one hand, we must beware of vague and exaggerated opinions. We must maintain firmly that God hates wickedness, and that the end of all who persist in wickedness will be destruction. It is not true that God's love is 'lower than hell.' It is not true that God so loved the world that all mankind will be finally saved, but that he so loved the world that he gave his Son to be the Saviour of all who believe. His love is offered to all men freely, fully, honestly, and unreservedly, but it is only through the one channel of Christ's redemption. He that rejects Christ cuts himself off from God's love, and will perish everlastingly.—On the other hand, we must beware of narrow and contracted opinions. We must not hesitate to tell any sinner that God loves him. It is not true that God cares for none but his own elect, or that Christ is not offered to any but those who are ordained to eternal life. There is a 'kindness and love' in God towards all mankind. It was in consequence of that love that Christ came into the world, and died upon the cross. Let us not be wise above that which is written, or more systematic in our statements than Scripture itself. God has no pleasure in the death of the wicked. God is not willing that any should perish. God would have all men to be saved. God loves the world (*John* 6:32; *Titus* 3:4; *1 John* 4:10; *2 Pet.* 3:9; *1 Tim.* 2:4; *Ezek.* 33:11).

These verses show us, thirdly, *the peculiar plan by which the love of God has provided salvation for sinners.* That plan is the atoning death of Christ on the cross. Our Lord says to Nicodemus, 'As Moses lifted up the serpent in the wilderness, even so must the Son of man be lifted up: that whosoever believeth in him should not perish, but have eternal life.'

By being 'lifted up,' our Lord meant nothing less than his own death upon the cross. That death, he would have us know, was appointed by God to be 'the life of the world' (*John* 6:51). It was ordained from all eternity to be the great propitiation and satisfaction for man's sin. It was the payment, by an almighty Substitute and Representative, of man's enormous debt to God. When Christ died upon the cross, our many sins were laid upon him. He was made 'sin' for us. He was made 'a curse' for us (2 *Cor.* 5:21; *Gal.* 3:13). By his death he purchased pardon and complete redemption for sinners. The brazen serpent, lifted up in the camp of Israel, brought health and cure within the reach of all who were bitten by serpents. Christ crucified, in like manner, brought eternal life within the reach of lost mankind. Christ has been lifted up on the cross, and man looking to him by faith may be saved.

The truth before us is the very foundation stone of the Christian religion. Christ's death is the Christian's life. Christ's cross is the Christian's title to heaven. Christ 'lifted up' and put to shame on Calvary is the ladder by which Christians 'enter into the holiest,' and are at length landed in glory. It is true that we are sinners;—but Christ has suffered for us. It is true that we deserve death;—but Christ has died for us. It is true that we are guilty debtors;—but Christ has paid our debts with his own blood. This is the real gospel! This is the good news! On this let us lean while we live. To this let us cling when we die. Christ has been 'lifted up' on the cross, and has thrown open the gates of heaven to all believers.

These verses show us, fourthly, *the way in which the benefits of Christ's death are made our own*. That way is simply to put faith and trust in Christ. Faith is the same thing as believing. Three times our Lord repeats this glorious truth to Nicodemus. Twice he proclaims that 'whosoever believeth shall not perish.' Once he says, 'He that believeth on the Son of God is not condemned.'

Faith in the Lord Jesus is the very key of salvation. He that has it has life, and he that has it not has not life. Nothing whatever *beside* this faith is necessary to our complete justification; but nothing whatever *except* this faith, will give us an interest in Christ. We may fast and mourn for sin, and do many things that are right, and use religious ordinances, and give all our goods to feed the poor, and yet remain unpardoned, and lose our souls.—But if we will only come to Christ as guilty sinners, and believe on him, our sins shall at once be forgiven, and our iniquities shall be entirely put away. Without faith there is no salvation; but through faith in Jesus the vilest sinner may be saved.

If we would have a peaceful conscience in our religion, let us see that our views of saving faith are distinct and clear. Let us beware of supposing that justifying faith is anything more than a sinner's simple trust in a Saviour, the grasp of a drowning man on the hand held out for his relief.—Let us beware of mingling anything else with faith in the matter of *justification*. Here we must always remember faith stands entirely alone. A justified man, no doubt, will always be a holy man. True believing will always be accompanied by godly living. But that which gives a man an interest in Christ, is not his *living*, but his faith. If we would know whether our faith is genuine, we do well to ask ourselves how we are living. But if we would know whether we are justified by Christ, there is but one question to be asked. That question is, 'Do we believe?'

These verses show us, lastly, *the true cause of the loss of man's soul.* Our Lord says to Nicodemus, 'This is the condemnation, that light is come into the world, and men loved darkness rather than light, because their deeds were evil.'

The words before us form a suitable conclusion to the glorious tidings which we have just been considering. They completely clear God of injustice in the condemnation of sinners. They show in simple and unmistakable terms, that although man's salvation is entirely of God, his ruin, if he is lost, will be entirely from himself. He will reap the fruit of his own sowing.

The doctrine here laid down ought to be carefully remembered. It supplies an answer to a common cavil of the enemies of God's truth. There is no decreed reprobation, excluding anyone from heaven.

'God sent not his Son into the world to condemn the world, but that the world through him might be saved.' There is no unwillingness on God's part to receive any sinner, however great his sins. God has sent 'light' into the world, and if man will not come to the light, the fault is entirely on man's side. His blood will be on his own head, if he makes shipwreck of his soul. The blame will be at his own door, if he misses heaven. His eternal misery will be the result of his own choice. His destruction will be the work of his own hand. God loved him, and was willing to save him; but he 'loved darkness,' and therefore darkness must be his everlasting portion. He would not come to Christ, and therefore he could not have life (*John* 5:40).

The truths we have been considering are peculiarly weighty and solemn. Do we live as if we believed them?—Salvation by Christ's death is close to us today. Have we embraced it by faith, and made it our own?—Let us never rest till we know Christ as our own Saviour. Let us look to him without delay for pardon and peace, if we have never looked before. Let us go on believing on him, if we have already believed. 'Whosoever,' is his own gracious word,—'*whosoever* believeth on him, shall not perish, but have eternal life.'

Notes—John 3:9-21

9.—[*Nicodemus answered … How can these things be?*] This is the third and last time that Nicodemus speaks during his visit to Christ, so far as it is reported to us. His question here is a striking and instructive instance of the deep spiritual ignorance which may be found in the mind of a learned man. In four different ways our Lord had brought before him one and the same lesson. First, he had laid down the great principle that every man must be 'born again.'—Secondly, he had repeated the same thing in fuller words, and brought in the idea of 'water,' to illustrate the work of the Spirit.—Thirdly, he had shown the necessity of the new birth, from the natural corruption of man.—Fourthly, he had illustrated the work of the Spirit a second time by the instance of the 'wind.' And yet now, after all that our

Lord has said, this learned Pharisee seems utterly in the dark, and asks the pitiable question, 'How can these things be?' We have no right to be surprised at the vast ignorance of saving religion which we see on all sides, when we consider the history of Nicodemus. We should make up our minds to expect to find spiritual darkness the rule, and spiritual light the exception. Few things in the long run give so much trouble to ministers, missionaries, teachers, and district-visitors, as beginning work with extravagant and unscriptural expectations.

10.—[*Jesus answered and said.*] It will be observed, that our Lord does not answer the question of Nicodemus directly, but rebukes him sharply for his ignorance. Yet it ought to be carefully noted, as Melanchthon remarks, that before he concludes what he now begins to say, he supplies a complete answer to his inquirer. He shows him the true root and spring of regeneration, namely, faith in himself. He answers his groping inquiry, 'How can these things be?' by showing him the first step in saving religion, viz., to believe in the Son of God. Let Nicodemus begin like a little child, by simply believing on him who was to be lifted up on the cross, and he would soon understand 'how' a man could be born again, even in his old age.

[*Art thou a master of Israel?*] The English version of this question hardly gives the full force of the original. It should be literally rendered, 'Art thou *the* master of Israel?' i.e., 'Art thou the famous teacher and instructor of the Jews?' 'Dost thou profess to be a light of them that sit in darkness, and an instructor of others?'—The expression certainly seems to indicate that Nicodemus was a man of established reputation as a teacher among the Pharisees. When the teachers were so ignorant, what must have been the state of the taught?

[*Knowest not these things?*] These words unquestionably imply rebuke. The things which our Lord had just mentioned, Nicodemus ought to have known and understood. He professed to be a religious teacher. He professed to know the Old Testament Scriptures. The doctrine, therefore, of the necessity of a new birth ought not to have appeared strange to him. 'A clean heart,—circumcision of the heart,—a new heart,—a heart of stone instead of a heart of flesh,' were expressions and ideas which he must have read in the Prophets, and which all pointed towards the new birth (*Psa.* 51:10; *Jer.* 4:4; *Ezek.* 18:31; 36:26). His ignorance consequently was deserving of blame.

The verse before us appears to me to supply a strong argument against the idea that the expression, 'born of water and the Spirit' means baptism. I do not see how Nicodemus could possibly have known this doctrine, as it is nowhere revealed in the Old Testament, and even its own advocates confine it to New Testament times. To blame a man for not knowing 'things' which he could not possibly know, would

be obviously most unjust, and entirely at variance with the general tenor of our Lord's dealings.

11.—[*We speak that we do know, etc.*] Whom does our Lord mean here when he says 'We'? The answers to this question are various.

a. Some think, as Luther, Brentius, Bucer, Gualter, Aretius, Hutcheson, Musculus, Gomarus, Piscator, and Cartwright, that 'We' means, 'I, and John the Baptist.'

b. Some think, as Calvin, Beza, and Scott, that it means, 'I, and the Old Testament prophets.'

c. Some think, as Alcuin (according to Maldonatus), and Wesley, that it means, 'I, and all who are born of the Spirit.'

d. Some think, as Chrysostom, Cyril, Rupertus, Calovius, Glassius, Chemnitius, Lampe, Leigh, Nifanius, Cornelius à Lapide, Cocceius, Stier, and Bengel, that it means either, 'I, and the Father,'—or 'I, and the Holy Ghost,'—or 'I, and both the Father and the Spirit.'

e. Some think, as Theophylact, Zwingle, Poole, and Doddridge, that our Lord only means himself when he says 'We,' and that he uses the plural number in order to give weight and dignity to what he says, as kings do. So also he says, 'Whereunto shall we liken the kingdom of God? or with what comparison shall we compare it?' (*Mark* 4:30). 'We,' in that text, evidently stands for 'I.'—In St John's first epistle, the first person plural is used instead of the singular repeatedly in the first five verses of the first chapter.

The last of these five opinions appears to me by far the most probable and satisfactory.—The three first seem to me to be entirely overthrown by John the Baptist's words in this chapter (3:32), where he mentions it as a peculiar mark of our Lord's superiority to all other teachers, that he testifieth 'what he hath seen and heard.'—The fourth opinion appears to me untenable. The fear of Socinianism must not make us wrest texts in order to apply them to the Trinity. There is a fitness in our Lord's saying, during his earthly ministry, after his incarnation, 'I speak and testify what I have known and seen from all eternity with my Father.' But there is no apparent fitness in saying that he and the two other persons in the Trinity 'speak what they have seen.'

The meaning of the sentence appears to be this, 'I declare with authority, and bear witness to truths, which from all eternity I have known and seen, as God in union with the Father and the Holy Ghost. I do not speak (as all merely human ministers must) what I have been taught by others. I do not testify things which I have received as God's servant, as ordinary prophets have, and which I should not have known without God's inspiration. I testify what I have seen with my Father, and knew before the world began.' It is like the expression, 'I speak that which I have seen with my Father' (*John* 8:38).

Melanchthon thinks that our Lord, in this verse, contrasts the uncertain traditions and human inventions which the Pharisees taught, with the sure, certain, and irrefragable truths of God, which he came to preach.

Bucer remarks that the verse contains a practical lesson for all religious teachers. No man has a right to teach, unless he is thoroughly persuaded of the truth of what he teaches.

[*Ye receive not our witness.*] This sentence corresponds so exactly with John the Baptist's words, at verse 32, that it confirms me in the opinion that our Lord, in this verse, only speaks of himself. The words before us, as well as those of John the Baptist, must be taken with some qualification: 'The greater part of you receive not our testimony.'—The object of the verse is to rebuke the unbelief of Nicodemus and all who were like-minded with him among the Jews. The use of the plural number 'Ye,' makes it probable that our Lord in this verse refers not merely to what he had just been saying to Nicodemus, but to all his public teaching at Jerusalem from the time of his casting out the buyers and sellers in the temple. If we do not adopt this theory, we must suppose him to mean, 'What I have spoken and testified to you about regeneration, is what I continually say to all who come, like you, to inquire of me; and yet neither you nor they believe what I say. You all

alike stumble at this stumbling-stone, the new birth.'

Calvin remarks on this expression, that we ought never to be surprised at unbelief. If men would not receive Christ's testimony, it is no wonder if they will not receive ours.

12.—[*If I have told ... earthly ... heavenly things?*] To see the full force of this verse, we should paraphrase it thus: 'If ye do not believe what I say when I tell you, as I have done, things that are earthly, how will you believe if I go on, as I shall do, to tell you of things that are heavenly? If you will not believe when ye hear my first lesson, what will ye do when ye hear my second? If ye are stumbled at the very alphabet of my gospel, what will ye do when I proceed to show you higher and deeper truths?'

The difficulty of the verse lies in the two expressions, 'earthly things' and 'heavenly things.' Our Lord does not explain them, and we are therefore left to conjecture their true meaning.—I offer the following explanation with some diffidence, as the most satisfactory one.

By 'earthly things' I believe our Lord means the doctrine of the 'new birth,' which he had just been expounding to Nicodemus. By 'heavenly things' I believe he means the great and solemn truths which he was about immediately to declare, and which he does declare in rapid succession from this verse down to the end of the conversation.—These truths were his own divinity,—the plan of redemption by his own death on the cross,—the love of God to the whole world, and his consequent provision of salvation,—faith in the Son of God, as the only way to escape hell,—and man's wilful rejection of light, the only cause of man's condemnation.

But why does our Lord call the new birth an 'earthly thing'? I reply, that he does so because it is an 'earthly' thing compared with his own divinity and atonement. Regeneration is a thing that takes place in man, here upon earth. The atonement is a transaction that was done for man, and of which the special effect is on man's position before God in heaven.—In regeneration God comes down to man, and dwells in him upon earth. In the atonement Christ takes up man's nature as man's representative,

106

and as man's forerunner goes up into heaven.—Regeneration is a change of which even the men of this world have some faint inkling, and which can be illustrated by such earthly figures as water and wind. Almost everyone allows, as Bucer remarks, that he is not so good as he should be, and that he needs some change to fit him for heaven. Christ's divinity, and the incarnation, and the atonement, and justification by faith, are such high and heavenly things that man has no natural conception of them.—Regeneration is so far an 'earthly' idea that even irreligious men borrow the word, and talk of regenerating nations, and society. Salvation by faith in Christ's blood is so entirely a 'heavenly thing,' that it is constantly misunderstood, hated, and sneered at by unconverted men.—When therefore our Lord calls the new birth an 'earthly thing,' we must understand that he does so comparatively. In itself the new birth is a high, holy, and 'heavenly thing.' But compared with the doctrine of the incarnation and the atonement, it is an 'earthly thing.'

13.—[*And no man hath ascended, etc.*] This verse, according to my view, contains the first 'heavenly thing' which our Lord displays to Nicodemus. But the sentence is undeniably a difficult one, and commentators differ widely as to its meaning.

Some think, as Calvin, Musculus, Bullinger, Hutcheson, Poole, Quesnel, Schoettgen, Dyke, Lightfoot, Leigh, Doddridge, A. Clark, and Stier, that our Lord here shows to Nicodemus, in highly figurative language, the necessity of divine teaching, in order to understand spiritual truth.—'No child of Adam has ever reached the lofty mysteries of heaven, and made himself acquainted with its high and holy truths, by his own natural understanding. Such knowledge is only possessed by the incarnate Saviour, the Son of man, who has come down from heaven. If you would know spiritual truth, you must sit at his feet and learn of him.' This view of the text is supported by Proverbs 30:4. According to this view, the verse must be taken in close connection with the preceding one, where the ignorance of Nicodemus is exposed.

Some think, as Zwingle, Melanchthon, Brentius, Aretius, Flacius, and Ferus, that our Lord here shows to Nicodemus (and again in highly figurative language), the impossibility of human merit, and the utter inability of man justifying himself, and obtaining an entrance into heaven by his own righteousness.—'No one can possibly ascend into God's presence in heaven, and stand perfect and complete before him, except the incarnate Saviour, who has come down from heaven to fulfil all righteousness. I am the way to heaven. If you would enter heaven, you must believe on the Son of man, and become a member of his body by faith.'—This view of the text appeals for support to Romans 10:6-9. According to this view, the verse must be taken in close connection with the following verse, in which the way of justification is explained.

The true view of the text, I venture to think, is as follows. The words of the text are to be taken literally. Our Lord begins his list of 'heavenly things' by declaring to Nicodemus his own divine nature and dignity. He reminds him that no one has ever ascended literally into that heaven where God dwells. Enoch, and Elijah, and David, for instance, were doubtless in a place of bliss when they left this world, but they had not 'ascended into heaven' (*Acts* 2:34). But that which no man, not even the holiest saint, had attained, was the right and prerogative of him in whose company Nicodemus was. The Son of man had dwelt from all eternity in heaven, had come down from heaven, would one day ascend again into heaven, and in his divine nature was actually in heaven, one with God the Father, at that very moment.—'Know who it is to whom you are speaking. I am not merely a teacher come from God, as you say. I am the Messiah, the Son of man, foretold by Daniel. I have come down from heaven, according to promise, to save sinners. I shall one day ascend again into heaven, as the victorious forerunner of a saved people. Above all, I am God in heaven at this moment. I am he who fills heaven and earth.'—I prefer this view of the verse to any other, for two reasons. For one thing, it gives a literal meaning to every word in the text. For another, it seems a fitting answer to the first idea which Nicodemus had put

107

forward in the conversation, viz., that our Lord was only 'a teacher come from God.' It is the view which is in the main held by Rollock, Calovius, and Gomarus, and expounded by them with much ability.

The Greek word which we render 'but,' I am inclined to think, ought to be taken in an *adversative* rather than in an *exceptive* sense. Instances of this usage will be found in Matthew 12:4; Mark 13:32; Luke 4:26, 27; John 17:12; Revelation 9:4; 21:27. The thought appears to be, 'Man has not, and cannot ascend into heaven. But that which man cannot do, I the Son of man can do.'

'Heaven,' throughout this verse, must be taken in the sense of that immediate and peculiar presence of God, which we can conceive of and express in no other form than by the word 'heaven.'

The expression 'which is in heaven,' deserves particular notice. It is one of those many expressions in the New Testament which can be explained in no other way than by the doctrine of Christ's divinity. It would be utterly absurd and untrue to say of any mere man, that at the very time he was speaking to another on earth he was in heaven! But it can be said of Christ with perfect truth and propriety. He never ceased to be very God, when he became incarnate. He was 'with God and was God.' As God he was in heaven while he was speaking to Nicodemus.

The expression is one which no Socinian can explain away. If Christ was only a very holy man and nothing more, he could not have used these words. The Socinian explanation of the former part of the verse, viz., that Christ was caught up into heaven after his baptism, and there instructed about the gospel he was to teach, would be of itself utterly absurd, and a mere theory invented to get over a difficulty. But the conclusion of the verse is a blow at the very root of the Socinian system. It is written not only that Christ 'came down from heaven,' but that 'he is in heaven.'

It admits of a question whether the Greek words which we translate 'which is,' do not, both here and in chapter 1:18, point to that peculiar name of Jehovah, which was doubtless familiar to Nicodemus, 'The Ever-existing One; the Living One.' It is the same phrase which forms part of Christ's name in Revelation, 'him which is' (*Rev.* 1:4).

Much of the difficulty of the verse is removed by remembering that the past tense, 'hath ascended,' admits of being rendered with equal grammatical correctness, 'does ascend, can ascend, or will ascend.' Pearce takes this view, and quotes in support of it John 1:26; 3:18; 5:24; 6:69; 11:27; 20:29.

Whitby thinks that throughout this verse our Lord has in view a rabbinical tradition,—that Moses had been into heaven to receive the law; and that he declares the falsehood of this tradition by saying, 'No man, not even Moses, had ascended into heaven.'

14.—[*As Moses lifted ... serpent ... so must, etc., etc.*] In this verse our Lord proceeds to show Nicodemus another 'heavenly thing,' viz., the necessity of his own crucifixion. Nicodemus probably thought, like most Jews, that when Messiah appeared, he would come with power and glory, to be exalted and honoured by men. Jesus tells him that so far from this being the case, Messiah must be 'cut off' at his first advent, and put to an open shame by being hanged on a tree. He illustrates this by a well-known event in the history of Israel's wanderings,—the story of the brazen serpent (*Num.* 21:9). 'Are you expecting me to take to myself power and to restore the kingdom of Israel? Cast away such a vain expectation. I have come to do very different work. I have come to suffer, and to offer up myself as a sacrifice for sin.'

The mention of Moses, of whom the Pharisees thought so much, was eminently calculated to arrest the attention of Nicodemus. 'Even Moses, in whom ye trust, has supplied a most vivid type of my great work on earth—the crucifixion.'

[*The Son of man must be lifted up.*] The expression 'Son of man,' was doubtless intended to remind Nicodemus of Daniel's prophecy of the Messiah.—The Greek word rendered 'must,' signifies 'it behoveth that,' 'it is necessary that.' It is necessary in order that God's promises of a Redeemer may be fulfilled,—the types of the Old

Testament sacrifices be accomplished,—the law of God be satisfied,—and a way for God's mercy be provided. In order to all this, Messiah must suffer in our stead. The phrase 'lifted up,' appears to me most decidedly to mean 'lifted up on the cross.' For one thing we find it so explained in this Gospel (*John* 12:32, 33). For another the illustration of the brazen serpent makes it absolutely necessary to explain it so. To apply the phrase, as Calvin and others do, to the 'necessity of lifting up and exalting Christ's atonement in Christian teaching,' seems to me a mistake. It is needlessly dragging in an idea which the words were not intended to convey. It is truth no doubt, and truth abundantly taught in Scripture, but not the truth of this text.

The main points of resemblance in the comparison,—'As Moses lifted up the serpent in the wilderness,'—form a subject which requires careful handling. The lifting up of the serpent of brass for the relief of Israel when bitten by serpents, is evidently selected by our Lord as an apt illustration of his own crucifixion for sinners. But how far may we press this illustration? Where are we to stop? What are the exact points at which the type and antitype meet? These questions require consideration.

Some see a meaning in the 'brass' of which the serpent was made, as a shining metal, a strong metal, etc., etc. I cannot see it. Our Lord does not even mention the brass.

Some see in the 'serpent' hanging on the pole, a type of the devil, the old serpent, bruised by Christ's death on the cross, and openly triumphed over on it (*Col.* 2:15). I cannot see this at all. It appears to me to confound and mingle up two scriptural truths, which ought to be kept distinct. Moreover, there is something revolting in the idea, that in order to be healed the Israelite had to look at a figure of the devil.

Some see in 'Moses' lifting up the serpent, a type of the law of God requiring payment of its demands, and becoming the cause of Christ dying on the cross. On this I will content myself with saying that I am not satisfied that this idea was in Christ's mind.

The points of resemblance appear to me to be these. —

a. As the Israelites were in sore distress, and dying from the bites of poisonous serpents, so is man in great spiritual danger, and dying from the poisonous effects of sin.

b. As the serpent of brass was lifted up on a pole in the sight of the camp of Israel, so Christ was to be lifted up on the cross publicly, and in the sight of the whole nation, at the passover.

c. As the serpent, lifted up on the pole, was an image of the very thing which had poisoned the Israelites, even so Christ had in himself no sin, and yet was made and crucified 'in the likeness of sinful flesh,' and counted sin (*Rom.* 8:3). The brazen serpent was a serpent without poison, and Christ was a man without sin. The thing which we should specially see in Christ crucified, is our sin laid upon him, and him counted as a sinner, and treated as a sinner, and punished as a sinner, for our redemption. In fact, we see on the cross our sins punished, crucified, borne, and carried by our Redeemer.

d. Finally, as the one way by which Israelites obtained relief from the brazen serpent was by looking at it, so the one way to get benefit from Christ is to look at him by faith. The feeblest look brought cure to an Israelite, and the weakest faith, if true and sincere, brings salvation to sinners.

It should be carefully noted, that it seems impossible to reconcile this verse with that modern divinity which can see nothing in Christ's death but a great act of self-sacrifice, and which denies Christ's substitution for us on the cross, and the imputation of our sins to him. Such divinity withers up such a verse as this entirely, and cuts out the life, heart, and marrow of its meaning. Unless words are most violently wrested from their ordinary signification, the illustration before us points directly towards two great truths of the gospel. One of them is that Christ's death upon the cross was meant to have a medicinal, health-conferring effect upon our souls, and that there was something in it far above a mere martyr's example. The other truth is, that when Christ died upon the cross, he was dealt with as our Substitute and

Representative, and punished, through the imputation of our sins, in our place. The thing that Israel saw on the pole, and from which they got health, was an image of the very serpent that bit them. The object that Christians should see on the cross, is a divine person, made sin and a curse for them, and allowing that very sin that has poisoned the world to be imputed to him, and laid upon his head.—It is easy work to sneer at the *words* 'vicarious sacrifice,' and 'imputed merit,' as nowhere to be found in Scripture. But it is not so easy to disprove the fact that the '*ideas*' are constantly to be met with in the Bible.

The use of the brazen serpent in this verse, as an illustration of Christ's death and its purpose, must not be abused and made an excuse for turning every incident of the history of Israel in the wilderness into an allegory. It is very important not to attach an allegorical meaning to Bible facts without authority. Such things as the manna, the smitten rock, and the brazen serpent, are allegorized for us by the Holy Ghost. But where the Holy Ghost has not pointed out any allegory, we ought to be very cautious in our assertions that allegory exists. Bucer's remarks on this subject deserve reading.

15.—[*That whosoever believeth* ... *not perish* ... *life.*] In this verse our Lord declares to Nicodemus the great end and purpose for which the Son of man was to be 'lifted up' on the cross, and the way in which the benefits of his crucifixion become our own. In interpreting the verse, we should carefully remember that the comparison of the serpent lifted up in the wilderness must be carried through to the end of the sentence. The Son of man must be lifted up on the cross, that whosoever believeth on him, or looks to him by faith, as the Israelite looked to the brazen serpent, should not perish in hell.

The expression 'whosoever,' deserves special notice. It might have been equally well translated 'everyone.' It is intended to show us the width and breadth of Christ's offers of salvation. They are for 'everyone,' without exception, that 'believeth.'

The expression, 'believeth in him,' is deeply important. It describes that one act of man's soul which is needful to give him an interest in Jesus Christ. It is not a mere belief of the head that there is such a person as Jesus Christ, and that he is a Saviour. It is a belief of the heart and will. When a person, feeling his desperate need by reason of sin, flees to Jesus Christ, and trusts in him, leans on him, and commits his soul entirely to him as his Saviour and Redeemer, he is said, in the language of the text, to 'believe on him.'—The simpler our views of faith are, the better. The more steadily we keep in view the Israelites looking at the brazen serpent, the more we shall understand the words before us. 'Believing' is neither more nor less than heart-looking. Whosoever looked at the brazen serpent was made well, however ill he was, and however feeble his look. Just so, whosoever looks to Jesus by faith, is pardoned, however great his sins may have been, and however feeble his faith.—Did the Israelite *look*? That was the only question in the matter of being healed from the serpents' bite.—Does the sinner *believe*? That is the only question in the matter of being justified and pardoned.—Looking to Moses, or looking to the tabernacle, or looking even to the pole on which the serpent hung, or looking to anything except the brazen serpent, the bitten Israelite would not have been cured. Just so, looking to anything but Christ crucified, however holy the object looked at may be, the sinner cannot be saved.

The expression, 'should not perish, but have eternal life,' is peculiarly strong. As the Israelite who looked to the brazen serpent not only did not die of his wounds, but recovered complete health, so the sinner who looks to Jesus not only escapes hell and condemnation, but has a seed of eternal life at once put in his heart, receives a complete title to an eternal life of glory and blessedness in heaven, and enters into that life after death.—The salvation of the gospel is exceedingly full. It is not merely being pardoned. It is being counted completely righteous, and made a citizen of heaven. It is not merely an escape from hell, but the reception of a title to heaven. It has been well remarked, that the Old Testament generally promised only 'length of days,' but the gospel promises 'everlasting life.'

16.—[*For God so loved the world, etc.*] Our Lord, in this verse, shows Nicodemus another 'heavenly thing.'—Nicodemus probably thought, like many Jews, that God's purposes of mercy were entirely confined to his chosen people Israel, and that when Messiah appeared, he would appear only for the special benefit of the Jewish nation. Our Lord here declares to him that God loves all the world, without any exception; that the Messiah, the only begotten Son of God, is the Father's gift to the whole family of Adam; and that everyone, whether Jew or Gentile, who believes on him for salvation, may have eternal life.—A more startling declaration to the ears of a rigid Pharisee it is impossible to conceive! A more wonderful verse is not to be found in the Bible! That God should love such a wicked world as this, and not hate it,—that he should love it so as to provide salvation,—that in order to provide salvation he should give, not an angel, or any created being, but such a priceless gift as his only begotten Son,—that this great salvation should be freely offered to everyone that believeth,—all, all this is wonderful indeed! This was indeed a 'heavenly thing.'

The words, 'God loved the world,' have received two very different interpretations. The importance of the subject in the present day makes it desirable to state both views fully.

Some think, as Hutcheson, Lampe, and Gill, that the 'world' here means God's elect out of every nation, whether Jews or Gentiles, and that the 'love' with which God is said to love them is that eternal love with which the elect were loved before creation began, and by which their calling, justification, preservation and final salvation are completely secured.—This view, though supported by many and great divines, does not appear to me to be our Lord's meaning. For one thing, it seems to me a violent straining of language to confine the word 'world' to the elect. 'The world' is undoubtedly a name sometimes given to the 'wicked' exclusively. But I cannot see that it is a name ever given to the saints.—For

another thing, to interpret the word 'world' of the elect only is to ignore the distinction which, to my eyes, is plainly drawn in the text between the whole of mankind and those out of mankind who 'believe.' If the 'world' means only the believing portion of mankind, it would have been quite enough to say, 'God so loved the world, that he gave his only begotten Son, that the world should not perish.' But our Lord does not say so. He says, 'that whosoever believeth: i.e., that whosoever out of the world believeth.'—Lastly, to confine God's love to the elect, is taking a harsh and narrow view of God's character, and fairly lays Christianity open to the modern charges brought against it as cruel and unjust to the ungodly. If God takes no thought for any but his elect, and cares for none beside, how shall God judge the world?—I believe in the electing love of God the Father as strongly as anyone. I regard the special love with which God loves the sheep whom he has given to Christ from all eternity, as a most blessed and comfortable truth, and one most cheering and profitable to believers. I only say, that it is not the truth of this text.

The true view of the words, 'God loved the world,' I believe to be this. The 'world' means the whole race of mankind, both saints and sinners, without any exception. The word, in my opinion, is so used in John 1:10, 29; 6:33, 51; 8:12; Romans 3:19; 2 Corinthians 5:19; 1 John 2:2; 4:14. The 'love' spoken of is that love of pity and compassion with which God regards all his creatures, and specially regards mankind. It is the same feeling of 'love' which appears in Psalm 145:9; Ezekiel 33:11; John 12:32; Titus 3:4; 1 John 4:10; 2 Peter 3:9; 1 Timothy 2:4. It is a love unquestionably distinct and separate from the special love with which God regards his saints. It is a love of pity and not of approbation or complaisance. But it is not the less a real love. It is a love which clears God of injustice in judging the world.

I am quite familiar with the objections commonly brought against the theory I have just propounded. I find no weight in them, and am not careful to answer them. Those who confine God's love exclusively to the elect appear to me to take a narrow and contracted view of God's character and attributes. They refuse to God that attribute of compassion with which even an earthly father can regard a profligate son, and can offer to him pardon, even though his compassion is despised and his offers refused. I have long come to the conclusion that men may be more systematic in their statements than the Bible, and may be led into grave error by idolatrous veneration of a system. The following quotations from one whom for convenience' sake I must call a thorough Calvinist, I mean Bishop Davenant, will show that the view I advocate is not new.

'The general love of God toward mankind is so clearly testified in Holy Scripture, and so demonstrated by the manifold effects of God's goodness and mercy extended to every particular man in this world, that to doubt thereof were infidelity, and to deny it plain blasphemy.'—Davenant's *Answer to Hoard*, p. 1.

'God hateth nothing which himself created. And yet it is most true that he hateth sin in any creature, and hateth the creature infected with sin, in such manner as hatred may be attributed to God. But for all this he so generally loved mankind, fallen in Adam, that he hath given his only begotten Son, that what sinner soever believeth in him should not perish but have everlasting life. And this everlasting life is so provided for man by God, that no decrees of his can bring any man thither without faith and repentance; and no decrees of his can keep any man out who repenteth and believeth. As for the measure of God's love exhibited in the external effect unto man, it must not be denied that God poureth out his grace more abundantly on some men than on others, and worketh more powerfully and effectually in the hearts of some men than of others, and that out of his alone will and pleasure. But yet, when this more special love is not extended, his less special love is not restrained to outward and temporal mercies, but reacheth to internal and spiritual blessings, even such as will bring men to an eternal blessedness, if their voluntary wickedness hinders not.'—Davenant's *Answer to Hoard*, p. 469.

'No divine of the Reformed church, of sound judgment, will deny a general intention or appointment concerning the salvation of all men individually by the death of Christ, on the condition if they should believe. For the intention or appointment of God is general, and is plainly revealed in Holy Scripture, although the absolute and not to be frustrated intention of God concerning the gift of faith and eternal life to some persons, is special, and limited to the elect alone.—So I have maintained and do maintain.'—Davenant's *Opinion on the Gallican Controversy*.

Calvin observes on this text, 'Christ brought life, because the heavenly Father loves the human race, and wishes that they should not perish.' Again he says, 'Christ employed the universal term *whosoever*, both to invite indiscriminately all to partake of life, and to cut off every excuse from unbelievers. Such also is the import of the term *world*. Though there is nothing in the world that is worthy of God's favour, yet he shows himself to be reconciled to the whole world, when he invites all men without exception to the faith of Christ.'

The same view of God's 'love' and the 'world,' in this text, is taken by Brentius, Bucer, Calovius, Glassius, Chemnitius, Musculus, Bullinger, Bengel, Nifanius, Dyke, Scott, Henry, and Manton.

The little word 'so,' in this verse, has called forth many remarks, on account of its depth of meaning. It doubtless signifies 'so greatly, so much, so dearly.' Bishop Sanderson, quoted by Ford, observes, 'How much that "so" containeth, no tongue or wit of man can reach: nothing expresseth it better to the life, than the work itself doth.'

[*That he gave his only begotten Son.*] The gift of Christ, be it here noted, is the result of God's love to the world, and not the cause. To say that God loves us because Christ died for us, is wretched theology indeed. But to say that Christ came into the world in consequence of the love of God, is scriptural truth.

The expression, 'he gave,' is a remarkable one. Christ is God the Father's gift to a lost and sinful world. He was given generally to be the Saviour, the Redeemer, the Friend of sinners,—to make an atonement sufficient for all,—and to provide a redemption large enough for all. To effect this, the Father freely gave him up to be despised, rejected, mocked, crucified, and counted guilty and accursed for our sakes. It is written that he was 'delivered for our offences,' and that God spared him not, 'but delivered him up for us all' (*Rom.* 4:25; 8:32). Christ is the 'gift of God,' spoken of to the Samaritan woman (*John* 4:10), and the 'unspeakable gift' spoken of by St Paul (2 *Cor.* 9:15). He himself says to the wicked Jews, 'My Father *giveth you* the true bread from heaven' (*John* 6:32). This last text, be it noted, was one with which Erskine silenced the General Assembly in Scotland, when he was accused of offering Christ too freely to sinners.

It should be observed that our Lord calls himself 'the only begotten Son of God' in this verse. In the verse but one before this, he called himself the 'Son of man.' Both the names were used in order to impress upon the mind of Nicodemus the two natures of Messiah. He was not only the Son of man but the Son of God. But it is striking to remark that precisely the same words are used in both places about faith in Christ. If we would be saved, we must believe in him both as the Son of man and the Son of God.

[*That whosoever believeth ... life.*] These words are exactly the same as those in the preceding verse. Why our translators should have rendered the same Greek word by 'everlasting' in one place, and 'eternal' in the other, it is hard to say. In Matthew 25:46, they did just the same.

The repetition of this glorious saying, 'whosoever believeth,' is very instructive. For one thing it serves to show that mighty and broad as is the love of God, it will prove useless to everyone who does not believe in Christ. God loves all the world, but God will save none in the world who refuse to believe in his only begotten Son.—For another thing it shows us the great point to which every Christian should direct his attention. He must see to it that he believes on Christ. It is mere waste of time to be constantly asking ourselves whether God loves us, and whether Christ died for us; and it argues gross ignorance of Scripture

to trouble ourselves with such questions. The Bible never tells men to look at these questions, but commands them to believe. Salvation, it always teaches, does not turn on the point, 'Did Christ die for me?' but on the point 'Do I believe on Christ?' If men do not 'have eternal life,' it is never because God did not love them, or because Christ was not given for them, but because they do not believe on Christ.

In leaving this verse, I may remark, that the idea maintained by Erasmus, Olshausen, Wetstein, Rosenmuller, and others, that it does not contain our Lord's words, and that from this verse down to verse 21 we have St John's comments or observations, appears to me utterly destitute of foundation, and unsupported by a single argument worth noticing. That our Lord would not have used the third person in speaking of himself is no argument. We find him frequently speaking of himself in the third person. See for instance John 5:19-27. There is literally nothing to be gained by adopting the theory, while it contradicts the common belief of nearly all believers in every age of the world.

Flacius observes that this verse and the two preceding ones comprise all the causes of justification: (1) the remote and efficient cause, God's love; (2) the approximate efficient cause, the gift of God's Son; (3) the material cause, Christ's exaltation on the cross; (4) the instrumental cause, faith; (5) the final cause, eternal life.

17.—[*God sent not ... condemn the world.*] In this verse our Lord shows Nicodemus another 'heavenly thing.' He shows him the main object of Messiah coming into the world. It was not to judge men, but to die for them; not to condemn, but to save.

I have a strong impression that when our Lord spoke these words, he had in view the prophecy of David about Messiah bruising the nations with a rod of iron, and Daniel's prophecy about the judgment, where he speaks of the thrones being cast down, and the Ancient of Days judging the world (*Psa.* 2:6-9; *Dan.* 7:9-22). I think that Nicodemus, like most Jews, was filled with the expectation that when Messiah came he would come with power and great glory, and *judge* all men. Our Lord corrects this notion in this verse. He declares that Messiah's first advent was not to judge, but to save people from their sins. He says in another place, 'I came not to judge the world, but to save the world' (*John* 12:47). The Greek word for judging and condemning, it must be remembered, is one and the same. Judgment and the condemnation of the ungodly, our Lord would have us know, are not the work of the first advent, but of the second. The special work of the first advent was to seek and save that which was lost.

[*That* the **world through him ... saved.**] This sentence must clearly be interpreted with some qualification. It would contradict other plain texts of Scripture if we took it to mean, 'God sent his Son into the world, that all the world might finally be saved through him, and none be lost.' In fact, our Lord himself declares in the very next verse, that 'he that believeth not is *condemned* already.'

The meaning of the sentence evidently is, that 'all the world might have a door of salvation opened through Christ,—that salvation might be provided for all the world,—and that so any one in the world believing on Christ, might be saved.' In this view it is like the expression of St John, 'The Father sent the Son to be the Saviour of the world' (1 *John* 4:14).

The expression, 'God hath sent,' in this verse, ought not to be overlooked. It is very frequently applied, in St John's Gospel, to our Lord. At least thirty-eight times we find him speaking of himself as him 'whom God hath sent.' It is probably from this expression that St Paul derives the peculiar name which he gives to our Lord, 'The Apostle . . . of our profession' (*Heb.* 3:1). 'The Apostle' means simply, 'The sent one.'

The readiness of natural man everywhere to regard Christ as a Judge much more than as a Saviour, is a curious fact. The whole system of the Roman Catholic Church is full of the idea. People are taught to be afraid of Christ, and to flee to the Virgin Mary! Ignorant Protestants are not much better. They often regard Christ as a kind of Judge, whose demands they will have to satisfy at the last day, much more than as a present personal Saviour and Friend.

Our Lord seems to foresee this error, and to correct it in the words of this text.

Calvin observes on this verse, 'Whenever our sins press us, whenever Satan would drive us to despair, we ought to hold out this shield,—that God is unwilling that we should be overwhelmed with everlasting destruction, because he has appointed his Son to be the salvation of the world.'

18.—[*He that believeth on him is not condemned.*] In this verse our Lord shows Nicodemus another 'heavenly thing.' He declares the privileges of believing, and the peril of not believing in the Son of God. Nicodemus had addressed him as a 'teacher come from God.' He would have Nicodemus know that he was that high and holy One, to believe on whom was life eternal, and not to believe on whom was everlasting destruction. Life or death was before men. If they believed and received him as the Messiah, they would be saved. If they believed not, they would die in their sins.

The expression, 'He that believeth,' deserves special notice. It is the third time that our Lord speaks of 'believing' on himself, and the consequence of believing, within four verses. It shows the immense importance of faith in the sinner's justification. It is that one thing, without which eternal life cannot be had.—It shows the amazing graciousness of the gospel, and its admirable suitableness to the wants of human nature. A man may have been the worst of sinners, but if he will only 'believe,' he is at once pardoned.—Last, but not least, it shows the need of clear, distinct views of the nature of saving faith, and the importance of keeping it entirely distinct from works of any kind, in the matter of justification. Faith, and faith only, gives an interest in Christ. The old sentence of Luther's days is perfectly true, paradoxical and startling as it may sound: 'The faith which justifies is not the faith which includes charity, but the faith which lays hold on Christ.'

The expression, 'is not condemned,' is equivalent to saying, 'he is pardoned, acquitted, justified, cleared from all guilt, delivered from the curse of a broken law, no longer counted a sinner, but reckoned perfectly righteous in the sight of God.' The *presentness* of the phrase, if one may coin a word, should be specially noticed. It is not said, that the believer 'shall not be condemned at the last day,' but that 'he is not condemned.' The very moment a sinner believes on Christ, his iniquities are taken away, and he is counted righteous. 'All that believe are justified from all things' (*Acts* 13:39).

[*He that believeth not is condemned already.*] This sentence means that the man who refuses to believe on Christ is in a state of condemnation before God, even while he lives. The curse of a broken law, which we all deserve, is upon him. His sins are upon his head. He is reckoned guilty and dead before God, and there is but a step between him and hell. Faith takes all a man's sins away. Unbelief keeps them all on him. Through faith a man is made an heir of heaven, though kept outside till he dies. Through unbelief a man is already a subject of the devil, though not yet entirely in his power and within hell. The moment a man believes, all charges are completely wiped away from his name. So long as a man does not believe, his sins cover him over, and make him abominable before God, and the just wrath of God abides upon him.

Melanchthon remarks that the sentence of God's condemnation, which was passed at the beginning, 'Thou shalt surely die,' remains in full force and unrepealed, against everyone who does not believe on Christ. No new condemnation is needful. Every man or woman who does not believe, is under the curse, and condemned already.

[*Because ... not believed ... name ... Son of God.*] This sentence is justly thought to prove that no sin is so great, so damning and ruinous to the soul, as unbelief. In one sense it is the only unpardonable sin. All other sins may be forgiven, however many and great, and a man may stand complete before God. But if a man will not believe on Christ, there is no hope for him; and if he persists in his unbelief he cannot be saved. Nothing is so provoking and offensive to God as to refuse the glorious salvation he has provided at so mighty a cost, by the death of his only begotten Son. Nothing is so suicidal on the part of

man as to turn away from the only remedy which can heal his soul. Other sins may be scarlet, filthy, and abominable. But not to believe on Christ is to bar the door in our own way, and to cut off ourselves entirely from heaven. It has been truly remarked that it was a greater sin in Judas Iscariot not to believe on Christ for pardon, after he had betrayed him, than to betray him into the hands of his enemies. To betray him no doubt was an act of enormous covetousness, wickedness, and ingratitude. But not to seek him afterwards by faith for pardon, was to disbelieve his mercy, love, and power to save.

The expression, 'the name,' as the object of faith, is explained in chapter 1:12. Here, as frequently, it stands for the attributes, character, and office of the Son of God.

Luther, quoted by Brown, remarks, 'Henceforward, he who is condemned must not complain of Adam and his inborn sin. The seed of the woman, promised by God to bruise the head of the serpent, is now come, and has atoned for sin, and taken away condemnation. But he must cry out against himself for not having accepted and believed in the Christ, the devil's head-bruiser and sin-strangler. If I do not believe the same, sin and condemnation must continue.'

19.—[*This is the condemnation, etc.*] In this verse our Lord shows Nicodemus one more 'heavenly thing.' He unfolds to him the true cause of the ruin of those who are lost. Primarily, I think, our Lord had in view the unbelieving Jews of his own day, and the real reason of their rejection of himself. It was not that there was any want of evidence of his Messiahship. They had evidence enough and to spare. The real reason was that they had no mind to give up their sins. Secondarily, I think, our Lord had in view the future history of all Christians, and the true cause of the ruin of all who are not saved in every age. It is not because there is any want of light to guide men to heaven. It is not because God is wanting in love and unwilling to save. The real reason is that men in every age love their own sins, and will not come to Christ that they may be delivered from them.

115

The expression 'this is the condemnation,' is evidently very elliptical, and the full meaning must be supplied. It is probably equivalent to saying 'this is the cause of the condemnation, this is the true account of it.' The following elliptical expressions are somewhat similar, and all found in St John's first epistle. 'This is the promise,' 'This is the love of God,' 'This is the victory,' 'This is the confidence' (1 John 2:25; 5:3-14).

[*That light is come into the world.*] It is a question in this sentence whether 'light' means Christ himself, or the light of Christ's gospel. I am inclined to think that our Lord meant to include both ideas. He has come as a light into the world, and the gospel that he has brought with him, is, like its author, a strong contrast to the ignorance and wickedness of the earth.

[*Men loved darkness rather than light.*] The darkness in this sentence means moral darkness and mental darkness,—sin, ignorance, superstition, and irreligion. Men cannot come to Christ and receive his gospel without parting with all this, and they love it too well to part with it.

[*Because their deeds were evil.*] This sentence means that their habits of life were wicked, and any doctrine which necessitated a change of these habits they naturally hated.

Throughout this verse I am inclined to think that the past tense, 'loved,' ought to be taken in a present sense (proleptically, to use a grammarian's phrase), as is frequently the case in the New Testament (see *John* 15:8, and *Rom.* 8:30). The meaning will then be, 'Men have loved, do love, and always will love darkness, in consequence of the corruption of human nature, as long as the world stands.' The sentence then becomes a solemn description of a state of things which was not only to be seen among the Jews while our Lord was on earth, but would be seen everywhere to the end of time.

The verse is one which deserves special notice, because of the deep mystery it unfolds. It tells us the true reason why men miss heaven and are lost in hell. The origin of evil we are not told. The reason why evil men are lost, we are told plainly. There is not a word about any decree of God predestinating men to destruction. There is not a syllable about anything deficient or wanting either in God's love or in Christ's atonement. On the contrary, our Lord tells us that 'light has come into the world,' that God has revealed enough of the way of salvation to make men inexcusable if they are not saved. But the real account of the matter is that men have naturally no will or inclination to use the light. They love their own dark and corrupt ways more than the ways which God proposes to them. They therefore reap the fruit of their own ways, and will have at last what they loved. They loved darkness, and they will be cast into outer darkness. They did not like the light, and so they will be shut out from light eternally. In short, lost souls will be what they willed to be, and will have what they loved.

The words, 'because their deeds were evil,' are very instructive. They teach us that where men have no love to Christ and his gospel, and will not receive them, their lives and their works will prove at last to have been evil. Their habits of life may not be gross and immoral. They may be even comparatively decent and pure. But the last day will prove them to have been in reality 'evil.' Pride of intellect, or selfishness, or love of man's applause, or dislike to submission of will, or self-righteousness, or some other false principle will be found to have run through all their conduct. In one way or another, when men refuse to come to Christ, their deeds will always prove to be 'evil.' Rejection of the gospel will always be found to be connected with some moral obliquity. When Christ is refused we may be quite sure that there is something or other in life or heart, which is not right. If a man does not love light his 'deeds are evil.' Human eyes may not detect the flaw; but the eyes of an all-seeing God do.

The whole verse is a deeply humbling one. It shows the folly of all excuses for not receiving the gospel, drawn from intellectual difficulties, from God's predestination, from our own inability to change ourselves, or to see things with the eyes of others. All such excuses are scattered to the winds by this solemn verse. People do not come to Christ, and do continue unconverted, just because they do not wish and want to come to Christ. They love something else better than the light. The elect of God prove themselves to be elect by 'choosing' the things which are according to God's mind. The wicked prove themselves to be only fit for destruction, by 'choosing, loving, and following' the things which must lead to destruction.

Quesnel says on this verse, 'The greatest misfortune of men does not consist in their being subject to sin, corruption, and blindness; but in their rejecting the Deliverer, the Physician, and the Light itself.'

20.—[*Every one that doeth evil, etc.*] This verse and the following one form a practical application of all that our Lord has been saying to Nicodemus, and are also a logical consequence of the preceding verse. Like the preceding verse these two verses apply primarily to the Jews in our Lord's day, and secondarily to every nation to which the light of the gospel comes. They are a most remarkable appeal to an inquirer's conscience, and supply a most searching test of the sincerity of a man in Nicodemus' state of mind.

The words 'every one that doeth evil,' mean every unconverted person, everyone whose heart is not right and honest in God's sight, and whose actions are consequently evil, and ungodly. Every such person 'hateth the light, neither cometh to the light.' He cannot really love Christ, and the gospel, and will not honestly, and with his whole heart, seek Christ by faith and embrace his gospel, until he is renewed. The reason for this is that every unconverted person shrinks from having his ungodliness exposed. He does not wish his wicked ways to be discovered, and his utter want of true righteousness and true preparedness for death, judgment, and eternity, to be put to shame. He does not like 'his deeds to be reproved,' and therefore he shrinks from the light, and keeps away from Christ.

The application of this verse must doubtless be made with caution. In the case of many unconverted persons, its truth is plain as noonday. They love sin and hate true religion, and get away from the gospel, the Bible, and religious people, as much as they possibly can. In the case of others,

its truth is not so apparent at first sight. There are many unconverted persons who profess to like the gospel, and seem to have no prejudice against it, and to hear it with pleasure, and yet remain unconverted. Yet even in the case of those persons the text would be found perfectly true if their hearts were really known. With all their seeming love to the light they do not really love it with all their heart. There is something or other which they love better, and which keeps them back from Christ. There is something or other which they do not want to give up, and do not like to be discovered and reproved. Man's eyes may not detect it; but the eyes of God can. The general principle of the text will be found true at last of every hearer of the gospel who dies unconverted. He did not thoroughly love the light. He did not really want to be changed. He did not truly and honestly seek salvation. All this was true of the Jews in the time of Nicodemus, and it is no less true of all mankind to whom the gospel comes in the present day. Right hearts will always come to Christ. If a man keeps away from the light, his heart is wrong. He is one who 'doeth evil.'

There is a curious difference between the Greek word translated 'doeth' in this verse, and the one translated 'doeth' in the next verse. Stier and Alford think the difference instructive and meaningful. They say that the Greek word used for 'doeth evil,' means the habit of action without fruit or result. On the contrary, the Greek word for 'doing truth,' signifies the true doing of good: good fruit, good that remains.

21.—[*He that doeth truth, etc.*] This verse, it is needless to say, is closely connected with the preceding one. The preceding verse describes the unconverted man. The verse before us describes the converted man.

The expression, 'he that doeth truth,' signifies the person whose heart is honest, the man who is truly converted, however weak and ignorant, and whose heart and actions are consequently true and right in the sight of God. The phrase is frequently found in St John's writings (see *John 18:37; 1 John 1:6-8; 2:4; 3:19; 2 John 1; 3 John 3, 4*). Every such person will always come to Christ and embrace his gospel, when it is brought near him. He will have an honest desire that 'his deeds may be made manifest,' and that his real character may be discovered to himself and to others. He will have an honest wish to know whether his habits of life are really godly, or 'wrought in God.'

The principle here laid down is of great importance, and experience shows that the assertion of the text is always confirmed by facts. I believe there was not a truly good man among the Jews in our Lord's day, who did not at once receive Christ, and welcome Christ's gospel as soon as it was brought before him. Nathanael was an example. He was a man 'who did truth' under the obscure light of the law of Moses, as ministered by scribes and Pharisees. But the moment the Messiah was brought before him, he received him and believed.—So also, I believe, when the gospel comes into a church, a parish, or a congregation, it is always gladly received and embraced by any whose hearts are true. To be a truly godly man, and yet to refuse to come to Christ, is an impossibility. He that hears of Christ and does not come to him and believe on him as God's appointed way of salvation, has something fatally wrong about him. He is not really 'doing truth.' He is not a converted man. Gospel light is a mighty magnet. If there is any one that has true religion within its sphere, it will attract to itself that person. To be truly religious and not to gravitate towards him who is the great centre of all light and truth, is impossible. If a man refuses Christ, he cannot be a godly man.

The application of the last two verses to the case of Nicodemus and those Jews who were in the same state of mind as Nicodemus, is plain and obvious. Our Lord leaves on the Pharisee's mind a solemn and heart-searching conclusion. 'Think not that you can stay away from me after hearing this discourse, and be saved. If you are a really earnest inquirer after truth, and your heart is honest and sincere, you must go on; you must come to the light, and embrace the light, and you will do so, however great your present ignorance. If, on the other hand, you are

not really desirous to serve God, you will prove it by keeping away from my gospel, and by not confessing me as the Messiah.' It is a pleasant reflection, that after-events proved that Nicodemus was one who 'did truth.' He used the light our Lord graciously imparted to him. He came forward and spoke for Christ in the council. And at last, when he boldly helped to bury Christ, he made it manifest to all Israel that 'his deeds were wrought in God.'

Let it be noted, that the two verses which conclude our Lord's address to Nicodemus, are a most instructive test of the sincerity and reality of persons who appear anxious inquirers in religion. If they are honest and true they will go on, and come to the full light of Christ. If they are not honest and sincere, but only influenced by temporary excitement, they will probably go back from the light, and will certainly not close with Christ and become his disciples. This should be pressed by ministers on all inquirers. 'If you are true, you will come to the light. If you are not true, you will go back, or stand still; you will not draw near and close with Christ.' The test will never be found to fail. Those who wish to see how exceedingly weak the beginnings of grace may be in a heart, and yet be true, as it proved in the case of Nicodemus, will find the matter most skilfully treated in a small work of Perkins, little known, called, *A Grain of Mustard Seed*. A man may have the beginning of regeneration in his heart, and yet be so ignorant as not to know what regeneration is.

In concluding these long notes, for the length of which the immense importance of the passage must be my apology, I think we should remark that we never hear a word about Nicodemus being baptized! This fact is a strong incidental evidence to my mind, that the baptism of water was not the subject which our Lord had in view when he told Nicodemus that he must be born of water and the Spirit.

One other thing ought to be remarked, in leaving this subject of our Lord's conversation with Nicodemus. That thing is the singular fulness of matter by which the whole of our Lord's address is characterized. Within the space of twenty verses we read of the work of all three persons in the Trinity,—the Father's love, the Son's death on the cross, and the Spirit's operation in the new birth of man,—the corruption of man's nature, the nature of regeneration, and the efficacy of faith in Christ,—the way to escape perishing in hell, the true cause of man's condemnation if he is lost, and the true marks of sincerity in an inquirer. A fuller sermon was never delivered than that which was here preached to Nicodemus in one evening! There is hardly a single important point in divinity which is left untouched!

JOHN 3:22-36

22 After these things came Jesus and his disciples into the land of Judæa; and there he tarried with them, and baptized.

23 And John also was baptizing in Ænon near to Salim, because there was much water there: and they came, and were baptized.

24 For John was not yet cast into prison.

25 Then there arose a question between *some* of John's disciples and the Jews about purifying.

26 And they came unto John, and said unto him, Rabbi, he that was with thee beyond Jordan, to whom thou barest witness, behold, the same baptizeth, and all *men* come to him.

27 John answered and said, A man can receive nothing, except it be given him from heaven.

28 Ye yourselves bear me witness, that I said, I am not the Christ, but that I am sent before him.

29 He that hath the bride is the bridegroom: but the friend of the bridegroom, which standeth and heareth him, rejoiceth greatly because of the bridegroom's voice: this my joy therefore is fulfilled.

30 He must increase, but I *must* decrease.

31 He that cometh from above is above all: he that is of the earth is earthly, and speaketh of the earth: he that cometh from heaven is above all.

32 And what he hath seen and heard, that he testifieth; and no man receiveth his testimony.

33 He that hath received his testimony hath set to his seal that God is true.

34 For he whom God hath sent speaketh the words of God: for God giveth not the Spirit by measure *unto him.*

35 The Father loveth the Son, and hath given all things into his hand.

36 He that believeth on the Son hath everlasting life: and he that believeth not the Son shall not see life; but the wrath of God abideth on him.

ON one account this passage deserves the special attention of all devout readers of the Bible. It contains the last testimony of John the Baptist concerning our Lord Jesus Christ. That faithful man of God was the same at the end of his ministry that he was at the beginning,—the same in his views of self,—the same in his views of Christ. Happy is that church whose ministers are as steady, bold, and constant to one thing, as John the Baptist!

We have, firstly, in these verses, *a humbling example of the petty jealousies and party-spirit which may exist among professors of religion.* We are told that the disciples of John the Baptist were offended, because the ministry of Jesus began to attract more attention than that of their master. 'They came unto John, and said unto him, Rabbi, he that was with thee beyond Jordan, to whom thou barest witness, behold the same baptizeth, and all men come to him.'

The spirit exhibited in this complaint, is unhappily too common in the churches of Christ. The succession of these complainers has never failed. There are never wanting religious professors who care far more for the increase of their own party, than for the increase of true Christianity; and who cannot rejoice in the spread of religion, if it spreads anywhere except within their own pale. There is a generation which can see no good doing except in the ranks of its own congregations; and which seems ready to shut men out of heaven, if they will not enter therein under its banner.

The true Christian must watch and pray against the spirit here manifested by John's disciples. It is very insidious, very contagious, and very injurious to the cause of religion. Nothing so defiles Christianity and gives the enemies of truth such occasion to blaspheme, as jealousy and party-spirit among Christians. Wherever there is real grace, we should be ready and willing to acknowledge it, even though it may be outside our own pale. We should strive to say with the apostle, 'If Christ be preached, I rejoice: yea, and will rejoice' (*Phil.* 1:18). If good is done, we ought to be thankful, though it even may not be done in what we think the best way. If souls are saved, we ought to be glad, whatever be the means that God may think fit to employ.

We have, secondly, in these verses, *a splendid pattern of true and godly humility.* We see in John the Baptist a very different spirit from that displayed by his disciples. He begins by laying down the great principle, that acceptance with man is a special gift of God; and that we must therefore not presume to find fault, when others have more acceptance than ourselves. 'A man can receive nothing except it be given him from heaven.' He goes on to remind his followers of his repeated declaration, that One greater than himself was coming: 'I said, I am not the Christ.' He tells them that his office compared to that of Christ, is that of the bridegroom's friend, compared to the bridegroom. And finally, he solemnly affirms, that Christ must and will become greater and greater, and that he himself must become less and less important, until, like a star eclipsed by the rising sun, he has completely disappeared.

A frame of mind like this is the highest degree of grace to which mortal man can attain. The greatest saint in the sight of God is the man who is most thoroughly 'clothed with humility' (1 Pet. 5:5). Would we know the prime secret of being men of the stamp of Abraham, and Moses, and Job, and David, and Daniel, and St Paul, and John the Baptist? They were all eminently humble men. Living at different ages, and enjoying very different degrees of light, in this matter at least they were all agreed. In themselves they saw nothing but sin and weakness. To God they gave all the praise of what they were. Let us walk in their steps. Let us covet earnestly the best gifts; but above all, let us covet humility. The way to true honour is to be humble. No man ever was so praised by Christ as the very man who says here, 'I must decrease,'—the humble John the Baptist.

We have, thirdly, in these verses, *an instructive declaration of Christ's honour and dignity*. John the Baptist teaches his disciples once more the true greatness of the person whose growing popularity offended them. Once more, and perhaps for the last time, he proclaims him as one worthy of all honour and praise. He uses one striking expression after another, to convey a correct idea of the majesty of Christ. He speaks of him as 'the bridegroom' of the church,—as 'him that cometh from above,'—as 'him whom God hath sent,'—as 'him to whom the Spirit is given without measure,'—as him 'whom the Father loves,' and into 'whose hands all things are given,'—to believe in whom is life everlasting, and to reject whom is eternal ruin. Each of these phrases is full of deep meaning, and would supply matter for a long sermon. All show the depth and height of John's spiritual attainments. More honourable things are nowhere written concerning Jesus, than these verses recorded as spoken by John the Baptist.

Let us endeavour in life and death, to hold the same views of the Lord Jesus, to which John here gives expression. We can never make too much of Christ. Our thoughts about the church, the ministry, and the sacraments, may easily become too high and extravagant. We can never have too high thoughts about Christ, can never love him too much, trust him too implicitly, lay too much weight upon him, and speak too highly in his praise. He is worthy of all the honour that we can give him. He will be all in heaven. Let us see to it, that he is all in our hearts on earth.

We have, lastly, in these verses, *a broad assertion of the nearness and presentness of the salvation of true Christians.* John the Baptist declares, 'He that believeth on the Son hath everlasting life.' He is not intended to look forward with a sick heart to a far distant privilege. He 'hath' everlasting life as soon as he believes. Pardon, peace, and a complete title to heaven, are an immediate possession. They become a believer's own from the very moment he puts faith in Christ. They will not be more completely his own if he lives to the age of Methuselah.

The truth before us is one of the most glorious privileges of the gospel. There are no works to be done, no conditions to be fulfilled, no price to be paid, no wearing years of probation to be passed, before a sinner can be accepted with God. Let him only believe on Christ, and he is at once forgiven. Salvation is close to the chief of sinners. Let him only repent and believe, and this day it is his own. By Christ all that believe are at once justified from all things.

Let us leave the whole passage with one grave and heart-searching thought. If faith in Christ brings with it present and immediate privileges, to remain unbelieving is to be in a state of tremendous peril. If heaven is very near to the believer, hell must be very near to the unbeliever. The greater the mercy that the Lord Jesus offers, the greater will be the guilt of those who neglect and reject it. 'He that believeth not the Son shall not see life; but the wrath of God abideth on him.'

Notes—John 3:22-36

22.—[*Came Jesus ... into ... land of Judæa.*] Some have thought, from this expression, that the conversation between Christ and Nicodemus did not take place in Jerusalem or Judæa, but in Galilee. Others have thought that a long interval must be supposed to have elapsed between the conversation and the events which are here narrated.—I can agree with neither view. I believe the true explanation is, that 'the land' here spoken of means the rural part or territory of Judæa, in contradistinction to the capital town of the territory, Jerusalem. The meaning will then be, that Jesus left the city and went into the country districts. The expression, 'Thou Bethlehem, in the land of Juda,' is similar (*Matt.* 2:6).

[*He tarried.*] The Greek word so rendered signifies a lengthened stay. It is translated in other places, 'continued' or 'abode.' It is noteworthy that many of the events of our Lord's ministry in Jerusalem and the surrounding district, are evidently not recorded in any of the Gospels.

[*And baptized.*] That our Lord did not baptize with his own hands, but left the ordinance to be administered by his disciples, as a work inferior to that of preaching, we may learn from the next chapter (*John* 4:2).

Lightfoot observes that 'The administration of Christ's ordinances by his ministers, according to his institution, is as his own work. The disciples' baptizing is called his baptizing.'

The questions have often been raised, 'In what name was this baptism administered? Was it a baptism that needed to be repeated after the day of Pentecost?'—The most probable answer to the first question is, that it was a baptism in the name of Jesus, upon profession of belief that he was the Messiah. The most probable answer to the second question is, that it was certainly not a baptism that required repetition. To suppose that a baptism, administered by our Lord's disciples, under our Lord's own eye, and by our Lord's own command, was not as effectual and profitable an ordinance as any baptism

that was ever afterwards administered is a most improbable supposition.

It may be remarked here, that there is no ground for the common idea, that it is absolutely necessary that baptism should be administered in the name of the Trinity, in order to be a valid and Christian baptism. In three cases recorded in the Acts we are expressly told that baptism was administered in the name of Jesus Christ, and no mention is made of all three persons in the Trinity (see *Acts* 2:38; 8:37; 10:48). In all these cases, however, it will be remembered, baptism in the name of Christ was practically baptism in the name of the Trinity. It was confession of faith in him whom the Father sent, and who was the giver of the Holy Ghost.

As a general rule in the church of Christ, no doubt baptism ought to be in the name of the Trinity (*Matt.* 28:19). But that our Lord's disciples, in the place now before us, did not baptize in the name of the Trinity, is pretty certain; and that baptism in the name of Jesus is valid Christian baptism seems clear from the places referred to in the Acts.

Hutcheson remarks, that 'Christ's own bodily presence, filled with the Spirit without measure, did not take away the use of external ordinances,' such as baptism. The Quakers' opinion, that we need no external ordinances under the gospel, is hard to reconcile with such a text as this.

23.—[*John also was baptizing.*] We can hardly doubt that John baptized all who came to him, at this period of his ministry, in the name of Jesus, upon confession of faith that Jesus was the Messiah. It seems most improbable that after publicly pointing out Jesus Christ as the Lamb of God, and the promised Saviour, he would be content to baptize with the baptism of repentance, which he had administered before Christ appeared. In short, John's baptism at this period, and the baptism administered by Christ's disciples, must have been precisely the same.

I may remark here, that the opinion maintained by Roman Catholics, and those who agree with them, that there was an essential difference between John's baptism and Christian baptism, seems to me entirely destitute of foundation.—I agree with Brentius, Lightfoot, and most of the Protestant commentators, that John's baptism and Christian baptism differed only in circumstantials, but were the same in substance, and that a person baptized by John the Baptist had no need to be re-baptized after the day of Pentecost. Unless we take this view, I cannot see any evidence that Peter, and Andrew, and James, and John ever received Christian baptism at all. There is not a single word in the Gospel to show that they were ever baptized again after leaving John the Baptist's company, and becoming Christ's disciples. Moreover, we are expressly told that 'Jesus himself baptized not' (*John* 4:2). The only baptism that the first apostles received appears to have been John the Baptist's baptism. This fact seems to me to prove irresistibly, that John's baptism was essentially of equal value with Christian baptism, and that a person baptized by John had no need to be baptized again.

The well-known passage in Acts (*Acts* 19:1-6), which is always quoted in opposition to the view I maintain, does not appear to me at all conclusive and decisive upon the question now before us.—For one thing, the persons described in that passage as having only been baptized with John's baptism, seem to have been ignorant of the first principles of Christianity. They said, 'We have not so much as heard whether there be any Holy Ghost.' That expression shows pretty clearly that they had not been hearers of John the Baptist, who frequently spoke of the Holy Ghost (*Matt.* 3:11), and had not been baptized by John himself.—It is most probable that they were inhabitants of Ephesus, who had only heard Apollos preaching, and knew even less than their teacher. Whether St Paul might not think it needful to administer baptism to such ignorant disciples as these, who could give no intelligent account of Christianity, is a question I would not undertake to decide.—But beside this, it is by no means certain that these disciples were really baptized again with water at all. Brentius holds that the words, 'They were baptized

in the name of the Lord Jesus,' mean the baptism of the Spirit. Streso maintains that the words are the concluding sentence of St Paul's address to these ignorant men. I cannot say that either of these last views is altogether satisfactory. All I say is, that I would infinitely rather adopt either of them, than hold such a monstrous opinion as the Romish one, that John's baptism was not Christian baptism at all, and needed to be repeated. The difficulties in the way of this last view appear to me far greater than the difficulties in the way of the one which I support. To say that the first five apostles never received any Christian baptism at all, is really preposterous. To assert that Christ himself baptized them, is to assert what the Bible never even hints at. There is not a shadow of proof that Jesus ever baptized a single person. I see no escape from the conclusion that Andrew, John, Peter, Philip, and Nathanael, either received John's baptism or no baptism at all.

Whatever men may think about John's baptism before the time when our Lord appeared, they will never prove that the baptism he administered in the text before us was not Christian baptism. To suppose that John would go on administering an ordinance which he knew was imperfect, while Christian baptism was being administered by Christ's disciples a few miles off, is simply absurd.

[*Ænon near to Salim.*] It is not certainly known where this place was. The probability is that it was somewhere in Judæa. In the list of the cities given to the tribe of Judah, we find together 'Shilhim and Ain' (*Josh.* 15:32). It is very possible that these two may be the 'Ænon and Salim' now before us. The changes which proper names undergo in passing from one language to another, everyone knows, are very great.

[*Because there was much water.*] It is frequently assumed from this expression, that John's baptism was immersion and not sprinkling, and that on this account a great supply of water was absolutely needful. It may perhaps have been so. The point is one of no importance. That immersion, however, is necessary to the validity of baptism, and that sprinkling alone is not sufficient, are points that can never be demonstrated from Scripture. So long as water is used, it seems to be left a matter of indifference whether the person baptized is dipped or sprinkled. I should find it very hard to believe that the three thousand baptized on the day of Pentecost, or the jailor and his family, baptized at midnight in the Philippian prison, were all immersed. The Church of England wisely allows either mode of applying water to be used. To suppose that dipping is forbidden to English Churchmen is mere ignorance.

[*They came ... baptized.*] This is an elliptical sentence. We are not told who are meant by 'they.' It is like 'men,' in Matthew 5:15, and means generally 'people.'

24.—[*John ... not yet ... prison.*] John's diligence in his Master's work is here pointed out. He doubtless knew that his ministry was fulfilled when Christ appeared, and that the time of his own departure, and violent death under Herod's hands, was at hand. Yet he worked on to the very last. 'Blessed is that servant, whom his Lord when he cometh shall find so doing' (*Matt.* 24:46).

Theophylact thinks that John's early death was permitted in God's providence, in order to prevent any distraction in people's minds between him and Christ.

25.—[*There arose a question ... disciples ... Jews ... purifying.*] The nature and particulars of this dispute must be left to conjecture. We can only form an idea of it from the context. It seems probable that it was a dispute between the unbelieving Jews and the disciples of John the Baptist, about the comparative value of the two baptisms which were being administered in Judæa: viz., John's baptism and Christ's.—Which was the most purifying? Which was the most efficacious? Which was the most valuable of the two?—The Jews probably taunted John's disciples with the decline of their master's popularity. John's disciples, in ignorant zeal and heat for their master, probably contended that no new teacher's baptism could possibly be more purifying and valuable than their own master's.

Wordsworth remarks upon the word 'purifying,' that St John never uses the word 'baptism,' and never calls John the Baptist by his common surname, 'the Baptist.' He says, 'John was no longer the Baptist, when St John wrote. His baptism had passed away.'

Musculus, on this verse, observes the excessive readiness of men in every age to raise questions, controversies, and persecutions about ceremonies of merely human institution, while about faith, and hope, and love, and humility, and patience, and mortification of the flesh, and renewal of the Spirit, they exhibit no zeal at all. Controversies about baptism certainly appear to be among the oldest and most mischievous by which the church has been plagued.

26.—[*They came unto John, etc.*] The language of the whole verse seems intended to show that John's disciples were jealous for their master's ministry, and that its declining popularity, in consequence of our Lord's appearance in Judæa as a public teacher, was a cause of annoyance to them. The verse is an instructive instance of that littleness and party-spirit which are so painfully common among Christians when one minister's popularity is interfered with by the appearance of another.

[*He ... with thee ... thou barest witness.*] This expression shows the publicity and notoriety of John's testimony to our Lord as the Messiah and the Lamb of God. It was testimony not borne privately in a corner, but in the hearing and full knowledge of all John's disciples. It would seem to have had very little effect on their minds. The words fell on their ears, but went no further.

[*Behold the same baptizeth.*] This expression implies partly surprise and partly complaint. In any case it shows how little the bulk of John's disciples understood that Jesus was really the Messiah promised in the prophecies. If they had understood it, they would surely neither have been surprised nor annoyed at him for baptizing and becoming popular. They would rather have expected it and rejoiced at it. It is one among many proofs that ministers may be loved by their hearers, and may tell them the truth faithfully, and yet be utterly unable to make their hearers understand or believe. Few are like Andrew, and 'follow

Jesus,' when their minister says, 'Behold the Lamb.' The most are as though they did not hear at all.

[*All men come to him.*] These words must doubtless be taken with qualification. The expression, 'all men,' only means, 'many persons.' We know as a fact that not all men came to Christ. Moreover, we must remember, that out of those who did come to Christ, very few believed. John says in his reply to his disciples, 'No man receiveth his testimony.'—Allowance must be made for the irritation under which John's disciples spoke. When men are vexed in spirit, by seeing their own party diminishing, they are often tempted to use exaggerated and incorrect expressions.

Hutcheson remarks on this verse, that 'Carnal emulation is an old and great sin in the church, and even among professors; it being the foul fruit of a carnal temper to look on the success of one man's gifts as the debasing of another's who is faithful, and to count the thriving of God's work in one minister's hand the disgracing of another who is not so much flocked to.'

Cyril remarks on this verse, how admirably God can bring good out of apparent evil. Here, as in many cases, a carnal and unkind saying of John's disciples gives occasion to John's admirable testimony about Christ.

27.—[*John answered ... A man can receive nothing, etc.*] This sentence is the statement of a general truth in religion. Success, promotion, and growth of influence, are gifts which God keeps entirely in his own hands. If one faithful minister's popularity wanes, while another's popularity and influence over men's hearts increases, the thing is of God, and we must submit to his appointment (*Psa.* 75:6, 7).

The application of the sentence is not to Christ, as Chrysostom thought, but to John the Baptist himself, as Augustine thought. They are meant to imply, 'I cannot command continued success in my ministry. I can only receive what God gives me. If he thinks fit to give anyone more acceptance with men than myself, I cannot prevent it, and have no right to complain. All success is of God. All that I have had, at any period of my ministry, has been

received, and none deserved.'—To apply the sentence to our Lord, seems to me an unsatisfactory interpretation, and derogatory to the dignity of Christ's ministry. Those who take this view, would probably prefer the marginal reading of the word 'receive,' and would render it, 'No man can take to himself anything.' The sentence would then be like St Paul's words to the Hebrews: 'No man taketh this honour unto himself, but he that is called of God, as was Aaron' (*Heb.* 5:4). But the translation, 'receive,' and the application to John the Baptist, appear to me more agreeable to the context, and the general spirit of John's reply. And although the word, a 'man,' ought not to have much stress laid upon it, I cannot help thinking that John uses it intentionally, in order to point to himself. 'A mere *man* like me can receive nothing but what is given him from heaven.'

Lightfoot thinks that the Greek word rendered 'receive,' means 'perceive,' or 'apprehend;' and that John meant, 'I see by this instance of yourselves, that no man can learn or understand anything, unless it be given him from heaven.' He regards the sentence as John's rebuke to his disciples for incredulity and stupidity. I doubt myself whether the Greek word will bear the sense Lightfoot would put on it.

The expression, 'from heaven,' is equivalent to saying, 'from God' (see *Dan.* 4:26; *Luke* 15:21).

The whole verse is a most useful antidote to that jealousy which sometimes springs up in a minister's mind, when he sees a brother's ministry prospering more than his own.

28.—[*Ye yourselves bear me witness ... I said, etc.*] John here reminds his disciples that he had repeatedly told them that he was not the Christ, and that he was only a forerunner sent before him. They ought to have remembered this. If they had done so, they would not have been surprised at the rise and progress of Christ's ministry, but would rather have expected him to outshine and surpass their master, as a matter of course.

The verse is an instructive illustration of the forgetfulness of hearers. John's testimony to the dignity of Christ and his superiority to himself had been constantly repeated. But it had been all thrown away on his disciples, and when Christ began to receive greater honours than their master, and their own party began to grow smaller than that of Christ's disciples, they were offended. People soon forget what they do not like.

29.—[*He that hath ... bride ... bridegroom, etc.*] In this verse John the Baptist explains the relative positions occupied by himself and Christ, by a familiar illustration. In tracing it out, it is of great importance not to press the points of resemblance too far. The illustration is one which specially requires to be handled with reverence, decency, and discretion.

The 'bride,' in the verse, signifies the whole company of believers: the Lamb's wife (*Rev.* 21:9). The 'bridegroom' is the Lord Jesus Christ himself. The 'friend of the bridegroom' means John the Baptist, and all other faithful ministers of Christ. According to the marriage customs of the Jews, there were certain persons called the bridegroom's *friends*, who were the means of communication between him and the bride before the marriage. Their duty was simply to set forward and promote the bridegroom's interests, and to remove all obstacles, as far as possible, to a speedy union of the parties. To accomplish this end and promote a thoroughly good understanding between the bride and bridegroom, was their sole office. If they saw the bridegroom's suit prospering, and at last saw him received favourably and gladly by the bride, their end was accomplished and their work was done. To all this John the Baptist makes allusion in the verse now before us. He tells his disciples that his sole work was to set forward and promote a good understanding between Christ and men. If he saw that work prospering he was thankful and would rejoice, even though the result was that his own personal importance was diminished. He would have his disciples know that the growing popularity of Christ which offended them, was the very thing which he longed to see. He had no greater joy than to hear of the voice of Christ, the Bridegroom, being listened to by believers, the bride. It was the very thing for which he had been preaching and ministering. His 'joy was fulfilled.'

The word 'hath' means 'possesses as his own.' Possession of the bride, as 'bone of his bones and flesh of his flesh,' is the peculiar prerogative of the bridegroom (*Gen.* 2:23). With this his friends have nothing to do.

The expression 'standeth,' must probably not be pressed too far. Some think that it is taken from the position occupied by the bridegroom's friends on the day when the bridegroom was first formally introduced to the bride. They stood at a respectful distance and looked on. The expression certainly implies inferiority. St Paul says that the Jewish priests '*stand*' daily ministering, but Christ '*sat down*' on the right hand of God (*Heb.* 10:12).

The expression, 'heareth the bridegroom's voice,' like the last, is one that must not be pressed too far. It is a part of the drapery of the illustration. When report was brought to John the Baptist, that Jesus Christ's ministry was accepted by some, and that he found favour with many disciples, then was fulfilled what is here meant. John heard 'the bridegroom's voice,' and saw the successful progress of his mission, and seeing and hearing this 'rejoiced.'

The whole verse is a most instructive picture of a true minister's work and character. He is a friend of Christ, and is ordained in order to promote a union between Christ and souls (2 *Cor.* 11:2). He must rigidly adhere to that office, and must never take to himself that which does not belong to him. The minister who allows honour to be given to himself which only belongs to Jesus, and exalts his own office into that of a mediator and priest, is treacherously usurping a position which is not his but his Master's. The professing Christian who treats ministers as if they were priests and mediators, is dishonouring Jesus Christ, and basely giving that honour to the Bridegroom's friends which belongs exclusively to the Bridegroom himself.

The expression, 'this my joy is fulfilled,' is a very instructive one for ministers. It shows that the truest happiness of a minister should consist in Christ's voice

127

being heard by souls. 'Now we live,' says St Paul, 'if ye stand fast in the Lord' (*1 Thess.* 3:8, etc.).

It deserves notice, that when our Lord at another period of his ministry expressly speaks of himself as 'the bridegroom,' in his reply to the disciples of John the Baptist (*Matt.* 9:15), he seems purposely to remind them of their master's words.

Musculus, on this verse, observes, 'The day of the Lord will declare what kind of zeal that is in our popish bishops, who profess to be influenced by zeal for the love of the church, which is Christ's bride, against Christ's enemies. The day will declare whether a zeal which makes them shed innocent blood and persecute the members of Christ, is the zeal of true friends of the Bridegroom, or of treacherous suitors of the bride.'

30.—[*He must increase ... I ... decrease.*] In this sentence John the Baptist tells his complaining disciples that it is right and proper and necessary that Christ should grow in dignity, and that he himself should be less thought of. He was only the servant; Christ was the Master. He was only the forerunner and ambassador; Christ was the King. He was only the morning star; Christ was the Sun. The idea implied appears to be that of the stars gradually fading away, as the sun rises, after the break of day. The stars do not really perish or really become less, but they pale and become invisible before the superior brightness of the great centre of light. The sun does not really become larger, or really increase in brightness, but it becomes more fully visible, and occupies a position in which it more completely fills our vision. So was it with John the Baptist and Christ.—Every faithful minister ought to be like-minded with John. He must be content to be less thought of by his believing hearers, in proportion as they grow in knowledge and faith, and see Christ himself more clearly. As churches decay and fall away, they think less of Christ and more of their ministers. As churches revive and receive spiritual life, they think less of ministers and more of Christ. To a decaying church the sun is going down, and the stars are beginning to appear. To a reviving church the stars are waning, and the sun appearing.

31.—[*He ... cometh ... above ... above all.*] In this sentence John the Baptist asserts the infinite superiority of Christ over himself or any other child of Adam, whatever office he may fill. Christ is 'from above.' He is not merely man, but God. He came from heaven, when he took our nature on him, and was born. As God, he is as far above all his ministers and servants as the Creator is above the creature. He is 'far above all principality, and power ... and every name that is named.' He is 'head over all things to the church,' and richly deserves all the honour, and dignity, and respect, and reverence that man can give (*Eph.* 1:21, 22).

[*He that is of the earth ... earthly ... speaketh ... earth.*] In this sentence John the Baptist expresses in strong language the comparative inferiority to Christ of himself or of any other minister. 'All who, like me,' he seems to say, 'are only men, mere dust and clay, descended from a father who was made out of the dust of the ground, are comparatively earthly. The weakness and feebleness of our origin pervade all our doings. By nature earthly, our works are earthly, and our speaking and preaching earthly.'—In short, there will be a savour of humanity about the ministry of everyone who is naturally engendered of the seed of Adam.

The difficulty that some see in John the Baptist calling his own ministry 'earthly,' is quite needlessly raised. It is evident that he calls it so 'comparatively.' Compared to the teaching of scribes and Pharisees, it was not earthly, but heavenly. Compared to the teaching of him who came from heaven, it was earthly. A candle compared to darkness is light; but the same candle compared to the sun is a poor dim spark.

[*He that cometh ... heaven ... above all.*] This sentence is only a repetition of the beginning of the verse. It is a second assertion of Christ's greatness and superiority over any mere man, in order to impress the matter more deeply on those who heard it. 'Mark what I tell you,' John the Baptist seems to say to his disciples: 'I repeat emphatically, that Christ having come from heaven, and being by nature God as well as man, is far above me and all other ministers, who are only men, and nothing more.'

Some think, as Erasmus, Bengel, Wetstein, Olshausen, and Tholuck, that John the Baptist's words end with the verse preceding the one now before us, and that the words, 'He that cometh from above,' begin the comment of John the Evangelist. I cannot for a moment admit this idea to be correct. I see no necessity for it. The whole passage runs on naturally, as the language of John the Baptist, to the end of the chapter. I see nothing unsuitable to John the Baptist in the concluding verses. They contain no truth which he was not likely to know. I see nothing gained by this idea. It throws no new light on the passage, and is an awkward break which would never occur to a simple reader of the Bible.

32.—[*What ... seen ... heard ... testifieth.*] In this sentence John the Baptist shows the divinity of Christ, and his consequent superiority over himself in another point of view. He says that Christ bears witness to truths which he has 'seen and heard.' He is not like mere human ministers who only declare what they have been taught by the Holy Spirit, and inspired to communicate to others. As God, he declares with authority truths which he had seen and heard and known from all eternity with the Father (*John* 5:19-30; 8:38).

Some draw a distinction between what our Lord has seen and what he has heard. They think that what Christ has 'seen,' means what he has seen as one with God the Father in essence, and what Christ has 'heard,' means what he has heard as a distinct person in the Trinity.—Or else they think that what Christ has 'seen,' means what he has seen with the Father as God; and what he has 'heard,' what he has heard from the Father as man.—I doubt the correctness of either view. I think it more probable that the expression 'seen and heard,' is only a proverbial way of signifying perfect knowledge, such as a person has intuitively or at first hand.

Euthymius thinks that the expression 'seen and heard,' was purposely used, because of the weakness of John's hearers;

and that such expressions were necessary, in order to give such hearers any adequate idea of Christ's divine nature.

The word 'testifieth' deserves notice, as an expression peculiarly characteristic of Christ's ministry. He told Pilate, 'For this cause came I into the world, that I should bear witness unto the truth' (*John* 18:27).

[*And no man receiveth his testimony.*] The expression, 'no man,' in this sentence, must evidently, from the following verses, be taken with qualification. It must mean 'very few.' Andrew, Peter, Philip, and others, had received Christ's testimony. The sentence seems intended to rebuke the complaint uttered by John's disciples: 'All men come unto him.' John seems to say, 'However many persons come to hear Jesus, you will yet see that very few believe on him. Great as he is, and deserving of far more reverence than myself, you have yet to learn that even he is really believed on by few. The crowds who follow him are, unhappily, not true believers. The temporary popularity which attends his ministry, is as worthless as that which attended my own.'

Pearce thinks that the Greek word rendered 'and,' would have been better translated 'and yet,' as in John 7:19 and 9:30.

The notion of Augustine's, that 'no man,' in this sentence means, 'none of the wicked,' seems very untenable and unsatisfactory.

33.—[*He that hath received, etc.*] In this verse John shows the great importance of receiving Christ's testimony. So far from being offended by the crowd which attended Christ's ministry, John's disciples should be thankful that so many heard him, and that some few received his teaching into their hearts.

[*Hath set to his seal.*] This expression is peculiar, and found nowhere else in the New Testament, in the same sense. Of course it does not mean any literal sealing. It only means, 'hath formally declared his belief,—hath publicly professed his conviction,'—just as a man puts his seal to a document, as a testimony that he consents to its contents. In ancient days, when few comparatively could write, to affix a seal to a paper, was a more common mode of expressing assent to it, than to sign a name.—The sentence is equivalent to saying, 'He that receives Christ's testimony, has set down his name as one who believes that God is true.'

[*That God is true.*] These words may be taken two ways. According to some they mean, 'He that receives Christ, declares his belief that it is the true God who has sent Christ; and that Christ is no impostor, but the Messiah, whom the true God of the Old Testament prophets promised to send.'—According to others they mean, 'He that receives Christ, declares his belief that God is true to his word, and has kept the promise that he made to Adam, Abraham, and David.' That the Greek word rendered 'true,' will bear this last meaning, seems proved by the expression, 'Let God be true, but every man a liar' (*Rom.* 3:4). Either view makes good sense and good divinity; but on the whole, I prefer the second one. It seems to me strongly confirmed by the expression in St John's first epistle: 'He that believeth not God hath made him a liar; because he believeth not the record that God gave of his Son' (*1 John* 5:10).

Some have thought that the sentence may mean, 'He that receives Christ, declares his belief that Christ is the true God,' and that it is parallel to 1 John 5:20: 'This is the true God.'—But I do not think the Greek words will admit of the interpretation. If they would, the Greek Fathers would never have overlooked this text in writing against the Arians.—Maldonatus seems to favour this opinion, and says that Cyril holds it. But it certainly does not clearly appear in Cyril's commentary on the place.

34.—[*He whom God hath sent.*] In this verse John the Baptist shows the dignity of Christ, and his superiority over all other teachers, by another striking declaration about him. He begins by giving him the well-known epithet which was peculiarly applied to Messiah. 'He whom God hath sent,—the sent One: the One whom God has sent into the world according to promise.'

[*Speaketh the words of God.*] This sentence means that Christ's words were not the words of a mere man, like John himself, or one of the prophets. They were nothing less than the words of God. He who heard them heard nothing less than God speaking. The unity of the Father and the Son is so close that he who hears the teaching of the Son hears the teaching of the Father also (compare *John* 7:16; 5:19; 14:10, 11; 8:28; 12:49). When John the Baptist spoke, he spoke merely human words, however true and good and scriptural. But when Christ spoke, he spoke divine words; even the words of God himself. As Quesnel says, 'He spoke by the Holy Ghost, who is his own Spirit, who inseparably dwelleth in him, and by the possession of whose fulness he receives his unction and consecration.'

Theophylact remarks on this sentence and others like it in St John's Gospel, that we must not suppose that Christ needed to be taught by God the Father what to speak, because whatever the Father knows the Son also knows, as consubstantial with him. So also when we read of the Son being 'sent,' we must think of him as a ray sent from the sun, which is not in reality separate from the sun, but a part of the sun itself.

Some think that the expression, 'speaketh the words of God,' in this place, has special reference to the promise given to Moses about Messiah: 'I . . . will put my words in his mouth' (*Deut.* 18:18).

[*For God giveth not ... Spirit by measure ... him.*] The expression, 'by measure,' in this sentence, means, 'partially, scantily, stintedly, in small degree.' It is the opposite to 'fully, completely, in unmeasured abundance.' Thus we read in Ezekiel's description of a time of scarcity at Jerusalem, 'They shall drink water by measure' (*Ezek.* 4:16).

The whole sentence is peculiar, and requires careful interpretation. The object of John the Baptist is to show once more the infinite superiority of the Lord Jesus over himself or any other man. To all others, even to the most eminent prophets and apostles, God gives the Holy Spirit, 'by measure.' Their gifts and graces are both imperfect. As St Paul says, they 'know in part' and 'prophesy in part' (*1 Cor.* 13:9). But with him whom God hath sent, it is very different. To him the Holy Ghost is given without measure, in infinite fulness and completeness. In his human nature the gifts and graces of the Spirit are present without the slightest shadow of imperfection. As man, Jesus of Nazareth was anointed with the Holy Ghost, and fitted for his office as our Priest and Prophet and King, in a way and degree never granted to any other man (*Acts* 10:38).

All this is undoubtedly true, but it is not, in my opinion, the whole truth of the sentence. I believe that John the Baptist points not only to our Lord's human nature, but to his divinity. I believe his meaning to be, 'He whom God hath sent, is One far above prophets and ministers, to whom the Spirit is only given by measure. He is One who is himself very God. In him dwelleth all the fulness of the Godhead bodily. He is One who, as a person in the Trinity, is eternally and ineffably united with God the Holy Spirit. From him the Holy Spirit proceeds as well as from the Father, and is the Spirit of Christ and the Spirit of the Son. As God, it is impossible that he can be separated from the Holy Spirit. To him therefore the Spirit is not given by measure, as if he were only a man. He is God as well as man, and as such he needeth not that the Spirit should be *given* to him. He has the Spirit without measure, because in the divine essence, he, and the Spirit, and the Father, are One and undivided.'

I am inclined to hold the view just stated, because of the verse which follows. The object of John the Baptist, in this last testimony to Christ, appears to be to lead his disciples step by step to the highest view of Messiah's dignity. He would have them recognize in him One who was very God as well as very man. The view of the sentence before us which is commonly adopted, appears to me of an unsafe tendency. That the Spirit was *given* to our Lord as man, and given without measure, is doubtless true. But we must be very careful that we never forget a truth of no less importance. That truth is, that our Lord Jesus Christ never ceased to be God as well as man, and that as God he was never separate from the Spirit. As Henry says, 'The Spirit dwelt in him, not as in a vessel, but as in a fountain, as in a bottomless ocean.'

It deserves remark that the concluding words of the verse, 'unto him,' are not found in the original Greek. This has led some to maintain that the second clause of the verse is only a general statement: 'God is not a God who gives the Spirit by measure.' But all the best commentators, from Augustine downwards, hold the view of our translators, that it is Christ who is signified, and that 'unto him' ought to be supplied in any translation.

Chemnitius thinks that this verse specially refers to Isaiah 11:2, where it is predicted that the seven-fold gifts of the Spirit shall rest on Messiah.

35.—[*The Father loveth the Son ... given all ... hand.*] There is something, at first sight, abrupt and elliptical in this verse. The full meaning of it I believe to be as follows: 'He whom God hath sent is One far above me or any other prophet. He is the eternal Son of God, whom the Father loved from all eternity, and into whose hands all things concerning man's salvation have been given and committed by an everlasting covenant. He is no mere man, as you, my disciples, ignorantly suppose. He is the Son of whom it is written, "Kiss the Son lest he be angry, and ye perish from the way" (*Psa.* 2:12). He is the Son to whom the Father has said, "I shall give thee the heathen for thine inheritance, and the uttermost parts of the earth for thy possession" (*Psa.* 2:8). Instead of being jealous of his present popularity, you should serve him with fear, and rejoice before him with trembling.'

The 'love of the Father toward the Son' here spoken of, is a subject far too deep for man to fathom. It is an expression graciously accommodated to man's feeble understanding, and intended to signify that most intimate and ineffable union which exists between the first and second persons in the blessed Trinity, and the entire approbation and complacency with which the Father regards the work of redemption undertaken by the Son. It is that love to which our Lord refers in the words, 'Thou lovedst me before the foundation of the world' (*John* 17:24), and which the Father expressly asserted at the beginning of the Son's earthly ministry: 'This is my beloved Son, in whom I am well pleased' (*Matt.* 3:17).

When it says that the Father hath given all things into the Son's hand, we must understand that mediatorial kingdom which in the eternal counsels of the Trinity has been appointed to Christ. By the terms of the everlasting covenant, the Father has given to the Son power over all flesh, to quicken whom he will,—to justify, to sanctify, to keep, and to glorify his people,—to judge, and finally punish the wicked and unbelieving,—and at last to take to himself a kingdom over all the world, and put down every enemy under his feet. These are the 'all things,' of which John speaks. Christ, he would have us know, has the keys of death and hell in his hand, and to him alone men must go, if they want anything for their souls.

Calvin observes on this verse, 'The love here spoken of is that peculiar love of God, which, beginning with the Son, flows from him to all the creatures. For that love, with which, embracing his Son he embraces us also in him, leads him to communicate all his benefits to us by his hand.'

Quesnel remarks, 'God loved the prophets as his servants; but he loves Christ as his only Son, and communicates himself to him in proportion to his love.'—'The prophets had only particular commissions, limited to a certain time and certain purposes; but Christ has full power given him as the general disposer of all his Father's works, the executor of his designs, the Head of his church, the universal High Priest of good things to come, the steward and disposer of all his graces.'

Chemnitius, on this verse, remarks the infinite wisdom and love of God in giving the management of our soul's affairs into Christ's hand. We are all naturally so weak and feeble, that if anything was left in our hands we should never be saved. We should lose all, even sooner than Adam did in paradise. But Christ will take care of all committed to his charge, and our wisdom is to commit all things to him, as St Paul did (2 Tim. 1:12).

36.—[*He that believeth ... Son hath ... life.*] In this verse John the Baptist concludes his testimony to Christ, by a solemn declaration of the unspeakable importance of believing on him. Whether his disciples would receive it or not, he tells them that life or death, heaven or hell, all turned on believing in this Jesus who had 'been with him beyond Jordan.'

The excellence of faith should be noted here. Like his divine Master, John teaches that 'believing on the Son,' is the principal thing in saving religion. Believing is the way to heaven, and not believing the way to hell.

The 'presentness' of the salvation which is in Christ should be here noted. Again, like his divine Master, John teaches that a believer 'hath' everlasting life. Pardon, peace, and a title to heaven, are at once and immediately a man's possession, the very moment that he lays his sins on Jesus, and puts his trust in him.

[*He that believeth not ... not see life.*] The Greek word here rendered 'believeth not,' is quite different from the one translated 'believeth,' at the beginning of the verse. It means something much stronger than 'not trusting.' It would be more literally rendered, 'He that does not obey, or is disobedient to.' It is the same word so rendered in Romans 2:8; 10:21; 1 Peter 2:8; 3:1, 20.

The expression, 'shall not see life,' must of course mean 'shall not see life, if he continues impenitent and unbelieving, and dies in that state.' The phrase, 'to see life,' most probably means, 'to taste, enter, enjoy, possess life,' and must not be literally interpreted as seeing either with bodily or mental eyes.

[*The wrath of God abideth on him.*] This concluding sentence of John the Baptist's testimony, is again very like his Master's teaching: 'He that believeth not is condemned already.' The meaning of the sentence is, that so long as a man is not a believer in Christ, the just wrath of God hangs over him, and he is under the curse of God's broken law. We are all by nature born in sin, and children of wrath; and our sins are all upon us, unpardoned, unforgiven, and untaken away, until that day when we believe on the Son of God, and are made children of grace.

The sentence is a very instructive one, and especially so in the present day. I see in it an unanswerable reply to some grievous errors which are very prevalent in some quarters.

a. It condemns the notion, upheld by some, that under the gospel there is no more anger in God, and that he is only love, mercy, and compassion, and nothing else. Here we are plainly told of 'the wrath of God.' It is clear that God hates sin. There is a hell. God can be angry. Sinners ought to be afraid.

b. It condemns the notion, maintained by some, that the elect are justified from all eternity, or justified before they believe. Here we are plainly told that if a man believe not on the Son, God's wrath abideth on him. We know nothing of anyone's justification until he believes. Those whom God predestinates, God calls and justifies in due season. But there is no justification until there is faith.

c. It condemns the modern idea, that Christ by his death justified all mankind, and removed God's wrath from the whole seed of Adam; and that all men and women are justified in reality, though they do not know it, and will all finally be saved. This idea sounds very amiable, but is flatly contrary to the text before us. Here we are plainly told, that until a man 'believeth on the Son of God, the wrath of God abideth on him.'

d. Finally, it condemns the weak and false charity of those who say that preachers of the gospel should never speak of God's wrath, and should never mention hell. Here we find that the last words of one of Christ's best servants, consist of a solemn declaration of the danger of unbelief. 'The wrath of God' is John's last thought. To warn men of God's wrath, and of their danger of hell, is not harshness, but true charity. Many will go to hell, because their ministers never told them about hell.

In leaving the passage, the variety of expressions used by John the Baptist concerning our Lord Jesus Christ, is very worthy of notice. He calls him the Christ,—the Bridegroom,—him that cometh from above,—him that testifieth what he hath seen and heard,—him whom God hath sent,—him who has the Spirit without measure,—him whom the Father loves,—him into whose hands all things are given,—him in whom to believe is everlasting life. To talk of John the Baptist's knowledge of divine things as meagre and scanty, in the face of such a passage as this, is, to say the least, not wise, and argues a very slight acquaintance with Scripture. To suppose, as some do, that the man who had such clear views of our Lord's nature and office, could afterwards doubt whether Jesus was the Christ, is to suppose what is grossly improbable. The message that John sent to Jesus when he was in prison, was for the sake of his disciples, and not for his own satisfaction (*Matt.* 11:3, etc).

JOHN 4:1-6

1 When therefore the Lord knew how the Pharisees had heard that Jesus made and baptized more disciples than John,

2 (Though Jesus himself baptized not, but his disciples,)

3 He left Judæa, and departed again into Galilee.

4 And he must needs go through Samaria.

5 Then cometh he to a city of Samaria, which is called Sychar, near to the parcel of ground that Jacob gave to his son Joseph.

6 Now Jacob's well was there. Jesus therefore, being wearied with *his* journey, sat thus on the well: *and* it was about the sixth hour.

THERE are two sayings in these verses which deserve particular notice. They throw light on two subjects in religion, on which clear and well-defined opinions are of great importance.

We should observe, for one thing, *what is said about baptism*. We read that 'Jesus himself baptized not, but his disciples.'

The expression here used is a very remarkable one. In reading it we seem irresistibly led to one instructive conclusion. That conclusion is, that baptism is not the principal part of Christianity, and that to baptize is not the principal work for which Christian ministers are ordained. Frequently we read of our Lord preaching and praying. Once we read of his administering the Lord's supper. But we have not a single instance recorded of his ever baptizing anyone. And here we are distinctly told that it was a subordinate work, which he left to others. Jesus 'himself baptized not, but his disciples.'

The lesson is one of peculiar importance in the present day. Baptism, as a sacrament ordained by Christ himself, is an honourable ordinance, and ought never to be lightly esteemed in the churches. It cannot be neglected or despised without great sin. When rightly used, with faith and prayer, it is calculated to convey the highest blessings. But baptism was never meant to be exalted to the position which many nowadays assign to it in religion. It does not act as a charm. It does not necessarily convey the grace of the Holy Ghost. The benefit of it depends greatly on the manner in which it is used. The doctrine taught, and the language employed about it in some quarters, are utterly inconsistent with the fact announced in the text. If baptism was all that some say it is, we should never have been told that 'Jesus himself baptized not.'

Let it be a settled principle in our minds that the first and chief business of the church of Christ is to preach the gospel. The words of St Paul ought to be constantly remembered: 'Christ sent me not to baptize, but to preach the gospel' (*1 Cor.* 1:17). When the gospel of Christ is faithfully and fully preached we need not fear that the sacraments will be undervalued. Baptism and the Lord's supper will always be most truly reverenced in those churches where the truth as it is in Jesus is most fully taught and known.

We should observe, for another thing, in this passage, *what is said about our Lord's human nature*. We read that Jesus was 'wearied with his journey.'

We learn from this, as well as many other expressions in the Gospels, that our Lord had a body exactly like our own. When 'the Word became flesh,' he took on him a nature like our own in all things, sin only excepted. Like ourselves, he grew from infancy to youth, and from youth to man's estate. Like ourselves, he hungered, thirsted, felt pain, and needed sleep. He was liable to every sinless infirmity to which we are liable. In all things his body was framed like our own.

The truth before us is full of comfort for all who are true Christians. He to whom sinners are bid to come for pardon and peace, is one who is man as well as God. He had a real human nature when he was upon earth. He took a real human nature with him, when he ascended up into heaven. We have at the right hand of God a High Priest who can be touched with the feeling of our infirmities, because he has suffered himself being tempted. When we cry to him in the hour of bodily pain and weakness, he knows well what we mean. When our prayers and praises are feeble through bodily weariness, he can understand our condition. He knows our frame. He has learned by experience what it is to be a man. To say that the Virgin Mary, or anyone else, can feel more sympathy for us than Christ, is ignorance no less than blasphemy. The man Christ Jesus can enter fully into everything that belongs to man's condition. The poor, the sick, and the suffering, have in heaven One who is not only an almighty Saviour, but a most feeling Friend.

The servant of Christ should grasp firmly this great truth, that there are two perfect and complete natures in the one person whom he serves. The Lord Jesus, in whom the gospel bids us believe, is, without doubt, almighty God,—equal to the Father in all things, and able to save to the uttermost all those that come unto God by him. But that same Jesus is no less certainly perfect man,—able to sympathize with man in all his bodily sufferings, and acquainted by experience with all that man's body has to endure. Power and sympathy are marvellously combined in him who died for us on the cross. Because he is God, we may repose the weight of our souls upon him with unhesitating confidence. He is mighty to save.— Because he is man, we may speak to him with freedom, about the many trials to which flesh is heir. He knows the heart of a man.— Here is rest for the weary! Here is good news! Our Redeemer is man as well as God, and God as well as man. He that believeth on him, has everything that a child of Adam can possibly require, either for safety or for peace.

Notes—John 4:1-6

1.—[*When therefore the Lord knew, etc.*] The connection between this chapter and the last, will be found at verse 25 of the last chapter. The controversy between John's disciples and the Jews was the means of calling public attention to our Lord's ministry. It became a subject of common conversation, and attracted the notice of the principal religious teachers of the Jews: viz., the Pharisees. They had been already disturbed by the ministry of John the Baptist, and the crowds which attended it (*John* 1:19-28). The deputation which they sent to John had been distinctly told by him that One greater than himself was about to appear. When therefore 'the Pharisees heard' that Jesus was actually baptizing more disciples, and attracting more attention than John, we can well imagine that their minds would be even more disturbed than before. A vague, uncomfortable feeling would arise in their hearts, that this mysterious person, who had cast out of the temple the buyers and sellers in so miraculous a manner, and was now baptizing so many disciples, might possibly be the Christ. And then would come the attendant feeling, that if this was the Christ, he was not the Christ they either expected or wanted.

The result of both feelings would probably be a bitter enmity against our Lord, and a secret determination, if possible, to settle all doubts by putting him to death.

In what manner our Lord 'knew' what the Pharisees had heard, we need not be careful to inquire. Possibly he knew it from information obtained by his disciples. We can hardly doubt that some of them kept up intercourse with their old master, John the Baptist, and so learned what was going on at Ænon.—It is more probable that he knew it from his omniscience as God. We are frequently told that 'he knew the thoughts' of his enemies, and acted and spoke accordingly. It is good for us all to remember that nothing is spoken, talked of, or reported among men, however secretly, which Christ does not know.

2.—[*Though Jesus himself baptized not, etc.*] The fact that our Lord did not actually administer baptism with his own hands, is only mentioned here in the Gospels, and is noteworthy. It shows, at any rate, that what is done by Christ's ministers, at Christ's command, in the administration of ordinances, is regarded as done by Christ himself. The preceding verse says, that 'Jesus baptized,' while the present one says, that he 'baptized not.' Lightfoot remarks,

'It is ordinary, both in Scripture phrase and in other language, to speak of a thing as done by a man himself, which is done by another at his appointment. So Pharaoh's daughter is said to "nurse Moses," and Solomon is said to "build the temple and his own house." So David "took Saul's spear and cruse," meaning Abishai by David's appointment' (*1 Sam.* 26:12).

The reasons assigned for our Lord's not administering baptism with his own hands, are various. Lightfoot mentions four. '1. Because he was not sent so much to baptize as to preach. 2. Because it might have been taken as a thing somewhat improper for Christ to baptize in his own name. 3. Because the baptizing that was most proper for Christ to use, was not with water, but with the Holy Ghost. 4. Because he would prevent all quarrels and disputes among men about their baptism, which might have arisen if some had been baptized by Christ, and others only by his disciples.'

To these reasons we may add another of considerable importance. Our Lord would show us that the effect and benefit of baptism do not depend on the person who administers it. We cannot doubt that Judas Iscariot baptized some. The intention of the minister does not affect the validity of the sacrament.

One thing seems abundantly clear, and that is, that baptism is not an ordinance of primary, but of subordinate importance in Christianity. The high-flown and extravagant language used by some divines about the sacrament of baptism and its effects, is quite irreconcilable with the text before us, as well as with the general teaching of Scripture (see *Acts* 10:48; *1 Cor.* 1:17).

3.—[*He left Judæa, etc.*] The context of the preceding verses seems to show that this movement was intended to avoid the designs of the Pharisees against our Lord. If he had remained in Judæa, he would have been cut off, and put to death before the appointed time. He therefore withdrew into the province of Galilee, where he was further off from Jerusalem, and where his ministry would attract less public notice.

Our Lord's conduct on this occasion shows us that it is not obligatory on a Christian to await danger to life and person, when he sees it coming, and that it is not cowardice to use all reasonable means to avoid it. We are not to court martyrdom, or needlessly to throw our lives away. There is a time for all things,—a time to live and work, as well as a time to suffer and to die. Whether some of the primitive martyrs would have acted as our Lord did here may be questioned. Their zeal for martyrdom seems sometimes to have partaken of the character of fanaticism.

4.—[*He must needs go through Samaria.*] Many pious and profitable remarks have been made on this expression. It has been thought to teach that our Lord went purposely, and out of the regular road, in order to save the soul of the Samaritan woman. It admits of grave question whether this opinion is well founded.—There was no other way by which a person could conveniently go from Judæa to Galilee, excepting through Samaria.—The expression, therefore, is probably nothing more than a natural introduction to the story of the Samaritan woman. The first in the train of circumstances which led to her conversion, was the circumstance that Jesus was obliged to pass through Samaria, on his journey towards Galilee. This accounted for his meeting with a Samaritan woman.

5.—[*Then cometh ... city ... called Sychar.*] The common opinion is that the city here spoken of is the same as Sichem or Shechem (*Gen.* 33:18, 19). Few places in Palestine, after Jerusalem, have had so much of Bible history connected with them. Here God first appeared to Abraham (*Gen.* 12:6, 7). Here Jacob dwelt when he first returned from Padan-aram, and here the disgraceful history of Dinah, and the consequent murder of the Shechemites took place (*Gen.* 34:2, etc.). Here Joseph's brethren fed their flocks when Jacob sent him to them, little thinking he would not see him again for many years (*Gen.* 37:12). Here, when Israel took possession of the land of Canaan, was one of the cities of refuge (*Josh.* 20:7, 8). Here Joshua gathered all the tribes, when he addressed them for the last time (*Josh.* 24:1). Here the bones of Joseph were buried, and all the patriarchs were interred (*Josh.* 24:32; *Acts* 7:16). Here the principal events in the history of Abimelech took place (*Judg.* 9:1, etc). Here Rehoboam met the tribes of Israel after Solomon's death, and gave the answer which rent his kingdom in two (*1 Kings* 12:1). Here Jeroboam first dwelt, when he was made King of Israel (*1 Kings* 12:25). And finally, close by Shechem was the city of Samaria itself, and the two hills of Ebal and Gerizim, where the solemn blessings and cursings were recited, after Israel entered Canaan (*Josh.* 8:33). A more interesting neighbourhood it is difficult to imagine. Whichever way the eye of a wearied traveller looked, he would see something to remind him of Israel's history.

It is only fair to say that one of the latest travellers in Palestine (Dr Thomson, author of *The Land and the Book*) doubts whether Sychar and Shechem really were the same place. He grounds his doubt on the fact that the well now called Jacob's well is two miles from the ruins of Shechem, and that close to these ruins are beautiful fountains of water. He thinks it highly improbable that a woman of Shechem would go two miles to draw water, if she could find it close by. He therefore thinks it more likely that a place now called Aschar, which is close to Jacob's well, must be the ancient Sychar, and that Sychar and Shechem were two different places.

The subject is one on which it is impossible to attain a conclusive decision. Whether the ruins now called the ruins of Shechem are really on the site of ancient Shechem,—whether the well now called Jacob's well is really the well spoken of in this chapter,—whether ancient Shechem may not have been nearer the well than it now appears,—are all points on which, after eighteen hundred years have passed away, it is impossible to speak positively. It ought however to be remembered, that the opinion of most competent judges is almost entirely against Dr Thomson's theory. Moreover, it is worth noticing that the Samaritan woman's words, 'neither come hither to draw,' seem to imply that she had to come some distance to Jacob's well when she drew water.

[*Near ... parcel of ground ... Jacob ... Joseph.*] The ground here spoken of

seems to consist of two parts. One part was bought by Jacob of Hamor, Shechem's father, for a hundred pieces of silver (*Gen.* 33:19). The other seems to have been his by conquest, when his sons slew the Shechemites for dishonouring Dinah (*Gen.* 34:28 and 48:22).

Let it be carefully noted that St John here speaks of Jacob and Joseph and the events of their lives, as if the history contained in Genesis was all simple matter of fact. It is always so in the New Testament. The modern theory, that the histories of the Old Testament are only fables, destitute of any foundation in fact, is a mere baseless invention, without a single respectable argument to be adduced in its favour.

6.—[*Jacob's well.*] It is not known how or when this well received its name. In Genesis we find mention of Abraham and Isaac digging wells, but not of Jacob doing so. All we know about it is what we read in the chapter before us.

A well called Jacob's well is still shown to all travellers in Palestine, near the ruins of Shechem, and is commonly supposed to be one of the oldest and most genuine remains of ancient times in the Holy Land. In fact there seems no reason for disputing the common belief, that it is the very identical well at which our Lord sat and held the conversation recorded in this chapter. It is in good preservation, and about thirty yards deep.

[*Wearied with his journey.*] This expression deserves notice. It shows the reality of our Lord's human nature. He had a body like our own, subject to all the conditions of flesh and blood.—It shows our Lord's infinite compassion, humility, and condescension, when he became flesh, and came on earth to live and die for our sins. Though he was rich he became poor. He who had made the world, and whose were 'the cattle on a thousand hills,' was content to be a weary traveller on foot, in order to provide eternal redemption for us. We never read of Jesus travelling in a carriage, and only once of his riding on a beast.—It supplies the poor with the strongest argument for contentment. If Christ was willing to be poor, we may surely be willing to submit to poverty. Men need not be ashamed

138

of poverty, if they have not brought it on themselves by misconduct. It is disgraceful to be profligate and immoral. But it is no sin to be poor.—Finally, it shows believers what a sympathizing Saviour Christ is. He knows what it is to have a weak and weary body. He can be touched with the feeling of our infirmities. When our work wearies us, though we are not weary of our work, we may confidently tell Jesus, and ask him for help. He knows the heart of a weary man.

[*Sat thus on the well.*] The general meaning of these words is, that our Lord sat down on the stones, which, according to Eastern custom, formed a wall or battlement round the mouth of the well. The particular meaning of the word 'thus' in the sentence, is a point that has perplexed commentators in every age, and will perhaps never be settled.

Some think, as De Dieu, A. Clarke, and Schleusner, that 'thus' is a pleonasm, or elegant expletive and redundancy in the Greek original, and that although a Greek would see a meaning in it, as giving a finish to the sentence, it has no special meaning that can be attached to it in the English translation.

Some think, as Chrysostom, Theophylact, Euthymius, Musculus, Bengel, Glassius, and Wordsworth, that 'thus' means 'just as he was,' without any regular seat, without looking for any convenient position, without any pride or formality; not upon a throne, not upon a cushion, but simply upon the ground.

Some think, as Doddridge, that 'thus' means immediately, and find a parallel for it in Acts 20:11.

Some think, as Calvin, Lightfoot, Dyke, Bullinger, Beza, Parkhurst, Stier, Alford, and Burgon, that 'thus' refers to the weariness just mentioned. Jesus, being wearied, sat down on the well accordingly, after the manner and according to the fashion that any weary person would sit. He was weary, and *so* he sat on the well.

The question is one that I feel unable to settle. The last meaning seems to me, on the whole, the most probable one, though it fails to carry complete conviction with it. The use of the word 'so,' in Acts 7:8, is somewhat like it. The Greek word for 'so' in that case is the same as the one here rendered 'thus.'

Burgon remarks on this sentence, 'that Jacob and Moses each found his future wife beside a well of water; and here it is seen that One greater than they, their divine Antitype, the Bridegroom takes to himself his alien spouse, the Samaritan church, at a well likewise.'

Quesnel remarks, 'The rest of Jesus Christ is as mysterious and full of kindness and beneficence as his weariness.—It is a great matter for a man to learn how to rest himself without being idle, and to make his necessary repose subservient to the glory of God.'

[*It was about the sixth hour.*] What time of the day was this, according to our calculation of time?—By far the most common opinion is, that the sixth hour here means twelve o'clock, the hottest and sultriest time of the day. It is notorious that the Jewish day began at six o'clock in the evening. Our seven o'clock was their one o'clock, and their sixth hour would be our twelve o'clock.

It is however only just and right to say, that some commentators, as Wordsworth and Burgon, maintain strongly that in St John's Gospel the Jewish mode of reckoning the hours of the day is not observed. They say that, writing later than the other Evangelists, and in Asia Minor, St John uses the Roman or Asiatic mode of reckoning time, and that the Roman mode was like our own. They say therefore, that when the disciples followed Jesus (*John* 1:39) at the tenth hour, it was ten o'clock in the morning; and when the fever left the ruler's son at the seventh hour, it was seven o'clock in the evening (*John* 4:52). They say that when Pilate brought forth Jesus to the Jews, on the day of the crucifixion, at the sixth hour (*John* 19:14), it was six o'clock in the morning. And finally, they say that when Jesus, in the passage before us, sat wearied on the well at the sixth hour, it means six o'clock in the evening. Moreover, they plead in support of their view, that it is infinitely more likely that a woman would come to a well to draw water at six o'clock in the evening than at twelve o'clock in the day. In Genesis it is distinctly said that the 'evening' is the 'time that women go out to draw water' (*Gen.* 24:11).

These arguments are undoubtedly weighty and ingenious, and the matter is one that admits of doubt. Nevertheless, for several reasons, I am disposed to think that the common view of the question is the correct one, and that the sixth hour in this place means twelve o'clock in the day. I purposely omit the consideration of the other places where St John mentions hours in his Gospel. None of them seem to me to present any difficulty, except the 'sixth hour,' in St John's account of the crucifixion. That difficulty I shall be prepared to examine in its proper place. I think then that the 'sixth hour' in the text before us, means twelve o'clock, for the following reasons.

a. It seems exceedingly improbable that St John would reckon time in a manner different to the other three Gospel writers.

b. It is by no means clear that the Romans did reckon time in our way, and not in the Jewish way. When the Roman poet Horace describes himself as lying late in bed in a morning, he says, 'I lie till the fourth hour.' He must surely mean ten o'clock, and not four in the afternoon.—When the Roman poet Martial describes the Roman day, he says, 'The first and second hours are employed by clients in attending levees, and the third hour exercises the advocates in the law-courts.'—He surely cannot mean that Roman law-courts did not open till two o'clock in the afternoon. About the custom of the Asiatics I offer no opinion. It is a doubtful point.

c. It is entirely a gratuitous assumption to say that no woman ever came to draw water except in the evening. There must surely be exceptions to every rule. The fact of the woman coming *alone*, seems of itself to indicate that she came at an unusual hour, and not in the evening.

d. Last, but not least, it seems far more probable that our Lord would hold a conversation alone with such a person as the Samaritan woman at twelve o'clock in the day, than at six o'clock in the evening. The conversation was not a very short one. There is little or no twilight in Eastern countries. The night soon comes on. And yet, on the theory I oppose, our Lord begins a conversation about six o'clock, and carries it on till the woman is converted. Then the woman goes away to the city, and tells the men what has happened, and they all come out to the well to see Jesus. Yet by this time, in all reasonable probability, it would be quite dark, and the night would have begun. And yet, after all this, our Lord says to the disciples, 'Lift up your eyes, and look on the fields' (4:35).

This last reason weighs very heavily in my mind, in forming a conclusion on the subject. Our Lord appears to me to have reached a resting-place for the middle of the day, according to the Eastern custom in travelling, and to have intended staying by the well for a short time, till the heat of the day was past. The arrival of the Samaritan woman at this hour of the day gave ample time for the conversation, for her rapid return to the city, and for the coming of the inhabitants to the well.

I must say that I see a peculiar beauty and fitness in the mention of the sixth hour, if it means twelve o'clock, which I should not see so strongly if it meant six in the evening. To my eyes there is a special seemliness and propriety in the fact that our Lord held his conversation with such a person as this Samaritan woman at noonday. When he talked to Nicodemus, in the preceding chapter, we are told that it was at night. But when he talked to a woman of impure life, we are carefully told that it was twelve o'clock in the day. I see in this fact a beautiful carefulness to avoid even the appearance of evil, which I should entirely miss if the sixth hour meant six o'clock in the evening. I see even more than this. I see a lesson to all ministers and teachers of the gospel about the right mode of carrying on the work of trying to do good to souls like that of the Samaritan woman. Like their Master, they must be careful about times and hours, and specially if they work alone. If a man will try to do good to a person like the Samaritan woman, alone and without witnesses, let him take heed that he walks in his Master's footsteps, both as to the time of his proceedings as well as to the message he delivers. I believe there was a deep meaning in the little sentence, 'It was about the sixth hour.'

Augustine thinks that 'the sixth hour' here was meant to represent, allegorically, the sixth age of the world. He says that the first hour was from Adam to Noah, the second from Noah to Abraham, the third from Abraham to David, the fourth from David to the Babylonian captivity, the fifth from the captivity to the baptism of John, and the sixth the time of the Lord Jesus. I can see no foundation for these things in the text. If such interpretations of Scripture are correct, it is easy to make the Bible mean anything.

JOHN 4:7-26

7 There cometh a woman of Samaria to draw water: Jesus saith unto her, Give me to drink.

8 (For his disciples were gone away unto the city to buy meat.)

9 Then saith the woman of Samaria unto him, How is it that thou, being a Jew, askest drink of me, which am a woman of Samaria? for the Jews have no dealings with the Samaritans.

10 Jesus answered and said unto her, If thou knewest the gift of God, and who it is that saith to thee, Give me to drink; thou wouldest have asked of him, and he would have given thee living water.

11 The woman saith unto him, Sir, thou hast nothing to draw with, and the well is deep: from whence then hast thou that living water?

12 Art thou greater than our father Jacob, which gave us the well, and drank thereof himself, and his children, and his cattle?

13 Jesus answered and said unto her, Whosoever drinketh of this water shall thirst again:

14 But whosoever drinketh of the water that I shall give him shall never thirst; but the water that I shall give him shall be in him a well of water springing up into everlasting life.

15 The woman saith unto him, Sir, give me this water, that I thirst not, neither come hither to draw.

16 Jesus saith unto her, Go, call thy husband, and come hither.

17 The woman answered and said, I have no husband. Jesus said unto her, Thou hast well said, I have no husband:

18 For thou hast had five husbands; and he whom thou now hast is not thy husband: in that saidst thou truly.

19 The woman saith unto him, Sir, I perceive that thou art a prophet.

20 Our fathers worshipped in this mountain; and ye say, that in Jerusalem is the place where men ought to worship.

21 Jesus saith unto her, Woman, believe me, the hour cometh, when ye shall neither in this mountain, nor yet at Jerusalem, worship the Father.

22 Ye worship ye know not what: we know what we worship: for salvation is of the Jews.

23 But the hour cometh, and now is, when the true worshippers shall worship the Father in spirit and in truth: for the Father seeketh such to worship him.

24 God is a Spirit: and they that worship him must worship him in spirit and in truth.

25 The woman saith unto him, I know that Messias cometh, which is called Christ: when he is come, he will tell us all things.

26 Jesus saith unto her, I that speak unto thee am he.

THE history of the Samaritan woman, contained in these verses, is one of the most interesting and instructive passages in St John's Gospel. St John has shown us, in the case of Nicodemus, how our Lord dealt with a self-righteous formalist. He now shows us how our Lord dealt with an ignorant, carnal-minded woman, whose moral character was more than ordinarily bad. There are lessons in the passage for ministers and teachers, which they would do well to ponder.

We should mark, firstly, *the mingled tact and condescension of Christ in dealing with a careless sinner.*

Our Lord was sitting by Jacob's well, when a woman of Samaria came thither to draw water. At once he says to her, 'Give me to drink.' He does not wait for her to speak to him. He does not begin by reproving her sins, though he doubtless knew them. He opens communication by asking a favour. He approaches the woman's mind by the subject of 'water,' which was naturally uppermost in her thoughts. Simple as this request may seem, it opened a door to spiritual conversation. It threw a bridge across the gulf which lay between her and him. It led to the conversion of her soul.

Our Lord's conduct in this place should be carefully remembered by all who want to do good to the thoughtless and spiritually ignorant. It is vain to expect that such persons will voluntarily come to us, and begin to seek knowledge. We must begin with them, and go down to them in the spirit of courteous and friendly aggression. It is vain to expect that such persons will be prepared for our instruction, and will at once see and acknowledge the wisdom of all we are doing. We must go to work wisely. We must study the best avenues to their hearts, and the most likely ways of arresting their attention. There is a handle to every mind, and our chief aim must be to get hold of it. Above all, we must be kind in manner, and beware of showing that we feel conscious of our own superiority. If we let ignorant people fancy that we think we are doing them a great favour in talking to them about religion, there is little hope of doing good to their souls.

We should mark, secondly, *Christ's readiness to give mercies to careless sinners.* He tells the Samaritan woman that if she had asked, 'he would have given her living water.' He knew the character of the person before him perfectly well. Yet he says, 'If she had asked, he would have given,'—he would have given the living water of grace, mercy, and peace.

The infinite willingness of Christ to receive sinners is a golden truth, which ought to be treasured up in our hearts, and diligently impressed on others. The Lord Jesus is far more ready to hear than we are to pray, and far more ready to give favours than we are to ask them. All day long he stretches out his hands to the disobedient and gainsaying. He has thoughts of pity and compassion towards the vilest of sinners, even when they have no thoughts of him. He stands waiting to bestow mercy and grace on the worst and most unworthy, if they will only cry to him. He will never draw back from that well-known promise, 'Ask and ye shall receive: seek and ye shall find.' The lost will discover at the last day, that they had not because they asked not.

We should mark, thirdly, *the priceless excellence of Christ's gifts when compared with the things of this world.* Our Lord tells the Samaritan woman, 'Whosoever drinketh of this water shall thirst again: but whosoever drinketh of the water that I shall give him shall never thirst.'

The truth of the principle here laid down may be seen on every side by all who are not blinded by prejudice or love of the world. Thousands of men have every temporal good thing that heart could wish, and are yet weary and dissatisfied. It is now as it was in David's time: 'There be many that say, Who will show us any good?' (*Psa.* 4:6). Riches, and rank, and place, and power, and learning, and amusements, are utterly unable to fill the soul. He that only drinks of these waters is sure to thirst again. Every Ahab finds a Naboth's vineyard hard by his palace, and every Haman sees a Mordecai at the gate. There is no heart-satisfaction in this world, until we believe on Christ. Jesus alone can fill up the empty places of our inward man. Jesus alone can give solid, lasting, enduring happiness. The peace that he imparts is a fountain, which, once set flowing within the soul, flows on to all eternity. Its waters may have their ebbing seasons; but they are living waters, and they shall never be completely dried.

We should mark, fourthly, *the absolute necessity of conviction of sin before a soul can be converted to God*. The Samaritan woman seems to have been comparatively unmoved until our Lord exposed her breach of the seventh commandment. Those heart-searching words, 'Go, call thy husband,' appear to have pierced her conscience like an arrow. From that moment, however ignorant, she speaks like an earnest, sincere inquirer after truth. And the reason is evident. She felt that her spiritual disease was discovered. For the first time in her life she saw herself.

To bring thoughtless people to this state of mind should be the principal aim of all teachers and ministers of the gospel. They should carefully copy their Master's example in this place. Till men and women are brought to feel their sinfulness and need, no real good is ever done to their souls. Till a sinner sees himself as God sees him, he will continue careless, trifling, and unmoved. By all means we must labour to convince the unconverted man of sin, to prick his conscience, to open his eyes, to show him himself. To this end we must expound the length and breadth of God's holy law. To this end we must denounce every practice contrary to that law, however fashionable and customary. This is the only way to do good. Never does a soul value the gospel medicine until it feels its disease. Never does a man see any beauty in Christ as a Saviour, until he discovers that he is himself a lost and ruined sinner. Ignorance of sin is invariably attended by neglect of Christ.

We should mark, fifthly, *the uselessness of any religion which only consists of formality*. The Samaritan woman, when awakened to spiritual concern, started questions about the comparative merits of the Samaritan and Jewish modes of worshipping God. Our Lord tells her that true and acceptable worship depends not on the place in which it is offered, but on the state of the worshipper's heart. He declares, 'The hour cometh, when ye shall neither in this mountain nor yet at

Jerusalem, worship the Father.' He adds that 'the true worshippers shall worship ... in spirit and in truth.'

The principle contained in these sentences can never be too strongly impressed on professing Christians. We are all naturally inclined to make religion a mere matter of outward forms and ceremonies, and to attach an excessive importance to our own particular manner of worshipping God. We must beware of this spirit, and especially when we first begin to think seriously about our souls. The heart is the principal thing in all our approaches to God. 'The Lord looketh on the heart' (1 Sam. 16:7). The most gorgeous cathedral service is offensive in God's sight, if all is gone through coldly, heartlessly, and without grace. The feeblest gathering of three or four poor believers in a cottage to read the Bible and pray, is a more acceptable sight to him who searches the heart than the fullest congregation which is ever gathered in St Peter's at Rome.

We should mark, lastly, *Christ's gracious willingness to reveal himself to the chief of sinners.* He concludes his conversation with the Samaritan woman by telling her openly and unreservedly that he is the Saviour of the world. 'I that speak to thee,' he says, 'am the Messiah.' Nowhere in all the Gospels do we find our Lord making such a full avowal of his nature and office as he does in this place. And this avowal, be it remembered, was made not to learned scribes, or moral Pharisees, but to one who up to that day had been an ignorant, thoughtless, and immoral person!

Dealings with sinners, such as these, form one of the grand peculiarities of the gospel. Whatever a man's past life may have been, there is hope and a remedy for him in Christ. If he is only willing to hear Christ's voice and follow him, Christ is willing to receive him at once as a friend, and to bestow on him the fullest measure of mercy and grace. The Samaritan woman, the penitent thief, the Philippian jailor, the publican Zacchæus, are all patterns of Christ's readiness to show mercy, and to confer full and immediate pardons. It is his glory that, like a great physician, he will undertake to cure those who are apparently incurable, and that none are too bad for him to love and heal. Let these things sink down into our hearts. Whatever else we doubt, let us never doubt that Christ's love to sinners passeth knowledge, and that Christ is as willing to receive as he is almighty to save.

What are we ourselves? This is the question, after all, which demands our attention. We may have been up to this day careless, thoughtless, sinful as the woman whose story we have been reading. But yet there is hope. He who talked with the Samaritan woman at the well is yet living at God's right hand, and never changes. Let us only ask, and he will 'give us living water.'

Notes—John 4:7-26

7.—[*There cometh a woman ... draw water.*] The scarcity of water in the hot climates of the East makes drawing water from the nearest well an important part of the daily business of an Eastern household. We learn from other parts of Scripture that it was a work ordinarily done by women (*Gen.* 24:11; *1 Sam.* 9:11). A well became naturally a common meeting place for the inhabitants of a neighbourhood, and especially for the young people (*Judg.* 5:11). The insinuation, however, of some writers, as Schoettgen, that the Samaritan woman's motives in coming to the well were possibly immoral, seems destitute of any foundation. Bad as her moral character evidently was, we have no right to heap upon her more blame than is warranted by facts.

Augustine regards this woman as a type of the Gentile church, 'not now justified, but even now at the point to be justified.' I doubt whether we were meant by the Holy Ghost to take this view. There is great danger in adopting such allegorical interpretations. They insensibly draw away the mind from the plain lessons of Scripture.

Musculus remarks what a wonderful instance it is of sovereign grace, that our Lord should turn away from learned scribes, Pharisees, and priests, to converse with and convert such a person as this woman, to all appearance so utterly unworthy of notice. He also observes how singularly our least movements are overruled by God's providence. Like Rebecca and Rachel, the woman came to the well knowing nothing of the importance of that day's visit to her soul.

[*Jesus saith ... Give me to drink.*] In this simple request of our Lord there are four things deserving notice. 1. It was a gracious act of spiritual aggression on a sinner. He did not wait for the woman to speak to him, but was the first to begin conversation. 2. It was an act of marvellous condescension. He by whom all things were made, the Creator of fountains, brooks, and rivers, is not ashamed to ask a draught of water from the hand of one of his sinful creatures. 3. It was an act full of wisdom and prudence. He does not at once force religion on the attention of the woman, and rebuke her for her sins. He begins with a subject apparently indifferent, and yet one of which the woman's mind was doubtless full. He asks her for water. 4. It was an act full of the nicest tact, and exhibiting perfect knowledge of the human mind. He asks a favour, and puts himself under an obligation. No line of proceeding, it is well known to all wise people, would be more likely to conciliate the woman's feelings towards him, and to make her willing to hear his teaching. Simple as the request was, it contains principles which deserve the closest attention of all who desire to do good to ignorant and thoughtless sinners.

The idea of Euthymius, that our Lord *pretended* thirst in order to introduce conversation is unworthy of notice.—Cyril thinks that our Lord intended to make a practical protest against the exclusiveness of the Jews, by asking drink of a Samaritan woman, and to show her that he disapproved the custom of his nation.

8.—[*His disciples ... gone ... buy meat.*] This verse is an instance of our Lord's general rule not to work a miracle in order to supply his own wants. He who could feed five thousand with a few loaves and fishes when he willed, was content to buy food, like any other man.—It is an instance of his lowly-mindedness. The Creator of all things, though rich, for our sakes became poor.—It ought to teach Christians that they are not meant to be so spiritual as to neglect the management of money, and a reasonable use of it for the supply of their wants. God could feed his children, as he fed Elijah, by a daily miracle. But he knows it is better for our souls, and more likely to call grace into exercise, not to feed them so, but to make them think, and use means. There is no real spirituality in being careless about money. Jesus himself allowed his disciples to 'buy.'

The word rendered 'meat' means nothing more than 'food or nourishment,' and must not be confined to 'flesh.' Out of the sixteen places where it is used in the New Testament, there is not one where it necessarily signifies 'flesh.' The meat offering of the Old Testament consisted of nothing but flour, oil, and incense (*Lev.* 2:1, 2). The meaning of the word 'meat,' in the English language, has evidently changed since the last revision of the English Bible.

The whole verse is an instance of one of those short, parenthetical, explanatory comments, which are common in St John's Gospel. Its object is to explain the circumstance of our Lord being alone at the well, and the fact that he did not ask a disciple to give him water.

9.—[*Then saith the woman ... How is it ... a Jew ... Samaria?*] This question implies that the woman was surprised at our Lord speaking to her. It was an unexpected act of condescension on his part, and as such arrested her attention. Thus one point, at any rate, was gained. It is a great matter if we can only get a careless sinner to give us a quiet hearing. We shall soon see how our Lord improved the opportunity.

How the woman knew our Lord to be a Jew, is matter of conjecture. Some think that she knew it by the dialect that he spoke. Some think that she knew it by the fringe upon his dress, which he probably wore in conformity to the Mosaic law (*Num.* 15:38, 39), and which the Samaritans very likely neglected. One thing is very clear. There was nothing in our Lord's personal appearance, when he was a man upon earth, to distinguish him from any other Jewish traveller who might have been found sitting at a well. There was nothing eccentric or peculiar about his dress. He looked like other men.

I venture the opinion that in the woman's question stress should be laid on the word 'woman.' She was not only surprised that a Jewish man asked drink of a Samaritan, but also that he asked it of a woman.

[*The Jews have no dealings with the Samaritans.*] This sentence is generally thought, with much reason, to be the explanatory comment of St John, and not the words of the Samaritan woman. It certainly seems more natural to take it so. The sentence should then be read as a parenthesis. Calvin thinks it is the woman's words, but his reasons are not convincing.

The enmity between the Jews and Samaritans, here referred to, no doubt originated in the separation of the ten tribes under Jeroboam, and the establishment of the kingdom of Israel. It was exceedingly increased after the ten tribes were carried into captivity by the Assyrians, by the fact that the Samaritans became mingled with foreigners, whom the king of Assyria sent to Samaria from Babylon and other places, and so lost their right to be called pure Jews (2 *Kings* 17:1, etc.). It was further aggravated by the opposition which the inhabitants of Samaria made to the rebuilding of Jerusalem, after the return from the captivity of Babylon, in the days of Ezra

(*Ezra* 4:10 etc.). In the days of our Lord the Jews seem to have gone into the extreme of regarding the Samaritans as entirely foreigners, and aliens from the common-wealth of Israel. When they told our Lord that he was 'a Samaritan,' and had 'a devil,' they meant the expression to convey the bitterest scorn and reproach (*John* 8:48). It is clear, however, from the conversation in this chapter, that the Samaritans, however mistaken on many points, were not ignorant heathens. They regarded themselves as descended from Jacob. They had a kind of Old Testament religion. They expected the coming Messias.

The bitter and exclusive spirit of the Jews towards all other nations, referred to in this verse, is curiously confirmed by the language used about the Jews by heathen writers at Rome. Exclusiveness was noted as one among their peculiarities.—The immense difficulty with which even the apostles got over this exclusive feeling, and went forth to preach to the Gentiles, is noticeable both in the Acts and the Epistles (*Acts* 10:28; 11:2, 3; *Gal.* 2:12; *1 Thess.* 2:16).

The utter absence of real charity and love among men in the days when our Lord was upon earth, ought not to be overlooked. Well would it be if men had never quarrelled about religion after he left the world! Quarrels among the crew of a sinking ship are not more hideous, unseemly, and irrational than the majority of quarrels among professors of religion. A historian might truly apply St John's words to many a period in church history, and say, 'The Romanists have no dealings with the Protestants,' or 'the Lutherans have no dealings with the Calvinists,' or 'the Calvinists have no dealings with the Arminians,' or 'the Episcopalians have no dealings with the Presbyterians,' or 'the Baptists have no dealings with those who baptize infants,' or 'the Plymouth Brethren have no dealings with anybody who does not join their company.' These things ought not so to be. They are the scandal of Christianity, the joy of the devil, and the greatest stumbling-block to the spread of the gospel.

The Greek words translated 'have no dealings,' mean literally 'use not anything together with' the Samaritans. Pearce says 'The Jews would not eat or drink with the Samaritans, would not drink out of the same cup, or eat of the same dish with them.' This fact throws much light on the woman's surprise at our Lord's request: 'Give me to drink.'

10.—[*Jesus answered, etc.*] In this verse our Lord proceeds to use the opportunity which the woman's question affords him. He passes over for the present her expression of surprise at a Jew speaking to a Samaritan. He begins by exciting her curiosity and raising her expectations, by speaking of something within her reach which he calls 'living water.' The first step to take with a careless sinner after his attention has been arrested, is to produce on his mind the impression that we can tell him of something to his advantage within his reach. There is a certain vagueness in our Lord's words which exhibits his consummate wisdom. A systematic statement of doctrinal truth would have been thrown away at this stage of the woman's feeling. The general and figurative language which our Lord employed, was exactly calculated to arouse her imagination, and to lead her on to further inquiry.

[*The gift of God.*] This expression is variously explained. Some think, as Augustine, Rupertus, Jansenius, Whitby, and Alford, that it means 'the Holy Spirit,'—that peculiar gift which it was the Messiah's special office to impart to men in greater abundance than it had before been imparted (*Acts* 2:38; 10:45).

Some think, as Brentius, Bucer, Musculus, Calovius, Grotius, and Barradius, that it means 'the gracious opportunity which God is graciously giving to thee.' If thou didst but know what a door of life is close to thee, thou wouldst joyfully use it.

Some think, as Euthymius, Toletus, Bullinger, Gualter, Hooker, Beza, Rollock, Lightfoot, Glassius, Dyke, Hildersam, and Gill, that it means 'Christ himself,'—God's gracious gift to a sinful world. If thou didst but know that God has actually given his only begotten Son, according to promise, and that he has come into the world, and that it is he who is speaking to thee, thou wouldst at once ask of him living water.

Some think that it means 'God's gifts, and especially his gift of grace,' which is now being proclaimed and made manifest to the world by the appearing on earth of his Son (see *Rom.* 5:15). This seems to be the view of Cyril, Lampe, Theophylact, Zwingle, and Calvin.

Of these four views the last seems to me, on the whole, the most probable and satisfactory. The first sounds strange and unlike the usual teaching of Scripture. 'If thou knewest the Holy Spirit, thou wouldst have asked,' is an expression we can hardly expect at this period of our Lord's ministry, when the mission of the Comforter had not yet been explained.—The second view seems hardly more natural than the first.—The third view is undoubtedly recommended by the fact that Christ is frequently spoken of as God's great gift to the world. If the woman had really known anything aright about Messiah, and had known that he was before her, she would have asked of him living water. Nevertheless, it is a strong objection to this view that it makes our Lord apparently say the same thing twice over. 'If thou knewest Christ, and that it is Christ who speaks.'

The last view makes the first clause *general*: 'If thou knewest the grace of God;' and the second *particular*: 'If thou also knewest that the Saviour himself is with thee.' Thus both clauses receive a meaning.

[*Living water.*] The meaning of this expression, like 'the gift of God,' is variously explained. Some, as Calovius and Chemnitius, seem to think it means the doctrine of God's mercy, pardon, cleansing, and justification. Others, as Chrysostom, Augustine, Cyril, Theophylact, Calvin, Beza, Gualter, Musculus, and Ferus, think it means the Holy Spirit, renewing, and sanctification.

I doubt whether either view is quite correct. I am inclined, with Bullinger and Rollock, to regard the expression as a general figurative description of everything which it is Christ's office to bestow on the soul of man,—pardon, peace, mercy, grace, justification, and sanctification. As water is cleansing, purifying, cooling, refreshing, thirst-satisfying to man's body, so are Christ's gifts to the soul. I think everything that a sinful soul needs is purposely included under the general words, 'living water.' It comprises not only the justifying 'blood which cleanses from all sin,' but the sanctifying grace of the Spirit, by which we 'cleanse ourselves from all filthiness,'—not only the inward peace which is the result of pardon, but the sense of inward comfort, which is the companion of renewal of heart.

The idea of 'water,' we should remember, is specially brought forward in some of the Old Testament promises of good things to come (see *Isa.* 12:3; 44:3; *Ezek.* 47:1, etc; *Zech.* 13:1; 14:8). A sprinkling of clean water was particularly mentioned as one of the things Messiah was to give (*Isa.* 52:15; *Ezek.* 36:25). To an intelligent reader of the Old Testament the mention of 'living water' would at once raise up the idea of Messiah's times.

The word 'living,' applied here to water, must not be pressed too far. It does not necessarily mean anything more than fresh, running waters. Thus it is said that Isaac's servants found a well of living waters (*Gen.* 26:19. See also *Num.* 19:17; *Song of Sol.* 4:15). There was undoubtedly a deep meaning in our Lord's words, and a tacit reference to the verse in Jeremiah, where God speaks of himself as 'the fountain of living waters' (*Jer.* 2:13). Nevertheless, the first idea that the words would convey to the woman's mind, would probably be no more than this, that he who sat before her had better, fresher, and more valuable water than that of the well. The fact is that our Lord purposely used a figurative, general expression, in order to lead the woman's mind gently on. If he had said, 'He would have given thee grace and mercy,' she would have been unprepared for such purely doctrinal language, and it would have called forth prejudice and dislike.

There is a vast quantity of deep truth contained in this verse. It is rich in first principles, linked together in a most instructive chain. 1. Christ has living water to give to men. 2. If men would only ask, Christ would at once give. 3. Men do not ask because they are ignorant.—The verse condemns all who die unpardoned. They have not because they ask not: they ask not because they are blind to their condition. To remove this blindness and ignorance must be the first object we should aim at in dealing with a thoughtless, unconverted man.

The notion of Ambrose, Cyprian, and Rupertus, that 'living water' here means baptism, is too monstrous to require refutation. It is only a sample of the preposterous views of some of the Fathers and their followers about the sacraments.

Bengel remarks on this verse our Lord's readiness to draw lessons of spiritual instruction from every object near him. To the Jews desiring bread, he spoke of the bread of life (*John* 6:33). To the people at Jerusalem at break of day, he speaks of the light of the world, referring probably to the rising sun (*John* 8:2, 12). To the woman coming to draw water, he speaks of living water.

11.—[*The woman saith, etc.*] The words of the woman, in this and the following verse, imply surprise, curiosity, and perhaps a slight sneer. At any rate they show that her attention was arrested. A strange Jew at a well suddenly speaks to her about 'living water.' What could he mean? Was he in earnest or not? With a woman's curiosity she desires to know.

[*Sir.*] The Greek word so rendered is generally translated 'Lord.' This leads some, as Chrysostom, to think, that the woman's heart was so far impressed with the woman that she purposely used a term of respect and reverence. We must not, however, lay too much stress on the word. It is certainly translated 'Sir,' in other places, where inferiors speak to superiors (*Matt.* 13:27; 21:30; 27:63; *John* 4:49; 5:7; 12:21; 20:15; *Rev.* 7:14). Yet it is difficult to see what other word the woman could have used in addressing a strange man, without rudeness and discourtesy.

[*Nothing to draw with.*] The Greek expression here is simply a substantive, meaning 'an instrument for drawing water.' What it was we are left to conjecture. Schleusner suggests from Nonnus that it must mean a cup fastened to a rope.

[*The well is deep.*] These words, according to the universal testimony of travellers

at this day, are still literally true. The well is at least thirty yards deep, and to a person not provided with a rope, as the woman doubtless saw was our Lord's case, the water would be inaccessible.

[*Whence then ... that living water?*] The Greek word here rendered 'that' is simply the article commonly translated 'the.' It is like 'that prophet' (*John* 1:21).

The ignorance of the woman in thinking of nothing but material water, naturally strikes us. Yet it is nothing more than we see in many other instances in the Gospels. Nicodemus could not see any but a carnal meaning in the new birth; the disciples could not understand our Lord's having 'meat to eat,' unless it was literal meat; the Jews thought the 'bread from heaven' was literal bread (*John* 3:4; 4:33; 6:34). The natural heart of man always tries to put a carnal and material sense on spiritual expressions. Hence have arisen the greatest errors about the sacraments.

12.—[*Art thou greater?*] This question exhibits the woman's curiosity to know who the stranger before her could be. Who art thou that speakest of living water? It also savours of a sneer and incredulity. Dost thou mean to say that thou canst give me better and more abundant supplies of water, than a well which the patriarch Jacob found sufficient for himself and all his numerous company? Dost thou pretend to know of a better well? Art thou, a poor weary traveller in appearance, so great a person that thou dost possess a better well than Jacob possessed?

[*Our father Jacob ... gave us the well.*] Let it be noted that the woman carefully claimed relationship with Jacob, and called him 'our father,' though, after all the intermixture of the Samaritans with heathen nations, the relationship was not very easy of proof. But it is common to find people shutting their eyes to difficulties when they want to prove a connection or relationship. The advocates of an extreme view of apostolical succession seldom condescend to notice difficulties when they assert that episcopally ordained ministers can trace their order up to the apostles.

When it says that 'Jacob gave' the well, there is probably a reference to the grant which Jacob made to his son Joseph of the district near the well. From Joseph came the tribe of Ephraim, to which, no doubt, the Samaritan woman claimed to belong (*Gen.* 48:22).

[*Drank ... himself ... children ... cattle.*] These words were doubtless said to show the goodness and abundance of the water. Did the stranger at the well really mean to say that he could really give any better water?

Bucer on this verse, remarks how the Samaritans prided themselves on their relationship to Jacob, and the possession of his well, while they made no effort to imitate his goodness, and points out the tendency of superstition to the same thing, in every age. 'True piety,' he says, 'does not consist in having Jacob's well and Jacob's land,—but Jacob's spirit; not in keeping the bones of the saints, but in imitating their lives.'

13.—[*Jesus answered, etc.*] In this and the following verse our Lord proceeds to raise the desires of the woman by exalting the value of the living water of which he had spoken. He still refrains from distinct statements of doctrinal truth: he still adheres to the figurative expression, 'water.' And yet he makes an advance, and leads on the woman gently and almost imperceptibly to glorious spiritual things. Now, for the first time, he begins to speak of 'everlasting life.'

[*Whosoever drinketh of this water ... thirst again.*] It will be noted that our Lord does not answer the woman's questions directly. He keeps steadily to the one point he desires to fasten on her mind: viz., the infinite excellence of a certain 'living water' which he had to give. And first he reminds her of what she knew well by laborious experience: the water of Jacob's well might be good and plentiful; but still he who drank of it was only satisfied for a few hours. He soon thirsted again.

We cannot doubt that there was a deep latent thought in our Lord's words, in this sentence. He would have us know that the waters of Jacob's well are typical of all temporal and material good things: they cannot satisfy the soul; they have no power to fill the heart of an immortal creature like man. He who only drinks of them is sure to thirst again.

Some have thought that there is a tacit reference in these words to the woman's insatiable love of sin.

The similarity ought to be noticed between our Lord's line of argument in this verse, and the line he adopts in recommending to the Jews the bread of life in the sixth chapter. He showed the Jews the superiority of the bread of life over the manna, by the words, 'Your fathers did eat manna and are dead' (*John* 6:49). Just so in this place, he shows the inferiority of the water of Jacob's well to the living water, by saying, 'He that drinks of this water shall thirst again.' The two passages deserve a careful comparison.

14.—[*Whosoever drinketh ... never thirst.*] These words contain a precious promise, and declare a glorious truth of the gospel. The benefits of Christ's gifts are promised to everyone who is willing to receive them, whosoever and whatsoever he may be. He may have been as bad as the Samaritan woman; but the promise is for him as well as for her: 'whosoever drinketh, shall never thirst.'—The declaration 'shall never thirst' does not mean, 'shall never feel any spiritual want at all.' It simply asserts the abiding and enduring nature of the benefits which Christ gives. He that drinks of the living water which Christ gives, shall never entirely and completely lose the cleansing, purifying, and soul-refreshing effects which it produces.

Our English translation of this sentence hardly gives the full sense of the Greek. Literally rendered, it would be 'shall never thirst unto eternity.' The same expression is used frequently in St John's Gospel. See John 6:51-58; 8:51; 10:28; 11:26; 14:16.

[*The water ... I ... give ... well ... everlasting life.*] To see the full meaning of this figurative sentence, it must be paraphrased. The meaning seems to be something of this kind. 'The gift of grace, mercy, and peace which I am ready to give, shall be in the heart of him who receives it an overflowing source of comfort, satisfaction, and spiritual refreshment; continuing and flowing on, not only through this life, but unto life eternal. He that receives my gift of living water has a fountain opened in his soul of spiritual satisfaction, which shall neither be dried up in this life or the life to come, but shall flow on to all eternity.'

Let it be noted that the whole verse is a strong argument in favour of the doctrine of the perpetuity of grace, and the consequent perseverance in the faith of believers. It is difficult to understand how the Arminian doctrine of the possibility of believers completely falling away, and being lost, can be reconciled with any natural interpretation of this verse.

Zwingle thinks, with much probability, that the words 'a fountain in him,' point to the benefits which grace once received makes a man impart to others, as well as enjoy himself (see *John* 7:38).

Rollock remarks on this verse, 'Let me say in a word what I feel. You will find nothing either in heaven or in earth, with which you will be satisfied and feel supplied, except Jesus Christ alone, with all that fulness of the Godhead which dwells in him bodily.'

Poole says, 'He who receiveth the Holy Spirit and the grace thereof, though he will be daily saying Give, give, and continually desiring further supplies of grace, yet he shall never wholly want, never want any good thing that shall be needful for him. The seed of God shall abide in him, and his water shall be in him a spring supplying him until he comes to heaven.'

15.—[*The woman saith, etc.*] In this verse, I think, we see the first sparks of good in the woman's soul. Our Lord's words aroused a desire in her heart for this living water of which he had spoken. She does what our Lord said she ought to have done at first. She 'asks' him to give her the water.

[*Give me this water, that I thirst not ... draw.*] The motives of the woman in making this request are variously explained.

Some think, as Musculus, Calvin, Bucer, Brentius, Gualter, Lightfoot, Poole, and Dyke, that the request was made in a sarcastic and sneering spirit, as though she would say, 'Truly this water would be a fine thing, if we could get it! Give it me, if you have it to give.'

Some think, as Augustine, Cyril, Bullinger, Rollock, Hildersam, Jansenius, and Nifanius, that the request was only the lazy, indolent wish of one who was weary of this world's labour, and yet could see nothing but the things of this world in our Lord's sayings; like the request of the Jews, 'Evermore give us this bread' (*John* 6:34). It was as though she would say, 'Anything to save me the trouble of coming to draw water would be a boon. If you can do that for me, do it.' As Bengel says, 'She wished to have this living fountain at her own house.'

Some think, as Chrysostom, Theophylact, and Euthymius, that the request was really the prayer of an anxious soul, aroused to some faint spiritual desires by the mention of eternal life. 'Hast thou eternal life to bestow? Give it to me.'

I venture to think that none of these three views is quite correct. The true motive of the request was probably a vague feeling of desire that the woman herself could hardly have defined. It is useless to analyse and scrutinize too closely the first languid and imperfect desires that arise in souls when the Spirit begins his work of conversion. It is folly to say that the first movings of a heart towards God must be free from all imperfect motives and all mixture of infirmity. The woman's motives in saying 'Give me this water,' were probably mixed and indefinite. Material water was not out of her thoughts, and yet she had probably some desires after everlasting life. Enough for us to know that she asked and received, she sought and found. Our great aim must be to persuade sinners to apply to Jesus, and to say to him, 'Give me to drink.' If we forbid them to ask anything until they can prove that they ask in a perfect spirit, we should do no good at all. It would be as foolish to scrutinize the grammatical construction of an infant's cries, as to analyse the precise motives of a soul's first breathings after God. If it breathes at all and says, 'Give,' we ought to be thankful.

16.—[*Jesus saith ... Go, call thy husband ... hither.*] This verse begins an entirely new stage in the history of the woman's conversion. From this point we hear no more of 'living water.' Figurative language is dropped entirely. Our Lord's words become direct, personal, and plain. The woman had asked at last for 'living water.' At once our Lord proceeds to give it to her.

Our Lord's reasons for bidding the woman call her husband, have been variously interpreted. Some think that he only meant her to understand that he had spoken long enough to her, a solitary woman; and that before he proceeded further, she must call her husband to be a witness of the conversation, and to partake of the benefits he was going to confer. This seems the view of Chrysostom and Theophylact.—Others think, with far more probability, in my judgment, that our Lord's main object in naming the woman's husband, was to produce in her mind conviction of sin, and to show her his own divine knowledge of all things. He knew that she had no husband, and he purposely named him in order to touch her conscience. He always knew the thoughts of those to whom he spoke; and he knew, in the present case, what the effect of his words would be. It would bring to light the woman's besetting sin.—It is as though he said, 'Thou dost ask me for living water. Thou dost at last express a desire for that great spiritual gift which I am able to bestow. Well then, I begin by bidding thee know thyself and thy sinfulness. I will show thee that I know thy spiritual disease, and can lay my finger on the most dangerous ailment of thy soul. Go, call thy husband and come hither.'

Let it be noted that the first draught of living water which our Lord gave to the Samaritan woman was conviction of sin. That fact is a lesson for all who desire to benefit ignorant and careless sinners. The first thing to be taught to such persons, when once we have got their attention, is their own sinfulness, and their consequent need of a Saviour. No one values the physician until he feels his disease.

Augustine thinks that when our Lord said, 'Call thy husband,' he meant, 'Cause thine understanding to be forthcoming. Thy understanding is not with thee. I am speaking after the spirit, and thou hearest

after the flesh!' I can see no wisdom in this fanciful idea.

17.—[*The woman answered ... no husband.*] These words were an honest and truthful confession, so far as they went. Whether the woman wished it to be supposed that she was a widow, it would perhaps be hardly fair to inquire. Theophylact and Euthymius suggest that she did wish to deceive our Lord. The way in which our Lord received her declaration makes it probable that she did not profess to be a widow, and very likely her dress showed that she was not. In this point of view the honesty of her confession is noteworthy. There is always more hope of one who honestly and bluntly confesses sin, than of a smooth-tongued hypocrite.

[*Jesus said ... Thou hast well said ... husband.*] Our Lord's commendation of the woman's honest confession deserves notice. It teaches us that we should make the best of an ignorant sinner's words. An unskilful physician of souls would probably have rebuked the woman sharply for her wickedness, if her words led him to suspect it. Our Lord on the contrary says, 'Thou hast well said.'

18.—[*Thou hast had five husbands.*] Many foolish and unseemly things have been written about this sentence, which it is not worthwhile to bring forward. Of course it is utterly improbable that the woman had lost five husbands by death, and had been five times a widow. The more likely explanation is that she had been divorced and put away by several husbands in succession. Divorces were notoriously common among the Jews, and in all probability among the Samaritans, for very trivial causes. In the case, however, of the woman before us, the second clause of the verse before us makes it likely that she had been justly divorced for adultery.

Augustine regards these five husbands as significant of 'the five senses of the body,' which are as five husbands by which the soul of the natural man is ruled! I cannot think that our Lord meant anything of the kind.—Euthymius mentions another allegorical view, making the woman to typify human nature, and the five husbands five different dispensations, and him with whom she now lived the Mosaic Law! This seems to me simply absurd. Origen says much the same. It is well to know what patristic interpretation is!

[*He whom ... hast is not thy husband.*] These words show plainly that the Samaritan woman was living in adultery up to the very day when our Lord spoke to her.

Our Lord's perfect knowledge of the woman's past and present life is very noteworthy. It ought to remind us how perfectly he is acquainted with every transaction of our own lives. From him no secrets are hid.

[*In that saidst thou truly.*] There is a kindness very worthy of notice in these words. Wicked and abandoned as this Samaritan woman was, our Lord deals gently and kindly with her, and twice in one breath commends her confession: 'Thou hast well said.—In that thou saidst truly.' Kindness of manner like this will always be found a most important point in dealing with the ungodly. Scolding and sharp rebuke, however well deserved, have a tendency to harden and shut up hearts, and to make people bolt their doors. Kindness, on the contrary, wins, softens, conciliates, and disarms prejudice. An unskilful soul-physician would probably have ended his sentence by saying, 'Thou art a wicked woman; and if thou dost not repent, thou wilt be lost.' All this would have been true no doubt. But how different our Lord's grave and gentle remark: 'Thou saidst truly!'

19.—[*The woman saith ... I perceive ... prophet.*] I think we see in this verse a great change in the Samaritan woman's mind. She evidently confesses the entire truth of what our Lord has just said, and turns to him as an anxious inquirer about her soul. It is as though she said, 'I perceive at last that thou art indeed no common person. Thou hast told me what thou couldst not have known, if thou wert not a prophet sent from God. Thou hast exposed sins which I cannot deny, and aroused spiritual concern which I would now fain have relieved. Now give me instruction.'

Let it be noted that the thing which first struck the Samaritan woman, and made her call Jesus 'a prophet,' was the same that struck Nathanael, viz., our Lord's perfect knowledge.—To call our Lord 'a prophet' at first sight may seem not much. But it must be remembered that even after his resurrection, the two disciples going to Emmaus only described Jesus as a 'prophet mighty in deed and word' (*Luke* 24:19). A clear knowledge of the divine nature of Messiah seems to have been one of the points on which almost the whole Jewish nation was ignorant. Even the learned scribes could not explain how Messiah was to be David's Lord and also David's Son (*Mark* 12:37).

20.—[*Our fathers worshipped, etc.*] To see the full drift of this verse, we must carefully remember the state of the Samaritan woman's mind at this moment. I think that she spoke under spiritual anxiety. She was alarmed by having her sins suddenly exposed. She found herself for the first time in the presence of a prophet. She felt for the first time the necessity of religion. But at once the old question between the Jews and Samaritans arose before her mind. How was she to know what was truth? What was she to believe? Her own people said that the Samaritan mode of worshipping God was correct. The Jews said that Jerusalem was the only place where men ought to worship. Between these two conflicting opinions what was she to do?

The natural ignorance of almost all unconverted people, when first aroused to thought about religion, appears strikingly in the woman's words. Man's first idea is to attach great importance to the outward mode of worshipping God. The first refuge of an awakened conscience is strict adherence to some outward form, and zeal for the external part of religion.

The woman's readiness to quote 'the fathers' and their customs is an instructive instance of man's readiness to make custom and tradition his only rule of faith. 'Our fathers did so,' is one of the natural man's favourite arguments. Calvin's comments on the expression 'fathers' in this verse are very useful. He remarks among other things, 'None should be reckoned Fathers but those who are manifestly the sons of God.'

154

When the woman spoke of 'this mountain,' she doubtless meant the hill on which the rival temple of Samaria was built, to the bitter annoyance of the Jerusalem Jews. It is said that this temple was first built in the days of Nehemiah by Sanballat, and that his son-in-law, the son of Joiada, whom Nehemiah 'chased from him,' was its first high priest (*Neh.* 13:28). Some have gone so far as to maintain that the hill Gerizim at Samaria was the hill on which Abraham offered up Isaac, and that the words of the woman refer to this. The more common opinion is that Mount Moriah at Jerusalem was the place.

When the woman says, 'Ye say,' she doubtless includes the whole Jewish nation, of whom she regards our Lord as a representative.

Musculus, Baxter, Scott, and Barnes, think that the woman, in this verse, desired to turn away the conversation from her own sins to a subject of public controversy, and in this way to change the subject. I am not however satisfied that this view is correct. I prefer the view of Brentius, which I have already set forth, that she was truly impressed by our Lord's exposure of her wickedness, and made a serious inquiry about the things needful to salvation. She was aroused to seriousness, and asked what was true religion. Her own nation said one thing. The Jews said another. What was truth? In short, her words were only another form of the jailer's question, 'What shall I do to be saved?'

21.—[*Jesus saith ... Woman, believe me.*] The calmness, gravity, and solemnity of these opening words are very noteworthy. 'I tell you a great truth, which I ask you to credit and believe.'

Jansenius thinks that our Lord uses the expression 'believe me,' because the truth he was about to impart was so new and strange, that the woman would be apt to think it incredible.

Stier remarks that this is the only time our Lord ever uses this expression, 'believe me,' in the Gospels.

[*The hour cometh.*] The hour, or time here spoken of, means the time of the gospel, the hour of the Christian dispensation.

[*Ye shall neither in this mountain ... Jerusalem, worship, etc.*] Our Lord here declares that under the gospel there was to be no more distinction of places, like Jerusalem. The old dispensation under which men were bound to go up to Jerusalem three times a year, to attend the feasts and worship in the temple, was about to pass away. All questions about the superior sanctity of Samaria or Jerusalem would soon be at an end. A church was about to be founded, whose members would find access to the Father everywhere, and would need no temple service, and no priests or sacrifices or altars in order to approach God. It was therefore mere waste of time to be disputing about the comparative claims of either Samaria or Jerusalem. Under the gospel all places would soon be alike.

It seems far from improbable that our Lord referred in this verse to the prophecy of Malachi: 'In every place incense shall be offered unto my name' (*Mal.* 1:11).

The utter passing away of the whole Jewish system seems clearly pointed at in this verse. To bring into the Christian church holy places, sanctuaries, altars, priests, sacrifices, gorgeous vestments, and the like, is to dig up that which has been long buried, and to turn to candles for light under the noonday sun. The favourite theory of the Irvingites, that we ought as far as possible, in our public worship, to copy the Jewish temple services and ceremonial, seems incapable of reconciliation with this verse.

Calvin says, 'By calling God the Father in this verse, Christ seems indirectly to contrast him with the "fathers" whom the woman had mentioned, and to convey this instruction, that God will be a common Father to all, so that he will be generally worshipped without distinction of place or nation.'

22.—[*Ye worship ye know not what.*] In this verse our Lord unhesitatingly condemns the religious system of the Samaritans, as compared with that of the Jews. The Samaritans could show no scriptural authority, no revelation of God, commanding and sanctioning their worship. Whatever it was, it was purely an invention of man, which God had never formally authorized or accredited. They had no warrant for believing that it was accepted. They had no right to feel sure that their prayers, praises, and offerings were received. In short, all was uncertainty. They were practically worshipping an 'unknown God.'

Mede remarks that the Samaritan woman overlooked the *object* of worship in her question about the *place*. 'You inquire concerning the place of worshipping. But a far more important question is at issue between us, viz., the Being to be worshipped, respecting whom you are ignorant.'

[*We know what we worship.*] In contrast to the Samaritan religious system, our Lord declares that the Jews at any rate could show divine warrant and scriptural authority for all they did in their religion. They could render a reason of their hope. They knew whom they approached in their religious services.

[*Salvation is of the Jews.*] Our Lord here declares that God's promises of a Saviour and Redeemer specially belong to the Jerusalem Jews. They were the descendants of the tribe of Judah, and to them belonged the house and lineage of David. On this point at any rate the Samaritans had no right whatever to claim equality with the Jews. Granting that the Samaritans had any right to be called Israelites, they were of the tribe of Ephraim, from which it was nowhere said that Messiah should spring. And in truth the Samaritans were of such mixed origin that they had no right to be called Israelites at all.

I believe, with Olshausen, that 'salvation' in this verse, was really intended to mean 'the Saviour' himself. The use of the article in the Greek is striking. It is literally 'the salvation.' Does not the saying to Zacchæus point the same way? 'This day is salvation come to this house' (*Luke* 19:9).

The expression 'we' in this verse is very interesting. It is a wonderful instance of our Lord's condescension, and one that stands almost alone. He was pleased to speak of himself, just in the light that he appeared to the woman, as one of the Jewish nation. 'I and all other Jews know what we worship.'

The folly of supposing that ignorance is to be praised and commended in religion, as the mother of devotion, is strongly condemned in this verse. Christ would have Christians 'know what they worship.'

The testimony borne to the general truth of the religious system of the Jews in this place is very striking. Corrupt and wicked as scribes and Pharisees were, Jesus declares that the Jewish religion was true and scriptural. It is a mournful proof that a church may retain a sound creed, and yet be on the high road to destruction.

Hildersam has a long note which is well worth reading on the words 'salvation is of the Jews.' Considering the times in which he lived, it shows singularly clear views of God's continual purposes concerning the Jewish nation. He sees in the words the great truth that all God's revelations to man in every age have been made through the Jews.

23.—[*The hour cometh, and now is.*] These words mean that the times of the gospel approach, and indeed have already begun. 'They have begun by the preaching of the kingdom of God. They will be fully brought in by my death and ascension, and the establishment of the New Testament church.'

[*True worshippers ... worship ... spirit and in truth.*] Our Lord here declares who alone would be considered true worshippers in the coming dispensation of the gospel. They would not be merely those who worshipped in this place or in that place. They would not be exclusively Jews, or exclusively Gentiles, or exclusively Samaritans. The external part of the worship would be of no value compared to the internal state of the worshippers. They only would be counted true worshippers who worshipped in spirit and in truth.

The words 'in spirit and in truth' are variously interpreted, and much has been written about them. I believe the simplest explanation to be this. The word 'spirit' must not be taken to mean the Holy Spirit, but the intellectual or mental part of man, in contradistinction to the material or carnal part of man. This distinction is clearly marked in 1 Corinthians 7:34: 'Holy . . . in body and in spirit.'—'Worship in spirit' is heart-worship in contradistinction to all formal, material, carnal worship, consisting only of ceremonies, offerings, sacrifices, and the like. When a Jew offered a formal meat-offering, with his heart far away, it was worship after the flesh. When David offered in prayer a broken and a contrite heart, it was worship in spirit.—'Worship in truth' means worship through the one true way of access to God, without the medium of the sacrifices or priesthood, which were ordained till Christ died on the cross. When the veil was rent, and the way into the holiest made manifest by Christ's death, then, and not till then, men 'worshipped in truth.' Before Christ they worshipped through types, and shadows, and figures, and emblems. After Christ they worshipped in truth.—Spirit is opposed to 'flesh;' truth to 'shadow.' 'Spirit,' in short, is heart-service contrasted with lip-worship and formal devotion. 'Truth' is the full light of the Christian dispensation contrasted with the twilight of the law of Moses.

The view I have endeavoured to give is substantially that of Chrysostom and Euthymius.

Caryl, quoted by Ford, says, 'In *spirit* regard the inward power, in *truth* the outward form. The first strikes at hypocrisy, the second at idolatry.'

[*The Father seeketh such to worship him.*] This is a remarkable sentence. I believe it to mean that 'the hour is come, in which the Father has ordained from eternity that he will gather out of the world a company of true and spiritual worshippers. He is even now seeking out and gathering in such worshippers.'—The expression 'seeketh' is peculiar. There is something like it in the sentence, 'The Son of man is come to *seek* and to save that which was lost' (*Luke* 19:10). It seems to show the exceeding compassion of the Father, and his infinite willingness to save souls. He does not merely 'wait' for men to come to him. He 'seeks' for them. It also shows the wide opening of God the Father's mercy under the gospel. He no longer confines his grace to the Jews. He now *seeks* and desires to gather in everywhere true worshippers out of every nation.

The clause appears to me specially intended to encourage the Samaritan woman. Let her not trouble herself with difficulties about the comparative claims of the Samaritan and Jewish systems. Was she willing to be a spiritual worshipper? That was the one question which deserved her attention.

Trapp observes, 'How should this fire up our hearts to spiritual worship! That God *seeks* for such worshippers!'

24.—[*God is a Spirit.*] Our Lord here declares to the Samaritan woman the true nature of God. Let her cease to think that God was such a one as man, and that he could not be found, or approached, or addressed, like a mere earthly monarch, except at one particular place. Let her learn to have higher, nobler, and more exalted views of the Being with whom sinners have to do. Let her know this day that God was a Spirit.

The declaration before us is one of the most lofty and definite sayings about God's nature which is to be found in the whole Bible. That such a declaration should have been made to such a person as the Samaritan woman is a wonderful instance of Christ's condescension! To define precisely the full meaning of the expression is past man's understanding. The leading idea most probably is, that 'God is an immaterial being, that he dwelleth not in temples made with hands, and that he is not, like ourselves, therefore, absent from one place when he is present at another.' These things are all true, but how little we can realize them!

Cornelius à Lapide gives an excellent summary of the opinions of heathen philosophers on the nature of God, in his commentary on this verse.

[*They ... worship ... must worship ... spirit ... truth.*] Our Lord draws this broad conclusion from the statement of God's nature which he has just made. If 'God is a Spirit' it behoves those who would worship him acceptably, to worship in spirit and in truth. It is unreasonable to suppose that he can like any worship which does not come from the heart, or can be so well pleased with worship which is offered through types and ceremonies, as with worship offered through the true way which he has provided, and is now revealing.

The importance of the great principle laid down in this and the preceding verse, can never be overrated. Any religious teaching which tends to depreciate heart-worship, and to turn Christianity into a mere formal service, or which tends to bring back Jewish shadows, ceremonies, and services, and to introduce them into Christian worship, is on the face of these remarkable verses most unscriptural and deserving of reprobation.

Of course we must not admit the idea that in this and the preceding verse Jesus meant to pour contempt on the ceremonial law, which God himself had given. But he plainly teaches that it was an imperfect dispensation, given because of man's ignorance and infirmity, as we give pictures to children in teaching them. It was, in fact, a schoolmaster to Christ (*Gal.* 3:24). To want men to return to it is as absurd as to bid grown-up people begin learning the alphabet by pictures in an infant school.— On the other hand, as Beza remarks, we must not run into the extreme of despising all ordinances, sacraments, and outward ceremonies in religion. These things have their use and value, however much they may be abused.

25.—[*The woman saith ... I know ... Messias ... Christ, etc.*] This verse is an interesting one. It shows the woman at last brought to the very state of mind in which she would be prepared to welcome a revelation of Christ. She had been told of 'living water,' and had expressed a desire for it. She had been told her own sin, and had been unable to deny it. She had been told the uselessness of resting on any formal membership of the Samaritan church, and the necessity of spiritual and heart-worship of God. And now what can she say? It is all true, she feels: she cannot gainsay it. But what can she do? To whom is she to go? Whose teaching can she follow? All she can do is to say that she knows Messias is one day coming, and that he will make all things clear and plain. It is evident that she wishes for him. She is uncomfortable, and sees no relief for her newly-raised perplexities, unless Messias should appear.

The mention of Messias in this verse, makes it clear that the Samaritans were not altogether ignorant of the Old Testament, and that there was an expectation of a Redeemer of some kind among them, as well as among the Jews. The existence of a general expectation of this sort throughout the East, at the time when our Lord appeared on earth, is a fact to which even heathen writers have testified.

When the woman says, 'He will tell us all things,' we must probably not inquire too closely into what she meant. It is very likely that she had only a vague feeling that Messias would remove all doubts and show all things needful to salvation.

Chrysostom remarks on this verse, 'The woman was made dizzy by Christ's discourse, and fainted at the sublimity of what he said, and in her trouble saith, I know that Messias cometh.'

Wordsworth observes, that the Samaritan woman had a clearer knowledge of Messiah's office than the Jews generally showed. She looked for him as a Teacher. They looked for him as a conquering King.

Beza and A. Clarke think that the words, 'which is called Christ,' in this verse, are St John's parenthetical explanation of the word Messias. It is certainly rather unlikely that the woman would have used them in addressing a Jew. Yet most commentators think that they were her words.

26.—[*Jesus saith ... I ... speak ... am he.*] These words are the fullest declaration which our Lord ever made of his own Messiahship, which the Gospel writers have recorded. That such a full declaration should be made to such a person as the Samaritan woman is one of the most wonderful instances of our Lord's grace and condescension related in the New Testament! At last the woman obtained an answer to one of her first questions, 'Art thou greater than our father Jacob?' When the answer came it completely converted her soul.

Rollock remarks on this verse, how ready and willing Christ is to reveal himself to a sinner's soul. The very moment that this woman expressed any desire for Messiah, he at once revealed himself to her: 'I am he.'

Quesnel observes, 'It is a great mistake to suppose that the knowledge of the mysteries of religion ought not to be imparted to women by the reading of Scripture, considering this instance of the great confidence Christ reposed in this woman by his manifestation of himself. The abuse of the Scriptures and the sin of heresies, did not proceed from the simplicity of women, but from the conceited learning of men.'

In leaving the whole passage there are several striking points which ought never to be forgotten. 1. Our Lord's *mercy* is remarkable. That such a one as he should deal so graciously with such a sinner is a striking fact. 2. Our Lord's *wisdom* is remarkable. How wise was every step of his way in dealing with this sinful soul!

3. Our Lord's *patience* is remarkable. How he bore with the woman's ignorance, and what trouble he took to lead her to knowledge! 4. Our Lord's *power* is remarkable. What a complete victory he won at last! How almighty must that grace be which could soften and convert such a carnal and wicked heart!

We must never despise any soul, after reading this passage. None can be worse than this woman. But Christ did not despise her.

We must never despair of any soul, after reading this passage. If this woman was converted, anyone may be converted.

Finally, we must never condemn the use of all wise and reasonable means in dealing with souls. There is a 'wisdom which is profitable to direct' in approaching ignorant and ungodly people, which must be diligently sought.

JOHN 4:27-30

27 And upon this came his disciples, and marvelled that he talked with the woman: yet no man said, What seekest thou? or, Why talkest thou with her?

28 The woman then left her waterpot, and went her way into the city, and saith to the men,

29 Come, see a man, which told me all things that ever I did: is not this the Christ?

30 Then they went out of the city, and came unto him.

THESE verses continue the well-known story of the Samaritan woman's conversion. Short as the passage may appear, it contains points of deep interest and importance. The mere worldling, who cares nothing about experimental religion, may see nothing particular in these verses. To all who desire to know something of the experience of a converted person, they will be found full of food for thought.

We see, firstly, in this passage, *how marvellous in the eyes of man are Christ's dealings with souls*. We are told that the disciples 'marvelled

159

that he talked with the woman.' That their Master should take the trouble to talk to a woman at all, and to a Samaritan woman, and to a strange woman at a well, when he was wearied with his journey,—all this was wonderful to the eleven disciples. It was a sort of thing which they did not expect. It was contrary to their idea of what a religious teacher should do. It startled them and filled them with surprise.

The feeling displayed by the disciples on this occasion does not stand alone in the Bible. When our Lord allowed publicans and sinners to draw near to him and be in his company, the Pharisees marvelled: they exclaimed, 'This man receiveth sinners, and eateth with them' (*Luke* 15:2). When Saul came back from Damascus, a converted man and a new creature, the Christians at Jerusalem were astonished: they 'believed not that he was a disciple' (*Acts* 9:26). When Peter was delivered from Herod's prison by an angel, and brought to the door of the house where disciples were praying for his deliverance, they were so taken by surprise that they could not believe it was Peter: when they saw him 'they were astonished' (*Acts* 12:16).

But why should we stop short in Bible instances? The true Christian has only to look around him in this world in order to see abundant illustrations of the truth before us. How much astonishment every fresh conversion occasions! What surprise is expressed at the change in the heart, life, tastes, and habits of the converted person! What wonder is felt at the power, the mercy, the patience, the compassion of Christ! It is now as it was eighteen hundred years ago. The dealings of Christ are still a marvel both to the church and to the world.

If there was more real faith on the earth, there would be less surprise felt at the conversion of souls. If Christians believed more, they would expect more, and if they understood Christ better, they would be less startled and astonished when he calls and saves the chief of sinners. We should consider nothing impossible, and regard no sinner as beyond the reach of the grace of God. The astonishment expressed at conversions is a proof of the weak faith and ignorance of these latter days: the thing that ought to fill us with surprise is the obstinate unbelief of the ungodly, and their determined perseverance in the way to ruin. This was the mind of Christ. It is written that he thanked the Father for conversions: but he marvelled at unbelief (*Matt.* 11:25; *Mark* 6:6).

We see, secondly, in this passage, *how absorbing is the influence of grace, when it first comes into a believer's heart.* We are told that after our Lord had told the woman he was the Messiah, she 'left her waterpot, and went her way into the city, and saith to the men, Come, see a man, which told me all things that ever I did.' She had left her home for the express purpose of drawing water. She had carried a large vessel to the well, intending to bring it back filled. But she found at the well a new heart, and new objects of interest. She became a new creature. Old things passed away: all things became new. At once everything else was forgotten for the time: she could think of nothing but the truths she had heard, and the Saviour she had found. In the fulness of her heart she 'left her waterpot,' and hastened away to express her feelings to others.

We see here the expulsive power of the grace of the Holy Ghost. Grace once introduced into the heart drives out old tastes and interests. A converted person no longer cares for what he once cared for. A new tenant is in the house: a new pilot is at the helm. The whole world looks different. All things have become new. It was so with Matthew the publican: the moment that grace came into his heart he left the receipt of custom (*Matt.* 9:9).—It was so with Peter, James, and John, and Andrew: as soon as they were converted they forsook their nets and fishing boats (*Mark* 1:19, 20).—It was so with Saul the Pharisee: as soon as he became a Christian he gave up all his brilliant prospects as a Jew, in order to preach the faith he had once despised (*Acts* 9:20).—The conduct of the Samaritan woman was precisely of the same kind: for the time present the salvation she had found completely filled her mind. That she never returned for her waterpot would be more than we have a right to say. But under the first impressions of new spiritual life, she went away and 'left her waterpot' behind.

Conduct like that here described is doubtless uncommon in the present day. Rarely do we see a person so entirely taken up with spiritual matters, that attention to this world's affairs is made a secondary matter, or postponed. And why is it so? Simply because true conversions to God are uncommon. Few really feel their sins, and flee to Christ by faith. Few really pass from death to life, and become new creatures. Yet these few are the real Christians of the world: these are the people whose religion, like the Samaritan woman's, tells on others. Happy are they who know something by experience of this woman's feelings, and can say with Paul, 'I count all things but loss for the excellency of the knowledge of Christ!' Happy are they who have given up everything for Christ's sake, or at any rate have altered the relative importance of all things in their minds! 'If . . . thine eye be single, thy whole body shall be full of light' (*Phil.* 3:8; *Matt.* 6:22).

We see, lastly, in this passage, *how zealous a truly converted person is to do good to others*. We are told that the Samaritan woman went 'into the city, and saith to the men, Come, see a man, which told me all things that ever I did: is not this the Christ?' In the day of her conversion she became a missionary. She felt so deeply the amazing benefit she had received from Christ, that she could not hold her peace about him. Just as Andrew told his brother Peter about Jesus, and Philip told Nathanael that he had found Messiah, and Saul, when converted, straightway preached Christ, so, in the same way, the Samaritan woman said, 'Come and see' Christ. She used no abstruse arguments: she attempted no deep reasoning about our Lord's claim to be the Messiah. She only said, 'Come and see.' Out of the abundance of her heart her mouth spoke.

That which the Samaritan woman here did, all true Christians ought to do likewise. The church needs it: the state of the world demands it. Common sense points out that it is right. Everyone who has received the grace of God, and tasted that Christ is gracious, ought to find words to testify of Christ to others. Where is our faith, if we believe that souls around us are perishing, and that Christ alone can save them, and yet hold our peace? Where is our charity, if we can see others going down to hell and yet say nothing to them about Christ and salvation?—We may well doubt our own love to Christ if our hearts are never moved to speak of him. We may well doubt the safety of our own souls if we feel no concern about the souls of others.

What are we ourselves? This is the question, after all, which demands our notice. Do we feel the supreme importance of spiritual things, and the comparative nothingness of the things of the world? Do we ever talk to others about God, and Christ, and eternity, and the soul, and heaven, and hell? If not, what is the value of our faith? Where is the reality of our Christianity? Let us take heed lest we awake too late, and find that we are lost for ever; a wonder to angels and devils, and, above all, a wonder to ourselves, because of our own obstinate blindness and folly.

Notes—John 4:27-30

27.—[*Upon this.*] The true idea contained in this expression seems to be, 'At this point, at this critical juncture in the conversation between our Lord and the woman.'—What the woman would have said next after our Lord's marvellous discovery of himself, we are left to conjecture. But just as our Lord said, 'I am the Messiah,' the disciples returned from buying food, and their appearance stopped the conversation. The woman's heart was probably too full, and her mind too much excited to say more in the presence of witnesses, and especially of strangers. Therefore no more was said, and she withdrew. The soul, in the beginning of a work of grace, shrinks from discovering its workings before strangers.

[*Marvelled ... talked with the woman.*] I am inclined to think that these words would have been more correctly rendered, 'talked with a woman.' There is no article in the original Greek. The wonder of the disciples was excited, not so much by our Lord talking to this woman, as by his talking to a woman at all. It is clear from babbinical writings, that there was a common opinion among the Jews that both in understanding and religion women were an inferior order of beings to men. This ignorant prejudice had most likely leavened the minds of the disciples, and is probably referred to in this place. Of the woman's moral character it is not clear that the disciples could know anything at all.

Rupertus thinks that our Lord, by conversing openly with a Samaritan woman, wished to show his disciples by an example, that the wall between Jews and other people was to be broken down by the gospel, just as he taught Peter the same lesson after his ascension, by the vision of the sheet full of clean and unclean beasts (*Acts* 10:11-15). He thinks that the

163

wonder of the disciples arose from the same Jewish prejudice against intercourse with uncircumcised Gentiles which appeared so strongly in after-times.

Lightfoot, Schoettgen, and Tholuck quote proverbial sayings from rabbinical writers, showing the Jewish feeling about women. The following are instances. 'He who instructs his daughter in the law plays the fool.' 'Do not multiply discourses with a woman.' 'Let no one talk with a woman in the street, no not with his own wife.'— Whitby also says, from Buxtorf, that the rabbins say that 'talking with a woman is one of the six things which make a disciple impure.'

[*No man said, What seekest ... why talkest? etc.*] We are left to conjecture whether both these questions apply to our Lord, or whether the first applied to the woman: 'What seekest thou of him?' and the second to our Lord: 'Why talkest thou with her?' The point is of no particular importance. To me, however, it appears that both questions apply to Christ. 'No man said, "What art thou seeking from her? Why art thou talking with her?"'

Grotius suggests that the disciples supposed our Lord might have been seeking meat or drink from the Samaritan woman, and meant, 'Why seekest thou any meat or drink from her?'

I venture to doubt whether both questions had not better have been translated alike: 'What art thou seeking from her? What art thou talking about with her?' The Greek word is the same which our translators have rendered 'what' in the first question, and 'why' in the second.

The expression, 'No man said,' seems to imply that no man ventured to ask any question what was our Lord's reason for talking with the woman. It is not very clear why the sentence is introduced. The object probably is, as Cyril and Chrysostom remark, to show us the deep reverence and respect with which the disciples regarded our Lord and all his actions, even at this early period of his ministry. It also shows us that they sometimes thought things about him to which they dared not give expression, and saw deeds of his which they could not understand, but were content silently to wonder at them. There is a lesson for us in their conduct. When we cannot understand the reason of our Lord's dealings with souls, let us hold our peace, and try to believe that there are reasons which we shall know one day. A good servant in a great house must do his own duty, and ask no questions. A young student of medicine must take many things on trust.

28.—[*The woman ... left ... waterpot.*] The Greek word here rendered 'waterpot' is the same that is used in the account of the miracle at Cana in Galilee (*John* 2:6). It does not mean a small drinking vessel, but a large jar, such as a woman in Eastern countries would carry on her head. We can therefore well understand that if the woman wished to return in haste to the city she would leave her waterpot. So large a vessel could not be carried quickly, whether empty or full.

The mind of the woman in leaving her waterpot seems to me clear and unmistakable. She was entirely absorbed in the things which she had heard from our Lord's mouth. She was anxious to tell them without delay to her friends and neighbours. She therefore postponed her business of drawing water, for which she had left her house, as a matter of secondary importance, and hurried off to tell others what she had been told. The sentence is deeply instructive.

Lightfoot thinks, besides this, that the woman left her waterpot out of kindness to our Lord, 'that Jesus and his disciples might have wherewithal to drink.'

[*Went her way ... city.*] The Greek word rendered 'went her way,' means simply, 'departed' or 'went.' The city must of course mean 'Sychar.'

[*Saith to the men.*] We must not suppose that the woman spoke to the men only, and not to her own sex. But it is probable that the men of the place would be the first persons she would see, and that the women would not be in the streets, but at home. Moreover it is not unlikely that the expression is meant to show us the woman's zeal and anxiety to spread the good tidings. She did not hesitate to speak to men, though she well knew that anything a woman might say about religion was not likely to command attention.

Cyril, on this verse, remarks the power of Christ's grace. He began by bidding the woman go and 'call her husband.' The end of the conversation which ensued was her going and calling all the men of the city to come and see Christ.

29.—[*Come, see a man.*] The missionary spirit of the woman, in this verse, deserves special notice. Having found Christ herself, she invites others to come and be acquainted with him. Origen calls her 'the apostle of the Samaritans.'

Let it be noted that her words are simple in the extreme. She enters into no argument. She only asks the men to 'come and see.' This, after all, is often the best way of dealing with souls. A bold invitation to come and make trial of the gospel often produces more effect than the most elaborate arguments in support of its doctrines. Most men do not want their reason convinced so much as their will bent, and their conscience aroused. A simple-minded, hearty, unlearned young disciple will often touch hearts that would hear an abstruse argument without being moved.—This fact is most encouraging to all believers who try to do good. All cannot argue: but all believers may say, 'Come and see Christ. If you would only look at him and see him, you would soon believe.'

Barradius remarks what a practical illustration the woman affords of one of the concluding sentences of Revelation: 'Let him that heareth say, Come' (*Rev.* 22:17). The Samaritan woman having heard, said, 'Come,' and the result was that many souls came and took the water of life freely.

Cyril remarks the difference between the woman's conduct and that of the servant who buried his talent in the ground. She received the talent of the good tidings of the gospel, and at once put it out at interest.

Chrysostom remarks the wisdom of the woman. 'She did not say, Come, *believe*; but Come, *see*: a gentler expression than the other, and one which more attracted them.'

[*Told me all things ... ever I did.*] These words must be taken with some qualifications. Of course they cannot mean that

our Lord had literally told the woman 'all things that ever she did in her life.' This would have been physically impossible in the space of a single afternoon.—The probable meaning is, 'He has told me all the principal sins that I have committed. He has shown a perfect knowledge of the chief events of my life. He has shown such thorough acquaintance with my history, that I doubt not he could have told me anything I ever did.'

Some allowance must probably be made for the warm and excited feelings of the woman when she spoke these words. She used hyperbolical and extravagant language, under the influence of these feelings, which she would probably not have used in a calm state of mind, and which we must therefore not judge too strictly. Moreover, as Poole remarks, it admits of doubt whether our Lord may not have spoken of other things in the conversation, which St John has not been inspired to record.

Let it be noted, that the Samaritan woman, in saying that our Lord had told her all things she had ever done, very probably referred to the common opinion about Messiah's omniscience. The rabbinical writers, according to Lightfoot, especially applied to Messiah the words of Isaiah: 'He shall make him of quick understanding in the fear of the Lord. He shall not judge by the sight of his eyes' (*Isa.* 11:3). Her words, therefore, were a well-known argument, that our Lord must be the Christ, and her object in using them would be thoroughly understood.

[*Is not this the Christ?*] The Greek words so rendered would be translated with equal correctness, 'Is this the Christ? Can this be the Christ?' A similar form of interrogative sentence is found in thirteen other places in the New Testament. In twelve of them the interrogative is used without 'not:' viz., Matthew 7:16; 26:22, 25; Mark 4:21; 14:19; Luke 6:39; John 7:31; 8:22; 18:35; Acts 10:47; 2 Corinthians 1:17; James 3:11.—In only one place is the interrogative used with 'not:' Matthew 12:23. I am inclined, on the whole, to think that 'not' would have been better omitted in the sentence before us. Euthymius takes this view.

165

The value of questions, if we want to do good to souls, is well illustrated in this verse. A question often sets working a mind which would be utterly unmoved by an affirmation. It drives the mind to exertion, and by a gentle compulsion arouses it to think. Men are far less able to go to sleep under religious teaching, when they are invited to answer a question. The number of questions in the New Testament is a striking and instructive fact. Had the woman said, 'This is the Christ!' she might have excited prejudice and dislike. By asking, 'Is this the Christ?' she got the men to inquire and judge for themselves.

30.—[*Then they went out of the city.*] This sentence is full of encouragement to all who try to do good to souls. The words of one single woman were the means of arousing a whole city to go forth and inquire about Christ. We must never despise the smallest and meanest efforts. We never know to what the least beginnings may grow. The grain of mustard seed at Sychar was the word of a feeble woman: 'Come and see.'

Specially we ought to observe the encouragement the verse affords to the efforts of women. A woman may be the means, under God, of founding a church. The first person baptized by Paul in Europe was not a man, but a woman: Lydia, the seller of purple. Let women never suppose that men only can do good. Women also, in their way, can evangelize as really and truly as men. Every believing woman who has a tongue can speak to others about Christ.— The Samaritan woman was far less learned than Nicodemus. But she was far bolder, and so did far more good.

[*And came unto him.*] Perhaps the sentence would be more literally rendered, 'were coming,' or 'began to come to him.' It was while they were coming that the conversation which immediately follows, between Christ and his disciples, took place, and perhaps it was the sight of the crowd coming which made our Lord say some of the things that he did.

Calvin remarks on this part of the woman's history, that some may think her blameable, in that 'while she is still ignorant and imperfectly taught, she goes beyond the limits of her faith. I reply that she would have acted inconsiderately if she had assumed the office of a teacher; but when she desires nothing more than to excite her fellow-citizens to hear Christ speaking, we will not say that she forgot herself, or proceeded further than she had a right to do. She merely does the office of a trumpet or a bell, to invite others to come to Christ.'

The concluding verse shows us most forcibly that ministers and teachers of religion ought never to be above taking pains and trouble with a single soul. A conversation with one person was the means of leading a whole city to come and hear Christ, and resulted in the salvation of many souls.

Cornelius à Lapide, at this point of his commentary, gravely informs us that the name of the Samaritan woman was Photina; that after her conversion she preached the gospel at Carthage, and that she suffered martyrdom there on 20 March, on which day the Romish Martyrology makes special mention of her name! He also tells us that her head is kept as a relic at Rome, in the Basilica of St Paul, and that it was actually shown to him there!—It is well to know what ridiculous and lying legends the Church of Rome palms upon Roman Catholics as truths, while she withholds from them the Bible!

JOHN 4:31-42

31 In the mean while his disciples prayed him, saying, Master, eat.

32 But he said unto them, I have meat to eat that ye know not of.

33 Therefore said the disciples one to another, Hath any man brought him *aught* to eat?

34 Jesus saith unto them, My meat is to do the will of him that sent me, and to finish his work.

35 Say not ye, There are yet four months, and *then* cometh harvest? behold, I say unto you, Lift up your eyes, and look on the fields; for they are white already to harvest.

36 And he that reapeth receiveth wages, and gathereth fruit unto life eternal: that both he that soweth and he that reapeth may rejoice together.

37 And herein is that saying true, One soweth, and another reapeth.

38 I sent you to reap that whereon ye bestowed no labour: other men laboured, and ye are entered into their labours.

39 And many of the Samaritans of that city believed on him for the saying of the woman, which testified, He told me all that ever I did.

40 So when the Samaritans were come unto him, they besought him that he would tarry with them: and he abode there two days.

41 And many more believed because of his own word;

42 And said unto the woman, Now we believe, not because of thy saying: for we have heard *him* ourselves, and know that this is indeed the Christ, the Saviour of the world.

WE have, for one thing, in these verses, *an instructive pattern of zeal for the good of others.* We read, that our Lord Jesus Christ declares, 'My meat is to do the will of him that sent me, and to finish his work.' To do good was not merely duty and pleasure to him. He counted it as his food, meat and drink. Job, one of the holiest Old Testament saints, could say that he esteemed God's *Word* 'more than [his] necessary food' (*Job* 23:12). The great Head of the New Testament church went even further: he could say the same of God's *work.*

Do we do any work for God? Do we try, however feebly, to set forward his cause on earth,—to check that which is evil, to promote that which is good? If we do, let us never be ashamed of doing it with all our heart, and soul, and mind, and strength. Whatsoever our hand finds to do for the souls of others, let us do it with our might (*Eccles.* 9:10). The world may mock and sneer, and call us enthusiasts. The world can admire zeal in any service but that of God, and can praise enthusiasm on any subject but that of religion. Let us work on unmoved. Whatever men may say and think, we are walking in the steps of our Lord Jesus Christ.

Let us, beside this, take comfort in the thought that Jesus Christ never changes. He that sat by the well of Samaria, and found it 'meat and drink' to do good to an ignorant soul, is always in one mind. High in heaven at God's right hand, he still delights to save sinners, and still approves zeal and labour in the cause of God. The work of the missionary and the evangelist may be despised and ridiculed in many quarters; but while man is mocking, Christ is well pleased. Thanks be to God, Jesus is the same yesterday, and today, and for ever.

We have, for another thing, in these verses, *strong encouragement held out to those who labour to do good to souls*. We read that our Lord described the world as a field 'white already to harvest;' and then said to his disciples, 'He that reapeth receiveth wages, and gathereth fruit unto life eternal.'

Work for the souls of men, is undoubtedly attended by great discouragements. The heart of natural man is very hard and unbelieving. The blindness of most men to their own lost condition and peril of ruin, is something past description. 'The carnal mind is enmity against God' (*Rom.* 8:7). No one can have any just idea of the desperate hardness of men and women, until he has tried to do good. No one can have any conception of the small number of those who repent and believe, until he has personally endeavoured to 'save some' (*1 Cor.* 9:22). To suppose that everybody will become a true Christian, who is told about Christ, and entreated to believe, is mere childish ignorance. 'Few there be that find the narrow way!' The labourer for Christ will find the vast majority of those among whom he labours, unbelieving and impenitent, in spite of all that he can do. 'The many' will not turn to Christ. These are discouraging facts. But they are facts, and facts that ought to be known.

The true antidote against despondency in God's work, is an abiding recollection of such promises as that before us. There are 'wages' laid up for faithful reapers. They shall receive a reward at the last day, far exceeding anything they have done for Christ,—a reward proportioned not to their success, but to the quantity of their work.

They are gathering 'fruit,' which shall endure when this world has passed away,—fruit, in some souls saved, if many will not believe, and fruit in evidences of their own faithfulness, to be brought out before assembled worlds. Do our hands ever hang down, and our knees wax faint? Do we feel disposed to say, 'My labour is in vain and my words without profit'? Let us lean back at such seasons on this glorious promise. There are 'wages' yet to be paid. There is 'fruit' yet to be exhibited. 'We are . . . a sweet savour of Christ, in them that are saved, and in them that perish' (2 *Cor.* 2:15). Let us work on. 'He that goeth forth and weepeth, bearing precious seed, shall doubtless come again with rejoicing, bringing his sheaves with him' (*Psa.* 126:6). One single soul saved, shall outlive and outweigh all the kingdoms of the world.

We have, lastly, in these verses, *a most teaching instance of the variety of ways by which men are led to believe Christ.* We read that 'many of the Samaritans . . . believed on [Christ] for the saying of the woman.' But this is not all. We read again, 'Many more believed because of [Christ's] own word.' In short, some were converted through the means of the woman's testimony, and some were converted by hearing Christ himself.

The words of St Paul should never be forgotten: 'There are diversities of operations, but it is the same God which worketh all in all' (1 *Cor.* 12:6). The way in which the Spirit leads all God's people is always one and the same. But the paths by which they are severally brought into that road are often widely different. There are some in whom the work of conversion is sudden and instantaneous: there are others in whom it goes on slowly, quietly, and by imperceptible degrees. Some have their hearts gently opened, like Lydia: others are aroused by violent alarm, like the jailer at Philippi. All are finally brought to repentance toward God, faith toward our Lord Jesus Christ, and holiness of conversation: but all do not begin with the same experience. The weapon which carries conviction to one believer's soul, is not the one which first pierces another. The arrows of the Holy Ghost are all drawn from the same quiver; but he uses sometimes one and sometimes another, according to his own sovereign will.

Are we converted ourselves? This is the one point to which our attention ought to be directed. Our experience may not tally with that of other believers. But that is not the question. Do we feel sin, hate it, and flee from it? Do we love Christ, and rest solely on him for salvation? Are we bringing forth fruits of the Spirit in righteousness and true holiness? If these things are so, we may thank God and take courage.

Notes—John 4:31-42

31.—[*In the mean while.*] This expression means, 'during the time when the Samaritans were coming out of the city to the well:' between the time when the woman went her way, and the time when her fellow-countrymen, aroused by her testimony, appeared at the well. It is highly probable that they were already in sight.

[*Prayed.*] The Greek word so rendered is remarkable. It is frequently used to convey the idea of 'asking, or making inquiry.' It is a curious fact that it is not used in describing any person's address to God in prayer, except in the case of our Lord Jesus Christ (*John* 14:16; 16:26; 17:9, 15, 20). There is one remarkable instance where it seems to be used in describing a believer's prayer (*1 John* 5:16). But this instance stands so entirely alone that it is probable the meaning is not 'pray,' but 'make curious inquiry.'

[*Master, eat.*] The difference between our Lord and his disciples appears here in a striking manner. Their weak minds were preoccupied with the idea of food and bodily sustenance. His heart was filled with the great object of his ministry: 'doing good to souls.' It is a striking illustration of a difference that may frequently be seen between a believer of great grace and a believer of little grace. The latter, with the best possible intentions, will often attach an importance to bodily and temporal things, with which the strong believer will feel no sympathy.

32.—[*I have meat, etc.*] The meaning of our Lord's words in this verse must

evidently be figurative. He had soul-nourishment and soul-sustenance of which his disciples were ignorant. He found such refreshment in doing good to ignorant souls that for the time present he did not feel bodily hunger.

There is no necessity for supposing that our Lord referred to any miraculous supply of his bodily wants in this place. His words appear to me only to indicate that he found such delight and comfort in doing good to souls, that it was as good as meat and drink to him. Many of his holiest servants in every age, I believe, could testify much the same. The joy and happiness of spiritual success has for the time lifted them above all bodily wants, and supplied the place of material meat and drink. I see no reason why this may not have been the case with our Lord. He had a body in all respects constituted like our own.

The idea of some writers that these words show that our Lord's 'thirst' was only simulated and pretended, seems to me utterly unworthy of notice.

The application of the words which every believer ought to endeavour to make to himself, is familiar to every well-instructed Christian. He has supplies of spiritual nourishment and support, which are hidden and unknown to the world. These supplies he ought to use at all times, and specially in times of sorrow and trial.

33.—[*Therefore said ... one to another, etc.*] These words seem to have been spoken privately, or whispered one to another, by the disciples. Their inability to put any but a carnal sense on their Master's words, has been already remarked. In slowness to see a spiritual sense in his language they do not appear at all unlike Nicodemus and the Samaritan woman. 'What wonder is it,' says Augustine, 'if the woman could not understand our Lord, speaking about living water, when the disciples could not understand him speaking about meat?'

The original Greek of the expression, 'Hath any man brought him aught to eat?' is remarkable. There is a negative left out in our translation. It seems to show that the question of the woman, at verse 29, would have been better rendered, 'Is this the Christ? Can this be the Christ?'

34.—[*Jesus saith, etc.*] The leading idea of this verse is, 'that doing God's will, and finishing God's work, was so soul-refreshing and pleasant to our Lord that he found it equivalent to meat and drink.'

The Greek expression rendered 'to do,' and 'to finish,' would have been more literally rendered, 'that I should do,' and, 'that I should finish.' But there can be little doubt, as Winer remarks, that the language is intended to have an infinitive sense. Precisely the same construction is employed in another remarkable place, John 17:3. It seems a matter of regret that our translators did not render that verse as they have rendered the verse before us. It should have been, 'This is life eternal to know thee,' etc.

The 'will of God,' which it was Christ's meat to 'do,' must mean God's will, that salvation by faith in a Saviour should be proclaimed and a door of mercy set wide open to the chief of sinners. 'It is my meat,' says our Lord, 'to do that will, and to proclaim to everyone with whom I speak, that whosoever believeth on the Son shall not perish.' The view that it simply means, 'My meat is to obey God's commandments and do what he has told me to do,' appears to me to fall short of the full meaning of the expression. The leading idea seems to me to be specially God's will about proclaiming salvation by Christ. Compare John 6:39, 40.

The 'work of God,' which it was Christ's meat to 'finish,' must mean that work of complete fulfilment of a Saviour's office which Christ came on earth to perform, and that obedience to God's law which he came to render. 'It is my meat,' says our Lord, 'to be daily doing that great work which I came into the world to do for man's soul, to be daily preaching peace, and daily fulfilling all righteousness.' Compare John 17:4.

The utter unlikeness between Christ and all ministers of the gospel who perform their duties in a mere perfunctory way, and care more for the world, and its pleasures or gains, than for saving souls, is strikingly brought out in this and the preceding verse. How many professing teachers of religion know nothing whatever of the spirit and habits of mind which our Lord here displays! It can never be said of hunting, shooting, ball-going, card-playing, farming clergymen, that it is their meat and drink to do God's will and finish his work! With what face will they meet Christ in the day of judgment?

Cyril says, on this verse, 'We learn from hence how great is the love of God towards men. He calls the conversion of lost people his meat.'

35.—[*Say not ye, etc.*] This saying is interpreted in two different ways.

Some think, as Origen, Rupertus, Brentius, Beza, Jansenius, Cyril, Lightfoot, Lampe, Suicer, and many others, that our Lord really meant that there were four literal months to harvest, at the time when he spoke; and that as the harvest began about May, he spoke in February. The sense would then be, 'Ye say at this time of the year that it will be harvest in four months. But I tell you there is a spiritual harvest already before you, if you will only lift up your eyes and see it.'

Others think, as De Dieu, Maldonatus, Calovius, Whitby, Schoettgen, Pearce, Tittman, Stier, Alford, Barnes, and Tholuck, that our Lord only meant that it was a proverbial saying among the Jews,—'four months between seed time and harvest,' and that he did not mean the words to be literally taken. The sense would then be, 'Ye have a common saying that it is four months from seed time to harvest. But I tell you that in spiritual works the harvest ripens far more quickly. Behold those Samaritans coming out already to hear the word, the very day that seed has been sown among them. The fields are already white for harvest.'

Either of the above views makes good sense and good divinity. Yet on the whole I prefer the second view: viz., that our Lord quoted a proverb. To suppose that he really meant that there were literally four months to pass away before harvest, appears to me to involve serious chronological difficulties. It necessitates the assumption that at least three-quarters of a year had passed away since the passover, when our Lord purified the temple (*John* 2:23). No doubt this possibly may have been the case. But it does not appear to me probable. In addition, we must remember that our Lord on another occasion referred to a proverbial saying about the weather, beginning much as he does here, 'Ye say' (*Matt.* 16:2, 3). Moreover, in this very passage he quotes a proverb about 'one sowing and another reaping,' within two verses. The expression therefore, 'Say not ye,' seems to me to point to a proverbial saying much more than to a fact. The antithesis to it is the 'I say,' which immediately follows.

Calvin says, 'By this expression, *Do not ye say?* Christ intended indirectly to point out how much more attentive the minds of men are to earthly than to heavenly things, for they burn with so intense a desire of harvest that they carefully reckon up months and days, while it is astonishing how drowsy and indolent they are in gathering the heavenly wheat.'

Cornelius à Lapide conjectures that the disciples had been talking to one another about the prospects of harvest, as they came to the well, and that our Lord, knowing the conversation, referred to it by the words, 'Do not ye say?'

[*Lift up your eyes, and look on the fields ... white ... harvest.*] There can be little doubt that this saying must be interpreted figuratively. The sense is, 'There is a harvest of souls before you ready to be gathered in.' The same figure is used elsewhere (*Matt.* 9:37; *Luke* 10:2).

Some think, as Chrysostom, that when our Lord said, 'Behold, ... lift up your eyes ... look,' he spoke with especial reference to the crowd of Samaritans whom he saw coming from the city to the well. If this be so, it is hard to suppose that he first began conversation with the woman at six o'clock in the evening.

Others think that our Lord spoke these words with reference to the whole world, and specially the Jewish nation, at the time of his ministry. They were so ready and prepared for the preaching of the gospel, that they were like a field white for harvest. The expression, 'lift up your eyes,' is used elsewhere in Scripture, when mental attention is being called to something remarkable (see *Isa.* 49:18; 60:4; *Gen.* 13:14, 15).

I am disposed to think that both views are correct. Our Lord wished his disciples to notice that both at Samaria and elsewhere the minds of men were everywhere ready to receive the message of the gospel in an unusual degree. Let them mark how willing the multitude was everywhere to listen to the truth. Let them know that everywhere, as in the apparently hopeless field of Samaria, they would find a harvest of souls ready to be reaped, if only they would be reapers.

Chrysostom, on this verse, remarks, 'Christ leads his disciples as his custom is, from low things to high. *Fields* and *harvests* here express the great number of souls which are ready to receive the word. The *eyes* are both spiritual and bodily ones, for they saw a great multitude of Samaritans now approaching. This expectant crowd he calls, very suitably, white fields. For as the corn when it grows white is ready for harvest, so were those ready for salvation. But why does he not say all this in direct language? Because by making use of the objects around them he gave great vividness and power to his words, and also caused his discourse to be more pleasant and sink deeper into their memories.'

36.—[*He that reapeth, etc.*] This verse seems to me to show that our Lord is speaking generally of the field of this world, and of the whole work which his apostles would have to do in it, not only in Samaria, but to the ends of the earth. The verse is a general promise for the encouragement of all labourers of Christ. The full meaning of it can hardly be brought out without a paraphrase. 'The reaper of the spiritual harvest has a far more honourable and satisfactory office than the reaper of the natural harvest. He receives wages and gathers fruit not for this life only, but for the life to come. The wages that he receives are eternal wages: a crown of glory that fadeth not away (1 Pet. 5:4). The fruit that he gathers is eternal fruit: souls plucked from destruction and saved for evermore' (see Dan. 12:3; John 15:16; and 1 Cor. 9:17).

Burkitt, and several other writers, call attention to the fact that the harvestman's wages are much more than the wages of any other labourer, and hence draw the conclusion that no Christian will receive so glorious a reward as the man who labours to win souls to Christ.

[*That both he that soweth ... reapeth may rejoice together.*] These words appear to me to refer to the common joy that there will be in heaven among all who have laboured for Christ, when the whole harvest of saved souls is finally gathered in. The Old Testament prophets and John the Baptist, who *sowed*, will all rejoice together with the apostles, who *reaped*.— The results of the spiritual harvest are not like those of the natural harvest, temporal; but eternal: so that a day will come when all who have laboured for it in any way, either by sowing or reaping, will sit down and rejoice together to all eternity. Here in this world the sower sometimes does not live to see the fruit of his labour, and the reaper who gathers in the harvest rejoices alone. But work done in the spiritual harvest is eternal work, and consequently both sowers and reapers are sure at last to 'rejoice together,' and to see the fruit of their toil.

Let it be noted, that in heaven there will at last be no jealousy and envy among Christ's labourers. Some will have been sowers and some will have been reapers. But all will have done that part of the work allotted to them, and all will finally 'rejoice together.' Envious feelings will be absorbed in common joy.

Let it be noted, that in doing work for Christ, and labouring for souls, there are sowers as well as reapers. The work of the reaper makes far more show than the work of the sower: yet it is perfectly clear that if there was no sowing there would be no reaping. It is of great importance to remember this. The church is often disposed to give an excessive honour to Christ's reapers, and to overlook the labours of Christ's sowers.

37.—[*Herein is that saying true, etc., etc.*] Our Lord here quotes a proverbial saying, which appears to me to confirm the view I have already maintained, that the expression of verse 35, 'Say not ye there are yet four months,' etc., refers to a proverb.

The phrase 'herein' means literally, 'in this,' and seems to me to refer to the verse which immediately follows. 'That common saying, one soweth and another reapeth, is made good in this way,—is fulfilled by this circumstance,—is verified in the following manner: viz., 'I sent you to reap,' etc.

The meaning of the proverb is plain. 'It is a common saying among men that it often falls to one to sow the field and to another to reap it. The sower and the reaper are not always the same person.'

The frequent use of proverbial sayings in the New Testament deserves notice. It shows the value of proverbs, and the importance of teaching them to children and young people. A pointed proverb is often remembered when a long moral lesson is forgotten.

38.—[*I sent you to reap, etc.*] Our Lord here states the manner in which the proverbial saying of the preceding verse is true. He tells the apostles that they were sent to reap a spiritual harvest on which they had bestowed no labour. Other men had laboured: viz., the prophets of the Old Testament and John the Baptist. They had broken up the ground: they had sown the seed. The result of their labour was that the minds of men in the apostles' times were prepared to expect the Messiah, and the apostles had only to go forth and proclaim the glad tidings that Messiah was come.

Pearce maintains the strange notion that our Lord, in this verse, only means, 'I sent you away into the city to buy meat. While you were absent I sowed spiritual seed in the heart of a Samaritan woman. She is now gone to call others. These and many more will be the harvest which you will reap, without having bestowed any labour on it.' This interpretation seems to me quite untenable.

The past tense in this verse, 'I have sent,' is used, as a grammarian would say, proleptically. It means, 'I do send you.' Such a use of the past tense is common in Scripture, and especially when God speaks of a thing about to be done. With God there is no uncertainty. When he undertakes a thing, it may be regarded as done and finished, because in his counsels it is certain to be finished. Our Lord's meaning is, 'I send you throughout Samaria, Galilee, and Judæa, to reap the fruit of the labours of the prophets and John the Baptist. They have sowed, and you have now only to reap.'

Some think, as Stier and Alford, that when our Lord said, 'other men have laboured,' he referred rather to himself than to the prophets. I am unable to see this. It appears to me a forced and unnatural interpretation. I hold decidedly, with Chrysostom, Cyril, Theophylact, Calvin, Zwingle, Melanchthon, Brentius, Lampe, and Poole, that it applies principally to the law and prophets.—'If the prophets were not the sowers,' says Augustine, 'whence had that saying come to the woman, I know that Messias cometh?'—Origen says, 'Did not Moses and Elias, the sowers, rejoice with the reapers, Peter, James, and John, when they saw the glory of the Son of God at the transfiguration?'

Theophylact sees in this verse a strong argument against the heretical view of the Marcionites, Manichees, and others, that the New Testament is contrary to the Old. Here the prophets and apostles are spoken of together, as labourers under one common Master in one common field.

The idea propounded by Bucer, that our Lord alludes here to the heathen philosophers as well as the prophets, seems to me unwarrantable and unsafe.

39.—[*Many ... Samaritans ... believed.*] About the exact nature of the belief mentioned here and in verse 41, we have no materials for forming an opinion. Whether it was only an intellectual belief that Christ was the Messiah, or whether it was that true faith of the heart which justifies a sinner before God, we are left to conjecture. The more probable opinion appears to be that it was true faith, though very weak and unintelligent, like that of the apostles themselves. It is a strong confirmation of this view, that when Philip, after the day of Pentecost, went down to Samaria and preached Christ, his preaching was received with joy, and many were baptized, both men and women (*Acts* 8:5-12). The gospel was received without prejudice, and embraced at once as an acknowledged truth.

[*For ... saying ... woman ... testified, etc.*] These words show the importance of merely human testimony to Christ's gospel. The word of one weak woman was made the instrumental means of belief to many souls. There was nothing remarkable in the woman's word. It contained no elaborate reasoning, and no striking eloquence. It was only a hearty, earnest testimony of a believing heart. Yet God was pleased to use it to the conversion of souls. We must never despise the use of means. If the woman had not spoken, the Samaritans would not have been converted.—Above all, we must never despise means because of their apparent weakness, feebleness, and inaptness to do good. God can make the weakest instruments powerful to pull down the strongholds of sin and Satan, just as he made David's sling and stone prevail over Goliath.

Theophylact points out that the Samaritan woman's past wicked life was well known to her fellow-citizens, and that their attention must have been aroused by her publicly proclaiming that she had found One who knew her former life, although a stranger. They rightly concluded that he must be no common person.

Melanchthon remarks that the belief which resulted from the testimony of a woman in this case, is a clear proof that it is not absolutely necessary to have regular ministerial orders in order to do good to souls, and that episcopal orders are not absolutely needful in order to give effect to the word when spoken.

40.—[*So when ... Samaritans ... come
... besought ... tarry, etc.*] The desire of
the Samaritans for instruction is shown in
this verse, and the willingness of Christ
to assist inquirers is strikingly exhibited.
He waits to be entreated. If we have him
not abiding with us, it is because we do
not ask him. The two disciples journeying
to Emmaus would have missed a great
privilege if they had not said, 'Abide with
us' (*Luke* 24:29).

Ferus on this verse remarks the wide
difference between the Samaritans and the
Gergesenes. The Gergesenes prayed our
Lord to 'depart' from them, the Samaritans
to 'tarry' with them (*Matt.* 8:34).

[*He abode ... two days.*] We can only
suppose that these two days were spent
in teaching and preaching the gospel. One
would like to know all that was taught and
said in those two days. But it is an instance
of the occasional 'silences' of Scripture,
which every attentive Bible reader must
have noticed. The first thirty years of our
Lord's life at Nazareth,—the way in which
St Paul spent his time in Arabia,—and his
employment during his two years' impris-
onment in Cæsarea, are similar silences
(*Gal.* 1:17; *Acts* 24:27).

It is an interesting fact, which has been
observed by some writers, that at this very
day Nablous and its neighbourhood, occu-
pying the site of Samaria and Sychar, are in a
more flourishing and prosperous condition
than almost any place in Palestine. While
Capernaum, and Chorazin, and Bethsaida,
which rejected Christ, have almost entirely
passed away, Samaria, which believed and
received him, flourishes still.

41.—[*Many more believed ... own
word.*] This verse shows the sovereignty
of God in saving souls. One is called in
one way and another in another. Some
Samaritans believed when they heard
the woman testify. Others did not believe
till they heard Christ himself.—We must
be careful that we do not bind down the
Holy Ghost to one mode of operation. The
experience of saved souls often differs
widely. If people are brought to repentance
and faith in Christ, we must not be stumbled because they are not all brought in the
same way.

Olshausen remarks on this verse, 'Here
is a rare instance in which the ministry
of the Lord produced an awakening on a
large scale. Ordinarily we find that a few
individuals only were aroused by him, and
that these, like grains of seed scattered here
and there, became the germs of a new and
higher order of things among the people at
large.'

42.—[*Now we believe, not ... thy saying.*]
The Greek words so rendered would be translated more literally, 'Not any longer because
of thy saying do we believe.'

Calvin thinks that the Greek word here
rendered 'saying,' means literally, 'talk,
or talkativeness,' and that 'the Samaritans
appear to boast that they have now a
stronger foundation than a woman's
tongue.' In the only other three places
where it is used, it is translated 'speech'
(*Matt.* 26:73; *Mark* 14:70; *John* 8:43).

[*This is indeed ... Christ ... Saviour
... world.*] The Greek words so rendered
would be translated more literally, 'This is
the Saviour of the world, the Christ.'

The singular fulness of the confession
made by these Samaritans deserves special
notice. A more full declaration of our Lord's
office as 'Saviour of the world' is nowhere
to be found in the Gospels. Whether the
Samaritans clearly understood what they
meant when they spoke of our Lord as
'the Saviour,' may be reasonably doubted.
But that they saw with peculiar clearness
a truth which the Jews were specially
backward in seeing,—that he had come
to be a Redeemer for all mankind, and
not for the 'Jews' only,—seems evident
from the expression, 'the world.' That
such a testimony should have been borne
to Christ by a mixed race of semi-heathen
origin, like the Samaritans, and not by the
Jews, is a remarkable instance of the grace
of God.

The inference drawn by Calvin from this
verse, that 'within two days the sense of the
gospel was more plainly taught by Christ
at Samaria than he had hitherto taught it
at Jerusalem,' seems both unwarrantable
and needless. Ought we not rather to fix
our eyes on the difference between the Jews
and Samaritans? Christ's teaching was the
same, but the hearts of his hearers were

widely different. The Jews were hardened. The Samaritans believed.

Chemnitius, on this verse, thinks that an emphasis is meant to be laid on the Greek word rendered 'indeed.' Literally it is 'truly.' He thinks it was used of our Lord in contradistinction to the false Christs and Messiahs who had appeared before him, as well as to the typical Messiahs and Saviours, such as the judges.

In leaving the passage we may well wonder that so many 'Samaritans' should at once have believed on our Lord, when so few 'Jews' ever believed. Our wonder may well be increased when we consider that our Lord worked no miracle on this occasion, and that the word was the only instrument used to open the Samaritans' hearts.—We see for one thing the entire sovereignty of the grace of God. The last are often first and the first last: the most ignorant and unenlightened believe and are saved, while the most learned and enlightened continue unbelieving and are lost.—We see for another thing that it is not miracles and privileges, but grace, which converts souls. The Jews saw scores of mighty miracles worked by our Lord, and heard him preach for weeks and months, and yet with a few rare exceptions remained impenitent and hardened.

The Samaritans saw no miracles worked at all, and only had our Lord among them for two days, and yet many of them believed. If ever there was clear proof that the grace of the Holy Spirit is the chief thing needed in order to procure the conversion of souls, we have it in the verses we are now leaving.

The allegorical and typical meanings which some writers assign to the Samaritan woman and her history, as related in this chapter, are hardly worth recounting. Some regard the woman as a type of the Jewish synagogue, slavishly bound to the five books of the law, and drawn finally by Christ to drink the living water of the gospel.—Some regard the woman as a type of the Gentile nations, for five thousand years committing fornication with heathen idols, and at length purged by Christ, and casting away their empty waterpot in obedience to Christianity.—Some go even further, and regard the woman as a prophetical type of things yet to come. They consider her as a type of the Greek Church, which is yet to be brought in to the true faith of Christ! These views appear to me at best only fanciful speculations, and more likely to do harm than good, by drawing men away from the plain practical lessons which the passage contains.

JOHN 4:43-54

43 Now after two days he departed thence, and went into Galilee.

44 For Jesus himself testified, that a prophet hath no honour in his own country.

45 Then when he was come into Galilee, the Galilæans received him, having seen all the things that he did at Jerusalem at the feast: for they also went unto the feast.

46 So Jesus came again into Cana of Galilee, where he made the water wine. And there was a certain nobleman, whose son was sick at Capernaum.

47 When he heard that Jesus was come out of Judæa into Galilee, he went unto him, and besought him that he would come down, and heal his son: for he was at the point of death.

48 Then said Jesus unto him, Except ye see signs and wonders, ye will not believe.

49 The nobleman saith unto him, Sir, come down ere my child die.

50 Jesus saith unto him, Go thy way; thy son liveth. And the man believed the word that Jesus had spoken unto him, and he went his way.

51 And as he was now going down, his servants met him, and told *him*, saying, Thy son liveth.

52 Then enquired he of them the hour when he began to amend. And they said unto him, Yesterday at the seventh hour the fever left him.

53 So the father knew that *it was* at the same hour, in the which Jesus said unto him, Thy son liveth: and himself believed, and his whole house.

54 This *is* again the second miracle *that* Jesus did, when he was come out of Judæa into Galilee.

FOUR great lessons stand out boldly on the face of this passage. Let us fix them in our memories, and use them continually as we journey through life.

We learn, firstly, that *the rich have afflictions as well as the poor.* We read of a nobleman in deep anxiety because his son was sick. We need not doubt that every means of restoration was used that money could procure. But money is not almighty. The sickness increased, and the nobleman's son lay at the point of death.

The lesson is one which needs to be constantly impressed on the minds of men. There is no more common, or more mischievous error, than to suppose that the rich have no cares. The rich are as liable to sickness as the poor; and have a hundred anxieties beside, of which the poor know nothing at all. Silks and satins often cover very heavy hearts. The dwellers in palaces often sleep more uneasily than the dwellers in cottages. Gold and silver can lift no man beyond the reach of trouble: they may shut out debt and rags, but they cannot shut out care, disease, and death. The higher the tree, the more it is shaken by storms: the broader its branches, the greater is the mark which it exposes to the tempest. David was a happier man when he kept his father's sheep at Bethlehem, than when he dwelt as a king at Jerusalem, and governed the twelve tribes of Israel.

Let the servant of Christ beware of desiring riches. They are certain cares, and uncertain comforts. Let him pray for the rich, and not envy them. How hardly shall a rich man enter the kingdom of God! Above all, let him learn to be content with such things as he has. He only is truly rich who has treasure in heaven.

We learn, secondly, in this passage, that *sickness and death come to the young as well as to the old*. We read of a son sick unto death, and a father in trouble about him. We see the natural order of things inverted: the elder is obliged to minister to the younger, and not the younger to the elder. The child draws nigh to the grave before the parent, and not the parent before the child.

The lesson is one which we are all slow to learn. We are apt to shut our eyes to plain facts, and to speak and act as if young people, as a matter of course, never died when young. And yet the gravestones in every churchyard would tell us that few people out of a hundred ever live to be fifty years old, while many never grow up to man's estate at all. The first grave that ever was dug on this earth, was that of a young man: the first person who ever died, was not a father but a son. Aaron lost two sons at a stroke. David, the man after God's own heart, lived long enough to see three children buried. Job was deprived of all his children in one day. These things were carefully recorded for our learning.

He that is wise will never reckon confidently on long life. We never know what a day may bring forth. The strongest and fairest are often cut down and hurried away in a few hours, while the old and feeble linger on for many years. The only true wisdom is to be always prepared to meet God, to put nothing off which concerns eternity, and to live like men ready to depart at any moment. So living, it matters little whether we die young or old. Joined to the Lord Jesus, we are safe in any event.

We learn, thirdly, from this passage, *what benefits affliction can confer on the soul*. We read, that anxiety about a son led the nobleman to Christ, in order to obtain help in time of need. Once brought into Christ's company, he learned a lesson of priceless value: in the end, he 'believed, and his whole house.' All this, be it remembered, hinged upon the son's sickness. If the nobleman's son had never been ill, his father might have lived and died in his sins.

Affliction is one of God's medicines. By it he often teaches lessons which would be learned in no other way. By it he often draws souls away from sin and the world, which would otherwise have perished everlastingly. Health is a great blessing, but sanctified disease is a greater. Prosperity and worldly comfort are what all naturally desire; but losses and crosses are far better for us, if they lead us to Christ. Thousands at the last day, will testify with David, and the nobleman before us, 'It is good for me that I have been afflicted' (*Psa.* 119:71).

Let us beware of murmuring in the time of trouble. Let us settle it firmly in our minds that there is a meaning, a needs-be, and a message from God, in every sorrow that falls upon us. There are no lessons so useful as those learned in the school of affliction. There is no commentary that opens up the Bible so much as sickness and sorrow. 'No chastening for the present seemeth to be joyous, but grievous: nevertheless afterward it yieldeth . . . peaceable fruit' (*Heb.* 12:11). The resurrection morning will prove that many of the losses of God's people were in reality eternal gains.

We learn, lastly, from this passage, that *Christ's word is as good as Christ's presence.* We read that Jesus did not come down to Capernaum to see the sick young man, but only spoke the word: 'Thy son liveth.' Almighty power went with that little sentence: that very hour the patient began to amend. Christ only spoke, and the cure was done: Christ only commanded, and the deadly disease stood fast.

The fact before us is singularly full of comfort. It gives enormous value to every promise of mercy, grace, and peace, which ever fell from Christ's lips. He that by faith has laid hold on some word of Christ, has got his feet upon a rock. What Christ has said, he is able to do; and what he has undertaken, he will never fail to make good. The sinner who has really reposed his soul on the word of the Lord Jesus, is safe to all eternity. He could not be safer if he saw the book of life and his own name written in it. If Christ has said, 'Him that cometh to me, I will in no wise cast out,' and our hearts can testify, 'I have come,' we need not doubt that we are saved. In the things of this world, we say that seeing is believing. But in the things of the gospel, believing is as good as seeing. Christ's word is as good as man's deed.

EXPOSITORY THOUGHTS ON JOHN

He of whom Jesus says in the gospel, 'He liveth,' is alive for evermore, and shall never die.

And now let us remember that afflictions, like that of the nobleman, are very common. They will probably come to our door one day. Have we known anything of bearing affliction? Would we know where to turn for help and comfort when our time comes? Let us fill our minds and memories betimes with Christ's words. They are not the words of man only, but of God. The words that he speaks are spirit and life (*John* 6:63).

Notes—John 4:43-54

43.—[*After two days.*] The Greek words here would be more literally rendered, 'After the two days:' i.e., after the two days mentioned in the preceding verse.

[*Departed thence.*] Quesnel remarks, 'It is an instance of self-denial which is very uncommon, to leave those who respect and applaud us, that we may go to preach among others from whom we have reason to expect a quite different treatment.'

44.—[*For Jesus himself testified ... his own country.*] This verse has much perplexed commentators. What is meant by the expression, 'his own country'? If it means Galilee, as most suppose, how are we to reconcile it with the words which follow, 'the Galileans received him'?—And again, what is the connection between the verse before us and the one which precedes it? Why should our Lord go into Galilee, when it was a place where he had no honour? And finally, how are we to reconcile the statement that our Lord had no 'honour' in Galilee with the undeniable fact that nearly all his disciples and adherents were Galileans? All these points have given rise to much speculation and conjecture.

a. Some, as Origen and Maldonatus, get over the difficulty in the following manner. They say that the words, 'his own country,' must mean Judæa, and Bethlehem, where Christ was born. The sense will then be, 'After two days Jesus departed from Samaria, and went into Galilee, and not into Judæa, because in Judæa he received no honour,

and was not believed.' This solution seems to me unnatural and unsatisfactory. Our Lord's going to Galilee was a premeditated journey, and not a sudden plan decided on during his stay at Samaria. Beside this, there is no proof whatever that our Lord was not received and believed in Judæa. On the contrary, he 'made and baptized' so many disciples in Judæa, that it attracted the notice of the Pharisees, and made it necessary for him to 'depart into Galilee.'

b. Augustine holds that 'his own country' means Galilee, and seems to attach the following sense to the verse: 'And yet Jesus testified that a prophet hath no honour in his own country, for when he came into Galilee no one believed on him, except the nobleman and his house.' This appears to me a far-fetched and unnatural interpretation. Tittman and Blomfield take much the same view, and render it, 'Although Jesus had testified,' etc.

c. Chrysostom and Euthymius think that 'his own country' means Capernaum. This interpretation also seems to me improbable. We find Capernaum elsewhere called our Lord's 'own city,' but nowhere else 'his own country' (see *Matt.* 9:1).

d. Theophylact suggests that the verse before us is inserted in order to explain 'why our Lord did not always abide and continue in Galilee, but only came there at intervals. The reason was that he received no honour there.' This also seems to me an unsatisfactory interpretation.

e. Alford says, 'The only true and simple view is, that this verse refers to the next following, and indeed to the whole narrative which it introduces. It stands as a preliminary explanation of "Except ye see signs and wonders ye will not believe," and indicates the contrast between the Samaritans, who believed on him for his own word, and his own countrymen, who only received him because they had seen the miracles which he did at Jerusalem.' This view of the text seems to me as far-fetched and unsatisfactory as any of those I have mentioned. Moreover I doubt much whether the Greek word rendered 'for,' is ever used in the sense Alford puts on it, in the New Testament.

f. The following explanation appears to me by far the most probable one. The words, 'his own country,' mean neither Galilee nor Judæa, but 'Nazareth.' The sense is, 'Jesus departed from Samaria into Galilee, but not to his own country, Nazareth, because he testified, both now and on other occasions, that a prophet has no honour in his own country.'—In confirmation of the view I have maintained, it deserves notice, that in the six only places in which the Greek word here rendered 'country' is found in the Gospels, beside the one before us, it always means the town of Nazareth, and not the district in which Nazareth is situated (*Matt.* 13:54, 57; *Mark* 6:1, 4; *Luke* 4:23, 24). The view I have supported is that of Cyril, Calvin, Calovius, Lampe, Poole, De Dieu, Pearce, Doddridge, Dyke, and Olshausen.

Our Lord's use of a proverb in this verse is again worthy of notice. It is another proof of the value of proverbial sayings.

The lesson of the proverb is a very instructive one. It is one of the most melancholy proofs of man's fallen and corrupt state, that he never values what he is familiar with, and that familiarity breeds contempt. Ministers of the gospel discover this by painful experience, when they have resided many years in the same parish, and ministered long in the same congregation. Those who have the most abundant supply of gospel privileges are often the people who value them least. 'The nearer the church the further from God,' is often found to be literally true. Those who live furthest off, and are obliged to deny themselves most in order to hear the gospel, are often the very persons who take most pains to hear it.

One grain of comfort, however, may be extracted from this painful verse. A minister must not despair, and accuse himself of unfaithfulness, because the gospel he preaches is not honoured in his own congregation, and many remain hardened and unbelieving, after he has preached to them many years. Let him remember that he is sharing his Master's lot. He is drinking the very cup of which Christ drank. Christ had no honour in Nazareth, and faithful ministers have often less honour among their own people than they have elsewhere.

Pellican thinks that our Lord 'testified' the truth contained in this verse in reply to someone who asked him why he did not go to Nazareth. I prefer the opinion that it simply means our Lord 'always did testify, and made a practice of testifying.'

45.—[*Galilæans received him.*] The word 'received' probably means no more than that they 'received him with respect and reverence,' as One who was no common person. There is no warrant for supposing that they all received him with true faith, and experimentally believed on him as the Saviour of their souls.

[*Having seen ... things ... Jerusalem ... feast.*] This expression confirms the view already maintained (*John* 2:23), that our Lord did many other miracles at Jerusalem at the first passover, when he was there, beside casting the buyers and sellers out of the temple. It is probable that the miracles recorded in the four Gospels are only a selection out of the number that Christ worked.

Here, as elsewhere, we see the special use of miracles. They served to arrest men's attention, and gave the impression that he who wrought them deserved a hearing. The Galileans were ready to receive Christ respectfully, because they had seen his miracles.

[*They also went ... feast.*] This sentence is a useful proof of the universality of the Jewish custom of attending the great feasts at Jerusalem, and especially the feast of the passover. Even those who lived furthest off from Jerusalem, in Galilee, made a point of going to the passover. It serves to show the publicity of our Lord's ministry, both in life and death. When he was crucified at the passover, the event happened in the presence of myriads of witnesses from every part of the world. The overruling providence of God ordered things so that the facts of Christ's life and death could never be denied. 'This thing was not done in a corner' (*Acts* 26:26).

46.—[*Jesus came again ... Cana.*] The circumstance of our Lord going twice to Cana may be accounted for by remembering the fact that one of his disciples, 'Nathanael,' belonged to Cana, and that his mother, Mary, in all probability had relatives there (see note on *John* 2:1).

[*A certain nobleman.*] The Greek word rendered 'nobleman' is only found here in this sense, as a substantive, in the New Testament. The marginal reading, 'courtier or ruler,' hardly makes it more clear. Some have conjectured that the nobleman must have been someone attached to Herod's court, and is therefore called 'a royal person,' which is the literal meaning of the word. Some, as Luther, Chemnitius, Lightfoot, and Pearce, have also conjectured that 'Chuza, Herod's steward,' whose wife Joanna became one of our Lord's disciples, and 'ministered unto him' (*Luke* 8:3), must have been this nobleman. This is no doubt possible, and would be an interesting fact if it could be proved. But there is no authority for it, except conjecture. Lightfoot adds a conjecture, that if not Chuza it might have been Manaen (*Acts.* 13:1).

The rarity of a nobleman and a person connected with a royal court seeking Christ under any circumstances, is observed by Glassius and others. It shows us that Christ will have trophies of the power of his grace out of every rank, class, and condition. In the first chapter of St John's Gospel we see fishermen converted; in the third, a self-righteous Pharisee; in the beginning of the fourth, a fallen Samaritan woman; and in the end, a nobleman out of a king's court.

Pearce thinks that the nobleman was one of the class called Herodians (*Matt.* 22:16).

[*Son was sick at Capernaum.*] We should always notice the number and greatness of miracles which our Lord worked at Capernaum, and the dignity of the persons at whose instance they were worked. Here he healed the centurion's servant (*Matt.* 8:5). Here, in all probability, he restored to life the daughter of Jairus, the ruler of the synagogue (*Mark* 5:21, 22). And here, in the present instance, he healed the nobleman's son. Three distinct and leading classes had each of them a mighty miracle wrought among them. The centurion was a Gentile soldier. The ruler of the synagogue was a Jew of high ecclesiastical position. The nobleman was connected with the highest civil authorities. The consequence no doubt was that the name and power of Christ became known to every leading family in Capernaum. No wonder that our Lord says, 'Thou, Capernaum, that art exalted unto heaven' (*Matt.* 11:23). No place was so privileged as this city.

The idea entertained by some that this 'nobleman' was the same as the centurion in Matthew 8:5, and that the miracle here recorded is only the same miracle differently reported, seems to me entirely destitute of foundation. The details of the two miracles are entirely different. The miracle before us is nowhere else reported in the Gospels.

47.—[*Heard that Jesus was come, etc.*] This verse shows how widely spread was the fame of the miracle wrought at Cana upon the occasion of our Lord's former visit, and how great was the report of our Lord's miracles at Jerusalem, brought back by the Galileans who went to the feast. In no other way can we account for the nobleman going to our Lord and beseeching him to come and heal his son. Our Lord must have got the reputation of being One who was both able and willing to work such cures.

Musculus remarks on this verse, how much more love descends than ascends. In all the Gospels we never read of any sons or daughters coming to Christ on behalf of their parents.

Dyke observes, 'Some crosses drive men to Christ, especially in our children. This was the cross that subdued Egypt; and to great men, such as this ruler, who have much to leave their children, this cross is the greatest.'

48.—[Then said Jesus, Except ye see, etc.] Our Lord in this verse appears to refer to the common desire expressed by the Jews to see miracles and signs, as a proof of his Messiahship. 'Cannot you believe unless you actually see with your own eyes a miracle worked? Is your faith so small, that except you *see* something you cannot believe?'—No doubt our Lord knew the heart of the man before him. He wished to test his faith, and to draw out from him more earnest desires after the mercy that he wanted. The resemblance between our Lord's first answer to the nobleman and his first answer to the woman of Canaan, who came to him about her daughter, deserve comparison (*Matt.* 15:24).

Chrysostom remarks, 'Christ's meaning is, Ye have not yet the right faith, but still feel towards me as only a prophet. He rebuketh the state of mind with which the nobleman had come to him, because that before a miracle he believed not strongly. Thus too he drew him on the more to belief.—That the nobleman came and entreated was nothing wonderful, for parents in their great affection are wont to resort to, and talk with physicians. But that he came without any strong purpose appears from this, that he only came to Christ when Christ came into Galilee, whereas, if he had firmly believed, he would not have hesitated, when his child was at the point of death, to go into Judæa.'

Glassius thinks that our Lord, in these words, intends to contrast the faith of the Samaritans with the unbelief of the Galileans. The Samaritans believed without having seen any signs or wonders at all.

Chemnitius thinks that our Lord, in this verse, spoke with special reference to the state of mind in which he found the inhabitants of Cana upon his second visit. He thinks that he found them aroused to a state of expectation and curiosity by his miracle of changing water into wine, but still destitute of any real saving faith.

Poole compares the nobleman to Naaman, who had faith enough to come to Elisha's door to be healed of his leprosy, but was stumbled because Elisha did not put his hand on the diseased place, but only sent him a message (2 *Kings* 5:11).

49.—[*The nobleman saith, etc.*] This verse shows the earnestness of the nobleman's desire for relief, quickened and sharpened by the apparent rebuff contained in our Lord's reply to his first application. Yet it was a saying exhibiting much ignorance. It is clear that he did not discover what our Lord hinted at,—that possibly he might be helped without his coming down to see his sick son. He neither denies the truth of our Lord's words, nor enters into argument. He only knew that he felt in grievous distress, and begged our Lord to 'come down ere his child died.' That our Lord could heal him he did not doubt. But that he could heal him at a distance, without even seeing him, was something that he could not yet understand.

Chrysostom says, 'Observe how these very words show the weakness of the man. When he ought, after Christ had rebuked his state of mind, to have imagined something great concerning him, even if he did not before, listen how he drags along the ground! He speaks as though Christ could not raise his son after death, and as though he knew not in what state the child was.'

Brentius remarks that the nobleman did not bring to Christ faith, but merely a spark of faith.

50.—[*Jesus saith unto him, etc.*] Three things are very deserving of notice in this verse. 1. We should observe our Lord's marvellous kindness and compassion. He takes no notice of the nobleman's weak faith and slowness of understanding. He freely grants his request, and gives his son life and health without delay. 2. We should observe our Lord's almighty power. He simply speaks the words, 'Thy son liveth,' and at once a sick person, at several miles' distance, is cured and made well. He spake and it was done. 3. We should observe, not least, the unhesitating confidence which the nobleman reposed in our Lord's power. He asked no more questions after he heard the words, 'Thy son liveth.' At once he believed that all would be well, and went his way.

Cyril observes on this verse, that our Lord here healed two persons at one time by the same words. 'He brought the nobleman's mind to faith, and delivered the body of the young man from disease.'

Chrysostom remarks, 'What can be the reason why in the case of the centurion Christ undertook voluntarily to come and heal, while here, though invited, he came not? Because in the case of the centurion faith had been perfected, and therefore he undertook to go, that we might learn the right-mindedness of the man; but here the nobleman was imperfect. When therefore he continually urged him, saying, "Come down," and knew not clearly that even when absent he could heal, he showeth that even this was possible unto him, in order that this man might gain, from his not going, that knowledge which the centurion had of himself.'

Bishop Hall observes, 'The ruler's request was, Come and heal. Christ's answer was, "Go thy way: thy son liveth." Our merciful Saviour meets those in the end whom he crosses in the way. How sweetly doth he correct our prayers; and while he doth not give us what we asked, gives us better than we asked.'

51.—[*As he was now going down.*] The relative positions of Cana and Capernaum are not precisely known at the present day. The exact size of Capernaum is matter of dispute among travellers and geographers. All we can glean from the expression before us is, that Cana was probably in the hill country, and Capernaum on the Lake of Galilee. Hence a person leaving Cana for Capernaum would 'go down.'

[*Thy son liveth.*] The meaning of this expression must evidently be, 'Thy son is so much better, that he is comparatively alive from the dead. He was as one dead. He is now alive.'

52.—[*Then inquired he ... the hour.*] This man's mind seems at once to have laid hold on the nature of the miracle, and to have acknowledged the power of Christ's word.

[*He began to amend.*] The Greek expression so rendered is a very peculiar one, and only found in this place. It is literally, 'Had himself better: in more elegant order.'—Let it be noted, that here, as elsewhere, we find an expression which is only used once in the New Testament. This shows that it is no valid argument against the inspiration of any text or passage, that it contains Greek expressions nowhere else used.

[*Yesterday at the seventh hour.*] This expression has been differently interpreted, according to the view which commentators take of St John's mode of reckoning time. Those who think that he numbered hours in the same way that we do, maintain that it means, 'at seven o'clock in the evening.' Those, on the contrary, who maintain that St John observed the Jewish mode of computation, say that it means 'at one o'clock in the afternoon.'

I have already given it as my decided opinion, that John observes the Jewish mode of reckoning time; and I therefore hold with those who think, that 'the seventh hour' means one o'clock. The arguments of those who say that, if it had been one o'clock, the nobleman would never have taken till the next day to reach home, appear to my mind quite inconclusive. For one thing, we know nothing accurately of the distance from Cana to Capernaum.— For another thing, we forget the slow rate at which people travel in Eastern countries, on bad roads, in a hilly country.—For another thing, it is entirely an assumption to suppose that the nobleman had nothing else to do at Cana, when he came to Jesus about his son. For anything we know, he had, as a nobleman, business of various kinds, which made it impossible for him to reach home in the afternoon after Jesus had said, 'Thy son liveth.'—Last, but not least, it seems hardly probable that the nobleman would have asked our Lord to come down to Capernaum at so late an hour as seven o'clock in the evening; or would have set off on his own return at that hour, and met his servants in the night.

[*The fever left him.*] Trench remarks, that the words seem to indicate that there was not merely an abatement of the fever, but that it suddenly forsook him (compare *Luke* 4:39).

53.—[*Himself believed.*] Beda remarks, on the matter of the nobleman's believing, that 'there are three degrees of faith,—the beginning, the increase, and the perfection. There was a beginning in this man, when he first came to Christ; an increase, when our Lord told him that his son lived; and a perfection, when he found him to have recovered at that very time.'

[*His whole house.*] This expression probably means, 'his whole family,'—including children and servants. We have no right whatever to exclude children from the sense of the words. Remembering this, we shall better understand what is meant when it is written, St Paul baptized 'the household of Stephanas:' or when it is related, that the house of Lydia was baptized (*1 Cor.* 1:16; *Acts* 16:15).

There seems no reason for doubting that the nobleman, from this time forth, became a thorough, true-hearted, believer in Christ. If, as some suppose, he is the same as Chuza, Herod's steward, we may perhaps date the conversion of Joanna his wife to the period of the verse now before us.

Bishop Hall remarks on this verse, 'Great men cannot want clients. Their example sways some: their authority more. They cannot go to either of the other worlds alone. In vain do they pretend power over others who labour not to draw their families to God!'

54.—[*The second miracle that Jesus did.*] The plain meaning of these words is, that our Lord had worked no other miracle in Galilee before this one, excepting that of turning the water into wine at Cana. It appears likely that many of our Lord's earliest miracles were wrought in Judæa and Jerusalem; although we have no record of them, except in the second chapter of St John's Gospel (*John* 2:23). This fact is noteworthy, because it throws light on the wickedness of the Jews at Jerusalem, where at last Christ was condemned and crucified.

Chrysostom remarks, 'The word "second" is not added without cause, but to exalt yet more the praises of the Samaritans, by showing that even when a second miracle had been wrought, they who beheld it had not yet reached so high as those who had not seen one.'

Origen says, 'Mystically the two journeys of Christ into Galilee signify his two advents. At the first he makes us his guests at supper, and gives us wine to drink. At the second he raises up the nobleman's son at the point of death,—i.e., the Jewish people, who after the fulness of the Gentiles attain salvation. The sick son is the Jewish people fallen from the true religion.'—This is patristic interpretation! Allegorical expositions like this destroy the whole value of God's Word. At this rate the Bible may be made to mean anything.

Chemnitius thinks, that with this chapter ends the first year of our Lord's public ministry, and gives a useful summary of the principal events comprehended within it. These are the Lord's baptism,—the calling of the first disciples,—the miracle at Cana,—the miracle of casting out of the temple the buyers and sellers,—the conversation with Nicodemus,—the tarrying in Judæa and baptizing,—the testimony of John the Baptist,—the journey through Samaria,—the arrival in Galilee,—and the healing of the nobleman's son. Epiphanius, he observes, calls it the 'acceptable year' of our Lord's ministry, because it was the most quiet and peaceful.

Bengel, in closing this chapter, observes, that St John seems to arrange our Lord's miracles in threes. He relates three in Galilee,—the first at the marriage in Cana, the second on the nobleman's son, the third in feeding five thousand men (*John* 6);—three in Judæa,—the first at Bethesda at Pentecost (chapter 5), the second after the feast of tabernacles, on the blind man (chapter 9), the third on Lazarus before the passover (chapter 11).—So also after the ascension, he describes three appearances of our Lord to his disciples (*John* 21:14).

Dyke observes how God keeps account of all the gracious means he affords men for their good. 'The *second* miracle is specified to aggravate the infidelity of the Jews; that though Christ had now done another and a second miracle, yet only the ruler and his household believed. Two miracles wrought, and one household converted! God takes account not only how many men are won by a sermon (*Acts* 2:41), but of how many sermons are lost by men.'

JOHN 5:1-15

1 After this there was a feast of the Jews; and Jesus went up to Jerusalem.

2 Now there is at Jerusalem by the sheep *market* a pool, which is called in the Hebrew tongue Bethesda, having five porches.

3 In these lay a great multitude of impotent folk, of blind, halt, withered, waiting for the moving of the water.

4 For an angel went down at a certain season into the pool, and troubled the water: whosoever then first after the troubling of the water stepped in was made whole of whatsoever disease he had.

5 And a certain man was there, which had an infirmity thirty and eight years.

6 When Jesus saw him lie, and knew that he had been now a long time *in that case*, he saith unto him, Wilt thou be made whole?

7 The impotent man answered him, Sir, I have no man, when the water is troubled, to put me into the pool: but while I am coming, another steppeth down before me.

8 Jesus saith unto him, Rise, take up thy bed, and walk.

9 And immediately the man was made whole, and took up his bed, and walked: and on the same day was the sabbath.

10 The Jews therefore said unto him that was cured, It is the sabbath day: it is not lawful for thee to carry *thy* bed.

11 He answered them, He that made me whole, the same said unto me, Take up thy bed, and walk.

12 Then asked they him, What man is that which said unto thee, Take up thy bed, and walk?

13 And he that was healed wist not who it was: for Jesus had conveyed himself away, a multitude being in *that* place.

14 Afterward Jesus findeth him in the temple, and said unto him, Behold, thou art made whole: sin no more, lest a worse thing come unto thee.

15 The man departed, and told the Jews that it was Jesus, which had made him whole.

WE have in this passage one of the few miracles of Christ which St John records. Like every other miracle in this Gospel, it is described with great minuteness and particularity. And like more than one other miracle it leads on to a discourse full of singularly deep instruction.

We are taught, for one thing, in this passage, *what misery sin has brought into the world.* We read of a man who had been ill for no less than thirty-eight years! For eight-and-thirty weary summers and winters he had endured pain and infirmity. He had seen others healed at the waters of Bethesda, and going to their homes rejoicing. But for him there had been no healing. Friendless, helpless, and hopeless, he lay near the wonder-working waters, but derived no benefit from them. Year after year passed away, and left him still uncured. No relief or change for the better seemed likely to come, except from the grave.

When we read of cases of sickness like this, we should remember how deeply we ought to hate sin! Sin was the original root, and cause, and fountain of every disease in the world. God did not create man to be full of aches, and pains, and infirmities. These things are the fruits of the fall. There would have been no sickness, if there had been no sin.

No greater proof can be shown of man's inbred unbelief, than his carelessness about sin. 'Fools,' says the wise man, 'make a mock at sin' (*Prov.* 14:9). Thousands delight in things which are positively evil, and run greedily after that which is downright poison. They love that which God abhors, and dislike that which God loves. They are like the madman, who loves his enemies and hates his friends. Their eyes are blinded. Surely if men would only look at hospitals and infirmaries, and think what havoc sin has made on this earth, they would never take pleasure in sin as they do.

Well may we be told to pray for the coming of God's kingdom! Well may we be told to long for the second advent of Jesus Christ! Then, and not till then, shall there be no more curse on the earth, no more suffering, no more sorrow, and no more sin. Tears shall be wiped from the faces of all who love Christ's appearing, when their Master returns. Weakness and infirmity shall all pass away. Hope deferred shall no longer make hearts sick. There will be no chronic invalids and incurable cases, when Christ has renewed this earth.

We are taught, for another thing, in this passage, *how great is the mercy and compassion of Christ.* He 'saw' the poor sufferer lying in the crowd. Neglected, overlooked, and forgotten in the great multitude, this man was observed by the all-seeing eye of Christ. The Saviour 'knew' full well, by his divine knowledge, how long he had been 'in that case,' and pitied him. He spoke to him unexpectedly, with words of gracious sympathy. He healed him by miraculous power, at once and without tedious delay, and sent him home rejoicing.

This is just one among many examples of our Lord Jesus Christ's kindness and compassion. He is full of undeserved, unexpected, abounding love towards man. 'He delighteth in mercy' (*Mic.* 7:18).

187

He is far more ready to save than man is to be saved, far more willing to do good than man is to receive it.

No one ever need be afraid of beginning the life of a true Christian, if he feels disposed to begin. Let him not hang back and delay, under the vain idea that Christ is not willing to receive him. Let him come boldly, and trust confidently. He that healed the cripple at Bethesda is still the same.

We are taught, lastly, *the lesson that recovery from sickness ought to impress upon us*. That lesson is contained in the solemn words which our Saviour addressed to the man he had cured: 'Sin no more, lest a worse thing come unto thee.'

Every sickness and sorrow is the voice of God speaking to us. Each has its peculiar message. Happy are they who have an eye to see God's hand, and an ear to hear his voice, in all that happens to them. Nothing in this world happens by chance.

And as it is with sickness, so it is with recovery. Renewed health should send us back to our post in the world with a deeper hatred of sin, a more thorough watchfulness over our own ways, and a more constant purpose of mind to live to God. Far too often the excitement and novelty of returning health tempt us to forget the vows and intentions of the sick-room. There are spiritual dangers attending a recovery! Well would it be for us all after illness to grave these words on our hearts, 'Let me sin no more, lest a worse thing come unto me.'

Let us leave the passage with grateful hearts, and bless God that we have such a gospel and such a Saviour as the Bible reveals.—Are we ever sick and ill? Let us remember that Christ sees, and knows, and can heal if he thinks fit.—Are we ever in trouble? Let us hear in our trouble the voice of God, and learn to hate sin more.

Notes—John 5:1-15

1.—[*After this.*] Literally translated, this would be, 'after these things.' Some think that when St John is telling some event which follows immediately after the last thing narrated, he uses the expression, 'after this thing' (as *John* 2:12), but that when there has been an interval of time he uses the expression, 'after these things.'—If this be correct, we must suppose that some space of time elapsed between the healing of the nobleman's son and the visit to Jerusalem, recorded in this chapter.

[*A feast of the Jews.*] There is nothing to show what feast this was. Most commentators think it was the passover. Many however think it was the feast of Pentecost. Some few say it was the feast of tabernacles, some the feast of purim, and some the feast of the dedication. Each view has its advocates, and the question will probably never be settled. An argument in favour of the passover is the fact that none of the five Jewish feasts were so regularly attended by devout Jews as the passover. An argument against it is the fact that on three other occasions, when the feast of the passover is mentioned in St John, he carefully specifies it by name; and one would naturally expect that it would be named here.

The matter is really of no peculiar importance. In one point of view only it is interesting.—If the 'feast' was the passover, it proves that there were four passovers during the period of our Lord's ministry on earth. St John mentions three by name,— beside this 'feast' (*John* 2:23; 6:4; 12:1). This would make it certain that our Lord's ministry lasted three full years, or at any rate must have begun with a passover and ended with a passover.—If the 'feast' was not the passover, we have no proof that his ministry lasted longer than between two and three years (see notes on *John* 2:13).

The expression, 'a feast of the Jews,' is one of many incidental evidences that St John wrote specially for the use of Gentile converts, and that he thought it needful for their benefit to explain Jewish ordinances.

[*Jesus went up.*] The frequency of our Lord's attendance at Jewish feasts, and the respect he showed for Mosaic ordinances, should always be noticed. They were appointed by God, and so long as they lasted, he gave them honour. It is an important proof to us that the unworthiness of ministers is no reason for neglecting God's ordinances, such as baptism and the Lord's supper. The benefit we receive from ordinances and sacraments does not depend on the character of those who administer them, but on the state of our own souls. The priests and officers of the temple, in our Lord's time, were probably very unworthy persons. But that did not prevent our Lord honouring the temple ordinances and feasts.—It does not however follow from this that we should be justified in habitually going to hear false doctrine preached. Our Lord never did this.

Let it be noted, that none of the four Gospel writers speak so much of our Lord's doings in Judæa and Jerusalem as St John does.

2.—[*There is at Jerusalem.*] These words, it is thought, show that Jerusalem was yet standing and not taken and destroyed by the Romans, when John wrote his Gospel. Otherwise, it is argued, he would have said, 'There *was* at Jerusalem.'

[*By the sheep market a pool.*] Nothing certain is known about this pool, or its precise situation. Modern travellers have professed to point out where it was. But there is little ground for determining the matter, except conjecture and tradition. After all the changes of eighteen centuries, points like these are almost incapable of a satisfactory solution. There is no place in the world, perhaps, where it is so difficult to settle anything decidedly about ancient buildings and sites as Jerusalem. Some propose to render the expression 'sheep market' the 'sheep gate,' because of Nehemiah 3:1. But we really have no certain ground for either expression.

[*Called in the Hebrew tongue Bethesda.*] The word 'Bethesda,' according to Cruden, means 'house of effusion,' or 'house of pity or mercy.' It is not mentioned anywhere else in the Bible. The mention of the 'Hebrew tongue,' shows again that John did not write for Jews so much as Gentiles.

[*Having five porches.*] These porches were probably covered arcades, piazzas, colonnades, or verandas, open at one side to the air, but protected against the sun or rain overhead. In a hot country like Palestine, such buildings are very necessary.

3.—[*In these lay a great multitude.*] The context seems to show that the multitude were assembled at this particular feast in this place, expecting a certain miracle to be wrought, which only took place at this particular time of the year.

[*Impotent folk.*] This expression evidently does not mean paralytic people, but merely people who were sick and ill. The mention of 'blind, halt, withered,' shows this.

[*Moving of the water.*] This 'moving' must have been something that could be seen and observed by persons standing by or looking on. There was no virtue or healing element in the water, until the movement took place.

4.—[*For an angel went down, etc.*] The thing we are here told is very curious. There is nothing like it in the Bible. Josephus, the Jewish writer, does not mention it. The simplest view is that it was a standing miracle wrought once every year, as Cyril says, or at any rate at some special season only, by God's appointment, to keep the Jews in mind of the wonderful works that had been done for them in time past, and to remind them that the God of miracles was unchanged.—But when this singular miracle first began,—on what occasion it began,—why we never hear anything else about it,—in what way the angel came down,—are questions which cannot be answered.—That angels did interpose in a miraculous manner in the days of the New Testament, is perfectly clear from many instances in the Gospels and Acts. That the Jews themselves had strong faith in the interposition of angels on certain occasions, is clear from the account of the vision of Zacharias, when we are simply told that the people 'perceived that he had seen a vision in the temple' (*Luke* 1:22). That from the days of Malachi, when inspiration ceased, God may have seen it good to keep up in the Jewish mind a faith in unseen things, by the grant of a standing miracle, is a very probable opinion. The wisest course is to take the passage as we find it, and to believe though we cannot explain.

All other attempts to get over the difficulties of the passage are thoroughly unsatisfactory. To condemn the passage as not genuine, is a lazy way of cutting the knot, and not at all clearly warranted by the authority of manuscripts.—To say that St John only used the popular language of the Jews in describing the miracle, and did not really believe it himself, is, to say the least, irreverent and profane.—To suppose, as Hammond and others have done, that the 'angel' only means a common human 'messenger' sent by the priests, and that the healing efficacy of the water arose from the blood of the many sacrifices which drained into the pool of Bethesda at the passover feast;—or to suppose, as others, that Bethesda was a pool where sacrifices were washed before they were offered, are all entirely gratuitous assumptions, and do not get over the main difficulty. There is no proof that the blood of the sacrifices did drain into the pool. There is no proof that the blood would give the water any healing virtue. There is no proof, as Lightfoot shows, that sacrifices were washed at all. (See Lightfoot's *Exercitations on John*, on this passage.) Moreover this hypothesis would not account for only one person being healed every time the waters were 'troubled,' or for St John's mention of the 'angel troubling' the waters. Here, as in many other instances, the simplest view, and the one which involves the fewest difficulties, is to take the passage as we find it, and to interpret it as narrating an actual fact: viz., a standing miracle which actually was literally wrought at a certain season, and perhaps every year.

After all there is no more real difficulty in the account before us, than in the history of our Lord's temptation in the wilderness, the various cases of satanic possession, or the release of Peter from prison by an angel. Once admit the existence of angels, their ministry on earth, and the possibility of their interposition to carry out God's designs, and there is nothing that ought to stumble us in the passage. The true secret of some of the objections to it, is the modern tendency to regard all miracles as useless lumber, which must be thrown overboard, if possible, and cast out of the sacred narrative on every occasion. Against this tendency we must watch and be on our guard.

Rollock remarks, 'The Jewish people at this time was in a state of great confusion, and the presence of God was in great measure withdrawn from it. The prophets whom God had been accustomed to raise up for extraordinary purposes, were no longer given to the Jews. Therefore God, that he might not appear altogether to cast off his people, was willing to heal some miraculously, and in an extraordinary way, in order that he might testify to the world that the nation was not yet entirely rejected.' Brentius and Calvin say much the same.

Poole thinks that this miracle only began a little before the birth of Christ, 'as a figure of him being about to come who was to be a fountain opened to the house of David.' Lightfoot takes the same view.

[*Troubled the water.*] This means, no doubt, 'disturbed, agitated, stirred up,' the water of the pool. There is no reason for supposing that the angel visibly appeared in doing this. It is enough to suppose that at a certain hour there was a sudden stir and agitation of the waters, immediately after which they possessed the miraculous virtue of healing,—just as the waters at Marah became sweet immediately after Moses cast the tree into them (*Exod.* 15:25).

[*Whosoever then first.*] This shows that the whole affair was miraculous. On no other supposition can we account for only one person being healed after the troubling of the water. That only 'one' was healed, is plain, I think, from the wording of the passage.

[*Of whatsoever disease he had.*] These words would be more literally translated, 'with whatsoever disease he was held.' Bengel thinks that the use of the past tense throughout this verse shows that the miracle had ceased when John wrote. He 'used to go down,'—'used to trouble the waters,' etc. Tertullian declares expressly that the miracle ceased from the time that the Jews rejected Christ.

5.—[*Infirmity thirty and eight years.*] This means the length of time during which the sick man had been ill. How old he was we do not know.

Baxter remarks, 'How great a mercy is it to live eight-and-thirty years under God's wholesome discipline! O my God, I thank thee for the like discipline of eight-and-fifty years. How safe a life is this compared to one spent in full prosperity and pleasure!'

Those who see typical and abstruse meanings in all the least details of the narratives of Scripture, observe that thirty-eight years was the exact time of Israel's wanderings in the wilderness. They see in the sick man,—helpless and hopeless till Christ came,—a type of the Jewish church. The pool of Bethesda is Old Testament religion. The small benefit it conferred,—viz., only healing one at a time,—represents the narrow and limited benefit which Judaism conferred on mankind. The merciful interference of Christ on the sick man's behalf, represents the bringing in of the gospel for all the world. These are pious thoughts, but it may well be doubted whether there is any warrant for them.

The notions that the pool of Bethesda was a type of baptism, and the five porches typical of the five books of the law, or the five wounds of Christ, appear to me mere ingenious inventions of man, without any solid foundation. Yet Chrysostom, Augustine, Theophylact, Euthymius, Burgon, Wordsworth, and many others, maintain them. Those who wish to see a full reply to the theory that the miracle at the pool of Bethesda is a typical proof of the doctrine of baptismal regeneration, will find it in Gomarus, the Dutch divine. He takes up Bellarmine's argument on the subject, and answers him completely.

6.—[*When Jesus saw ... knew ... long time.*] We need not doubt that our Lord knew this man's history by that divine knowledge which, as God, he possesses of all things in heaven and earth. To suppose that he ascertained by inquiry the state of his case before speaking to him, is a weak, meagre, and frigid interpretation. As a practical truth, it is a most comfortable doctrine that Jesus knows every sickness and disease, and all its weary history. Nothing is hid from him.

[*He saith unto him.*] This is an example of our Lord being the first to speak and begin conversation, as he did with the woman of Samaria (*John* 4:7). Unasked, unsolicited, unexpectedly, he mercifully addressed the sick man. No doubt he always begins in man's heart before man begins with him. But he does all things as a Sovereign, according to his own will: and it is not always that we see him taking the first step so entirely of himself as we do here.

[*Wilt thou be made whole?*] The English language here fails to give the full force of the Greek. It means, 'Hast thou a will? Dost thou wish? Dost thou desire to be made whole?' The question was perhaps meant to awaken desire and expectation in the man, and to prepare him in some sense for the blessing about to be bestowed on him.

Is not this, to take a spiritual view, the very language that Christ is continually addressing to every man and woman who hears his gospel? He sees us in a wretched, miserable, sin-sick condition. The one thing he asks us is, 'Hast thou any wish to be saved?'

7.—[*The impotent man answered him, Sir.*] The word rendered 'Sir' is the same that is more commonly rendered 'Lord'. It is the same that is rendered 'Sir' all through the fourth chapter, in the history of the Samaritan woman.

[*I have no man ... put me into the pool.*] This is no doubt mentioned as an intentional proof of the heartlessness and unkindness of human nature. Think of a poor invalid waiting for years by the water, and having not a single friend to help him! The longer we live on earth the more we shall find that it is a selfish world, and that the sick and afflicted have few real friends in time of need. 'The poor is hated even of his own neighbour' (*Prov.* 14:20). Christ is the only unfailing friend of the friendless and helper of the helpless.

8.—[*Rise, take up thy bed, and walk.*] Here, as in other similar cases, it is evident that miraculous healing power went forth with the words of our Lord. Thus, 'Stretch forth thine hand' (*Mark* 3:5); 'Go show yourselves unto the priests' (*Luke* 17:14). Commands like these tested the faith and obedience of those to whom they were given. How could they possibly do the things commanded, if impotent like the man before us? Where was the use of doing them, if still covered with leprosy, like the ten lepers? But it was precisely in the act

of obedience that the blessing came. The whole power is Christ's. But he loves to make us exert ourselves, and show our obedience and faith.

Augustine finds in the command, 'Take up thy bed,' an exhortation to the love of our neighbours, because we are to bear one another's burdens; and in the command, 'walk,' an exhortation to love God! Such allegorizing appears to me very unwarrantable, and calculated to bring the Bible into contempt, as a book that can be made to mean anything.

9.—[*Immediately ... made whole ... walked.*] Here we see the reality of the miracle wrought. Nothing but divine power could enable one who had been a cripple for so many years to move his limbs and carry a burden all at once. But it was as easy to our Lord to give immediate strength as it was to create muscles, nerves, and sinews in the day that Adam was made.

When we are told that the man 'took up his bed,' we must remember that this probably was nothing more than a light mattress, carpet, or thick cloth, such as is commonly used in hot countries for sleeping on.

10.—[*The Jews.*] Here, as in many places in St John's Gospel, the expression, 'the Jews,' when used of the Jews at Jerusalem, means the leaders of the people,—elders, rulers, and scribes. It does not mean vaguely the 'Jewish crowd' around our Lord, but the representatives of the whole nation,—the heads of Israel at the time.

[*It is not lawful ... carry ... bed.*] In support of this charge of unlawfulness, the Jew would allege not merely the general law of the fourth commandment, but the special passages in Nehemiah and Jeremiah, about 'bearing no burden' on the sabbath day (*Neh.* 13:19; *Jer.* 17:21). But they could not have proved that these passages applied to the case of the man before them.—For a man to carry merchandise and wares on the sabbath was one thing. For a sick man, suddenly and miraculously healed, to walk away to his home, carrying his mattress, was quite another.—To forbid the one man to carry his burden was scriptural and lawful. To forbid the other was cruel, and contrary to the spirit of the law of Moses.— The act of the one man was unnecessary. The act of the other was an act of necessity and mercy.—It might perhaps be urged, in defence of the Jews, that they only saw a man carrying off a burden, and knew nothing of his previous illness or his cure. But when we remember the many instances recorded in the Gospels of their extreme and harsh interpretation of the fourth commandment, it is doubtful whether this plea will stand.

11.—[*He that made me whole, the same said, etc.*] The answer of the man seems simple. But it contains a deep principle. 'He that has done so great a thing to me was surely to be obeyed, when he told me to take up my bed. If he had authority and power to heal, he was not likely to lay upon me an unlawful command. I only obeyed him who cured me.' If Christ has really healed our souls, should not this be our feeling towards him?—'Thou hast healed me. What thou commandest I will do.'

12.—[*What man is that which said ... Take up thy bed? etc.*] Ecolampadius, Grotius, and many others, remark what an example this question is of the malevolent and malicious spirit of the Jews. Instead of asking, 'Who healed thee?' they asked 'Who told thee to carry thy bed?' They cared not for knowing what they might admire as a work of mercy, but what they might make the ground of an accusation. How many are like them! They are always looking out for something to find fault with.

13.—[*Wist not who it was.*] It is most probable that the cripple really knew not who it was that had healed him, and had only seen our Lord that day for the first time. He was ignorant of his name, and only knew him as a kind person, who came up and said suddenly, 'Wilt thou be made whole?' and after curing him miraculously, suddenly disappeared in the crowd.

[*Conveyed himself away.*] The Greek word so rendered is peculiar, and only found in this place. Parkhurst thinks that it simply means 'departed, or went away.' Schleusner says that the root of the idea is, 'swimming out, or escaping by swimming,' and that the meaning here is, 'withdrew

himself secretly from the crowd that was in the place.' If so, it is not improbable that, as in Luke 4:30, at Nazareth, and John 10:39, in the temple, our Lord put forth a miraculous power in passing or gliding through the crowd without being observed or stopped.

14.—[*Afterward ... temple.*] It is not clear how long a time elapsed before our Lord found the man whom he had healed in the temple. If the theory be correct to which I adverted in the note on the first verse, there must have been an interval. The word 'afterward' is literally 'after these things.'

Chrysostom thinks that the circumstance of the man being found 'in the temple' is an indication of his piety.

[*Behold, thou art made whole: sin no more, etc.*] These words appear to point at something more than meets the eye. They are a solemn caution. One might fancy that our Lord knew that some sin had been the beginning of the man's illness, and that he meant to remind him of it. It certainly seems very unlikely that our Lord would say broadly and vaguely, 'sin no more,' unless he spoke with a significant reference to some sin which had been the primary cause of this man's long illness (see *1 Cor.* 11:30). There are sins which bring their own punishments on men's bodies: and I am strongly disposed to think that it may have been the case with this man. The expression, 'a worse thing,' would then come out with more force. It would be 'a heavier visitation,' a worse judgment even that this thirty-eight years' illness. A sick-bed is a sorrowful place, but hell is much worse.

Besser remarks,—'It is a dreadful thing, when the correction and mercy of divine love wearies itself with a man in vain. You that are sick, write over your beds, when you rise up from them in renewed health,— "Behold thou art made whole: sin no more, lest a worse thing come unto thee."' Brentius says much the same.

If sin was the cause of this man's disease, and he had been ill from the effects of it thirty-and-eight years, it is plain that it must have been committed before our Lord was born! It is an instance, in that case, of our Lord's perfect and divine knowledge of all things, past as well as future.

15.—[*Departed and told the Jews.*] There is no proof that the man did this with an evil design. Born a Jew, and taught to reverence his rulers and elders, he naturally wished to give them the information they desired, and had no reason to suppose, for anything we can see, that it would injure his benefactor.

JOHN 5:16-23

16 And therefore did the Jews persecute Jesus, and sought to slay him, because he had done these things on the sabbath day.

17 But Jesus answered them, My Father worketh hitherto, and I work.

18 Therefore the Jews sought the more to kill him, because he not only had broken the sabbath, but said also that God was his Father, making himself equal with God.

19 Then answered Jesus and said unto them, Verily, verily, I say unto you, The Son can do nothing of himself, but what he seeth the Father do: for what things soever he doeth, these also doeth the Son likewise.

20 For the Father loveth the Son, and sheweth him all things that himself doeth: and he will shew him greater works than these, that ye may marvel.

21 For as the Father raiseth up the dead, and quickeneth *them*; even so the Son quickeneth whom he will.

22 For the Father judgeth no man, but hath committed all judgment unto the Son:

23 That all *men* should honour the Son, even as they honour the Father. He that honoureth not the Son honoureth not the Father which hath sent him.

THESE verses begin one of the most deep and solemn passages in the four Gospels. They show us the Lord Jesus asserting his own divine nature, his unity with God the Father, and the high dignity of his office. Nowhere does our Lord dwell so fully on these subjects as in the chapter before us. And nowhere, we must confess, do we find out so thoroughly the weakness of man's understanding! There is much, we must all feel, that is far beyond our comprehension in our Lord's account of himself. Such knowledge, in short, is too wonderful for us. 'It is high: [we] cannot attain unto it' (*Psa.* 139:6). How often men say that they want clear explanations of such doctrines as the Trinity. Yet here we have our Lord handling the subject of his own person, and, behold, we cannot follow him! We seem only to touch his meaning with the tip of our fingers.

We learn, for one thing, from the verses before us, that *there are some works which it is lawful to do on the sabbath day.*

The Jews, as on many other occasions, found fault because Jesus healed a man who had been ill for thirty-eight years, on the sabbath. They charged our Lord with a breach of the fourth commandment.

Our Lord's reply to the Jews is very remarkable. 'My Father,' he says, 'worketh hitherto, and I also work.' It is as though he said:— 'Though my Father rested on the seventh day from his work of creation, he has never rested for a moment from his providential government of the world, and from his merciful work of supplying the daily wants of all his creatures. Were he to rest from such work, the whole frame of nature would stand still. And I also work works of mercy on the sabbath day. I do not break the fourth commandment when I heal the sick, any more than my Father breaks it when he causes the sun to rise and the grass to grow on the sabbath.'

We must distinctly understand, that neither here nor elsewhere does the Lord Jesus overthrow the obligation of the fourth commandment. Neither here nor elsewhere is there a word to justify the vague assertions of some modern teachers, that 'Christians ought not to keep a sabbath,' and that it is 'a Jewish institution which has passed away.' The utmost that our Lord does, is to place the claims of the sabbath on the right foundation. He clears the day of rest from the false and superstitious teaching of the Jews, about the right way of observing it. He shows us clearly that works of necessity and works of mercy are no breach of the fourth commandment.

After all, the errors of Christians on this subject, in these latter days, are of a very different kind from those of the Jews. There is little danger of men keeping the sabbath too strictly. The thing to be feared is the disposition to keep it loosely and partially, or not to keep it at all. The tendency of the age is not to exaggerate the fourth commandment, but to cut it out of the Decalogue, and throw it aside altogether. Against this tendency it becomes us all to be on our guard. The experience of eighteen centuries supplies abundant proofs that vital religion never flourishes when the sabbath is not well kept.

We learn, for another thing, from these verses, *the dignity and greatness of our Lord Jesus Christ.*

The Jews, we are told, sought to kill Jesus because he said 'that God was his Father, making himself equal with God.' Our Lord, in reply, on this special occasion, enters very fully into the question of his own divine nature. In reading his words, we must all feel that we are reading mysterious things, and treading on very holy ground. But we must feel a deep conviction, however little we may understand, that the things he says could never have been said by one who was only man. The speaker is nothing less than 'God . . . manifest in the flesh' (*1 Tim.* 3:16).

He asserts his own unity with God the Father. No other reasonable meaning can be put on the expressions,—'The Son can do nothing of himself, but what he seeth the Father do: for what things soever he doeth, these also doeth the Son likewise. The Father loveth the Son, and showeth him all things that himself doeth.' Such language, however deep and high, appears to mean that in operation, and knowledge, and heart, and will, the Father and the Son are one,—two persons, but one God. Truths such as these are of course beyond man's power to explain particularly. Enough for us to believe and rest upon them.

He asserts, in the next place, his own divine power to give life. He tells us, 'The Son quickeneth whom he will.' Life is the highest and greatest gift that can be bestowed. It is precisely that thing that man, with all his cleverness, can neither give to the work of his hands, nor restore when taken away. But life, we are told, is in the hands of the Lord Jesus, to bestow and give at his discretion. Dead bodies and dead souls are both alike under his dominion. He has the keys of death and hell. In him is life. He is the life (*John* 1:4; *Rev.* 1:18).

He asserts, in the last place, his own authority to judge the world. 'The Father,' we are told, 'has committed all judgment unto the Son.' All power and authority over the world is committed to Christ's hands. He is the King and the Judge of mankind. Before him every knee shall bow, and every tongue shall confess that he is Lord. He that was once despised and rejected of man, condemned and crucified as a malefactor, shall one day hold a great assize, and judge all the world. 'God shall judge the secrets of men by Jesus Christ' (*Rom.* 2:16).

And now let us think whether it is possible to make too much of Christ in our religion. If we have ever thought so, let us cast aside the thought for ever. Both in his own nature as God, and in his office as commissioned Mediator, he is worthy of all honour. He that is one with the Father,—the Giver of life,—the King of kings,—the coming Judge, can never be too much exalted. 'He that honoureth not the Son, honoureth not the Father which hath sent him.'

If we desire salvation, let us lean our whole weight on this mighty Saviour. So leaning, we never need be afraid. Christ is the rock of ages, and he that builds on him shall never be confounded,— neither in sickness, nor in death, nor in the judgment day. The hand that was nailed to the cross is almighty. The Saviour of sinners is 'mighty to save' (*Isa.* 63:1).

Notes—John 5:16-23

16.—[*Therefore ... Jews persecute, etc.*] The verbs in this verse are all in the imperfect tense. It may be doubted whether the meaning is not, strictly speaking, something of this kind: 'The Jews from this time began to persecute Jesus, and were always seeking to slay him, because he made a habit of doing these things on the sabbath day.' It is some confirmation of this view that our Lord at a much later period refers to this very miracle at Bethesda, as a thing which had specially angered the Jews of Jerusalem, and for which they hated him and sought still to kill him. It was long after the time of this miracle when he said,—'Are ye angry at me, because I have made a man every whit whole on the sabbath day?' (*John* 7:23).

17.—[*But Jesus answered.*] This seems to have been the first reply which our Lord made when charged with breaking the fourth commandment. It was a short, simple justification of the lawfulness of doing works of mercy on the sabbath. There seems to have been an interval between this reply and the long argumentative defence which begins in verse 19.

[*My Father worketh hitherto, and I work.*] The words rendered 'hitherto,' are, literally, 'until now:' that is, from the beginning of creation up to the present time.

I can only see one meaning in this pithy sentence: 'My Father in heaven is continually working works of mercy and kindness in his providential government of the world, in supplying the wants of all his creatures, in maintaining the whole fabric of the earth in perfection, in giving rain from heaven and fruitful seasons, in preserving and sustaining life. All this he does on sabbaths, as well as weekdays. Were he to cease from such works, the whole world would be full of confusion. When he rested from his works of creation he did not rest from his works of providence. I also, who am his beloved Son, claim the right to work works of mercy on the sabbath. In working such works I do not break the sabbath any more than my Father does. My Father appointed the fourth commandment to be honoured, and yet never ceased to cause the sun to rise and the grass to grow on the sabbath. I also, who claim to be one with the Father, honour the sabbath, but I do not abstain from works of mercy upon it.'

Two things should be observed in this sentence. One is the plain practical lesson that the sabbath was not meant to be a day of total idleness, and of entire cessation from all kinds and sorts of work. 'The sabbath was made for man,'—for his benefit, comfort, and advantage. Works of mercy and of real necessity to man's life and animal existence on the sabbath day, were never intended to be forbidden.—The other thing to be observed is our Lord's assertion of his own divinity and equality with God the Father. When he said, 'My Father worketh ... and I work,' he evidently meant much more than bringing forward his Father's *example*, though that of course is contained in his argument, and justifies all Christians in doing works of mercy on Sundays. What he meant was, 'I am the beloved Son of God: I and my Father are one in essence, dignity, honour, and authority: whatever he does I also do, and have right to do. He works and I also work. He gave you the sabbath, and it is his day. I too, as one with him, am Lord of the sabbath.' That the Jews saw this to be the meaning of his words seems clear from the next verse.

Chrysostom remarks on this verse: 'If anyone says, "How doth the Father *work*, who ceased on the seventh day from all his works?" let him learn the manner in which he worketh. What is it? He careth for, he

holdeth together all that hath been made. When thou beholdest the sun rising, and the moon running in her path, the lakes, the fountains, the rivers, the rains, the course of nature in seeds, and in our own bodies and those of irrational beings, and all the rest, by means of which this universe is made up, then learn the ceaseless working of the Father' (*Matt.* 5:45; 6:30).

Schoettgen quotes a remarkable saying of Philo Judæus: 'God never ceases to work. Just as it is the property of fire to burn and of snow to be cold, so is it the property of God to work.'

Ferus remarks on the great variety of arguments used by our Lord on various occasions, in reply to the superstitious views of the Jews about the sabbath. One time he adduces the example of David eating the shewbread, another time the example of the priests working in the temple on the sabbath, another time the readiness of the Jews to help an ox out of a pit on the sabbath. All these arguments were used in defence of works of necessity and mercy. Here he takes higher ground still,—the example of his Father.

18.—[*Therefore the Jews sought the more to kill him.*] This short defence which our Lord made seems to have rankled in the minds of the Jews, and to have made them even more bitter against him. What length of time is covered by this verse is not very plain. I am inclined to think that it implies some little pause between verses 17 and 19. Here again, as in verse 16, we have the imperfect tense all the way through. It must surely point at something of habit, both in the designs of the Jews against our Lord, and in our Lord's conduct, and in his language about his Father.

[*Said ... God ... his Father ... equal with God.*] It is clear that our Lord's words about his Sonship struck the Jews in a far more forcible way than they seem to strike us. In a certain sense all believers are 'sons of God' (*Rom.* 8:14). But it is evident that they are not so in the sense that our Lord meant when he talked of God as his Father, and himself as God's Son. The Greek undoubtedly might be translated more clearly, 'said that God was his own particular Father' (compare *Rom.* 8:32). The Jews at any rate accepted the words as meaning our Lord to assert his own peculiar Sonship, and his consequent entire equality with God the Father. Their charge and ground of anger against him amounted to this: 'Thou callest God thine own particular Father, and claimest authority to do whatsoever he does. By so doing thou makest thyself equal with God.' And our Lord seems to have accepted this charge as a correct statement of the case, and to have proceeded to argue that he had a right to say what he had said, and that he really was equal with God. As St Paul says,—He 'thought it not robbery to be equal with God' (*Phil.* 2:6).

Augustine remarks,—'Behold the Jews understood what the Arians would not understand.'

Whitby remarks that the Jews never accused our Lord of blasphemy for saying that he was the Messiah, but for saying that he was the Son of God, because they did not believe that Messiah when he appeared was to be a divine person.

Ferus remarks that the Jews probably took notice of our Lord calling God 'my Father,' and not 'our Father.'—Cartwright also thinks that there is much weight in the expression 'my,' and that the Jews gathered from it that Christ claimed to be the only begotten Son of God, and not merely a son by adoption and grace.

19.—[*Then answered Jesus and said unto them.*] This verse begins a long discourse, in which our Lord formally defends himself from the charge of the Jews of laying claim to what he had no right to claim. 1. He asserts his own divine authority, commission, dignity, and equality with God his Father. 2. He brings forward the evidence of his divine commission, which the Jews ought to consider and receive. 3. Finally, he tells the Jews plainly the reason of their unbelief, and charges home on their consciences their love of man's praise more than God's, and their inconsistency in pretending to honour Moses while they did not honour Christ. It is a discourse almost unrivalled in depth and majesty.

There are few chapters in the Bible, perhaps, where we feel our own shallowness of understanding so thoroughly, and discover so completely the insufficiency of all human language to express 'the deep things of God.' Men are often saying they want explanations of the mysteries of the Christian faith, the Trinity, the incarnation, the person of Christ, and the like. Let them just observe, when we do find a passage full of explanatory statements on a deep subject, how much there is that we have no line to fathom and no mind to take in. 'I want more light,' says proud man. God gives him his desire in this chapter, and lifts up the veil a little. But behold, we are dazzled by the very light we wanted, and find we have not eyes to take it in!

It has always been thought by many commentators that this solemn discourse of our Lord's was delivered before the Sanhedrim, or general Ecclesiastical Assembly of the Jews. They regard it as a formal defence of his divinity and Messiahship, and a statement of evidence why he should be received, before a regularly constituted ecclesiastical court.—It may be so. Probabilities seem in favour of the idea. But it must be remembered that we have nothing but internal evidence in favour of the theory. There is not a word said to show that our Lord was formally brought before the Sanhedrim, and made a formal defence.—Some writers lay much stress upon the opening words of verse 19,—'Then answered Jesus and said,'—and consider that these words imply a formal charge in court, and a formal reply from our Lord. It may be true. But we must remember that it is only a conjecture.

One thing only is certain. Nowhere else in the Gospels do we find our Lord making such a formal, systematic, orderly, regular statement of his own unity with the Father, his divine commission and authority, and the proofs of his Messiahship, as we find in this discourse. To me it seems one of the deepest things in the Bible.

[*Verily, verily, I say unto you.*] Here, as elsewhere the remark applies, that this form of expression always precedes some statement of more than ordinary depth and importance.

[*The Son can do nothing of himself, etc.*] This opening verse declares the complete unity there is between God the Father and God the Son. The Son, from his very nature and relation to the Father, 'can do noth-ing,' independently or separately from the Father. It is not that he lacks or *wants* the power to do, but that he *will* not do (com-pare *Gen.* 19:22). When the angel said, 'I cannot do anything till thou be come thither;' it means of course 'I will not do.'— 'Of himself' does not mean without help, or unassisted, but 'from himself, from his own independent will. He can only do such things as, from his unity with the Father, and consequent ineffable knowledge, he 'seeth' the Father doing. For the Father and the Son are so united,—one God though two persons,—that whatsoever the Father does the Son does also. The acts of the Son therefore are not his own independent acts, but the acts of his Father also.

The Greek word which we render 'likewise' must not be supposed to mean nothing more than 'also, as well.' It is liter-ally 'in like manner.'

Bishop Hall paraphrases this saying of our Lord thus:—'I and the Father are one indivisible essence, and our acts are no less inseparable. The Son can do nothing without the will and act of the Father; and, even as he is man, can do nothing but what he seeth agreeable to the will and purpose of his heavenly Father.'

Barnes remarks,—'The words "what things soever" are without limit; all that the Father does, the Son likewise does. This is as high an assertion as possible of his being equal with God. If one does all that another does, or can do, then there is proof of equality. If the Son does all that the Father does, then, like him, he must be almighty, omniscient, all-present, and infi-nite in every perfection; or, in other words, he must be God.'

Augustine remarks,—'Our Lord does not say, whatsoever the Father doeth the Son does other *things like* them, but the very *same things* . . . If the Son doeth the same things, and in like manner, then let the Jew be silenced, the Christian believe, the heretic be convinced: the Son is equal with the Father.'

Hilary, quoted in the *Catena Aurea*, remarks,—'Christ is the Son because he does nothing of himself. He is God because whatsoever things the Father doeth, he

doeth the same. They are one because they are equal in honour. He is not the Father, because he is sent.'

Diodati remarks,—'The phrase, "what he seeth the Father do," is a figurative term, showing the inseparable communion of will, wisdom, and power, between the Son and the Father in the internal order of the most holy Trinity.'

Toletus remarks,—'When it is said "the Son can do nothing of himself," this does not mean want of power, but the highest power. Just as it is a mark of omnipotence not to be able to die, or to be worn out, or to be annihilated, because there is nothing that can injure omnipotence, so likewise, "to be unable to do anything of himself" is no mark of impotence, but of the highest power. It means nothing less than having one and the same power with the Father, so that nothing can be done by the one which is not equally done by the other.'

20.—[*The Father loveth the Son, etc.*] This verse carries on the thought begun in the preceding verse,—the unity of the Father and the Son. When we read the words, 'the Father loveth,' and the 'Father sheweth,' we must not for a moment suppose them to imply any superiority in the Father, or any inferiority in the Son, as to their divine nature and essence.—The 'love' is not the love of an earthly parent to a beloved child. The 'showing' is not the showing of a teacher to an ignorant scholar. The 'love' is meant to show us that unspeakable unity of heart and affection (if such words may be reverently used) which eternally existed and exists between the Father and the Son. The 'showing' means that entire con-fidence and co-operation which there was between the Father and the Son, as to all the works which the Son should do when he came into the world to fill the office of Mediator and to save sinners. The 'greater works,' which remained to be shown, were evidently the works specified in the two following verses,—the works of quickening and of judging. That the Jews did 'marvel,' and were confounded at the works of 'quickening,' we know from the Acts of the Apostles. That they will 'marvel' even more at our Lord's work of judgment we shall see when Christ comes again to judge the heathen, to restore Jerusalem, to gather Israel, to convince the Jews of their unbelief, and to renew the face of the earth.

Both in this, and the preceding verse, we must carefully remember the utter inability of any human language, or human ideas, to express perfectly such matters as our Lord is speaking of. Language is intended specially to express the things of man. It fails greatly when used to express things about God. In the expressions 'seeth the Father do,'—'loveth the Son,'—'sheweth him all things,'—'will shew him greater works,'—we must carefully bear this is mind. We must remember that they are expressions accommodated to our weaker capacities. They are intended to explain the relation between two divine beings, who are one in essence, though two persons,—one in mind and will, though two in manifestation,—equal in all things as touching the Godhead, though the Son is inferior to the Father as touching his manhood. There must needs be immense difficulty in finding words to convey any idea of the relation between these two persons. Hence the language used by our Lord must be cautiously handled, with a constant recollection that we are not reading of an earthly father and son, but of God the Father and God the Son, who though one in essence as God, are at the same time two distinct persons.

Augustine wisely remarks, 'There are times when speech is deficient, even when the understanding is proficient. How much more doth speech suffer defect when the understanding hath nothing perfect!'

Augustine and Bernard both remark, that it is far 'greater work' to repair ruined human nature, than to make it at first, and to re-create it, than to create it.

21, 22.—[*As the Father raiseth up the dead, etc.*] Our Lord here proceeds to tell the Jews one of his mighty works which he had come to do, in proof of his divine nature, authority, and commission. Did they find fault with him for making himself equal with God? Let them know that he had the same power as God the Father to give 'life' and quicken the dead. Let them know furthermore, that all 'judgment' was committed to him. Surely he who had in his hand the mighty prerogatives of giving life and judging the world, had a right to speak of himself as equal with God!

When we read 'the Father raiseth up the dead, and quickeneth them,' we must either understand the words to refer generally to God's power to raise the dead at the last day, which the Jew would allow as an article of faith, and a special attribute of divinity,—or else we must understand it to apply to the power of spiritually quickening men's souls, which God had from the beginning exercised in calling men from death to life, or else we must simply take it to mean that to give life, whether bodily or spiritual, is notoriously the peculiar attribute of God. The last view appears to me the most probable one, and most in harmony with what follows in afterverses.

When we read 'the Son quickeneth whom he will,' we have a distinct assertion of the Son's authority to give life at his will, either bodily or spiritual, with the same irresistible power as the Father. The highest of all gifts he has but to 'will' and to bestow. The Greek word translated 'quickeneth,' is very strong. It is, literally, 'makes alive,' and seems to imply the power of making life of all kinds, both bodily and spiritual.

Burkitt remarks, that it is never said of any prophet or apostle, that he did mighty works 'at his will.'

When we read 'the Father judgeth no man, but hath committed all judgment to the Son,' we must understand that in the economy of redemption, the Father has honoured the Son by devolving on him the whole office of judging the world. It cannot of course mean that judgment is work with which the Father from his nature has nothing to do, but that it is work which he has completely and entirely committed to the Son's hands. He that died for sinners, is he that will judge them. Thus it is written,—'He will judge the world in righteousness by that man whom he hath ordained' (*Acts* 17:31).

Burgon remarks, 'There is an original, supreme, judicial power; and there is also a judicial power derived, given by commission. Christ, as God, hath the first together with the Father; Christ, as man, hath the second from the Father.'

I think it highly probable that the 'all judgment committed to the Son,' includes not merely the final judgment of the last day, but the whole work of ordering, governing, and deciding the affairs of God's kingdom. 'To judge' is an expression constantly used in the Old Testament in the sense of 'to rule.' The meaning then would be that the Father has given to the Son the office of King and Judge. The whole administration of the divine government of the world is put into the hands of the Son, Christ Jesus. Everything connected with the rule of the church and world, as well as the last judgment, is placed in the Son's hands.

We should carefully mark the distinction between 'quickening' and 'judging' in the language of these two verses.

a. It is *not* said that 'the Father quick-eneth no man,' but hath committed the power of giving life to the Son. Had this been said it would have contradicted the texts 'no man can come to me except the Father . . . draw him,' and 'the Spirit giveth life' (*John* 6:44; *2 Cor.* 3:6). Quickening is the work of all three persons in the Trinity, of one as much as another.

b. It *is said* that judgment is the special work of the second person in the Trinity. It is not the peculiar office either of the Father, or of the Spirit, but of the Son. There seems a fitness in this. He who was condemned by an unjust judgment, and died for sinners, is he whose office it will be to judge the world.

c. It is said that 'the Son quickeneth whom he will.' The power of giving life is as much the prerogative of the Son as of the Father, or of the Spirit. Surely this teaches us that to place the election of God the Father, or the work of the Spirit, before men, as the first and principal thing they should look at, is not good theology. Christ, after all, is the meeting point between the Trinity and the world. It is his office to quicken as well as pardon. No doubt he quickeneth by the Spirit whom he sends into man's heart. But it is his prerogative to give life as well as peace. This ought to be remembered. There are some in this day

who in a mistaken zeal put the work of the Father and the Spirit before the work of Christ.

23.—[*That all men should honour the Son, etc.*] By these words our Lord teaches us that the Father would have the Son to receive equal honour with himself. We are to understand distinctly that there is no inferiority in the Son to the Father. He is equal to him in dignity and authority. He is to be worshipped with equal worship. If any man fancies that to honour the Son equally with the Father detracts from the Father's honour, our Lord declares that such a man is entirely mistaken. On the contrary, 'He that honoureth not the Son, honoureth not the Father which hath sent him.' It was the mind and intention of the Father that the Son, as the Mediator between God and man, should receive honour from all men. The glory of his beloved Son is part of the Father's eternal counsels. Whenever therefore anyone through ignorance, or pride, or unbelief, neglects Christ, but professes at the same time to honour God, he is committing a mighty error, and so far from pleasing God, is greatly displeasing him. The more a man honours Christ, and makes much of him, the more the Father is pleased.

Evangelical Christians should mark the doctrine of this verse, and remember it. They are sometimes taunted with holding new views in religion, because they bring forward Christ so much more prominently than their fathers or grandfathers did. Let them see here that the more they exalt the Son of God and his office, the more honour they are doing to the Father who sent him.

To the deist and Socinian, the words of this verse are a strong condemnation. Not honouring Christ, they are angering God the Father. The Fatherhood of God, out of Christ, is a mere idol of man's invention, and incapable of comforting or saving.

Alford remarks, 'Whosoever does not honour the Son with equal honour to that which he pays to the Father, how-ever he may imagine that he honours or approaches God, does not honour him at all; because he can only be known by us as "the Father who sent his Son."'—Barnes remarks, 'If our Saviour here did not intend to teach that he ought to be worshipped and esteemed equal with God, it would be difficult to teach it by any language.'

Rollock remarks, 'The Jews and Turks in the present day profess to worship God earnestly, not only without the Son, but even with contempt of the Son Jesus Christ. But the whole of such worship is idolatrous, and that which they worship is an idol. There is no knowledge of the true God except in the face of the Son.'

Wordsworth remarks, 'They who profess zeal for the one God do not honour him aright, unless they honour the Son as they honour the Father. This is a warning to those who claim the title of Unitarians, and deny the divinity of Christ. No one can be said to believe in the divine unity who rejects the doctrine of the Trinity.'

The entire unity of the three persons in the Trinity is a subject that needs far more attention than many give to it. It may be feared that many well-meaning Christians are *tritheists*, or worshippers of three distinct Gods, without knowing it. They talk as if God the Father's mind towards sinners was one thing, and God the Son's another,—as if the Father hated man, and the Son loved him and protected him. Such persons would do well to study this part of Scripture, and to mark the unity of the Father and the Son.

After all, that deep truth, 'the eternal generation' of God the Son, whatever proud man may say of it, is the foundation truth which we must never forget in trying to understand a passage like that before us. In the Trinity 'none is afore or after other. The Father is eternal: the Son eternal: the Holy Ghost eternal. The Father is God: the Son is God: the Holy Ghost is God. And yet there are not three eternals, but one eternal: not three Gods, but one God.' As Burgon remarks 'There never was a time when any one of the three persons was not;' and it might be added, there never was a time when the three persons were not equal. And yet the Son was begotten of the Father from all eternity, and the Holy Ghost proceeded from all eternity from the Father and the Son.

JOHN 5:24-29

24 Verily, verily, I say unto you, He that heareth my word, and believeth on him that sent me, hath everlasting life, and shall not come into condemnation; but is passed from death unto life.

25 Verily, verily, I say unto you, The hour is coming, and now is, when the dead shall hear the voice of the Son of God: and they that hear shall live.

26 For as the Father hath life in himself; so hath he given to the Son to have life in himself;

27 And hath given him authority to execute judgment also, because he is the Son of man.

28 Marvel not at this: for the hour is coming, in the which all that are in the graves shall hear his voice,

29 And shall come forth; they that have done good, unto the resurrection of life; and they that have done evil, unto the resurrection of damnation.

THE passage before us is singularly rich in weighty truths. To the minds of Jews, who were familiar with the writings of Moses and

Daniel, it would come home with peculiar power. In the words of our Lord they would not fail to see fresh assertions of his claim to be received as the promised Messiah.

We see in these verses that *the salvation of our souls depends on hearing Christ*. It is the man, we are told, who 'hears Christ's word,' and believes that God the Father sent him to save sinners, 'who has everlasting life.' Such 'hearing' of course is something more than mere listening. It is hearing as a humble scholar,—hearing as an obedient disciple,—hearing with faith and love,—hearing with a heart ready to do Christ's will: this is the hearing that saves. It is the very hearing of which God spake in the famous prediction of a 'prophet like unto Moses:'—'Unto him ye shall hearken . . . whosoever will not hearken unto my words which he shall speak in my name, I will require it of him' (*Deut.* 18:15, 19).

To 'hear' Christ in this way, we must never forget, is just as needful now as it was eighteen hundred years ago. It is not enough to hear sermons, and run after preachers, though some people seem to think this makes up the whole of religion. We must go much further than this: we must 'hear Christ.' To submit our hearts to Christ's teaching,—to sit humbly at his feet by faith, and learn of him,—to enter his school as penitents, and become his believing scholars,—to hear his voice and follow him: this is the way to heaven. Till we know something experimentally of these things, there is no life in us.

We see, secondly, in these verses, *how rich and full are the privileges of the true hearer and believer*. Such a man enjoys a present salvation. Even now, at this present time, he 'hath everlasting life.'—Such a man is completely justified and forgiven. There remains no more condemnation for him. His sins are put away. 'He shall not come into condemnation.'—Such a man is in an entirely new position before God. He is like one who has moved from one side of a gulf to another: 'He is passed from death unto life.'

The privileges of a true Christian are greatly underrated by many. Chiefly from deplorable ignorance of Scripture, they have little idea of the spiritual treasures of every believer in Jesus. These treasures are brought together here in beautiful order, if we will only look at them. One of a true Christian's treasures is the 'presentness' of his salvation. It is not a far distant thing which he is to have at last, if he does his duty and is good. It is his own in title the moment he believes. He is already pardoned, forgiven, and saved, though not in heaven.—Another of a true Christian's treasures is the 'completeness' of his justification. His sins are entirely removed, taken away, and blotted out of God's book, by Christ's blood. He may look forward to judgment without fear, and say, 'Who is he that condemneth?' (*Rom.* 8:34). He shall stand without fault before the throne of God.— The last, but not the least, of a true Christian's treasures, is the entire change in his relation and position toward God. He is no longer as one dead before him,—dead legally, like a man sentenced to die, and dead in heart. He is 'alive unto God' (*Rom.* 6:11). 'He is a new creature: old things are passed away; behold, all things are become new' (*2 Cor.* 5:17). Well would it be for Christians if these things were better known! It is want of knowledge, in many cases, that is the secret of want of peace.

We see, thirdly, in these verses, *a striking declaration of Christ's power to give life to dead souls.* Our Lord tells us that 'the hour is coming, and now is, when the dead shall hear the voice of the Son of God: and they that hear shall live.' It seems most unlikely that these words were meant to be confined to the raising of men's bodies, and were fulfilled by such miracles as that of raising Lazarus from the grave. It appears far more probable that what our Lord had in view was the quickening of souls,—the resurrection of conversion (*Eph.* 2:1; *Col.* 2:13).

The words were fulfilled, in not a few cases, during our Lord's own ministry. They were fulfilled far more completely after the day of Pentecost, through the ministry of the apostles. The myriads of converts at Jerusalem, at Antioch, at Ephesus, at Corinth, and elsewhere, were all examples of their fulfilment. In all these cases, 'the voice of the Son of God' awakened dead hearts to spiritual life, and made them feel their need of salvation, repent, and believe.—They are fulfilled at this very day, in every instance of true conversion. Whenever any men or women among ourselves awaken to a sense of their souls' value, and become alive to God, the words are made good before our eyes. It is Christ who has spoken to their hearts by his Spirit. It is 'the dead hearing Christ's voice, and living.'

We see, lastly, in these verses, *a most solemn prophecy of the final resurrection of all the dead.* Our Lord tells us that 'the hour is coming, [when] all that are in the graves shall hear his voice, and shall come forth; they that have done good, unto the resurrection of life; and they that have done evil, unto the resurrection of damnation.'

The passage is one of those that ought to sink down very deeply into our hearts, and never be forgotten. All is not over when men die. Whether they like it or not, they will have to come forth from their graves at the last day, and to stand at Christ's bar. None can escape his summons. When his voice calls them before him, all must obey. When men rise again, they will not all rise in the same condition. There will be two classes—two parties—two bodies. Not all will go to heaven. Not all will be saved. Some will rise again to inherit eternal life, but some will rise again only to be condemned. These are terrible things! But the words of Christ are plain and unmistakable. Thus it is written, and thus it must be.

Let us make sure that we hear Christ's quickening voice now, and are numbered among his true disciples. Let us know the privileges of true believers, while we have life and health. Then, when his voice shakes heaven and earth, and is calling the dead from their graves, we shall feel confidence, and not be 'ashamed before him at his coming' (*1 John* 2:28).

Notes—John 5:24-29

24.—[*Verily, verily, I say.*] Here, as in other places, these words are the preface to a saying of more than ordinary solemnity and importance.

[*He that heareth my word.*] The 'hearing' here is much more than mere listening, or hearing with the ears. It means hearing with the heart, hearing with faith, hearing accompanied by obedient discipleship. He that so hears the doctrine, teaching, or 'word' of Christ, hath life. It is such hearing as that of true sheep: 'My sheep hear my voice' (*John* 10:27); or as that spoken of by St Paul: 'Ye have not so learned Christ; if so be that ye have heard him, and have been taught by him' (*Eph.* 4:20, 21).

[*Believeth on him that sent me.*] This must not be supposed to mean that a vague faith in God, such as the deist professes to have, is the way to everlasting life. The belief spoken of is a believing on God in Christ,—a believing on God as the God who sent Christ to save sinners,—a believing on God as the God and Father of our Lord Jesus Christ, who has planned and provided redemption by the blood of his Son. He who so believes on God the Father, is the same man that believes in God the Son. In this sense the Father is just as much the object of saving faith as the Son. Thus we read: '... it shall be imputed, if we believe on him that raised up Jesus our Lord from the dead' (*Rom.* 4:24). And again, 'Who by him do believe in God, that raised him up from the dead, and gave him glory; that your faith and hope might be in God (*1 Pet.* 1:21). He that rightly believes on Christ as his Saviour, with the same faith believes in God as his reconciled Father. The gospel that invites the sinner to believe in Jesus as his Redeemer and Advocate, invites him at the same time to believe in the Father, who is 'well pleased' with all who trust in his Son.

Henry remarks, 'Christ's design is to bring us to God (*1 Pet.* 3:18). As God is the first original of all grace, so is he the ultimate object of all faith. Christ is our way, and God is our rest. We must believe on God as having sent Jesus Christ, and recommended himself to our faith and love, by manifesting his glory in the face of Jesus Christ.'

Lightfoot remarks, 'He doth most properly centre the ultimate fixing and resting of belief in God the Father. For as from him, as from the fountain, do flow all those things that are the object of faith,—namely free grace, the gift of Christ, the way of redemption, the gracious promises,—so unto him as to that fountain doth faith betake itself in its final resting and repose,—namely, to God in Christ.'

Chemnitius remarks, that the expression 'believe on him that sent me,' shows 'that true faith embraces the word of the gospel, not as something thought out by Christ alone, but as something decreed in the secret counsel of the whole Trinity.'

[*Hath everlasting life.*] This means that he possesses a complete title to an everlasting life of glory hereafter, and is reckoned pardoned, forgiven, justified, and an heir of heaven even now upon earth. His soul is delivered from the second death.—The 'presentness' of the expression should be carefully noticed. Everlasting life is the present possession of every true believer from the moment he believes. It is not a thing he shall have at last. He has it at once, even in this world. 'All that believe *are* justified.'— 'Being justified by faith, we *have* peace with God' (*Acts* 8:39; *Rom.* 5:1).

[*Shall not come into condemnation.*] The Greek word for 'come' is in the present tense, and it would be more literally rendered 'does not come.' The meaning is, there is no condemnation for him. His guilt is removed even now. He has nothing to fear in looking forward to the judgment of the last day. 'There is therefore now no condemnation to them which are in Christ Jesus.'—'He that believeth on him is not condemned' (*Rom.* 8:1; *John* 3:18).

I cannot see in these words any warrant for the notion held by some, that the saints of God shall not be judged at the last day in any way at all. The notion itself is so utterly contradictory to some plain texts of Scripture (*2 Cor.* 5:10; *Rom.* 14:10; *Matt.* 25:31, 32), that I cannot understand anyone holding it. But even in the text before us it seems to me a violent straining of the words to apply them to the judgment day. The thing our Lord is speaking of is the present privilege of a believer. The tense he uses, as Chemnitius bids us specially observe, is the present and not the future. And even supposing that the words do apply to the judgment day, the utmost that can be fairly made of them is that a believer has no condemnation to fear at the last day. *Judged* according to his works he shall be. *Condemned* he may certainly feel assured he shall not be. From the day he believes all his condemnation is taken away.

Ecolampadius remarks how irreconcilable this verse is with the Romish doctrine of purgatory.

[*But is passed from death unto life.*] This means that a believer has passed from a state of spiritual death to a state of spiritual life. Before he believed he was dead legally,—dead as a guilty criminal condemned to die. In the day that he believed he received a free and full pardon. His sentence was reversed and put away. Instead of being legally dead, he became legally alive. But this is not all. His heart, which was dead in sins, is now renewed, and alive unto God. There is a change in his character as well as in his position toward God. Like the prodigal son, he 'was dead and is alive' (*Luke* 15:24).

We should mark carefully the strong language of Scripture in describing the immense difference between the position of a man who believes, and the man who does not believe. It is nothing else than the difference between life and death,—between being dead and being alive. Whatever some may think fit to say about the privileges of baptism, we must never shrink from maintaining, that so long as men do not hear Christ's voice and believe,—so long they are dead, whether baptized or not, and have no life in them. Faith, not baptism, is the turning point. He that has not yet believed is dead, and must be born again. When he believes, and not till then, he will pass from death to life.

Ferus remarks, 'Although it seems very easy to believe, and many think they do believe when they have only heard the name of believing,—supposing that to believe is the same as to understand, to remember, to know, to think,—yet this believing is in truth a hard and difficult thing. It is easy to fast, to say prayers, to go on pilgrimage, to give alms, and the like; but to believe is a thing impossible to our strength. Let superstitious people learn that God requires of us a far higher and more difficult kind of worship than they imagine. Let pious people learn to seek faith more than anything, saying,—Lord, increase our faith.'

25.—[*Verily, verily, I say unto you.*] This emphatic preface here begins a prophecy of the wonderful things that should yet be done by the Son of God. Did the Jews of Jerusalem desire to know what proofs of divine power and authority the Son of God would give? Let them hear what he would do.

[*The hour is coming, and now is.*] This meant that a time was coming, and in fact had already begun.

[*The dead shall hear the voice ... and ... live.*] It is thought by some that these words apply to the literal raising again of dead persons, such as Lazarus at Bethany. I cannot think it. I believe that the 'dead' here spoken of are the spiritually dead. I believe that the 'hearing the voice of the Son of God,' means the hearing of faith. I believe that the 'living' spoken of means the rising out of the death of sin to spiritual newness of life. And I believe that the whole verse is a prediction of the many conversions of dead sinners that were to take place soon, and had begun in some measure to take place already. The prediction was fulfilled when dead souls were converted during our Lord's own ministry, and was much more fulfilled after the day of Pentecost, when he was preached by his apostles to the Gentiles, and 'believed on in the world' (*1 Tim.* 3:16).

To confine the words to the few cases of miraculous raising of dead bodies which took place in the time of our Lord and his apostles, appears to supply a very inadequate interpretation, and to be rendered unnecessary by the succeeding verse.

Let it be noted that it is only those who 'hear,' or 'have heard' with faith the voice of Christ, that live. Spiritual life turns on believing. 'Ye also trusted, after that ye heard the word of truth' (*Eph.* 1:13).

Ferus and Cocceius think that the calling and conversion of the Gentiles was the principal thought in our Lord's mind when he spoke these words.

26.—[*For as the Father, etc.*] The first part of this verse needs no explanation. It is an admitted principle that God is the author and source of all life. He 'hath life in himself.' When it says further, that he hath 'given to the Son to have life in himself,' we must not suppose it means that he has bestowed it on his Son in the same way that he gives gifts to mere men, such as prophets and apostles. It rather means that in his everlasting counsels concerning man's redemption, he has appointed that the second person of the Trinity, his beloved Son, should be the dispenser and giver of life to all mankind. 'God hath given to us eternal life, and this life is in his Son' (1 John 5:11).

Both here and in the following verse we must remember that 'giving' does not imply any inferiority in the Son to the Father, so far as concerns his divine essence. The things 'given' to the Son were things solemnly appointed, deputed, and laid upon him when he assumed the office of Mediator, in virtue of his office.

Burgon remarks: 'Both the Father and the Son have the same life; both have it in themselves; both in the same degree: as the one so the other; but only with this difference,—the Father from all eternity *giveth* it, the Son from all eternity *receiveth* it.'

27.—[*And hath given him authority, etc.*] This means that in virtue of his mediatorial office the second person of the Trinity is specially appointed to be the Judge of all mankind. In the counsels of God concerning man 'judgment' is assigned to the Son, and not to the Father, or the Holy Spirit. It is undoubtedly true that God is 'the Judge of all' (*Heb.* 12:23). But it is also true that it is God the Son who will execute judgment, and sit on the throne at the last day.

[*Because he is the Son of man.*] These words seem to imply that there is a connection between our Lord's incarnation and his filling the office of the Judge. It is because he humbled himself to take our nature on him, and be born of the Virgin Mary, that he will at length be exalted to execute judgment at the last day. It appears to be the same thought that St Paul expresses when he tells the Philippians that *because* of Christ's humiliation, 'God also hath highly exalted him, and given him a name which is above every name,' etc. (*Phil.* 2:9).

Burgon remarks: 'Because of his alliance with man's nature, because of his sense of man's infirmities, because of all he did and suffered for man's sake as the Son of man, the Son is that person of the Trinity who is most fit, as well as most worthy, to be man's judge.'

The expression, 'the Son of man,' would be rendered more literally, 'a Son of man,' or, 'Son of man.' Campbell remarks that the absence of the article 'the' before the words 'Son of man,' occurs nowhere in the Gospels except in this passage.

Both in this and the preceding verse we should observe an example of the great truth, that 'order is heaven's first law.' Even the second person in the Trinity, one with the Father, very and eternal God, does not *take on himself* the office of giving life and executing judgment, but receives it through the solemn appointment of God the Father. Just as it is written, 'Christ glorified not himself to be made an high priest; but he that said unto him, Thou art my Son' (*Heb.* 5:5), so we find it written here, that in taking on him the office of Mediator, it was '*given*' to him to have life in himself, and 'authority *given* to him' to judge. Those who take on themselves offices without either divine or human commission are very unlike our Lord.

Toletus quotes a remarkable passage from Athanasius, in which he points out that such expressions as, '*given* to the Son by the Father,' '*received* by the Son from the Father,' are purposely used in order to prevent the Sabellian heresy of supposing that the Father and the Son are one and the same person.—Such expressions are an unanswerable proof that the Father and the Son are two distinct persons, though one God. We must never forget the words of the Athanasian Creed: 'Neither confounding the persons nor dividing the substance.'

28, 29.—[*Marvel not at this.*] These words imply that the hearers of our Lord were astonished at the things he had spoken concerning his divine commission to give life and to judge. He proceeds to tell them that they have not yet heard all. If they wondered at what they had already heard, what would they think when he told them one thing more?

[*The hour is coming.*] This means the last day. To use the present tense of a time so distant as this is characteristic of one who is very God, to whom time past, time present, and time to come, are all alike, and a thousand years are as one day.

[*All that are in the graves shall hear his voice ... come forth ... damnation, etc.*] These words are singularly like those in Daniel 12:2. They contain one of the most distinct statements in Scripture of that great truth,—the resurrection of the dead.—It shall be universal, and not confined to a few only. 'All' in the graves shall come forth, whether old or young, rich or poor.—It shall take place at Christ's command and bidding. His 'voice' shall be the call that shall summon the dead from their graves.— There shall be a distinction of those who rise again, into two classes. Some shall rise to glory and happiness,—to what is called a 'resurrection of life.' Some shall rise to be lost and ruined for ever,—to what is called a 'resurrection of damnation.' The doings of men shall be the test by which their final state shall be decided. 'Life' shall be the portion of those that have 'done good,' 'damnation' of those that 'have done evil,' in the resurrection day.

a. This passage condemns those who fancy that this world is all, and that this life ends everything, and that the grave is the conclusion. They are awfully mistaken. There is a resurrection and a life to come.

b. This passage condemns those who try to persuade us in the present day that there is no future punishment, no hell, no condemnation for the wicked in the world to come,—that the love of God is lower than hell,—that God is too merciful and compassionate to punish anyone. There is a 'resurrection,' we are told, 'of damnation.'

c. This passage condemns those who try to make out that resurrection is the peculiar privilege of believers and saints, and that the wicked will be punished by complete annihilation. Both here and in Acts 24:15, we are distinctly told that both bad and good shall rise again. In St Paul's famous chapter about the resurrection (*1 Cor.* 15), the resurrection of believers only is treated of.

d. This passage condemns those who try to make out that men's lives and conduct are of little importance so long as they profess to have faith and to believe in Christ.

Christ himself tells us expressly that the 'doings' of men, whether good or evil, will be the evidence that shall decide whether they rise again to glory or condemnation.

Musculus remarks that the goodness which God requires of us is not such as only begins in the next world, after the resurrection. We must have it now, and it must precede the time of judgment. It is not said, 'some shall rise again that they may be made good and partakers of life,' but, 'they that *have done* good shall come forth to a resurrection of life.' We should take care to be such in this life as we desire to be found in the day of judgment.—He also remarks that our Lord does not say, 'those who have known or talked what is good,' but 'those who have actually *done* good' shall come forth to a resurrection of life. Those only will be found to have 'done good' who are God's elect, born again, and true believers. Nothing but true faith will bear the fruit of good works.

Calvin remarks that our Lord is not here speaking of the cause of salvation, but of the marks of the saved, and that one great mark which distinguishes the elect from the reprobate is good-doing.

There are two different Greek words used to express the English words 'they that have done,' and it is difficult to say why. Precisely the same difference exists in John 3:20, 21. The attempts made to explain the distinction between the two words do not appear to me very successful. For instance, Wordsworth remarks: 'Good made and done has permanence for ever. Evil is practised, but produces no fruit for eternity.' Yet I doubt whether this remark will apply to Romans 1:32, and 2:3, where both the two Greeks words for 'doing' are used together, and applied to the same class of persons: viz., the wicked.

It is thought by some that this passage supports the doctrine of the first resurrection as the peculiar privilege of the saints (*Rev.* 20:5). But it must in fairness be remembered that there is nothing said here about distinction of time in the resurrection of the good and bad.

As to the manner in which Christ's 'voice' will be heard by the dead 'in the graves' we are told nothing. It is remarkable that there are two other places beside this in which a 'voice' or sound is mentioned as accompanying the resurrection. In Corinthians we read of the 'last trumpet' (*1 Cor.* 15:52). In Thessalonians we are told of 'a shout,' of the 'voice of the archangel,' and the trump of God' (*1 Thess.* 4:16). Nothing, however, but conjecture can be brought forward about the subject. No doubt the latent thought is that the dead bodies of men are sleeping, and need to be awakened, as sleepers are roused by a voice.

As to the nature of risen bodies we are told nothing. Enough for us to know that this passage clearly shows it will be a resurrection of 'bodies' as well as souls. It is those who are 'in the graves' that shall come forth.

JOHN 5:30-39

30 I can of mine own self do nothing: as I hear, I judge: and my judgment is just; because I seek not mine own will, but the will of the Father which hath sent me.

31 If I bear witness of myself, my witness is not true.

32 There is another that beareth witness of me; and I know that the witness which he witnesseth of me is true.

33 Ye sent unto John, and he bare witness unto the truth.

34 But I receive not testimony from man: but these things I say, that ye might be saved.

35 He was a burning and a shining light: and ye were willing for a season to rejoice in his light.

36 But I have greater witness than *that* of John: for the works which the Father hath given me to finish, the same works that I do, bear witness of me, that the Father hath sent me.

37 And the Father himself, which hath sent me, hath borne witness of me. Ye have neither heard his voice at any time, nor seen his shape.

38 And ye have not his word abiding in you: for whom he hath sent, him ye believe not.

39 Search the scriptures; for in them ye think ye have eternal life: and they are they which testify of me.

IN these verses we see the proofs of our Lord Jesus Christ being the promised Messiah, set forth before the Jews in one view. Four different witnesses are brought forward. Four kinds of evidence are offered. His Father in heaven,—his forerunner, John the Baptist,—the miraculous works he had done,—the Scriptures, which the Jews professed to honour,—each and all are named by our Lord, as testifying that he was the Christ, the Son of God. Hard must those hearts have been which could hear such testimony, and yet remain unmoved! But it only proves the truth of the old saying,—that unbelief does not arise so much from want of evidence, as from want of will to believe.

Let us observe, for one thing, in this passage, *the honour Christ puts on his faithful servants*. See how he speaks of John the Baptist—'He bare witness unto the truth;'—'He was a burning and a shining light.'—John had probably passed away from his earthly labours when these words were spoken. He had been persecuted, imprisoned, and put to death by Herod,—none interfering, none trying to prevent his murder. But this murdered disciple was not forgotten by his divine Master. If no one else remembered him, Jesus did. He had honoured Christ, and Christ honoured him.

These things ought not to be overlooked. They are written to teach us that Christ cares for all his believing people, and never forgets them. Forgotten and despised by the world, perhaps, they are never forgotten by their Saviour. He knows where they dwell, and what their trials are. A book of remembrance is written for them. Their tears are all in his bottle (*Psa.* 56:8). Their names are graven on the palms of his hands. He notices all they do for him in this evil world, though they think it not worth notice, and he will confess it one day publicly, before his Father and the holy angels. He that bore witness to John the Baptist never changes. Let believers remember this. In their worst estate they may boldly say with David, 'I am poor and needy; yet the Lord thinketh upon me' (*Psa.* 40:17).

Let us observe, for another thing, *the honour Christ puts upon miracles, as an evidence of his being the Messiah*. He says, 'The works which the Father hath given me to finish, the same works that I do, bear witness of me that the Father hath sent me.'

The miracles of the Lord receive far less attention, in the present day, as proofs of his divine mission, than they ought to do. Too many regard them with a silent incredulity, as things which, not having seen, they cannot be expected to care for. Not a few openly avow that they do not believe in the possibility of such things as miracles, and would fain strike them out of the Bible as weak stories, which, like burdensome lumber, should be cast overboard, to lighten the ship.

But, after all, there is no getting over the fact that in the days when our Lord was upon earth his miracles produced an immense effect on the minds of men. They aroused attention to him that worked them. They excited inquiry, if they did not convert. They were so many, so public, and so incapable of being explained away, that our Lord's enemies could only say that they were done by Satanic agency. That they were done they could not deny. 'This man,' they said, 'doeth many miracles' (*John* 11:47). The facts which wise men pretend to deny now, no one pretended to deny eighteen hundred years ago.

Let the enemies of the Bible take our Lord's last and greatest miracle—his own resurrection from the dead—and disprove it if they can. When they have done that, it will be time to consider what they say about miracles in general. They have never answered the evidence of it yet, and they never will. Let the friends of the Bible not be moved by objections against miracles, until that one miracle has been fairly disposed of. If that is proved unassailable, they need not care much for quibbling arguments against other miracles. If Christ did really rise from the dead by his own power, there is none of his mighty works which man need hesitate to believe.

Let us observe, lastly, in these verses, *the honour that Christ puts upon the Scriptures*. He refers to them in concluding his list of evidences, as the great witnesses to him. 'Search the scriptures,' he says:—'they are they which testify of me.'

The 'scriptures' of which our Lord speaks are of course the Old Testament. And his words show the important truth which too many are apt to overlook,—that every part of our Bibles is meant to teach us about Christ. Christ is not merely in the Gospels and Epistles, Christ is to be found directly and indirectly in the Law, the Psalms, and the Prophets. In the promises to Adam, Abraham, Moses, and David,—in the types and emblems of the ceremonial law,—in the predictions of Isaiah and the other prophets,—Jesus, the Messiah, is everywhere to be found in the Old Testament.

How is it that men see these things so little? The answer is plain. They do not 'search the scriptures.' They do not dig into that wondrous mine of wisdom and knowledge, and seek to become acquainted with its contents. Simple, regular reading of our Bibles is the grand secret of establishment in the faith. Ignorance of the Scriptures is the root of all error.

And now what will men believe, if they do not believe the divine mission of Christ? Great indeed is the obstinacy of infidelity. A cloud of witnesses testify that Jesus was the Son of God. To talk of wanting evidence is childish folly. The plain truth is that the chief seat of unbelief is the heart. Many do not wish to believe and therefore remain unbelievers.

Notes—John 5:30-39

30.—[*I can of mine own self, etc.*] This verse is perhaps one of the most difficult in Scripture. It is so because the subject of it is that great mystery, the unity of God the Father and God the Son. Man has no language to express adequately the idea that has to be conveyed. The general thought of the verse seems to be as follows:—

'In consequence of the close relation between me and the Father, I cannot do anything independently and separately from him. "I judge," and decide, and speak on all points, in entire harmony with the Father, as though I *heard* him continually at my side; and so judging and speaking, my judgment on all points is always right. It is right now, and will be seen right at the great account of the last day. For in all that I do I seek not to do my own will only, but the will of him that sent me, since there is an entire harmony between my will and his.'

Let it be carefully noted that at this part of his address our Lord ceases to speak in the third person of himself as 'the Son of man,' and begins to use the first person: 'I can,' 'I hear,' 'I judge,' etc.

'Of mine own self' does not mean 'unhelped and unassisted,' but 'from myself,'—from my own independent volition and action.

Chrysostom remarks, 'Just as when we say, it is *impossible* for God to do wrong, we do not impute to him any weakness, but confess in him an unutterable power;

so also when Christ saith "I can of my own self do nothing," the meaning is that it is impossible,—my nature admits not,—that I should do anything contrary to the Father.'

'As I hear' is an expression adapted to man's comprehension, to convey the idea of the unity between the Father and the Son. It is like verse 19, where it is said, 'The Son can do nothing of himself, but what *he seeth* the Father do.' It is also like the words used of the Holy Ghost: 'He shall not speak of himself; but whatsoever he shall *hear*, that shall he speak (*John* 16:13).

Chrysostom remarks, 'Just as when Christ said, "We speak that we do know, and testify that we have seen," and John the Baptist said, "What he hath seen and heard, that he testifieth" (*John* 3:11, 32), both expressions are used concerning exact knowledge, and not concerning mere "seeing" and "hearing;"—so in this place, when Christ speaks of "hearing," he declares nothing else than that it is impossible for him to desire anything save what the Father desireth.'

'I judge' applies not only to all Christ's judgments and decisions as Mediator when he was upon earth, but to his final judgment at the last day.

'My judgment is just' would probably remind the Jews of the prophecies about Messiah (*Isa.* 11:3, 4 and *Dan.* 7:10, 13).

'I seek not mine own will' must be interpreted with special reference to our Lord's divine nature as Son of God. Having as God one will with the Father, it was not possible for him to seek his own will independently of the Father. Hence the judgment was not his only, but his Father's also.—As Son of man he had a human will distinct from his divine will, as when he said, 'Let this cup pass from me: nevertheless not as I will, but as thou wilt' (*Matt.* 26:39). But the will here seems to be his divine will.

Chrysostom remarks, 'What Christ implieth is of this kind:—not that the will of the Father is one and his own another, but that as one will in one mind, so is mine own will and my Father's.'

Once more we must remember the extreme difficulty of handling such a subject as the one before us. The distinction between the persons in the Trinity, and the unity of their essence at the same time, must always be a deep thing to man, hard to conceive, and harder still to speak or write about.

31.—[*If I bear witness of myself, etc.*] This verse must be interpreted with caution and reasonable qualification. It would be folly and blasphemy to say that our Lord's testimony about himself must be false. What the verse does appear to mean is this: 'If I have no other testimony to bring forward in proof of my Messiahship but my own word, my testimony would be justly open to suspicion.' Our Lord knew that in any disputed question a man's assertions in his own favour are worth little or nothing. He tells the Jews that he did not want them to believe him merely because he said he was the Son of God. He would show them that he had other witnesses, and these witnesses he next proceeds to bring forward. A comparison of this verse with John 8:14 shows at once that the meaning of the words, 'My witness is not true,' must be qualified and restrained, or else one place of Scripture would contradict the other.

32.—[*There is another that beareth witness.*] There are two distinct and different views of this expression.

a. Some, as Chrysostom, Theophylact, Euthymius, Lightfoot, Brentius, Grotius, Ferus, Barradius, Quesnel, Whitby, Doddridge, Gill, think that the 'other witness' is John the Baptist.

b. Some, as Cyril, Athanasius, Calvin, Beza, Gualter, Bucer, Ecolampadius, Zwingle, Rupertus, Flacius, Calovius, Cocceius, Piscator, Musculus, Aretius, Toletus, Nifanius, Rollock, Poole, Leigh, Diodati, Hammond, Trapp, Hutcheson, Henry, Burkitt, Baxter, Blomfield, Lampe, Bengel, Pearce, A. Clarke, Scott, Barnes, Stier, Alford, Webster, think that 'the other witness,' is God the Father.

I feel no doubt in my own mind that this last is the correct view. The use of the present tense, 'witnesseth,'—is a strong proof of it. John the Baptist's testimony was a thing past and gone.—Our Lord declares that his Father had borne distinct testimony to him, and supplied abundant evidence, if they, the Jews, would only receive it. And he adds, 'his testimony is true.' He will never bear witness to a lie.—Then having laid down this general proposition, he goes on to show the three-fold testimony which God had provided:—first, John the Baptist;—secondly, the miracles which the Father had commissioned him to work;—and, thirdly, the Scriptures.

The expression, 'I know,' probably implies the deep consciousness which our Lord had, even in his humiliation, of his Father's perfect righteousness and truthfulness. It means much more than a mere man's 'I know.' 'I know, and have known from all eternity, that my Father's testimony is perfect truth.'

33.—[*Ye sent unto John, etc.*] In this sentence the word 'ye' must be taken emphatically. It is 'ye yourselves.' The meaning of the verse seems to be, 'My first witness is John the Baptist. Now ye yourselves sent unto him at an early period of his ministry, and ye know that he told you One greater than himself was coming, whose messenger he was, and that afterwards he said of me, "Behold the Lamb of God." You cannot deny that he was a prophet indeed. Yet he bore faithful witness unto me. He told you the truth.'

There can be no doubt that our Lord refers to the formal mission of 'priests and Levites from Jerusalem,' to John the Baptist, described in John 1:19.

34.—[*But I receive not testimony from man, etc.*] This sentence seems meant to remind the Jews that they must not suppose our Lord depended either solely or chiefly on man's testimony. 'Not that I would have you think I rest my claim to be received as the Messiah on the witness of John the Baptist, or of any other man. But I say these things about John and his witness to me in order to remind you of what you heard him say, and that remembering his testimony to me you may believe and be saved.'

Here, as elsewhere, we should note how our Lord presses home on the Jews the inconsistency of admitting John the Baptist to be a prophet sent from God, while they refused to believe himself as the Messiah. If they believed John they ought in consistency to have believed him (see *Matt.* 21:23-27).

35.—[*He was a burning ... light.*] This is very high testimony to John. Doubtless he was not 'the light,' as Christ was. But still he was not an ordinary lamp lighted from above, as all true believers are. He was pre-eminently 'the lamp': a lamp of peculiar power and brilliancy, a 'burning' and a 'shining' light, like a flaming beacon or lighthouse seen from afar.

I think the expression 'he was' shows that at the time when our Lord spoke John the Baptist was either in prison or dead. At any rate his public ministry was ended. 'He used to be a light. He is burning and shining no longer.'

Chrysostom remarks,—'He called John a torch or lamp: signifying that he had not light of himself, but by the grace of the Spirit.'

[*Ye were willing for a season to rejoice.*] This refers to the extraordinary popularity and acceptance of John the Baptist when his ministry first began. 'Then went out to him Jerusalem, and all Judæa, and all the region round about Jordan' (*Matt.* 3:5). 'Many of the Pharisees and Sadducees came to his baptism' (*Matt.* 3:7). It was an ignorant excitement that brought many of John's hearers to him. They thought, most probably, that the Messiah, of whom he spoke, and whose way he came to prepare, would be a temporal king and conqueror, and would give to Israel its old pre-eminence on earth. But be the motives what

they might, the fact remains that John's ministry attracted immense attention, and awakened the curiosity of the whole Jewish nation. 'They willingly rejoiced in the light which John lifted up.' They seemed to take pleasure in coming to him, hearing him, following him, and submitting to his baptism.

The expression, 'for a season,' seems purposely used to remind the Jews of the very temporary and transitory nature of the impressions which John's ministry produced on them.

Stier remarks, 'Man generally, even a prophet, can only give light by burning, like a lighted candle, until he is burnt out, and his mission on earth ceases. Thus did the Baptist burn, brightly but rapidly.'

Burkitt remarks, 'It has been an old practice among professors not to like their pastors long, though they have been never such burning and shining lights. John was not changed, but his hearers were changed. He did burn and shine in the candlestick with equal zeal and lustre to the last, but they had changed their thoughts of him.'

36.—[*But I have greater witness ... John.*] This means, 'although John the Baptist was a witness to my being the Messiah, and the Son of God, his was not the only testimony I bid you receive. There is testimony even more important than his, namely, that of my miracles.' The Greek means literally, 'the greater witness;'—'The witness that I have is greater.'

Flacius suggests that our Lord here and in the preceding verse reminds the Jews how willing they were at first to receive John's ministry, and almost seemed to think he was the Messiah. Yet all this time 'John did no miracle.'—But when the true Messiah appeared, doing mighty 'works,' the Jews did not show him even as much attention as they had shown to John.

[*The works ... Father hath given, etc.*] This is a distinct appeal to miracles, as an important proof of our Lord's Messiahship and divinity. Four times in this Gospel we find the same appeal (*John* 3:2; 10:25; 15:24). The evidence of miracles should never be lightly esteemed. We are apt to underrate their value because they were wrought so long ago. But in the days when they were wrought they were great facts, which demanded the attention of all who saw them, and could not be evaded. Unless the Jews could explain them away, they were bound, as honest and reasonable men, to believe our Lord's divine mission. That they really were wrought the Jews never appear to have denied. In fact they dared not attempt to deny them. What they did do was to ascribe them to Satanic agency. All who attempt to deny the reality of our Lord's miracles in the present day, would do well to remember that those who had the best opportunity of judging, namely, the men who saw these miracles, and lived within hearing of them, never disputed the fact that they were wrought. If the enemies of our Lord could have proved that his miracles were only tricks, legerdemain, and impostures, it stands to reason they would have been only too glad to show it to the world, and to silence him for ever.

Five things should always be noted about our Lord's miracles. 1. Their *number*: they were not a few only, but very many indeed. 2. Their *greatness*: they were not little, but mighty interferences with the ordinary course of nature. 3. Their *publicity*: they were generally not done in a corner, but in open day, and before many witnesses, and often before enemies. 4. Their *character*: they were almost always works of love, mercy, and compassion, helpful and beneficial to man, and not mere barren exhibitions of power. 5. Their *direct appeal to men's senses*: they were visible, and would bear any examination. The difference between them and the boasted miracles of the Church of Rome, on all these points, is striking and instructive.

The manner in which our Lord speaks of his miracles is very remarkable. He calls them, 'the works which the Father hath given me to finish.' He carefully avoids the appearance of want of unity between the Father and himself, even in the working of miracles. They are not works which he did of his own independent will, but 'works which the Father hath given me,' works which it had been arranged in the eternal counsels the Son should work, when he became man and dwelt upon earth. Precisely the same expression is used elsewhere about 'the words' our Lord

spake, as here about 'the works:'—'I have given unto them the words which *thou gavest* me' (*John* 17:8).

37.—[*And the Father himself .... witness of me.*] There is undeniable difficulty about these words. It is not clear to what 'witness of the Father' our Lord here refers.

a. Some, as Chrysostom, Brentius, Bullinger, Gualter, Ferus, Toletus, Barradius, Cartwright, Chemnitius, Rollock, Jansenius, Trapp, Baxter, Hammond, Burkitt, Lampe, Bengel, Henry, Scott, Gill, think that our Lord refers to the audible testimony borne to him by the Father at his baptism, and at the transfiguration, when he said, 'This is my beloved Son, hear him' (*Matt.* 3:17; 17:5). But it surely is a capital objection to this theory, that this voice of the Father was in all probability heard by nobody excepting John the Baptist at the baptism, and Peter, James, and John at the transfiguration. At this rate it would be entirely a private testimony, and of no avail to the general body of the Jewish nation.

b. Some, as Theophylact, Euthymius, Rupertus, Calvin, Cocceius, Pearce, Tholuck, Blomfield, Tittman, A. Clarke, D. Brown, Alford, Burgon, think that our Lord refers to the testimony the Father has borne to him generally throughout the Old Testament Scriptures, and that the sentence before us should be taken in close connection with the next verse but one, beginning, 'Search the scriptures.' In fact that expression would then be the explanation of our Lord's meaning.

Of the two views I decidedly prefer the second one. It certainly seems the least difficult, and open to the fewest objections. There is a third view, supported by Olshausen and Bucer: viz., that the 'witness' here means the inward witness of the Spirit, in the hearts of believers. This, however, appears to me wholly out of the question. It is a witness that would be useless to the world at large.

Both here and elsewhere we must take care that we do not attach the idea of 'inferiority' to the expression 'sent' by the Father. Rollock remarks, 'It is quite possible that an equal may send an equal to discharge some office.' Cyril remarks, 'Mission and obedience, being sent and obeying, do not take away equality of power in the sender and the sent one.'

[*Ye have neither heard ... seen his shape.*] This appears to be a parenthetical sentence, as well as the verse that follows. It certainly seems to strengthen the view that when our Lord spoke of his Father 'bearing witness,' he could not have meant the audible witness of his voice at the baptism or transfiguration. In fact the sentence seems purposely to preclude the notion. It is as though our Lord said, 'Do not suppose that I mean any audible testimony of voice, or apparition, or vision, when I speak of my Father bearing witness to me. I mean testimony of a very different kind, even the testimony of his Word.'

The expression 'not seen his shape,' teaches the same great truth we find elsewhere: viz., that the Father is invisible, and has never been seen by mortal man. He who appeared to Abraham was the second person of the Trinity, and not the Father. St Paul says distinctly of the Father, 'whom no man hath seen, nor can see' (*1 Tim.* 6:16). The idea of artists and painters, when they represent the Father as an aged man, is a mere irreverent invention of their own brains, without the slightest warrant of Scripture.

Rupertus and Ferus suggest that the latter part of this verse was spoken to prevent the Jews thinking that our Lord spoke of Joseph, his supposed father. This, however, seems a rather improbable and fanciful idea.

38.—[*And ye have not his word, etc.*] This verse seems meant to remind the Jews that with all their pretended reverence for God, and affected zeal against blasphemies of him, they were really ignorant of God's mind. Their reverence for him was only a form. Their zeal for him was a blind fanaticism. They knew no more of his mind than of his shape or voice. They were not acquainted with his Word; it did not dwell in their hearts and guide their religion. They proved their own ignorance by not believing him whom the Father had sent. Had they really been familiar with the writings of the Old Testament they would have believed.

Our Lord evidently implies that real knowledge of God's Word will always lead a man to faith in Christ. Where there is no faith we may rightly assume the Bible is either not read or read in a wrong spirit. Ignorance and unbelief will go together.

Locke holds the curious opinion, that the 'Word' in this verse means the 'personal Word,' as at John 1:1. 'Ye have not me, the eternal Word, dwelling in your hearts.' But Christ nowhere calls himself 'the Word,' and the idea does not harmonize with the context.

Ecolampadius thinks that in this and the preceding verse there is a reference to Deuteronomy 18:15-19, where the Lord promised a prophet to the Jews like unto Moses, because they had said, 'Let me not hear again the voice of the Lord my God, neither let me see this great fire any more, that I die not.' He thinks our Lord reminds them of this. God had fulfilled his promise, and sent them a prophet like unto Moses, and now they would not believe on him!

39.—[*Search the scriptures.*] This famous sentence is interpreted two different ways.

a. Some, as Cyril, Erasmus, Ecolampadius, Beza, Brentius, Piscator, Cameron, Poole, Toletus, Lightfoot, Lampe, Bengel, Doddridge, Blomfield, Tholuck, A. Clarke, Scholefield, Barnes, Burgon, D. Brown, Webster, think that our Lord spoke in the indicative mood, simply making an assertion: 'Ye do search.'

b. Some, as Chrysostom, Augustine, Theophylact, Euthymius, Luther, Calvin, Cartwright, Gualter, Grotius, Rollock, Ferus, Calovius, Jansenius, Cocceius, Barradius, Musculus, Nifanius, Maldonatus, Cornelius à Lapide, Leigh, Whitby, Hammond, Stier, Alford, Wordsworth, think that he spoke in the imperative mood, giving a command: 'Search,'—as our version gives it.

I decidedly prefer this latter view. It is more forcible, and more in keeping with our Lord's general style of address; above all it seems to me to agree far better with the context. Our Lord had told the Jews that his Father had borne witness of him, though not by audible voice, nor by visible apparition. How then had he borne witness? They would find it in his Word.

'Go and search your own Scriptures,' our Lord seems to say. 'Examine them, and become really acquainted with their contents; you will find that they testify clearly and distinctly of me. If you wish to know God the Father's testimony to me, search the Scriptures.'

The word rendered 'search' means 'search minutely and diligently.' It appears to me intentionally used, to show that the Jews should not be content with mere reading. The Septuagint version of Proverbs 2:4 has an expression like it.

Chrysostom remarks, 'When Christ referred the Jews to the Scriptures, he sent them not to a mere reading, but to a careful and considerate search. He said not, "read," but, "search." Since the sayings about him required great attention (for they had been concealed from the beginning for the advantage of men of that time), he bids them now dig down with care, that they might discern what lay in the depths below. These sayings were not on the surface, nor were they cast forth to open view, but lay like some treasure hidden very deep.'

Some, who think the word 'search' should be taken as an indicative, 'ye search,' maintain that our Lord spoke ironically, and meant, 'Ye pretend to make a minute investigation of Scripture, and search into the letter of it, but never get any further.' I can see little ground for this view. The word 'search' is never used in a bad sense in Scripture (1 Pet. 1:11). The chief argument in favour of the 'indicative' side of the question is the notorious rabbinical custom of minutely scrutinizing and reverencing every syllable of Scripture. To this custom of honouring the letter of Scripture, while neglecting its spirit, many advocates of the 'indicative' here think that our Lord referred. Brentius gives a full account of the length to which the Jews went in their reverence for the letter of Scripture, such as counting the letters of each book, etc., and thinks that this was in our Lord's mind. I cannot however agree with this view.

[*In them ye think ye have eternal life.*] In this sentence the first 'ye' must be taken emphatically, as in verse 33. 'Think' does not imply that it was a doubtful point, or mere matter of opinion. It is rather, 'Ye yourselves think, and think rightly,—it is one of the dogmas of your faith,—that ye have in the Scriptures the way to eternal life pointed out.'

Chemnitius remarks, 'The words "ye think" mean that common persuasion and opinion of all men concerning Scripture, which, like an axiom in science, is established, firm, and certain.'

Let it be noted that many Christians are just in the unsatisfactory state of the Jews here described. Like them, they 'think,' and hold it as a dogma of their creed, that they 'have eternal life in the Scriptures.' But like them, they never read, mark, learn, and inwardly digest what Scripture contains.

Ecolampadius remarks, 'Scripture alone does not make a man any the better, nor even preaching, by itself, except by the Holy Ghost aiding. It is the peculiar office of the external Word to supply testimony; but it is the Spirit of God alone that can make the heart of man assent.'

[*They are they which testify of me.*] This sentence is a strong and weighty declaration of the value of the Old Testament Scriptures. It was to them exclusively, of course, that our Lord referred. He says, 'they testify of me.' In direct prophecies, in promises, in typical persons, in typical ceremonies, the Old Testament Scripture all through testifies of Christ. We read them to very little purpose if we do not discern this.

Ferus remarks that there are three ways in which the Scriptures testify of Christ. 1. Generally: they are as it were the voice of the uncreated Word, ever speaking to man in every part of them. 2. In figures: the paschal lamb, the brazen serpent, and all the sacrifices of the law were witnesses of Christ. 3. In direct prophecies.

Let us note in this verse the high honour which our Lord puts on the Old Testament Scriptures. He distinctly endorses the Jewish canon of inspired writings. Those modern writers who labour to depreciate them, and bring them into disrepute, show very little of Christ's mind. Much infidelity begins with an ignorant contempt of the Old Testament. Stier remarks, 'Israel, possessing still the Old Testament, will enter into the kingdom, when the despisers of Scripture in the final unbelief of Christendom will be judged and condemned.'

Let us note further what a plain duty it is to read the Scriptures. Men have no right to expect spiritual light if they neglect the great treasury of all light. If even of the Old Testament our Lord said, 'Search,' 'it testifies of me,' how much more is it a duty to search the whole Bible! An idle neglect of the Bible is one secret of the ignorant formal Christianity which is so widely prevalent in these latter days. God's blessing on a diligent study of the Scriptures is strikingly illustrated in the case of the Bereans (*Acts* 17:11).

JOHN 5:40-47

40 And ye will not come to me, that ye might have life.

41 I receive not honour from men.

42 But I know you, that ye have not the love of God in you.

43 I am come in my Father's name, and ye receive me not: if another shall come in his own name, him ye will receive.

44 How can ye believe, which receive honour one of another, and seek not the honour that *cometh* from God only?

45 Do not think that I will accuse you to the Father: there is *one* that accuseth you, *even* Moses, in whom ye trust.

46 For had ye believed Moses, ye would have believed me: for he wrote of me.

47 But if ye believe not his writings, how shall ye believe my words?

T HIS passage concludes our Lord Jesus Christ's wondrous defence of his own divine mission. It is a conclusion worthy of the defence, full of heart-searching appeals to the consciences of his enemies, and rich in deep truths. A mighty sermon is followed by a mighty application.

Let us mark in this passage, *the reason why many souls are lost*. The Lord Jesus says to the unbelieving Jews, 'Ye will not come to me, that ye might have life.'

These words are a golden sentence, which ought to be engraven in our memories, and treasured up in our minds. It is want of will to come to Christ for salvation that will be found, at last, to have shut the many out of heaven. It is not men's sins: all manner of sin may be forgiven. It is not any decree of God: we are not told in the Bible of any whom God has only created to be destroyed. It is not any limit in Christ's work of redemption: he has paid a price sufficient for all mankind. It is something far more than this: it is man's own innate unwillingness to come to Christ, repent, and believe. Either from pride, or laziness, or love of sin, or love of the world, the many have no mind, or wish, or heart, or desire to seek life in Christ. 'God has given to us eternal life, and this life is in his Son' (1 John 5:11). But men stand still, and will not stir hand or foot to get life. And this is the whole reason why many of the lost are not saved.

This is a painful and solemn truth, but one that we can never know too well. It contains a first principle in Christian theology. Thousands, in every age, are constantly labouring to shift the blame of their condition from off themselves. They talk of their inability to change. They tell you complacently, that they *cannot help* being what they are! They know, forsooth, that they are wrong, but they *cannot* be different!—It will not do. Such talk will not stand the test of the Word of Christ before us. The unconverted are what they are because they have no will to be better. 'Light is come into the world, and men loved darkness rather than light' (John 3:19). The words of the Lord Jesus will silence many: 'How often would I have gathered [you], and ye would not!' (Matt. 23:37).

Let us mark, secondly, in this passage, *one principal cause of unbelief*. The Lord Jesus says to the Jews, 'How can ye believe, which receive honour one of another, and seek not the honour that cometh from God only?' He meant by that saying, that they were not honest in their religion. With all their apparent desire to hear and learn, they cared more in reality for pleasing man than God. In this state of mind they were never likely to believe.

A deep principle is contained in this saying of our Lord's and one that deserves special attention. True faith does not depend merely on the state of man's head and understanding, but on the state of his heart. His mind may be convinced: his conscience may be pricked: but so long as there is anything the man is secretly loving more than God, there will be no true faith. The man himself may be puzzled, and wonder why he does not believe. He does not see that he is like a child sitting on the lid of his box, and wishing to open it, but not considering that his own weight keeps it shut. Let a man make sure that he honestly and really desires first the praise of God. It is the want of an honest heart which makes many stick fast in their religion all their days, and die at length without peace. Those who complain that they hear, and approve, and assent, but make no progress, and cannot get any hold on Christ, should ask themselves this simple question,—'Am I honest?—Am I sincere?—Do I really desire first the praise of God?'

Let us mark, lastly, in this passage, *the manner in which Christ speaks of Moses*. He says to the Jews, 'Had ye believed Moses, ye would have believed me: for he wrote of me.'

These words demand our special attention in these latter days. That there really was such a person as Moses,—that he really was the author of the writings commonly ascribed to him,—on both these points our Lord's testimony is distinct. 'He wrote of me.' Can we suppose for a moment that our Lord was only accommodating himself to the prejudices and traditions of his hearers, and that he spoke of Moses as a writer, though he knew in his heart that Moses never wrote at all? Such an idea is profane. It would make out our Lord to have been dishonest.—Can we suppose for a moment that our Lord was ignorant about Moses, and did not know the wonderful discoveries which learned men, falsely so called, have made in the nineteenth century? Such an idea is ridiculous blasphemy. To imagine the Lord Jesus speaking ignorantly in such a chapter as the one before us, is to strike at the root of all Christianity.—There is but one conclusion about the matter. There was such a person as Moses. The writings commonly ascribed to him were written by him. The facts recorded in them are worthy of all credit. Our Lord's testimony is an unanswerable argument. The sceptical writers against Moses and the Pentateuch have greatly erred.

Let us beware of handling the Old Testament irreverently, and allowing our minds to doubt the truth of any part of it, because of alleged difficulties. The simple fact that the writers of the New Testament continually refer to the Old Testament, and speak even of the most miraculous events recorded in it as undoubtedly true, should silence our doubts. Is it at all likely, probable, or credible, that we of the nineteenth century are better informed about Moses than Jesus and his apostles? God forbid that we should think so! Then let us stand fast, and not doubt that every word in the Old Testament, as well as in the New, was given by inspiration of God.

Notes—John 5:40-47

40.—[*And ye will not come to me ... life.*] The connection between this verse and the preceding one is not very clear. It is one of those abrupt elliptical transitions which occur frequently in St John's writings. I conjecture the link must be something of this kind: 'The Scriptures testify plainly of me. *And yet* in the face of this testimony ye have no will or inclination to come to me by faith, that ye may have eternal life through me.'

This verse evidently begins the third part of our Lord's address to the Jews. He had declared the relation between himself and God the Father. He had brought forward the evidence of his own divine commission, and his claim to be received as the Messiah. And now he concludes by a most heart-piercing appeal to the consciences of his enemies, in which he exposes the true state of their hearts, and the real reasons why they did not believe in him. If ever men were plainly dealt with, and received home-thrusts as to their own spiritual condition, it was on this occasion. In reading the conclusion of this chapter, one cannot but feel that a miraculous restraint must have been put on our Lord's enemies. Otherwise it is difficult to understand how they could have allowed him to bring such cutting and truthful charges against them. If ministers desire a warrant for dealing plainly with their hearers and addressing them directly and personally about their sins, they have only to look at their divine Master's words in this passage.

The opening charge that our Lord makes, 'Ye will not come to me,' misses much of its force in the English language. It is not the future tense of 'come' that is used in the Greek. Two distinct verbs are employed. The right meaning is, 'Ye do not will to come,'—'Ye have no heart, desire, or inclination to come to me.'

Let it be noted here that (1) we are all by nature dead in sins;—that (2) spiritual life is laid up for sinners in Christ alone: he is the fountain of life;—that (3) in order to receive benefit from Christ men must come to him by faith, and believe: believing is coming;—and finally, (4) that the real reason why men do not come to Christ, and consequently die in their sins, is their want of will to come.

Let it be carefully noted, that both here and elsewhere the loss of man's soul is always attributed in Scripture to man's own want of will to be saved. It is not any decree of God. It is not God's unwillingness to receive. It is not any limitation of Christ's redeeming work and atonement. It is not any want of wide, broad, free, full invitations to repent and believe. It is simply and entirely man's own fault,—his want of will. For ever let us cleave to this doctrine. Man's salvation, if saved, is entirely of God. Man's ruin, if lost, is entirely of himself. He 'loves darkness rather than light.' He will have his own way.

We should observe in this concluding part of our Lord's address, that he charges the Jews with four distinct sins: (1) want of real will to come to him, (2) want of real love to God, (3) undue desire of man's praise, (4) want of real faith in Moses' writings.

41.—[*I receive not honour from men.*] The connection between these words and the preceding verse is again not very clear.

I conjecture that it must be as follows: 'I do not say these things, as if I desired the praise and honour of man. I do not complain of your not coming to me, as if I only came into the world to seek man's praise. It is not on my own account that I mention your unbelief, but on yours, because it shows the state of your hearts. Do not suppose that I stand in need of followers, and am covetous of man's favour.'

42.—[*But I know you ... not the love of God, etc.*] The sense and connection here appear to be as follows: 'But the plain truth is, that I know and have long known the state of your hearts, and I know that you have no real love of God in you. You profess to worship the one true God, and to give him honour; but you show by your conduct, that with all your profession you do not really love God.'

To a Jewish hearer this tremendous charge must have been peculiarly galling. It was a charge that none but our Lord could make with equal decision, because he read men's hearts, and knew what was in them.

The word 'I know' is literally 'I have known.' Alford paraphrases the sentence: 'By long trial and bearing with your manners these many generations, and personally also, I have known, and do know you.'

In another place we find our Lord naming this sin as one of the special sins of the Pharisees. 'Woe unto you, Pharisees! For ye tithe mint and rue and all manner of herbs, and pass over judgment and the *love of God*' (*Luke* 11:42).

Ferus remarks that the incredulity of the Jews did not arise from want of evidence, but want of love towards God.

43.—[*I am come in my Father's name ... receive me not.*] This sentence contains a proof of the assertion made in the preceding verse. 'You show that you have no real love for God, by your not receiving me who have come in my Father's name, and desire nothing so much as his honour. If you really loved and honoured God as you professed to do, you would gladly receive and honour his Son.'

[*If another ... in his own name, him ye will receive.*] In this sentence our Lord supposes a case to show the corrupt and carnal state of the Jews' hearts. 'If another public teacher shall appear, giving himself out to be some great one, not seeking God's honour, and doing all in God's name, but aiming to exalt himself, and get honour to himself, you will receive and believe him. You reject me, the true Son of God. You are ready to receive any false pretender who comes among you, though he may give no honour to the God whom you profess to worship. It is true then that you have no real love of God in you.'

I believe decidedly that our Lord spoke these words prophetically. He had in view the many false Christs and false Messiahs who arose within the first hundred years after his death, and by whom so many of the Jews were invariably deluded. According to Stier no fewer than sixty-four false Messiahs appeared to them, and were more or less believed.

The readiness with which they believed these impostors is a remarkable historical fact, and a striking fulfilment of the words before us. They proved as forward to believe these pretenders to a divine mission who came in their own names, as they had been backward to believe our Lord.

I may add, however, that I am one of those who doubt whether the words of our Lord have even yet received their complete fulfilment. I think it highly probable that the world may yet see a personal Antichrist arise, who will succeed in obtaining credence from a vast portion of the Jewish nation. Then, and not till then, when Antichrist has appeared, this verse will be completely accomplished. Chrysostom, Cyril, Theophylact, Euthymius, Alcuin, Heinsius, take this view.

Stier remarks, 'He of whom the Lord here prophesies, is finally Antichrist, with his open and avowed denial of God and of Christ; with his most daring "I," before which all the proud will humbly bow down, because they will find themselves in him, and will honour him as their true god. As the Father reveals himself in Christ, so will Satan manifest himself in Antichrist, and give him all his work and witness, and his own honour as the prince of this world; and the wicked will yield themselves to him, because through unbelief they have already fallen into his nature, and fitly belong to him.'

Wordsworth remarks, 'The Fathers were generally of opinion, grounded on this passage, that Antichrist would be received by the Jews.'

44.—[*How can ye believe? etc., etc.*] This verse contains a very important principle. The substance of the meaning seems to be as follows:—Our Lord tells the Jews that they were not likely to believe, so long as they cared more for the praise of man than the praise of God. The true cause of their unbelief was a want of honesty and godly sincerity. With all their professed zeal for God, they did not really care so much for pleasing him as for pleasing man. In this state of mind they were never likely to have faith, or to come to the knowledge of the truth. 'How can ye believe, receiving and seeking honour from one another as ye do now?' It is not possible that you can believe, until you cease from your present earthly-mindedness, and honestly desire God's praise more than man's.

The great principle contained in the verse is the close connection between the state of a man's heart and his possessing the gift of faith. Believing or not believing, to have faith or not to have faith, is not a thing that depends only on a man's head being satisfied, and his intellect convinced. It depends far more on the state of a man's heart. If a man is not thoroughly honest in his professed desire to find out the truth in religion,—if he secretly cherishes any idol which he is resolved not to give up,—if he privately cares for anything more than God's praise,—he will go on to the end of his days doubting, perplexed, dissatisfied, and restless, and will never find the way to peace. His insincerity of heart is an insuperable barrier in the way of his believing. There is a mine of wisdom in the expression, 'an honest and good heart' (*Luke* 8:15). For want of it many a one complains that he cannot get comfort in religion, and cannot see his way towards heaven, when the truth is that his own dishonesty of heart is the cause. There is something he loves more than God. The consequence is that he never feels an honest will to believe.

The 'can' in this verse should be compared with the 'will' in the fortieth verse. 'Ye cannot because ye will not.'

[*From God only.*] This expression would be more literally rendered, 'from the only God,'—the one true God whom the Jews boasted that they alone knew and worshipped.

Doddridge remarks that the whole verse 'has much more spirit in it, if we consider it as applied to the members of the Sanhedrim, who had such distinguished titles of honour, than if we only take it as spoken to a mixed multitude.' If, as many suppose, our Lord was making a formal defence of himself and his divine mission before the great Ecclesiastical Assembly of the Jews, his words in this verse would come home to his hearers with stinging power.

45.—[*Do not think that I will accuse, etc.*] We must not suppose that our Lord literally meant that there was any real likelihood of Moses or himself standing up to make a formal accusation against the Jews. What he did mean was, that not to believe him was not to believe Moses. There was no need for him to accuse them of unbelief. Moses himself, for whom they professed such respect, might be their accuser, and prove them guilty. 'Even now,' he says, 'Moses accuseth you. His writings, daily read in your synagogue, are a constant witness of your unbelief.' There may also, it is highly probable, be a reference here to the Song of Moses, where he predicts the unbelief of the people, and desires the book of the law to be put 'in the side of the ark . . . that it may be there for a witness against thee' (*Deut.* 31:26).

Chemnitius remarks, 'What the Lord says to the Jews, is exactly as if I were to say to the Papists, It is not I, but the very Fathers whose authority ye allege in favour of your superstition, who will accuse you of impiety. Or as if we were to say to the Pope, It is not we who accuse and condemn thee, but Christ himself, whose vicar thou callest thyself; and Peter whose successor thou wilt have thyself; and Paul whose sword thou pretendest to bear: they it is who will accuse thee.' Beza makes much the same remark, and observes, that none will be more opposed to the Roman Catholics in the judgment day than the Virgin Mary and the saints in whom they profess to trust!

The notion of some Romanists that the expression, 'Moses, in whom ye trust,' justifies the invocation of saints, and putting confidence in them as mediators is, as Chemnitius observes, too weak and groundless to need refutation.

46.—[*For had ye believed Moses ... me.*] These words are simply an amplification of the idea in the preceding verse. If the Jews had really believed Moses, they could not have helped believing Christ. The witness of Moses to Christ was so distinct, express, and unmistakable, that true belief in his writings must inevitably have led them to belief in Christ.

[*He wrote of me.*] These words are very remarkable. In what sense our Lord used them, we cannot exactly know. At the very least we may conclude he meant that throughout the five books of Moses, by direct prophecy, by typical persons, by typical ceremonies, in many ways, and in divers manners Moses had written of him. There is probably a depth of meaning in the Pentateuch that has never yet been fully fathomed. We shall probably find at the last day that Christ was in many a chapter and many a verse, and yet we knew it not. There is a fulness in all Scripture far beyond our conception.

Let us note carefully that our Lord distinctly speaks of Moses as a real person, who, as a matter of history, lived and wrote books, and of his writings as true genuine writings deserving of all credit, and of undeniable authority. In the face of such an expression as this, it is a mournful fact that any man called a Christian can throw doubt on the existence of Moses, or on the authority of the books attributed to him.

To say, as some have done, that our Lord was only accommodating himself to the conventional language of the times, and that he did not really mean to assert his own belief either in the existence of Moses or the authority of his writings, is to charge him with downright dishonesty. It represents him as One aiding and countenancing the dissemination of a lie!

To say, as some have done, that our Lord,

born of a Jewish woman, and brought up among Jews, was not above the ignorant prejudices of the Jews, and did not really know that Moses ever existed, and that his writings are full of mistakes, is to talk downright blasphemy and nonsense. Fancy the eternal Son of God at any time talking ignorantly! Fancy above all that any trace of Jewish ignorance would be likely to be found in this chapter of St John's Gospel, in which, above all other chapters perhaps, our Lord's divine knowledge is most strikingly brought out!

47.—[*If ye believe not his writings, etc.*] This verse is an extension of the thought contained in the preceding one, and a solemn and mournful conclusion of the whole address. There is evidently an intentional contrast between 'writings' and 'words,' as if our Lord would remind the Jews that 'writings' are generally more relied upon than 'sayings.'—'If you do not really believe what your own honoured lawgiver Moses WROTE,—and it is plain that you do not,—it is not likely that you will believe what I SAY. If you have no real faith in the things written in your Scriptures by that very Moses for whom you profess such reverence, your favourite teacher and lawgiver, it is not to be wondered at that you have no faith in what I say, and that I speak to you in vain.'

The Greek word used here for 'writings' is very remarkable. It is generally translated 'letters,' as Luke 23:38. In 2 Timothy 3:15, it is rendered 'scriptures.' To my mind it is a strong indirect evidence in favour of the verbal inspiration of Scripture.

There is a sense in which these words should ring painfully in the ears of all the modern assailants of the Mosaic writings. It is just as true now, I firmly believe, as it was eighteen hundred years ago. They cannot divide Moses and Christ. If they do not believe the one, they will find sooner or later that they do not believe the other. If they begin with casting off Moses and not believing his writings, they will find in the end that to be consistent they must cast off Christ. If they will not have the Old Testament, they will discover at last that they cannot have the New. The two are so linked together that they cannot be separated. 'What God hath joined together let no man put asunder.'

In concluding the notes on this wonderful chapter, one would like to know how this marvellous address was received by those who heard it. But here we meet with one of the peculiar 'silences' of Scripture. Not one word is written to tell us what the Jews at Jerusalem thought of our Lord's argument, or what effect it had upon them. Our own duty is clear. Let us take heed that it has some effect on ourselves.

The amazing fulness of our Lord's teaching appears most strikingly in the address contained in this chapter. Within the short span of twenty-nine verses, we find no fewer than eleven mighty subjects brought forward: 1. The intimate relation of the Father and the Son. 2. The divine commission and dignity of the Son. 3. The privileges of the man who believes. 4. The quickening of the spiritually dead. 5. The judgment. 6. The resurrection of the body. 7. The value of miracles. 8. The Scriptures. 9. The corruption of man's will the secret of man's ruin. 10. The love of man's praise the cause of unbelief. 11. The importance of the writings of Moses.

JOHN 6:1-14

1 After these things Jesus went over the sea of Galilee, which is *the sea* of Tiberias.

2 And a great multitude followed him, because they saw his miracles which he did on them that were diseased.

3 And Jesus went up into a mountain, and there he sat with his disciples.

4 And the passover, a feast of the Jews, was nigh.

5 When Jesus then lifted up *his* eyes, and saw a great company come unto him, he saith unto Philip, Whence shall we buy bread, that these may eat?

6 And this he said to prove him: for he himself knew what he would do.

7 Philip answered him, Two hundred pennyworth of bread is not sufficient for them, that every one of them may take a little.

8 One of his disciples, Andrew, Simon Peter's brother, saith unto him,

9 There is a lad here, which hath five barley loaves, and two small fishes: but what are they among so many?

10 And Jesus said, Make the men sit down. Now there was much grass in the place. So the men sat down, in number about five thousand.

11 And Jesus took the loaves; and when he had given thanks, he distributed to the disciples, and the disciples to them that were set down; and likewise of the fishes as much as they would.

12 When they were filled, he said unto his disciples, Gather up the fragments that remain, that nothing be lost.

13 Therefore they gathered *them* together, and filled twelve baskets with the fragments of the five barley loaves, which remained over and above unto them that had eaten.

14 Then those men, when they had seen the miracle that Jesus did, said, This is of a truth that prophet that should come into the world.

T HESE verses describe one of our Lord's most remarkable miracles. Of all the great works that he did, none was done so publicly as this, and before so many witnesses. Of all the miracles related in the

Gospels, this is the only one which all the four Gospel writers alike record. This fact alone (like the four-times-repeated account of the crucifixion and resurrection) is enough to show that it is a miracle demanding special attention.

We have, for one thing, in this miracle, *a lesson about Christ's almighty power*. We see our Lord feeding five thousand men with 'five barley loaves, and two small fishes.' We see clear proof that a miraculous event took place in the 'twelve baskets of fragments' that remained after all had eaten. Creative power was manifestly exercised. Food was called into existence that did not exist before. In healing the sick, and raising the dead, something was amended or restored that had already existed. In feeding five thousand men with five loaves, something must have been created which before had no existence.

Such a history as this ought to be specially instructive and encouraging to all who endeavour to do good to souls. It shows us the Lord Jesus 'able to save to the uttermost.' He is one who has all power over dead hearts. Not only can he mend that which is broken,—build up that which is ruined,—heal that which is sick, strengthen that which is weak, he can do even greater things than these. He can call into being that which was not before, and call it out of nothing. We must never despair of anyone being saved. So long as there is life there is hope. Reason and sense may say that some poor sinner is too hardened, or too old to be converted. Faith will reply, 'Our Master can create as well as renew. With a Saviour who, by his Spirit, can create a new heart, nothing is impossible.'

We have, for another thing, in this miracle, *a lesson about the office of ministers*. We see the apostles receiving the bread from our Lord's hands, after he had blessed it, and distributing it to the multitude. It was not their hands that made it increase and multiply, but their Master's. It was his almighty power that provided an unfailing supply. It was their work to receive humbly, and distribute faithfully.

Now here is a lively emblem of the work which a true minister of the New Testament is meant to do. He is not a mediator between God and man. He has no power to put away sin, or impart grace. His whole business is to receive the bread of life which his Master provides, and to distribute it among the souls among whom he labours. He cannot make men value the bread, or receive it. He cannot make it soul-saving, or life-giving, to anyone. This is not his work. For this he is not responsible. His whole business is to be a faithful distributor of the food which his divine Master has provided; and that done, his office is discharged.

We have, lastly, in this miracle, *a lesson about the sufficiency of the gospel for the wants of all mankind.* We see the Lord Jesus supplying the hunger of a huge multitude of five thousand men. The provision seemed, at first sight, utterly inadequate for the occasion. To satisfy so many craving mouths with such scanty fare, in such a wilderness, seemed impossible. But the event showed that there was enough and to spare. There was not one who could complain that he was not filled.

There can be no doubt that this was meant to teach the adequacy of Christ's gospel to supply the necessities of the whole world. Weak, and feeble, and foolish as it may seem to man, the simple story of the cross is enough for all the children of Adam in every part of the globe. The tidings of Christ's death for sinners, and the atonement made by that death, is able to meet the hearts and satisfy the consciences of all nations, and peoples, and kindreds, and tongues. Carried by faithful messengers, it feeds and supplies all ranks and classes. 'The preaching of the cross is to them that perish foolishness; but unto us which are saved it is the power of God' (*1 Cor.* 1:18). Five barley loaves and two small fishes seemed scanty provision for a hungry crowd. But blessed by Christ, and distributed by his disciples, they were more than sufficient.

Let us never doubt for a moment, that the preaching of Christ crucified—the old story of his blood, and righteousness, and substitution,—is enough for all the spiritual necessities of all mankind. It is not worn out. It is not obsolete. It has not lost its power. We want nothing new,—nothing more broad and kind,—nothing more intellectual,—nothing more efficacious. We want nothing but the true bread of life, which Christ bestows, distributed faithfully among starving souls. Let men sneer or ridicule as they will: nothing else can do good in this sinful world; no other teaching can fill hungry consciences, and give them peace. We are all in a wilderness. We must feed on Christ crucified, and the atonement made by his death, or we shall die in our sins.

Notes—John 6:1-14

1.—[*After these things.*] The remark made in chapter 5, verse 1, applies here. The expression denotes an interval of time having elapsed between the end of the fifth chapter and the beginning of the sixth. John passes over all the events which happened at the conclusion of our Lord's defence of himself at Jerusalem. In fact, if the feast spoken of at the beginning of the fifth chapter was really the passover, almost an entire year of our Lord's ministry is unnoticed by John.

The events in this chapter, we should remark, are the only events in our Lord's ministry in Galilee described by St John, excepting the miracle of turning the water into wine at Cana, and the healing of the ruler's son (chapters 2 and 4).

[*Went over the sea of Galilee ... Tiberias.*] This sea so called was a freshwater lake in Galilee, through which the Jordan runs. According to Thomson, one of the most recent and accurate travellers in the Holy Land, it is about fourteen miles long, and nine wide, at the widest part. It lies no less than six hundred feet below the level of the sea, and is often agitated by sudden and violent storms.

Tiberias was a town on the west side of the lake, built by Herod about the time of our Lord's birth, and comparatively a modern place in our Lord's time. In the days of Josephus, forty years after our Lord's crucifixion, Tiberias had become an important city. It was spared by the Romans, when Vespasian's army destroyed almost every other city in Galilee, for its adherence to the Roman cause, and was made capital of the province.

John is the only Gospel writer who calls the lake the 'sea of Tiberias.' His doing so is an incidental confirmation of the opinion that he wrote much later than Matthew, Mark, and Luke, and after the taking of Jerusalem. He naturally used the name by which the lake was best known when he wrote, and most familiar to the Gentile readers, whom he had especially in view.

The reason of our Lord going over the sea, would appear to be his desire to withdraw himself from public notice (*Mark* 6:31), and perhaps from the persecution of Herod's party, after the death of John the Baptist. Comparing John's account with those of Matthew, Mark, and Luke, it seems most likely that he 'went over the sea' from the west coast, and landed on the northeast side of the lake, not far from Bethsaida. Luke tells us distinctly that the miracle which John here records, was wrought in 'a desert place, belonging to the city called Bethsaida' (*Luke* 9:10). Add to this the fact that no fewer than three of our Lord's disciples were inhabitants of Bethsaida, viz., Philip, Andrew, and Peter, and our Lord's retirement to this neighbourhood seems natural and reasonable. The notion held by many that there were two Bethsaidas, one in Galilee, where Andrew, Peter, and Philip lived, and one in Gaulanitis, where this miracle of feeding the multitude was wrought, seems both groundless and needless. Bethsaida was at the head of the lake, in Galilee, near the point where the river Jordan entered the lake, and the district belonging to it extended most probably beyond the river into Gaulanitis. Thomson shows this satisfactorily.

2.—[*A great multitude followed ... diseased.*] There seems no reason to suppose that this multitude followed our Lord from any but low motives. They 'saw his miracles:' that was all. Some few, perhaps, were in doubt and suspense, wondering whether he who wrought such miracles could possibly be the Messiah. The great majority probably 'followed' from that vague idle curiosity and love of excitement, which are the principles that gather nearly every crowd in the world.

St Mark says that 'the people saw them departing, and many knew him, and ran afoot thither out of all cities, and outwent them, and came together unto him' (*Mark* 6:33). This they might easily do by going round the head of the lake, to the point where Bethsaida was.

3.—[*Jesus went up into a mountain.*] The Greek here would be more correctly rendered 'into *the* mountain.' Whether there is any special reason for this we cannot tell.—It may be the one mountain which stood there, in contradistinction to the more level ground composing the district. Thomson, the American traveller, expressly says that there is a 'bold headland' here, with 'a smooth grassy spot' at the base, 'capable of seating many thousand people.'—It may possibly be 'that particular hill' to which our Lord was in the habit of going when he visited the district near Bethsaida.—It may be 'the hill country' generally, or mountainous district near Bethsaida.

[*His disciples.*] This expression includes not only the twelve who had been chosen and set apart by our Lord by this time, but many others who professed themselves his disciples. Many of them, it would appear from this very chapter (verse 66), were not really believers, and in course of time fell away. If Christ himself had many such disciples and followers, ministers nowadays (even the very best) must not be surprised to find the same state of things among their people.

4.—[*The passover, a feast of the Jews, was nigh.*] John's habit of explaining Jewish customs for the benefit of Gentile readers, should here be noticed.

The approach of the passover feast is no doubt specially mentioned in order to show the suitableness of our Lord's discourse in this chapter to the season of the year. The minds of his hearers would doubtless be thinking of the passover lamb, and its flesh about to be eaten and blood about to be sprinkled. Our Lord takes occasion to speak of that 'flesh and blood' which must be eaten and drunk by all who would not perish in sin. It is an instance of that divine wisdom with which our Master spoke 'words in season,' and turned everything to account.

Let it be noted that our Lord did not keep this passover in Jerusalem to all appearance, but remained in Galilee. Yet he generally observed all the ordinances of the law of Moses most strictly, and 'fulfilled all righteousness.' The reason evidently is, as Rollock remarks, that the enmity and persecution of the leading Jews at Jerusalem made it impossible for him to go there. It would have cut short his ministry and brought on his death before the time. May we not also learn here that the use of outward ordinances and ceremonies is not so absolutely necessary that they can never be dispensed with? Grace, and repentance, and faith are absolutely needful to salvation. Sacraments and ordinances are not.

The near approach of the passover may possibly account in part for the crowds who were assembled on this occasion. Not a few of the people perhaps were on their way to Jerusalem, to keep the passover feast, and were drawn out of their road by hearing of our Lord's miracles.

5.—[*When Jesus then lifted up his eyes, and saw a great company.*] We must not conclude from these expressions, that our Lord was suddenly surprised by the appearance of a great crowd. On the contrary Matthew and Mark both tell us that before he wrought the miracle which we are about to read of, he had felt compassion for the multitude, because they were 'as sheep not having a shepherd,' and had taught 'them many things' (*Mark* 6:34). When this teaching was over, he seems to have taken a survey of the crowd before him, and seeing how large it was, proceeded to show his tender concern for the wants of men's bodies as well as of their souls. A great crowd is always an impressive and solemn sight.

It is an interesting thought that the same eyes which looked compassionately on the crowd here, are still looking at every crowd, and especially at every crowd of persons assembled in God's name.

[*He saith unto Philip, Whence ... buy ... eat?*] Our Lord's reason for asking this question is given in the next verse. But it is worth notice that there was a certain propriety in asking Philip this question, because Philip 'was of Bethsaida,' the very town near which they were all assembled (*John* 1:44). Our Lord therefore might reasonably appeal to Philip, as one most likely and able to answer his question, whether it were possible to buy bread for such a multitude. He would of course know the capabilities of the neighbourhood. The idea, maintained by Chrysostom, Burgon, and others, that Philip was a disciple peculiarly slow to recognize Christ's Godhead, and therefore requiring special appeals, seems to me a far less satisfactory solution.

6.—[*This he said to prove him.*] We find the same kind of procedure on other occasions. When our Lord appeared to the two disciples at Emmaus, we read that after his discourse with them, 'he made as though he would have gone further' (*Luke* 24:28). This was 'to prove' whether they really wished for more of his company.—When on another occasion he came to the disciples walking on the sea, St Mark says, he 'would have passed by them' (*Mark* 6:48). When in this very chapter he would draw forth an expression of faith from his disciples, he says, 'Will ye also go away?' (*John* 6:67). Our Lord knows the sluggishness and coldness of our hearts, and he sees it good to stir our spiritual senses, and draw forth our spiritual desires by such a mode of dealing with us.

Explanatory observations like this, made by the Gospel writer himself, are more frequent in St John's Gospel than in any of the other three.

[*He himself knew ... would do.*] This would be rendered more literally 'what he was about to do.' Our Lord's foreknowledge of the miracle he was about to do should be noted. The words he used in the last chapter should be remembered. They were not works which were done by

chance and accidentally, in consequence of unforeseen circumstances, but foreseen and pre-determined. They were 'the works which the Father [had given him] to finish' (*John* 5:36).

7.—[*Philip answered him, Two hundred pennyworth, etc.*] What quantity of bread this sum would have procured we have no accurate means of knowing. But we may remember that the Roman 'denarius,' or penny, represented a very much larger sum than a penny does among ourselves. We must remember also that bread was much cheaper then than it is now. The quantity Philip named was probably much larger than we suppose.

Burgon thinks that the sum named by Philip was the whole 'store of money contained in their common purse:' viz., about six or seven pounds. But this cannot be proved.

8.—[*One of his disciples, Andrew, etc.*] Let it be noted here that Andrew, as well as Philip, was a native of the district of Bethsaida, where all these things happened. There is a propriety therefore in his speaking and giving information on the present occasion.

9.—[*There is a lad ... five barley loaves, and two small fishes.*] We should note in this verse how small were the provisions which our Lord miraculously multiplied. The fact that one 'little boy' (for this is the meaning of the word we render 'lad') could carry all the supply that Andrew mentions, is a plain proof that the 'loaves' could not have been large nor the 'fish' of great size.

The 'fishes' were probably small dried fish, such as are not uncommonly used as food now in hot countries, and near the Sea of Galilee would be of course common.

Barley was regarded, according to the Talmud, as a coarse food, only fit for horses and asses.

[*What are they among so many?*] This expression of Andrew's is purposely reported, no doubt, in order to show how strong was the conviction of our Lord's disciples that they had not sufficient provision to feed the multitude, and then to bring out into clear light the greatness of the miracle which our Lord wrought. It also helps to prove that the wonderful feeding of the multitude was not a preconcerted and prepared thing, arranged by our Lord and his disciples. Even his own immediate followers were taken by surprise.

10.—[*Jesus said, Make the men sit down.*] This arrangement prevented confusion and preserved order, points of vast importance when any large assembly of people is gathered together. Moreover, it made it less easy to practise any imposition or deceit in the feeding of the multitude. When every man was sitting steadily in his appointed place, no one could be passed over in the distribution of food, without it being observed. St Mark tells us that they 'sat down in ranks, by hundreds, and by fifties' (*Mark* 6:40).

[*There was much grass in the place.*] The time of the year when these things happened would be the very time when there was most 'grass.' It was in the spring-time, just before the passover, when the winter was gone, and the parching heat of summer had not begun. Thomson, the American traveller, reports that at this very day there is an open space of green grass at the foot of a hill, at the very place where in all probability this miracle took place.

Let us note our Lord's consideration for the bodily comfort of his followers. He chooses a place where there was 'much grass' to sit down on.

[*So the men sat down ... five thousand.*] The word 'men' here is probably emphatic, in contradistinction to the 'women and children,' whom Matthew expressly mentions as having been present beside the five thousand men. In the Greek the word is not the same as that rendered 'men' in the first clause of this verse.

11.—[*Jesus took the loaves ... given thanks.*] The expression here seems rather to imply a solemn action of prayer and blessing, as well as of giving thanks, as the first preliminary to the mighty miracle about to follow. In fact St Luke says, 'he took the five loaves and the two fishes, and looking up to heaven, he blessed them, and brake, and gave,' etc. (*Luke* 9:16). This also seems implied in St John's subsequent reference to this miracle, where he speaks of 'the place where they did eat bread, after that the Lord had given thanks' (*John* 6:23). The

Greek word here used is precisely the same that is used in the account of the institution of the Lord's supper given by St Matthew, St Mark, St Luke, and St Paul. St Matthew and St Mark say that our Lord 'gave thanks' when he took 'the cup.' St Luke and St Paul say that he also did it when he took 'the bread.' So here we can hardly doubt that blessing and giving thanks went together. The Greek word is the one which we have borrowed and transferred to our own language in the expression 'Eucharist.'

[*He distributed to the disciples, etc.*] I think there can be no doubt that this was the point at which the mighty miracle here wrought by our Lord came in. As fast as he broke the loaves and the disciples carried them away to distribute them, so fast did the loaves multiply under his hands. It was in the act of breaking and distributing to the disciples that the miraculous multiplication took place. In fact there was a continual act of creation going on. Bread was continually called into existence which did not exist before. The greatness of this miracle is perhaps not sufficiently realized. One loaf and less than half a fish to every thousand men! It is evident there could not have been more than a small morsel for each one without a miraculous increase of the food.

Bishop Hall remarks, 'He could as well have multiplied the loaves whole; why would he rather do it in the breaking? Was it not to teach us that in the distribution of our goods we should expect his blessing, not in their entireness and reservation? There is that scattereth and yet increaseth.'

12.—[*When they were filled.*] That expression deserves notice. It is one of the strongest proofs of the reality of the miracle we are reading. It would be impossible to convince five thousand hungry men in a wilderness that they were really filled, if they were not. A few enthusiasts and fanatics might possibly have been found who might have fancied they had eaten when they had not. But it is absurd to suppose that so strong a bodily sensation as hunger could possibly be relieved in five thousand men if there had not been a real supply of food, and real eating of it.

[*He said unto his disciples, Gather up the fragments, etc.*] In this little circumstance again we have a proof that real food was supplied, and in sufficient quantity for all. There was not merely a morsel for each man, but an abundant supply, enough and to spare. Our Lord's care for little things, and dislike of waste and extravagance, appear strongly in this sentence. It would be well if the principle contained in the words was more remembered by Christians: 'Let nothing be lost.' It is a deep principle of very wide application. Time, money, and opportunities of showing kindness and doing good are specially to be remembered in applying the principle.

It admits of question whether the 'disciples' who distributed the bread on this occasion, and afterwards gathered the fragments, did not include other helpers beside the twelve apostles. The time necessary for the distribution of bread among five thousand people, if only twelve sets of hands were employed, would prove on calculation to be very great.

13.—[*Therefore they gathered ... filled twelve baskets, etc.*] This simple fact is enough to prove that a mighty miracle had been wrought. Our common sense can tell us that five loaves and two fishes alone could not have filled a single basket. Now if the fragments left after the meal were enough to fill 'twelve baskets,' there must evidently have been a miraculous multiplication of the food at some stage of the proceedings. The fragments alone were probably fifty times more bulky than the original supply of food with which the meal began. The identity between the number of the baskets filled, and the number of the apostles, will of course strike any reader. One might think that each apostle had a basket.

St Mark mentions that there were fragments of 'fishes' put into the baskets as well as loaves, so that the fishes also were miraculously multiplied as well as the bread.

Some early writers, not without justice, call this the greatest miracle that our Lord ever wrought. Perhaps we are poor judges of such points, and little able to make comparisons. But it is certain that on no other occasion did our Lord manifest so clearly his creative power. No doubt it was as easy to him to cause bread to be, as to say 'Let there be light,' or to make the earth bring forth herbs and corn at the creation of the world. But the miracle was clearly intended to be one which Christians should hold in special remembrance. It is at any rate noteworthy that this is the only passage in Christ's life which all the four Gospel writers alike record. In this respect the miracle stands alone.

The attempts of Neologians to explain away this miracle are simply contemptible and ridiculous. It requires more faith to believe their explanations than to believe the miracle and take it as we find it. None but a person *determined* to disbelieve all miracles, and cast them out of the sacred narrative, would ever try to make out (as some actually have tried) that the four-times-repeated story of the miraculous feeding which we have considered, only meant that the multitude brought out the hidden stores of provisions which they had carried with them, and shared them with one another!

14.—[*Then those men.*] This probably means the whole crowd and multitude which had been fed on this occasion.

[*When they had seen the miracle.*] Signs and wonders were expected to accompany the appearance of any prophet or messenger from God. Here was a mighty miracle, and at once the minds of all who saw it were excited.

[*This is of a truth that prophet, etc.*] This meant that 'prophet like unto Moses,' whom all well-instructed Jews expected to appear, and for whose speedy appearing the ministry of John the Baptist had prepared the minds of all the dwellers in Palestine.

'Of a truth' would be more literally rendered 'truly:' i.e., really and indeed.

'That prophet' would be more literally 'the prophet.'

JOHN 6:15-21

15 When Jesus therefore perceived that they would come and take him by force, to make him a king, he departed again into a mountain himself alone.

16 And when even was now come, his disciples went down unto the sea,

17 And entered into a ship, and went over the sea toward Capernaum. And it was now dark, and Jesus was not come to them.

18 And the sea arose by reason of a great wind that blew.

19 So when they had rowed about five and twenty or thirty furlongs, they see Jesus walking on the sea, and drawing nigh unto the ship: and they were afraid.

20 But he saith unto them, It is I; be not afraid.

21 Then they willingly received him into the ship: and immediately the ship was at the land whither they went.

WE should notice, in these verses, *our Lord Jesus Christ's humility.* We are told that, after feeding the multitude, he 'perceived that they would come and take him by force, to make him a king.' At once he departed, and left them. He wanted no such honours as these. He had come, 'not to be ministered unto, but to minister, and to give his life a ransom for many' (*Matt.* 20:28).

We see the same spirit and frame of mind all through our Lord's earthly ministry. From his cradle to his grave he was 'clothed with humility' (*1 Pet.* 5:5). He was born of a poor woman, and spent the first thirty years of his life in a carpenter's house at Nazareth. He was followed by poor companions,—many of them no better than fishermen. He was poor in his manner of living: 'The foxes [had] holes, and the birds of the air nests; but the Son of man [had] not where to lay his head' (*Matt.* 8:20). When he went on the Sea of Galilee, it was in a borrowed boat; when he rode into Jerusalem, it was on a borrowed ass; when he was buried, it was in a borrowed tomb. 'Though he was rich, yet for [our] sakes he became poor' (*2 Cor.* 8:9).

The example is one which ought to be far more remembered than it is. How common are pride, and ambition, and high-mindedness! How rare are humility and lowly-mindedness! How few ever refuse greatness when offered to them! How many are continually seeking great things for themselves, and forgetting the injunction,—'Seek them not!' (*Jer.* 45:5). Surely it was not for nothing that our Lord,

235

after washing the disciples' feet, said, 'I have given you an example, that ye should do as I have done' (*John* 13:15). There is little, it may be feared, of that feet-washing spirit among Christians. But whether men will hear or forbear, humility is the queen of the graces. 'Tell me,' it has been said, 'how much humility a man has, and I will tell you how much religion he has.' Humility is the first step toward heaven, and the true way to honour. 'He that humbleth himself shall be exalted' (*Luke* 18:14).

We should notice, secondly, in these verses, *the trials through which Christ's disciples had to pass*. We are told that they were sent over the lake by themselves, while their Master tarried behind. And then we see them alone in a dark night, tossed about by a great wind on stormy waters, and, worst of all, Christ not with them. It was a strange transition. From witnessing a mighty miracle, and helping it instrumentally, amidst an admiring crowd, to solitude, darkness, winds, waves, storm, anxiety, and danger, the change was very great! But Christ knew it, and Christ appointed it, and it was working for their good.

Trial, we must distinctly understand, is part of the diet which all true Christians must expect. It is one of the means by which their grace is proved, and by which they find out what there is in themselves. Winter as well as summer, cold as well as heat, clouds as well as sunshine,—are all necessary to bring the fruit of the Spirit to ripeness and maturity. We do not naturally like this. We would rather cross the lake with calm weather and favourable winds, with Christ always by our side, and the sun shining down on our faces. But it may not be. It is not in this way that God's children are made 'partakers of his holiness' (*Heb.* 12:10). Abraham, and Jacob, and Moses, and David, and Job were all men of many trials. Let us be content to walk in their footsteps, and to drink of their cup. In our darkest hours we may seem to be left,—but we are never really alone.

Let us notice, in the last place, *our Lord Jesus Christ's power over the waves of the sea*. He came to his disciples as they were rowing on the stormy lake, 'walking on' the waters. He walked on them as easily as we walk on dry land. They bore him as firmly as the pavement of the temple, or the hills around Nazareth. That which is contrary to all natural reason was perfectly possible to Christ.

The Lord Jesus, we must remember, is not only the Lord, but the Maker of all creation. 'All things were made by him; and without him was not anything made that was made' (*John* 1:3). It was just as easy for him to walk on the sea as to form the sea at the beginning,—just as easy to suspend the common laws of nature, as they are called, as to impose those laws at the first. Learned men talk solemn nonsense sometimes about the eternal fixity of the 'laws of nature,' as if they were above God himself and could never be suspended. It is well to be reminded sometimes by such miracles as that before us, that these so-called 'laws of nature' are neither immutable nor eternal. They had a beginning, and will one day have an end.

Let all true Christians take comfort in the thought that their Saviour is Lord of waves and winds, of storms and tempests, and can come to them in the darkest hour, 'walking upon the sea.' There are waves of trouble far heavier than any on the Lake of Galilee. There are days of darkness which try the faith of the holiest Christian. But let us never despair if Christ is our Friend. He can come to our aid in an hour when we think not, and in ways that we did not expect. And when he comes, all will be calm.

Notes—John 6:15-21

15.—[*When Jesus therefore perceived.*] This would be more literally rendered, 'Jesus knowing, or having known.' It seems to imply divine knowledge of the multitude's secret intentions. Jesus knew men's hearts and thoughts.

[*That they would come.*] This would be more literally, 'that they are about to come.'

[*Take him by force, to make him a king.*] The intention or wish was probably to place him at their head, and proclaim him their king, with or without his consent, and then to hurry him away to Jerusalem, so as to arrive there at the passover feast, and announce him as a Deliverer to the crowd assembled at that time.—The idea evidently in their mind was, that one who could work such a mighty miracle must be a mighty temporal Redeemer, raised up, like the judges of old, to break the bonds of the Romish government, and restore the old independence and kingdom to Israel. There is no reason to suppose that there was any more spiritual feeling in the minds of the multitude. Of sense of spiritual need, and of faith in our Lord as a Saviour from sin there is no trace. Popularity and the good opinion of excited crowds are both worthless and temporary things.

Rollock remarks that the Jews were very sensitive about the tyranny and dominion of the Romans, while they did not feel the far greater tyranny and dominion of sin. He points out that we who are expecting the second advent of Christ in the present day should take care that we increasingly feel the burden and yoke of sin from which Christ's second advent will deliver the creation. Otherwise Christ's second advent will do us no more good than his first advent did to the Jews.

[*He departed again into a mountain ... alone.*] This would be more literally rendered, 'the mountain,' as at verse 3.

St Matthew and St Mark both mention another reason why our Lord withdrew to the mountain, beside his desire to avoid the intention of the multitude. They tell us that he sent the multitude away and departed to pray (*Matt.* 14:23; *Mark* 6:46).

Some think that a miracle must have been wrought when our Lord withdrew himself from the multitude, and that he must have passed through them invisibly, as after the miracle at Bethesda, and at Nazareth. Yet it seems hardly necessary to suppose this.

It is worth noticing that after St Luke's account of this miracle, he immediately relates that our Lord asked the disciples, 'Whom say the people that I am?' (*Luke* 9:18). It does not however follow that he asked immediately, but after an interval of some days. But the wish of the multitude here related may have occasioned the question.

16.—[*When even ... disciples went down unto the sea.*] St Matthew and St Mark both say that our Lord 'constrained' them to embark in the ship and depart. He 'obliged' or 'compelled' them. He probably saw that in their ignorance of the spiritual nature of his kingdom they were ready to fall in with the wishes of the multitude, and to proclaim him a king.

17.—[*Entered into a ship.*] This would be more literally 'the ship.' It seems to mean that particular vessel or fishing-boat which our Lord and his disciples always used on the Lake of Galilee, and which probably was lent for his use by the relatives of those of his disciples who were fishermen, if not

by the four themselves,—viz., James, John, Andrew, and Peter. There is no necessity for supposing that when they left their calling to become disciples they gave up their boats so entirely as to have no more use of them when they wished. The last chapter of this very Gospel seems to prove the contrary. When Peter said, 'I go a fishing,' there was the 'boat' ready for them at once (*John* 21:3).

[*Went over the sea ... Capernaum.*] This would be more literally 'were going,' 'were in the act of going.' Capernaum lay on the north-west shore of the Lake of Galilee, and the point where the disciples embarked was on the north-east shore. To reach Capernaum they would pass the point where the Jordan ran into the lake, and leave that point and the town of Bethsaida on their right hand. The place where the miracle was wrought was not at Bethsaida itself, we must remember, but in the desert country and district lying to the east of Bethsaida. St Luke specially mentions this (*Luke* 9:10), and unless we keep it in mind we shall not understand St Mark's words, that our Lord made his disciples 'go to the other side before unto Bethsaida.' To go to Capernaum they must need go 'in the direction of' Bethsaida, though they would leave it on the right as they passed. Thomson, in *The Land and the Book*, maintains this view, and Rollock, 250 years ago, held the same opinion.

I repeat the opinion, that I see no necessity for the theory of Alford and other commentators, that there were two Bethsaidas.

Capernaum was the city where our Lord passed more time, and probably worked more miracles, than he did in any other place during his ministry. This is probably the reason why our Lord speaks of it as 'exalted unto heaven' (*Matt.* 11:23). No city had such privileges and saw so much of the Son of God while he was manifest in the flesh.

[*It was now dark, and Jesus was not come.*] The Greek word for 'dark' is always rendered 'darkness' in other places, except John 20:1. The simple circumstance of the disciples being alone in the boat, on the sea, and in darkness, has been felt in every age to be an instructive emblem of the position of the church of Christ between the first and second advents. Like them, the church is on a sea of trouble, and separate from its Head. In estimating, however, the position and feelings of the disciples, we must not forget that four of them at least were fishermen, and familiar from their youth with the management of boats, and all the dangers of the lake. We must not therefore think of them as inexperienced landsmen, or as little children unable to take care of themselves.

We learn to know the value of Christ's company, when we have it, by the discomfort we experience when we have it not.

18.—[*And the sea arose ... great wind that blew.*] The Greek word rendered 'arose' would be more literally rendered 'was being raised or stirred.'

At first sight it may seem surprising that the waters of an inland lake, like the Sea of Galilee, could be so much agitated. But it is remarkable that the testimony of travellers in modern times is distinct, that this lake is peculiarly liable to be visited by violent squalls of wind, and to become very rough while they last. Thomson, the American traveller, says,—'My experience in this region enabled me to sympathize with the disciples in their long night's contest with the wind. I have seen the face of the lake like a huge boiling cauldron. The wind howled down the valleys from the north-east and east with such fury that no efforts of rowers could have brought a boat to shore at any point along that coast. To understand the cause of these sudden and violent tempests we must remember the lake lies low,—six hundred feet lower than the ocean,—that water-courses have cut out profound ravines and wild gorges, converging to the head of the lake, and that these act like gigantic funnels to draw down the cold winds from the mountains. On the occasion referred to we pitched our tents on the shore, and remained for three days and nights exposed to this tremendous wind. We had to double-pin all the tent ropes, and frequently were obliged to hang with our whole weight upon them, to keep the quivering tabernacle from being carried up bodily into the air. No wonder the disci-

ples toiled and rowed hard all that night.' In another place he says,—'Small as the lake is, and placid in general as a molten mirror, I have repeatedly seen it quiver, and leap, and boil like a cauldron, when driven by fierce winds.'—Thomson's *The Land and the Book.*

Burkitt remarks that the position of the disciples, immediately tempest-tossed after witnessing and partaking in a mighty miracle, is an instructive type of the common experience of believers. After seasons of peculiar privileges there often come sharp trials of faith and patience.

This sudden trial of faith by danger was no doubt intended to be a lesson to the disciples as to what they must expect in the exercise of their ministry. Affliction and crosses are the grindstones on which God is constantly sharpening those instruments which he uses most.

19.—[*So when ... rowed about five and twenty or thirty furlongs.*] We might gather from the disciples 'rowing,' and not sailing, that the wind was against them, and we are expressly told, both by St Matthew and St Mark, that 'the wind was contrary.' From the distance they had rowed, and the known width of the lake, at that particular part of it, they were probably now about the middle of their passage. St Matthew says,—they were 'in the midst of the sea' (*Matt.* 14:24). This would make them at least two or three miles from shore: a fact which should be carefully noted with reference to what follows.

Let the expression 'twenty-five or thirty' be noted. It is not necessary to define to a hair's breadth distances and quantities in narrating an event. Even an inspired writer does not. He uses the common language of men, and such language as those present on the occasion would have used. In a dark night they could not possibly have spoken with precise accuracy. John was there himself, and knew that excessive accuracy is sometimes suspicious, and looks like a made-up story (*John* 2:6, is a similar expression).

Bengel says, 'The Holy Spirit knew, and could have told John precisely how many furlongs there were. But in Scripture he imitates popular modes of expression.'

[*They see Jesus walking on the sea, etc., etc.*] This was undoubtedly as great a miracle as any that our Lord wrought.

'Moses,' says Theophylact, 'as a servant, by the power of God divided the sea. But Christ, the Lord of all, by his own power walked on the sea.'

For a solid body to walk on the face of the water as on dry land, is an entire suspension of what are called the laws of nature. It was of course as easy for him by whom the waters were first created to walk upon them as to create them. But the whole proceeding was so entirely supernatural, that we can thoroughly understand the disciples being 'afraid.' Nothing is found to alarm human nature so much as being suddenly brought into contact with anything apparently supernatural and belonging to another world, and especially in the night. The feelings called forth on such occasions, even in ungodly and irreligious men, are one of the strongest indirect proofs that all men's consciences recognize an unseen world.

That a mighty miracle really was wrought upon this occasion is the only reasonable account that can be given of the fact that we are told. St Mark adds to St John's account, that when Jesus came near the ship, he 'would have passed by them' (*Mark* 6:48). St Matthew adds another fact of even greater importance. He tells us that Peter said, 'Lord, if it be thou, bid me come unto thee on the water. And he said, Come. And when Peter was come down out of the ship, he walked on the water, to go to Jesus' (*Matt.* 14:28, 29). Such a fact as this cannot possibly be explained away. Not only did our Lord walk on the water himself, but he also gave one of his twelve apostles power to do the same.

To say in the face of such facts as these, that there was in reality no miracle,—that the disciples were mistaken,—that our Lord was only walking on the shore near the vessel—that the superstitious fear of the disciples made them fancy that he was walking on the sea,—that they finally put to shore, and took him on board,—to say such things as these pleases some persons who profess not to believe any miracles at all! But such views cannot possibly be reconciled with the account of what really happened, given by two witnesses, Matthew and John, who were actually present on the occasion, and by another writer, viz., Mark, who was intimate with that very Peter who walked on the water himself.

If the disciples were 'in the midst of the sea,' and two or three miles from shore, how could they possibly have seen our Lord walking on the shore?

If it was 'dark' when these things happened, it stands to reason that they could not distinguish anyone on shore, even supposing that they were not two miles off.

If there was a heavy gale blowing, and the waves were rough, it is absurd to suppose that they could hold a conversation with anyone walking on shore.

The plain truth is that it requires far more faith to accept such improbable and preposterous explanations as these, than to take the whole account simply as we find it, and to believe that a real mighty miracle was wrought.—Unless men are prepared to say that Matthew, Mark, and John, wrote accounts of the events of this night which are incorrect and not trustworthy, it is impossible for any honest and unprejudiced person to avoid the conclusion that a miracle took place.—Of course, if Matthew, Mark, and John give incorrect accounts, and are not to be trusted here, they are not to be trusted anywhere, and all their records of our Lord's doings and sayings become utterly worthless. This unhappily is the very result to which many would be glad to lead us. From denying all miracles to downright infidelity is nothing but a regular succession of steps. If a man begins with throwing overboard the miracles, he cannot stop logically till he has given up the Bible and Christianity.

20.—[*But he saith ... It is I; be not afraid.*] Our Lord's tenderness for his disciples' feelings appears beautifully here. No sooner does he see fear than he proceeds to calm it. He assures them that the figure they see walking on the deep is no spirit or ghost,—no enemy or object of dread. It is their own beloved Master. His voice, well known as it must have been, would, of course, help to calm their fears. Yet even that was not enough till Peter had said, 'If it be thou, bid me come unto thee.'

The practical remark has often been made, that many of the things which now frighten Christians, and fill them with anxiety, would cease to frighten them if they would endeavour to see the Lord Jesus in all, ordering every providence, and over-ruling everything, so that not a hair falls to the ground without him. They are happy who can hear his voice through the thickest clouds and darkness, and above the loudest winds and storms, saying, 'It is I; be not afraid.'

It has been thought by some that the words, 'It is I,' might be more literally rendered, 'I am,' and that they are intended to refer to the name of God, so familiar to Jews: 'I am.' But I doubt the correctness of the idea. It is a pious thought, but hardly in keeping with the context and the circumstances of the occurrence. Our Lord desired first to relieve the fears of his disciples by showing them who it was that they feared: and the Greek words for 'It is I,' are the only words that he could well have used.

It may be noted here that there seems to be no feeling or passion to which Christians are so liable as 'fear.' There is none, certainly, against which our Lord so often exhorts his disciples. 'Fear not:—be not afraid:—let not your heart be troubled:' are very common sayings of his.

21.—[*Then they willingly received ... ship.*] This would be rendered more literally, 'Then they were willing:' 'they were glad, and wished.'—It evidently implies that at first the disciples were afraid of our Lord. But as soon as they recognized him their fears departed; and so far from wishing to be rid of the figure they had seen walking on the sea, their great desire now was to receive him on board.

[*Immediately the ship was at the land whither they went.*] This sentence either means that shortly after our Lord joined the disciples in the boat they reached their destination, or that immediately, by miraculous agency, they arrived at the shore. There is, perhaps, no occasion to suppose any other miracle. Both Matthew

and Mark distinctly say that 'the wind ceased,' as soon as our Lord entered the boat. The storm, according to the custom of storms on the lake, suddenly ceased, and the disciples consequently had no trouble in rowing to the shore. The wind was no longer against them; and the sea, in so small a compass as the Lake of Galilee, would naturally soon go down.

The old practical lesson still remains to be remembered. Christ's church is now a tossed ship, in the midst of a stormy sea. The great Master has gone up into heaven to intercede for his people, left alone for awhile, and to return. When Jesus returns again to his tossed and afflicted church, at the second advent, their troubles will soon be over. They will soon be in harbour. His voice, which will fill the wicked with terror, will fill his people with joy.

The place where they landed was evidently Capernaum, or close to it. The discourse which follows was at any rate finished (wherever it may have begun) in 'the synagogue at Capernaum,' and follows in unbroken succession after the events we have now been considering. The state-ment of St Matthew and St Mark, that our Lord and his disciples reached the shore in 'the land of Genesaret,' is quite reconcil-able with St John's account. The 'land of Genesaret' was a plain on the north-west coast of the Lake of Galilee, extending from Magdala at the south, to Capernaum at the north.

In leaving this passage, I call the reader's attention to the very marked and peculiar position which the two miracles recorded by St John in this chapter occupy. They immediately precede that wonderful dis-course in the synagogue of Capernaum, in which our Lord proclaims himself to be 'the living bread, which came down from heaven and giveth life to the world,' and declares that, except we eat his flesh and drink his blood we have no life in us.—I believe that the two miracles were intended to prepare the minds of the disciples to receive the mighty truths which the dis-course contained. Did they stumble at the announcement that he was the 'bread of God,' and 'gave life to the world'? It would surely help their weak faith to remember that the very day before, they had seen him suddenly supply the wants of a mighty multitude with five loaves and two fishes.— Did they stumble at the doctrine, that 'his flesh was meat indeed and his blood drink indeed'? It would surely assist their feeble spiritual apprehension to remember that the very night before, they had seen that body walking on the face of the sea. They had had ocular proof that there was a deep mystery about our Lord's human nature, and that although he was real and true man, there was at the same time something about him far above man. These things I believe are worth noticing. The connection between our Lord's miracles and his teaching is often far closer than at first sight appears.

JOHN 6:22-27

22 The day following, when the people which stood on the other side of the sea saw that there was none other boat there, save that one whereinto his disciples were entered, and that Jesus went not with his disciples into the boat, but *that* his disciples were gone away alone;

23 (Howbeit there came other boats from Tiberias nigh unto the place where they did eat bread, after that the Lord had given thanks:)

24 When the people therefore saw that Jesus was not there, neither his disciples, they also took shipping, and came to Capernaum, seeking for Jesus.

25 And when they had found him on the other side of the sea, they said unto him, Rabbi, when camest thou hither?

26 Jesus answered them and said, Verily, verily, I say unto you, Ye seek me, not because ye saw the miracles, but because ye did eat of the loaves, and were filled.

27 Labour not for the meat which perisheth, but for that meat which endureth unto everlasting life, which the Son of man shall give unto you: for him hath God the Father sealed.

WE should mark first, in this passage, *what knowledge of man's heart our Lord Jesus Christ possesses.* We see him exposing the false motives of those who followed him for the sake of the loaves and fishes. They had followed him across the Lake of Galilee. They seemed at first sight ready to believe in him, and do him honour. But he knew the inward springs of their conduct, and was not deceived. 'Ye seek me,' he said, 'not because ye saw the miracles, but because ye did eat of the loaves, and were filled.'

The Lord Jesus, we should never forget, is still the same. He never changes. He reads the secret motives of all who profess and call themselves Christians. He knows exactly why they do all they do in their religion. The reasons why they go to church, and why they receive the sacrament,—why they attend family prayers, and why they keep Sunday holy,—all are naked and opened to the eyes of the great Head of the church. By him actions are weighed as well as seen. 'Man looketh on the outward appearance, but the Lord looketh on the heart' (1 Sam. 16:7).

Let us be real, true, and sincere in our religion, whatever else we are. The sinfulness of hypocrisy is very great, but its folly is greater still. It is not hard to deceive ministers, relatives, and friends. A little decent outward profession will often go a long way. But it is impossible to deceive Christ. 'His eyes [are] as a flame of fire' (Rev. 1:14). He sees us through and through. Happy are those who can say, 'Lord, thou knowest all things; thou knowest that [we] love thee' (John 21:17).

We should mark, secondly, in this passage, *what Christ forbids*. He told the crowds who followed him so diligently for the loaves and fishes, 'not to labour for the meat that perisheth.' It was a remarkable saying, and demands explanation.

Our Lord, we may be sure, did not mean to encourage idleness. It would be a great mistake to suppose this. Labour was the appointed lot of Adam in paradise. Labour was ordained to be man's occupation after the fall. Labour is honourable in all men. No one need be ashamed of belonging to 'the working classes.' Our Lord himself worked in the carpenter's shop at Nazareth. St Paul wrought as a tent-maker with his own hands.

What our Lord did mean to rebuke was that excessive attention to labour for the body, while the soul is neglected, which prevails everywhere in the world. What he reproved was the common habit of labouring only for the things of time, and letting alone the things of eternity,—of minding only the life that now is, and disregarding the life to come. Against this habit he delivers a solemn warning.

Surely, we must all feel our Lord did not say the words before us without good cause. They are a startling caution which should ring in the ears of many in these latter days. How many in every rank of life are doing the very thing against which Jesus warns us! They are labouring night and day for 'the meat that perisheth,' and doing nothing for their immortal souls. Happy are those who learn betimes the respective values of soul and body, and give the first and best place in their thoughts to salvation. One thing is needful. He that seeks first the kingdom of God will never fail to find all other things added to him (*Matt.* 6:33).

We should mark, thirdly, in this passage, *what Christ advises*. He tells us to 'labour . . . for that meat which endureth unto everlasting life.' He would have us take pains to find food and satisfaction for our souls. That food is provided in rich abundance in him. But he that would have it must diligently seek it.

How are we to labour? There is but one answer. We must labour in the use of all appointed means. We must read our Bibles, like men digging for hidden treasure. We must wrestle earnestly in prayer, like men contending with a deadly enemy for life. We must take our whole heart to the house of God, and worship and hear like those who listen to the reading of a will. We must fight daily against sin, the world, and the devil, like those who fight for liberty, and must conquer or be slaves. These are the ways we must walk in if we would find Christ, and be found of him. This is 'labouring.' This is the secret of getting on about our souls.

Labour like this no doubt is very uncommon. In carrying it on we shall have little encouragement from man, and shall often be told that we are 'extreme,' and go too far. Strange and absurd as it is, the natural man is always fancying that we may take too much thought about religion, and refusing to see that we are far more likely to take too much thought about the world. But whatever man may say, the soul will never get spiritual food without labour. We must 'strive,' we must 'run,' we must 'fight,' we must throw our whole heart into our soul's affairs. It is 'the violent' who take the kingdom (*Matt.* 11:12).

We should mark, lastly, in this passage, *what a promise Christ holds out*. He tells us that he himself will give eternal food to all who seek it: 'the Son of man shall give you the meat that endureth unto everlasting life.'

How gracious and encouraging these words are! Whatever we need for the relief of our hungering souls, Christ is ready and willing to bestow. Whatever mercy, grace, peace, strength we require, the Son of man will give freely, immediately, abundantly, and eternally. He is 'sealed,' and appointed, and commissioned by God the Father for this very purpose. Like Joseph in the Egyptian famine, it is his office to be the Friend, and Almoner, and Reliever of a sinful world. He is far more willing to give than man is to receive. The more sinners apply to him, the better he is pleased.

And now, as we leave this rich passage, let us ask ourselves, what use do we make of it? For what are we labouring ourselves? What do we know of lasting food and satisfaction for our inward man? Never let us rest till we have eaten of the meat which Christ alone can give. They that are content with any other spiritual food will sooner or later 'lie down in sorrow' (*Isa.* 50:11).

Notes—John 6:22-27

22.—[*The day following, etc.*] In this, and the three following verses, we have an instance of the extreme minuteness with which St John describes all the particulars connected with any of the miracles of our Lord which he records.—Here, for example, he tells us that our Lord's remaining behind, and not accompanying his disciples when they went into the boat, was observed by the multitude; and that nevertheless they could not find our Lord the next morning, and were puzzled to account for his being found at Capernaum when they got there.—All these little things help to prove that the circumstance of our Lord's joining the disciples was something miraculous, and cannot be explained away, as some Rationalists pretend to say. In particular the question, 'When camest thou hither?' (verse 25) is plain evidence that the multitude did not think it possible for our Lord to have walked along the shore, as some modern writers suggest, and did

not understand how he got to Capernaum, except in a boat.

In each of the seven great miracles recorded by St John this fulness and minuteness is very noticeable. Had he been inspired to relate as many miracles as we find in Matthew and Mark, his Gospel would have been fifty chapters, instead of twenty-one. Writing long after the other Gospel writers, and at a time when many who witnessed our Lord's miracles were dead, there was a fitness and wisdom in his supplying the abundant particulars which characterize his descriptions.

[*The people which stood on the other side of the sea.*] This means the multitude, or some of them, whom Jesus had fed on the north-east shore of the lake, and whom the disciples had left standing near the banks when they embarked, before our Lord sent them away. Matthew and Mark both mention that our Lord first made the disciples embark, and *then* sent the multitude away, and retired to the mountain to pray.

23.—[*Howbeit there came other boats, etc.*] This verse either means that other boats came from Tiberias the morning after the miracle of feeding the multitude, which were not there the evening that the disciples embarked; or else it means that there were other boats from Tiberias not far from the place where the miracle was worked, though there were none actually at the spot where the disciples embarked, except their one boat. The verse is carefully inserted parenthetically, in order to account for the multitude following our Lord to Capernaum. Had it not been inserted the infidel would have asked us triumphantly to explain how the people could have followed our Lord, when they had no boats! We need not doubt that every apparent discrepancy and difficulty in the Gospel narrative would equally admit of explanation, if we only knew how to fill up the gaps.

[*After that the Lord had given thanks.*] This is purposely inserted to remind us that it was no common eating of bread that had taken place, but an eating of food miraculously multiplied after our Lord had blessed it.

24.—[*When the people.*] There is no occasion to suppose that this expression means the whole five thousand whom our Lord had fed. For one thing, we are distinctly told that our Lord 'sent them away,' and the greater part probably dispersed, and went their way to their homes, or to Jerusalem to the passover. For another thing, it is absurd to suppose that so large a multitude could find boats enough to convey them across the lake. It evidently means the remaining portion of the multitude, and probably included many who followed our Lord about from place to place, wherever he went in Galilee, without any spiritual feeling, from a vague love of excitement, and in the hope of ultimately getting something by it.

[*They also took shipping.*] This means that they embarked in the boats which came from Tiberias, and crossed over the lake.

25.—[*And when they had found him on the other side of the sea.*] The place where they found our Lord was on the north-west side of the Lake of Galilee, on the opposite side from that where the miracle of feeding the multitude was wrought. The precise spot however where they found him is a point which it is not very easy to decide.—Of course if we read the discourse which follows as one unbroken discourse, all spoken at one time without breaks or pauses, except such as arise from the remarks of the people who heard our Lord, there can be no doubt where our Lord was. The fifty-ninth verse settles the question: 'These things said he in the synagogue as he taught in Capernaum.'—But if we suppose a break at verse 40, where the Jews begin 'to murmur,' and a short interval before the discourse was resumed, it seems highly probable that the crowd found our Lord at the landing place of Capernaum, or just outside the city,—that the discourse began there and continued up to verse 40,—and that then, after a short pause, it was resumed 'in the synagogue of Capernaum.' It certainly does seem rather abrupt and unnatural to suppose the crowd landing at Capernaum, going up to the synagogue, and *there* beginning the conversation with the question, 'When camest thou hither?'

[*When camest thou hither?*] The question evidently implies surprise at finding our Lord, and inability to understand how he could possibly have got to Capernaum, if he did not go in the boat with his disciples. It is a question, be it remarked, to which our Lord returned no answer. He knew the state of mind of those who asked it, and knew that it would be of no use to tell them when he had come, or how.

Wordsworth's idea that there is a mystical reference in this question to the manner and time of Christ's presence in the sacrament of the Lord's supper, appears to me very fanciful and far-fetched.

26.—[*Jesus answered ... Verily, verily, I say.*] This solemn expression, as usual in St John's Gospel, introduces a series of sayings of the deepest importance. The very first was a sharp and cutting rebuke of the carnal-mindedness of those whom our Lord addressed.

[Ye seek me, not ... miracles ... eat ... filled.] This was a severe saying, and one which he, who knew all hearts and read all secret motives, could say with peculiar power. It is a sad exposure of the true reason why many followed our Lord, both on this occasion and on others. It was not now even desire to see miracles performed, as it had been the day before (see verse 2). These, after a time, when the novelty was past, would cease to astonish and attract. It was a lower and more carnal motive still: it was the mere wish to be fed again with loaves and fishes. They wanted to get something more out of our Lord. They had been fed once, and they would like to be fed again.

The poor, and mean, and carnal motives which induce men to make some religious profession, are painfully exhibited here. Perhaps we have but a faint notion how little the reasons of many for coming to public worship or communion would bear sifting and examination. We may be sure that all is not gold that glitters, and that many a professor is rotten at heart. It was so even under our Lord's ministry, and much more now. Augustine remarks how seldom 'Jesus is sought for the sake of Jesus.'

Our Lord's perfect knowledge of the secret springs of men's actions is strikingly exhibited here. We cannot deceive him even if we deceive man; and our true characters will be exposed in the day of judgment if they are not found out before we die. Whatever we are in religion, let us be honest and true.

To follow Christ for the sake of a few loaves and fishes seems miserable work. To some who know nothing of poverty, it may appear almost incredible that a crowd of people should have done it. Perhaps those only can thoroughly understand it who have seen much of the poor in pauperized rural parishes. They can understand the immense importance which a poor man attaches to having his belly filled, and getting a dinner or a supper. Most of our Lord's followers in Galilee were probably very poor.

To deal plainly with people about their spiritual condition, and faithfully expose their false motives, if we know them, is the positive duty of ministers and teachers. It is no kindness or charity to flatter professing Christians, and tell them they are children of God, and going to heaven, if we know that they only make a religious profession for the sake of what they can get.

Wisdom and discrimination in giving temporal relief to the poor are very necessary things in ministers, and indeed in all Christians. Unless we take heed what we do in such matters, we do more harm than good. To be always feeding the poor and giving money to those who make some profession of religion, is the surest way to train up a generation of hypocrites, and to inflict lasting injury on souls.

27.—*[Labour not, etc., ... sealed.]* This verse is peculiarly full of instructive lessons. 1. There is something *forbidden*. We are not to labour exclusively, or excessively, for the satisfaction of our bodily wants, for that food which only perishes in the using, and only does us a little temporary good. 2. There is something *commanded*. We ought to work hard and strive for that spiritual food,—that supply for the wants of our souls, which once obtained is an everlasting possession. 3. There is something *promised*. The Son of man, even Jesus Christ, is ready to give to everyone who desires to have it, that spiritual food which endures for ever. 4. There is something *declared*. The Son of man, Jesus Christ, has been designated and appointed by God the Father for this very purpose, to be the dispenser of this spiritual food to all who desire it.

The whole verse is a strong proof that however carnal and wicked men may be, we should never hesitate to offer to them freely and fully the salvation of the gospel. Bad as the motives of these Jews were, we see our Lord, in the same breath, first exposing their sin, and then showing them their remedy.

The figure of speech used by our Lord, which supplies the keynote to the whole subsequent discourse, is a beautiful instance of that divine wisdom with which he suited his language to the mental condition of those he spoke to. He saw the crowd coming to him for food. He seizes the idea, and bids them labour not for bodily but spiritual food. Just so when he saw the rich young man come to him, he bade him 'sell all and give to the poor.'—Just so when the Samaritan woman met him at the well, as she came to draw water, he told her of living water.—Just so when Nicodemus came to him, proud of his Jewish birth, he tells him of a new birth which he needed.

When our Lord said, 'labour not for the meat that perisheth,' we must not for a moment suppose that he meant to encourage idleness, and the neglect of all lawful means in order to get our living. It is a kind of expression which is not uncommon in the Bible, when two things are put in comparison. Thus, when our Lord says, 'If any man come to me, and hate not his father, and mother, and wife, and children . . . he cannot be my disciple,' we see at a glance that these words cannot be taken literally. They only mean 'If any man does not love me more than father,' etc. (*Luke* 14:26). So here the simple meaning is that we ought to take far more pains about the supply of the wants of our souls than of our bodies (see also *1 Cor.* 7:29; *2 Cor.* 4:18; *1 Sam.* 8:7; *John* 12:43).

When our Lord says, 'labour for the meat that endureth,' etc., I think he teaches very plainly that it is the duty of everyone to use every means, and endeavour in every way to promote the welfare of this soul. In the use of prayer, the Bible and the public preaching of God's Word, we are specially to labour. Our responsibility and accountableness, the duty of effort and exertion, appear to me to stand out unmistakably in the expression. It is like the commands, 'Strive, Repent, Believe, Be converted, Save yourselves from this untoward generation, Awake, Arise, Come, Pray.' It is nothing less than wicked to stand still, splitting hairs, raising difficulties, and pretending inability, in the face of such expressions as these. What God commands man must always try to obey. Whatever language Christ uses, ministers and teachers must never shrink from using likewise.

The 'meat which endureth unto everlasting life,' must doubtless mean that satisfaction of the cravings of soul and conscience, which is the grand want of human nature. Mercy and grace, pardon of sin and a new heart, are the two great gifts which alone can fill the soul, and once given are never taken away, but endure for ever. Both here and in many other places, we must always remember, that 'meat' did not mean exclusively 'flesh' in the days when the Bible was translated, as it does now. The Greek word rendered 'meat' here means simply 'food' of any kind.

When our Lord says, that the Son of man shall give you 'meat which endureth unto everlasting life,' he appears to me to make one of the widest and most general offers to unconverted sinners, that we have anywhere in the Bible. The men to whom he was speaking were, beyond question, carnal-minded and unconverted men. Yet even to them Jesus says, 'The Son of man shall give unto you.' To me it seems an unmistakable statement of Christ's willingness and readiness to give pardon and grace to any sinner. It seems to me to warrant ministers in proclaiming Christ's readiness to save anyone, and in offering salvation to anyone, if they will only repent and believe the gospel. The favourite notion of some, that Christ is to be offered only to the elect,—that grace and pardon are to be exhibited but not offered to a congregation,—that we ought not to say broadly and fully to all whom we preach to, Christ is ready and willing to save you,—such notions, I say, appear to me entirely irreconcilable with the language of our Lord. Election, no doubt, is a mighty truth and a precious privilege. Complete and full redemption no doubt is the possession of none but the elect. But how easy it is, in holding these glorious truths, to become more systematic than the Bible, and to spoil the gospel by cramping and limiting it!

When our Lord says, 'him hath God the Father sealed,' he probably refers to the custom of setting apart for any specific purpose, and marking for any peculiar use by a seal. So also deeds and public documents were sealed to testify their execution and validity, and give them authority. So it is said in Esther: 'The writing which is written in the king's name, and *sealed* with the king's ring, may no man reverse' (*Esther* 8:8). The expression applied to our Lord in this place certainly stands alone, but I think there can be little doubt as to its meaning. It signifies that in the eternal counsels of God the Father, he has sealed, commissioned, designated, and appointed the Son of man, the Incarnate Word, to be the Giver of everlasting life to man. It is an office for which he has been solemnly set apart by the Father.

Parkhurst thinks that the word means 'him hath God the Father authorized with sufficient evidence, particularly by the voice from heaven'; and he refers the sealing entirely to the testimony which the Father had borne to the Son's Messiahship. This also is Suicer's view, and Alford's.

Stier remarks, 'This sealing is not to be understood merely of miracles, but of the stamp of divinity which was impressed upon his whole life and teaching.' This is Poole's view, and Hutcheson's.

It has been thought by some that there is a tacit reference here to the history of Joseph; and that our Lord meant that as Joseph was appointed to be the great almoner and reliever of the Egyptians by the king of Egypt, so he is appointed by the King of kings to relieve the spiritual famine of mankind. At any rate it is an apt and suitable illustration.

The idea of Hilary, and some others, that the expression 'sealed' refers to our Lord being the 'express image of the Father's presence,' appears to me far-fetched and without foundation.

The last words of the verse would be rendered more literally, 'him hath the Father sealed, even God.' It almost suggests the idea that our Lord desired to prevent his hearers supposing that he referred to Joseph as his father. It is as if he said, 'the Father I mean, remember, is not an earthly father, but God.'

Rollock remarks on this verse, that our Lord does not confine himself to showing the folly of only seeking 'the meat that perisheth,' but is careful to show the true food of the soul, and to point out who alone can give it. He observes that this is an example to us in teaching man the gospel. The remedy must be as plainly taught and lifted up as the disease. He observes truly that none can speak better of the vanity of earthly things and the glory of heaven, than many Papists do. But it is when they come to the feeding of man's soul that they fail. They try to feed him with man's merits, the intercession of saints, purgatory, and the like, and do not show him Christ.

It is noteworthy that it was the remembrance of this verse which made Henry Martyn persevere in preaching to poor Hindoos at Dinapore, in India. He had found they only came for temporal relief, and cared nothing for his preaching, and he was on the point of giving up in despair. But this verse came across his mind. 'If the Lord Jesus was not ashamed to preach to mere bread-seekers,' he thought, 'who am I, that I should give over in disgust?'

JOHN 6:28-34

28 Then said they unto him, What shall we do, that we might work the works of God?

29 Jesus answered and said unto them, This is the work of God, that ye believe on him whom he hath sent.

30 They said therefore unto him, What sign shewest thou then, that we may see, and believe thee? what dost thou work?

31 Our fathers did eat manna in the desert; as it is written, He gave them bread from heaven to eat.

32 Then Jesus said unto them, Verily, verily, I say unto you, Moses gave you not that bread from heaven; but my Father giveth you the true bread from heaven.

33 For the bread of God is he which cometh down from heaven, and giveth life unto the world.

34 Then said they unto him, Lord, evermore give us this bread.

THESE verses form the beginning of one of the most remarkable passages in the Gospels. None, perhaps, of our Lord's discourses has occasioned more controversy, and been more misunderstood, than that which we find in the sixth chapter of John.

We should observe, for one thing, in these verses, *the spiritual ignorance and unbelief of the natural man.* Twice over we see this brought out and exemplified. When our Lord bade his hearers 'labour . . . for that meat which endureth unto eternal life,' they immediately began to think of works to be done, and a goodness of their own to be established. 'What shall we do, that we might work the works of God?' Doing, doing, doing, was their only idea of the way to heaven.—Again, when our Lord spoke of himself as one sent of God, and the need of believing on him at once, they turn round with the questions, 'What sign shewest thou? . . . what dost thou work?' Fresh from the mighty miracle of the loaves and fishes, one might have thought they had had a sign sufficient to convince them. Taught by our Lord Jesus Christ himself, one might have expected a greater readiness to believe. But alas! there are no limits to man's dullness, prejudice, and unbelief in spiritual matters. It is a striking fact that the only thing which our Lord is said to have 'marvelled' at during his earthly ministry, was man's 'unbelief' (*Mark* 6:6).

We shall do well to remember this, if we ever try to do good to others in the matter of religion. We must not be cast down because our words are not believed, and our efforts seem thrown away. We must not complain of it as a strange thing, and suppose that the people we have to deal with are peculiarly stubborn and hard. We must recollect that this is the very cup of which our Lord had to drink, and like him we must patiently work on. If even he, so perfect and so plain a Teacher, was not believed, what right have we to wonder if men do not believe us? Happy are the ministers, and missionaries, and teachers who keep these things in mind! It will save them much bitter disappointment. In working for God, it is of first importance to understand what we must expect in man. Few things are so little realized as the extent of human unbelief.

We should observe, for another thing, in these verses, *the high honour Christ puts on faith in himself.* The Jews had asked him, 'What shall we do, that we might work the works of God?' In reply he says, 'This is the work of God, that ye believe on him whom he hath sent.' A truly striking and remarkable expression! If any two things are put in strong contrast, in the New Testament, they are faith and works. Not working, but believing,—not of works but through faith,—are words familiar to all careful Bible readers. Yet here the great Head of the church declares that believing on him is the highest and greatest of all 'works'! It is 'the work of God.'

Doubtless our Lord did not mean that there is anything meritorious in believing. Man's faith, at the very best, is feeble and defective. Regarded as a 'work,' it cannot stand the severity of God's judgment, deserve pardon, or purchase heaven. But our Lord did mean that faith in himself, as the only Saviour, is the first act of the soul which God requires at a sinner's hands. Till a man believes on Jesus, and rests on Jesus as a lost sinner, he is nothing.—Our Lord did mean that faith in himself is that act of the soul which specially pleases God. When the Father sees a sinner casting aside his own righteousness, and simply trusting in his dear Son, he is well pleased. Without such faith it is impossible to please God. Our Lord did mean that faith in himself is the root of all saving religion. There is no life in a man till he believes.—Above all, our Lord did mean that faith in himself is the hardest of all spiritual acts to the natural man. Did the Jews want something to do in religion? Let them know that the greatest thing they had to do was to cast aside their pride, confess their guilt and need, and humbly believe.

Let all who know anything of true faith thank God and rejoice. Blessed are they that believe! It is an attainment which many of the wise of this world have never yet reached. We may feel ourselves poor, weak sinners. But do we believe?—We may fail and come short in many things. But do we believe?—He that has learned to feel his sins, and to trust Christ as a Saviour, has learned the two hardest and greatest lessons in Christianity. He has been in the best of schools. He has been taught by the Holy Ghost.

We should observe, lastly, in these verses, *the far greater privileges of Christ's hearers than of those who lived in the times of Moses.* Wonderful and miraculous as the manna was which fell from heaven, it was nothing in comparison to the true bread which Christ had to bestow on his disciples. He himself was the bread of God who had come down from heaven to give life to the world.—The bread which fell in the days of Moses could only feed and satisfy the body. The Son of man had come to feed the soul.—The bread which fell in the days of Moses was only for the benefit of Israel. The Son of man had come to offer eternal life to the world.—Those who ate the manna died and were buried, and many of them were lost for ever. But those who ate the bread which the Son of man provided, would be eternally saved.

And now let us take heed to ourselves, and make sure that we are among those who eat the bread of God and live. Let us not be content with lazy waiting, but let us actually come to Christ, and eat the bread of life, and believe to the saving of our souls. The Jews could say, 'Evermore give us this bread.' But it may be feared they went no further. Let us never rest till, by faith we have eaten this bread, and can say, 'Christ is mine. I have tasted that the Lord is gracious. I know and feel that I am his.'

Notes—John 6:28-34

28.—[*Then said they unto him.*] These words begin one of the most important of our Lord's discourses and one about which the widest differences of opinion prevail. These differences it will be time enough to consider when we come to the passage out of which they arise. In the meantime let us remember that the speakers before us were men whom our Lord had miraculously fed the day before, and on whom he had just urged the paramount importance of seeking food and satisfaction for their souls. For anything we can see they were Jews in a state of great spiritual ignorance and darkness. Yet even with them our Lord patiently condescends to hold a long conversation. Teachers who desire to walk in Christ's steps must aim at this kind of patience and be willing to talk with and teach the darkest and most ignorant men. It needs wisdom, faith, and patience.

[*What shall we do . . . works of God?*] This question is the language of men who were somewhat aroused and impressed, but still totally in the dark about the way to heaven. They feel that they are in the wrong road, and that they ought to do something. But they are utterly ignorant of what to do, and their only notion is the old self-righteous one of the natural man: 'I must do something. I must perform some works to please God and buy admission to heaven.'—This seems to me the leading idea of the question before us. 'Your command to labour or work for the meat that endureth pricks our conscience. We admit that we ought to do something. Tell us what we must do, and we will try to do it.'—It is a case of a conscience partially aroused and put on its defence, groping after light. It is like the rich young man who came running to our Lord and saying, 'What good thing shall I do?' (*Matt.* 19:16).

The expression 'What shall we do?' would be more literally rendered, 'What do we?' or 'What must we do?' or 'What are we to do?'

The expression 'that we might work,' might have been rendered 'that we might labour.' It is the same Greek word that is translated in the previous verse 'labour.' The expression 'the works of God,' cannot of course mean 'the same works that God works.' It means 'the works that please God, that are agreeable to God's mind, and in accordance with God's will' (thus 1 *Cor.* 15:58, and 16:10). This is the view of Glassius.

This question, 'What shall we do?' we must remember, ought never to be despised. Though it may often be the lazy expression of languid religious feeling, just half-awakened, it is at any rate much better than having no feeling at all. The worst part of many persons' spiritual condition lies here,—that they are quite indifferent about their salvation; they never ask 'What shall we do?'—Many no doubt content themselves with saying 'What shall we do?' and like those of whom we are reading, never get any further. But, on the other hand, in many cases, 'What shall I do?' is the beginning of eternal life, the first step toward heaven, the first breath of grace, the first spiritual pulsation. The Jews on the day of Pentecost said, 'What must we do?' Saul, when the Lord met him near Damascus, said, 'Lord, what wilt thou have me to do?' The Philippian jailor said, 'What must I do to be saved?' Whenever therefore we hear a person ask the question about his soul, 'What shall I do?' we must try to help him and put him in the right way. We never know what it may lead to. It may perhaps end in nothing, and prove a mere temporary feeling. But it may also come to something, and end in the conversion of a soul.

29.—[*Jesus answered ... this ... work ... believe ... sent.*] In this verse our Lord takes hold of the expression used by the Jews about 'work,' and answers them according to their state of mind. Did they ask what work they should do? Let them know that the first thing God called them to do was to believe in his Son, the Messiah whom he had sent, and whom they saw before them.

When our Lord calls faith 'the work of God,' we must not suppose he means here that it is the work of his Spirit, and his gift. This is undoubtedly true, but not the truth of the text. He only means that believing is 'the work that pleases God,' and is most agreeable to God's will and mind.

Of course every well-instructed Bible reader will remember, that, strictly speaking, believing is so far from being a 'work,' that it is the very opposite of working. 'To him that worketh not, but believeth on him that justifieth the ungodly, his faith is counted [to him] for righteousness' (*Rom.* 4:5). But it is evident that our Lord accommodates his manner of speaking to the ignorant minds with which he had to deal. Thus St Paul calls the doctrine of faith the 'law of faith' (*Rom.* 3:27). It is much the same as if we said to an ignorant but awakened inquirer after salvation, who fancies he can do great things for his soul, 'You talk of doing; but know that the first thing to be done is to believe on Christ. This is the first step toward heaven. You have done nothing until you believe. This is the thing that pleases God most. Without faith it is impossible to please him. This is the hardest thing after all. Nothing will test the reality of your feelings so much as a willingness to believe on Christ, and cease from your own works. Begin therefore by believing.' The very attempt to believe, in such a case, might prove useful.

Let us note in this verse the marvellous wisdom with which our Lord suited his language to the minds of those he spoke to. It should be the constant aim of a religious teacher not merely to teach truth, but to teach truth wisely and with tact, so as to arrest the attention of those he teaches. Half the religious teaching in the churches and schools of our day is entirely thrown away for want of tact and power of adaptation in imparting it. To profess truth is one thing: to be able to impart it wisely, quite another.

Let us note in this verse the high honour our Lord puts upon faith in himself. He makes it the root of all religion, the foundation stone of his kingdom, the very first step toward heaven. Christians sometimes talk ignorantly about faith and works, as if they were things that could be compared with one another as equals, or opposed to one another as enemies. But let them observe here that faith in Christ is so immeasurably the first thing in Christianity, that in a certain sense it is the great work of works. In a certain sense it is the seed and root of all religion, and we can do nothing until we believe. In short, the right answer to 'What must I do?' is 'Believe.'

30.—[*They said therefore unto him.*] The secret unbelief of the Jews begins to come out in this verse. Nothing so thoroughly reveals the hearts of men as a summons to believe on Christ. Exhortations to work excite no prejudice and enmity. It is the exhortation to believe that offends.

[*What sign shewest thou then?*] The word 'thou,' in this sentence is emphatic in the Greek. It is as though the Jews said, 'Who art THOU indeed to talk in this way? What miraculous evidence of thy Messiahship hast THOU got to show?' There is an evident sneer or sarcasm in the question.

[*That we may see, and believe thee.*] This seems to mean, 'that we may see, in the miracle wrought, unanswerable proof that thou art the Messiah, and seeing the miracle may thus be able to believe thee.' This is the common language of many unconverted hearts. They want to see first, and then to believe. But this is inverting God's order. Faith must come first, and sight will follow.

There is a difference that ought to be marked between the 'believing thee' of this verse, and the 'believing on him whom he hath sent,' of the preceding verse. 'Believing on' is saving faith. 'Believing' alone is merely believing a person to speak the truth. The devils 'believe Christ,' but do not believe 'on Christ.' We believe John, but do not believe 'on him.'

[*What dost thou work?*] It seems at first most extraordinary that men who had seen such a miracle as that of feeding the five thousand with five loaves, and had been themselves of the number fed, and this only twenty-four hours before, could ask such a question as this! Our first thought is that no greater sign or miracle could have been shown. But they speak as if it was forgotten! Surely when we see such proofs of the extreme dullness and deadness of man's heart, we have no reason to be surprised at what we see among professing Christians.

Bucer and Grotius suggest that the speakers here can hardly be those who were witnesses of the miracle of feeding the five thousand. But I see no need for the suggestion, when we look round us and observe what human nature is capable of, or even look at the book of Exodus, and see how soon Israel in the wilderness forgot the miracles they had seen.

Let us remember that this demand for 'a sign,' or great miracle, was common during our Lord's ministry. It seems to have been a habit of mind among the Jews. St Paul says, 'The Jews require a sign' (*1 Cor.* 1:22). They were always deceiving themselves with the idea that they wanted more evidence, and pretending that if they had this evidence they would believe. Thousands in every age do just the same. They live on waiting for something to convince them, and fancying that if they were convinced they would be different men in religion. The plain truth is that it is want of heart, not want of evidence, that keeps people back from Christ. The Jews had signs, and evidences, and proofs of Christ's Messiahship in abundance, but they would not see them. Just so, many a professed unbeliever of our day has plenty of evidence around him, but he will neither look at it nor examine it. So true it is that 'none are so blind as those that will not see.'

Quesnel remarks, 'The atheist is still seeking after proofs of a deity, though he walks every day amidst apparent miracles.'

We should observe that the Jews were willing enough to honour Christ as 'a prophet.' It was the doctrine of faith in him that they could not receive. Christ the 'teacher,' is always more popular than Christ the 'sacrifice and substitute.'

31.—[*Our fathers ... manna ... written ... to eat.*] The intention of the Jews in saying what they do in this verse is plain. They evidently implied a disparaging comparison between our Lord and Moses, and our Lord's miracle of feeding the multitude, and the feeding of Israel with manna. It is as though they said, 'Although thou didst work a miracle yesterday, thou hast done nothing greater than the thing that happened in the days when our fathers were fed with manna in the wilderness. The sign thou hast given is not so great a sign as that which Moses gave our fathers when he gave them bread from heaven to eat. Why then should we be called on to believe thee? What proof have we that thou art a prophet greater than Moses?' The word 'manna' would have been more correctly rendered 'the manna:' i.e., 'the well-known and famous manna.'

Let us note in this verse how prone men are to refer back at once to things done in the days of their 'fathers,' when saving religion is pressed home on their consciences. The woman of Samaria began talking about 'our father Jacob:' 'Art thou greater than our father Jacob?' (*John* 4:12). The Pharisees '[built] the sepulchres of the prophets' (*Luke* 11:47). Dead teachers have always more authority than living ones.

Let us mark that the miraculous feeding of Israel in the wilderness with manna is spoken of by the Jews as a notorious historical fact. Our Lord moreover in the following verse entirely assumes the truth of the miracle. The modern attempts to deny or explain away the miraculous facts recorded in the Old Testament, are here, as well as elsewhere, entirely irreconcilable with the manner in which they are always spoken of in the New Testament. He that denies Old Testament miracles, is assaulting the knowledge and veracity of Christ and the apostles. They believed them, and spoke of them, as historical facts. We never need be ashamed of being on their side.

Let us observe the acquaintance with Scripture which the Jews exhibit. They quote Psalm 78 (verses 24, 25) as a sufficient proof of the fact they had just mentioned. A certain knowledge of Scripture, unhappily, may often be found in a very unbelieving heart. Knowledge of the letter of Scripture at any rate seems to have been very common among the Jews (see *Deut.* 6:6, 7).

Whether or not they applied the sentence they quoted to Moses, rather than God, I think, admits of a question. Our Lord's words, in the following verse, would rather lead one to think that they meant that 'Moses gave them bread from heaven.'

32.—[*Then Jesus ... Verily ... Moses gave you not that bread.*] The object of our Lord in this verse is very plain. He replies to the argument of the Jews, that the miracle of the manna was a greater miracle than any he had come into the world to work, and that Moses was consequently a greater prophet than he was. Yet in the words he uses, it is not very easy to settle where the stress should be laid, and what is the precise word on which the point of the answer rests.

a. Some think that it means, 'It was not Moses who gave you the bread from heaven, but God.' They lay the stress on *Moses*.

b. Some think that it means, 'Moses did not give you bread from the real heaven of heavens, where God the Father dwells, but only a material food from the upper part of that atmosphere which surrounds this earth.' They lay the stress on *heaven*.

c. Some think that it means, 'Moses did not give the true spiritual bread from heaven, though he gave you bread.' They lay the stress on '*that* bread.'

The second of these opinions seems to me quite inadmissible. The distinction between the heaven where God dwells and the upper region of our atmosphere was not, I believe, in our Lord's mind when he used the language he uses here. Moreover it cannot be denied that the manna, though only material food, was heavenly food: i.e., food supplied by God's miraculous interposition.

The true view seems to me to be contained in the first and third opinions taken together. The Greek bears it out by putting the word 'not' in the very forefront of the sentence. 'It was not Moses who gave you that bread from heaven, and even the bread that was given you was not that true bread which endures to everlasting life.'

[*But my Father giveth you the true bread from heaven.*] The use of the present tense should be noticed in this sentence. The idea seems to be, 'What Moses could not give you, even the true bread which feeds the soul, my Father does give you, and is actually giving you at this moment, in that he gives you myself.'

The expression, 'giveth you,' must not be supposed to imply actual reception on the part of the Jews. It rather means 'giving' in the sense of 'offering for acceptance a thing which those to whom it is offered may not receive.—It is a very remarkable saying, and one of those which seems to me to prove unanswerably that Christ is God's gift to the whole world,—that his redemption was made for all mankind,—that he died for all,—and is offered to all. It is like the famous texts, 'God so loved the world that he gave his only begotten Son' (*John* 3:16); and, 'God hath given to us eternal life, and this life is in his Son' (*1 John* 5:11). It is a gift no doubt which is utterly thrown away, like many other gifts of God to man, and is profitable to none but those that believe. But that God nevertheless does in a certain sense actually 'give' his Son, as the true bread from heaven, even to the wicked and unbelieving,

appears to me incontrovertibly proved by the words before us. It is a remarkable fact that Erskine, the famous Scotch seceder, based his right to offer Christ to all, on these very words, and defended himself before the General Assembly of the Kirk of Scotland on the strength of them. He asked the Moderator to tell him what Christ meant when he said, 'My Father giveth you the true bread from heaven,' and got no answer. The truth is, I venture to think, that the text cannot be answered by the advocates of an extreme view of particular redemption. Fairly interpreted, the words mean that in some sense or another the Father does actually 'give' the Son to those who are not believers. They warrant preachers and teachers in making a wide, broad, full, free, unlimited offer of Christ to all mankind without exception.

Even Hutcheson, the Scotch divine, though a strong advocate of particular redemption, remarks, 'Even such as are, at present, but carnal and unsound, are not secluded from the offer of Christ; but upon right terms may expect that he will be gifted to them.'

The expression 'true,' in this place, when applied to bread means 'true' as opposed to that which is only typical, emblematical, and temporal. The manna was undoubtedly real true food for the body. But it was a type of a far better food, and was itself a thing which could not benefit the soul. Christ was the true spiritual food of which the manna was the type. (Examples of 'true' in this sense may be seen in *John* 1:9; 15:1; *Heb.* 8:2; 9:24.)

33.—[*The bread of God is he which, etc.*] At first sight this verse seems to mean that 'Christ coming down from heaven and giving life unto the world is the true bread of God: the divine food of man's soul.' But it may well be doubted whether this is the precise meaning of the Greek words. I think, with Rollock, Bengel, Scholefield, Alford, and others, they would be more correctly rendered, 'The bread of God is that bread which cometh down from heaven.'

a. For one thing, the Jews do not appear to have understood our Lord as yet to speak directly of himself, or of any person. Else why should they have said, 'Lord, give us this bread.' Moreover, they did not murmur when they heard these words.

b. For another thing, our Lord does not appear as yet to reveal fully that he was the bread of God. He reserves this till verse 35, and then declares it. At present he only gives a general intimation of a certain divine life-giving bread.

c. For another thing, it is more in keeping with the gradual unfolding of truth, which appears so strikingly in this chapter, to suppose that our Lord begins with a general statement, than to suppose that he speaks at once of himself personally. First (1), the bread generally,—then (2), I am the bread,—then (3), the bread is my flesh,—then (4), except ye eat the flesh, and drink the blood, no life, etc.: such seem the gradual steps by which our Lord leads on his hearers in this wonderful chapter. I freely admit that the point is doubtful. Happily, whether we read, 'the bread of God is he,' or 'the bread of God is that bread,' the doctrine is sound, and scriptural, and edifying.

The expression, 'the bread of God,' seems equivalent to the expression of the preceding verse, 'the true bread.' It is that real satisfying food for the soul which God has provided.

The expression, which 'cometh down from heaven,' is an assertion of the divine origin of that spiritual food which God had provided. Like the manna, it came down from heaven, but in a far higher, fuller, and deeper sense, than the manna did. It was 'that personal bread,' of which they would soon hear more distinctly.

The expression, 'giveth life to the world,' implies a contrast between the 'bread of God' and the manna. The manna only supplied the hunger of the twelve tribes of Israel: viz., 600,000 men and their families. The bread of God was for the whole world, and provided eternal life for every member of Adam's family who would eat of it, whether Jew or Gentile.

We should mark, again, what a strong argument these words supply in favour of the doctrine of Christ being God's gift to all. That all the world has not life from Christ, and does not believe in him, is undoubtedly true. But that life is provided in Christ, and salvation sufficient for all the world, appears to be the natural interpretation of the text.

34.—[*Then said they ... Lord, evermore give us this bread.*] There is a striking resemblance between the thought expressed in this verse, and the thought of the Samaritan woman, when she heard of the living water that Christ could give: 'Sir, give me this water, that I thirst not, neither come hither to draw' (*John* 4:15). In both cases we see desire called forth and excited by our Lord's words. There is a vague sense of something great and good being close at hand, and a vague wish expressed to have it. In the case of the Samaritan woman, the wish proved the first spark in a thorough conversion to God. In the case of the Jews before us, the wish seems to have been nothing more than the 'desire of the slothful,' and to have gone no further. Wishing and admiring are not conversion.

Let us note, carefully, that there is nothing hitherto to show that the Jews understood our Lord to call *himself* the 'bread of God,' or 'the true bread.' That there was such a thing as the true and satisfying bread,—that it must be the same as that 'meat which endureth unto everlasting life,' they seem to have concluded;—and that it was something which our Lord could give, they inferred. But there is not a word to make us think they saw it at present to mean Christ himself. This is a weighty argument in favour of that view of the preceding verse which I have tried to support: viz., that it ought to be translated 'the bread of God is that bread,' not 'he.'

There is some probability in Lightfoot's remark, that our Lord's hearers, like most Jews, had their minds stuffed with foolish and superstitious notions about great banquets and feasts, which they expected Messiah to give them whenever he appeared. They had a tradition that Leviathan and Behemoth were to be slain, and their flesh made into a great feast for Israel when Messiah came. Our Lord, possibly, had this tradition in his mind, and desired to turn the minds of the Jews to the true food which Messiah had come to give.

JOHN 6:35-40

35 And Jesus said unto them, I am the bread of life: he that cometh to me shall never hunger; and he that believeth on me shall never thirst.

36 But I said unto you, That ye also have seen me, and believe not.

37 All that the Father giveth me shall come to me; and him that cometh to me I will in no wise cast out.

38 For I came down from heaven, not to do mine own will, but the will of him that sent me.

39 And this is the Father's will which hath sent me, that of all which he hath given me I should lose nothing, but should raise it up again at the last day.

40 And this is the will of him that sent me, that every one which seeth the Son, and believeth on him, may have everlasting life: and I will raise him up at the last day.

THREE of our Lord Jesus Christ's greatest sayings are strung together, like pearls, in this passage. Each of them ought to be precious to every true Christian. All taken together they form a mine of truth, into which he that searches need never search in vain.

We have, first, in these verses, *a saying of Christ about himself.* We read that Jesus said, 'I am the bread of life: he that cometh to me shall never hunger; and he that believeth on me shall never thirst.'

Our Lord would have us know that he himself is the appointed food of man's soul. The soul of every man is naturally starving and famishing through sin. Christ is given by God the Father, to be the Satisfier, the Reliever, and the Physician of man's spiritual need. In him and his mediatorial office,—in him and his atoning death,—in him and his priesthood,—in him and his grace, love, and power,—in him alone will empty souls find their wants supplied. In him there is life. He is 'the bread of life.'

With what divine and perfect wisdom this name is chosen! Bread is necessary food. We can manage tolerably well without many things on our table, but not without bread. So is it with Christ. We must have Christ, or die in our own sins.—Bread is food that suits all. Some cannot eat meat, and some cannot eat vegetables. But all like bread. It is food both for the Queen and the pauper. So it is with Christ. He is just the Saviour that meets the wants of every class.—Bread is food that we need daily. Other kinds of food we take, perhaps, only occasionally. But we want bread every morning and evening in our lives. So it is with Christ. There is no day in our lives but we need his blood, his righteousness, his intercession, and his grace.—Well may he be called, 'the bread of life!'

Do we know anything of spiritual hunger? Do we feel anything of craving and emptiness in conscience, heart, and affections? Let us distinctly understand that Christ alone can relieve and supply us, and that it is his office to relieve. We must come to him by faith. We must believe on him, and commit our souls into his hands. So coming, he pledges his royal word we shall find lasting satisfaction both for time and eternity.—It is written, 'He that cometh to me shall never hunger; and he that believeth on me shall never thirst.'

We have, secondly, in these verses, *a saying of Christ about those who come to him*. We read that Jesus said, 'him that cometh to me I will in no wise cast out.'

What does 'coming' mean? It means that movement of the soul which takes place when a man, feeling his sins, and finding out that he cannot save himself, hears of Christ, applies to Christ, trusts in Christ, lays hold on Christ, and leans all his weight on Christ for salvation. When this happens, a man is said, in Scripture language, to 'come' to Christ.

What did our Lord mean by saying, 'I will in no wise cast him out'? He meant that he will not refuse to save anyone who comes to him, no matter what he may have been. His past sins may have been very great. His present weakness and infirmity may be very great. But does he come to Christ by faith? Then Christ will receive him graciously, pardon him freely, place him in the number of his dear children, and give him everlasting life.

These are golden words indeed! They have smoothed down many a dying pillow, and calmed many a troubled conscience. Let them sink down deeply into our memories, and abide there continually. A day will come when flesh and heart shall fail, and the world can help us no more. Happy shall we be in that day, if the Spirit witnesses with our spirit that we have really come to Christ!

We have, lastly, in these verses, *a saying of Christ about the will of his Father.* Twice over come the solemn words, 'This is the will of him that sent me.' Once we are told it is his will, 'that everyone which seeth the Son . . . may have everlasting life.' Once we are told it is his will that, of all which he hath given to Christ he shall lose nothing.

We are taught by these words that Christ has brought into the world a salvation open and free to everyone. Our Lord draws a picture of it from the story of the brazen serpent, by which bitten Israelites in the wilderness were healed. Everyone that chose to 'look' at the brazen serpent might live. Just in the same way everyone who desires eternal life may 'look' at Christ by faith, and have it freely. There is no barrier, no limit, no restriction. The terms of the gospel are wide and simple. Everyone may 'look and live.'

We are taught, furthermore, that Christ will never allow any soul that is committed to him to be lost and cast away. He will keep it safe, from grace to glory, in spite of the world, the flesh, and the devil. Not one bone of his mystical body shall ever be broken. Not one lamb of his flock shall ever be left behind in the wilderness. He will raise to glory, in the last day, the whole flock entrusted to his charge, and not one shall be found missing.

Let the true Christian feed on the truths contained in this passage, and thank God for them. Christ the Bread of life,—Christ the Receiver of all who come to him,—Christ the Preserver of all believers,—Christ is for every man who is willing to believe on him, and Christ is the eternal possession of all who so believe. Surely this is glad tidings and good news!

Notes—John 6:35-40

35.—[*Jesus said ... I am the bread of life.*] In this verse our Lord begins to speak in the first person. Henceforth in this discourse we hear directly of 'I' and 'me' no fewer than thirty-five times. He drops all further reserve as to his meaning, and tells the Jews plainly, 'I am the bread of life,'—the true bread from heaven,—the bread of God which, coming down from heaven, giveth life to the world.

The 'bread of life,' means that spiritual bread which conveys life to the soul,—that living bread which does not merely feed the body, like common bread, but supplies eternal sustenance and nourishment to the eternal soul. It is like 'the water of life' (*Rev.* 22:17), and 'living water' (*John* 4:10).

The reasons why Christ calls himself 'bread,' appear to be such as these. He is intended to be to the soul what bread is to the body: its food.—Bread is necessary food: when men can afford to eat nothing else, they eat bread.—It is food that all need: the king and the pauper both eat bread.—It is food that suits all: old and young, weak and strong, all like bread.—It is the most nourishing kind of food: nothing does so much good, and is so indispensable to bodily health, as bread.—It is food that we need daily and are never tired of: morning and night we go on all our lives eating bread.— The application of these various points to Christ is too plain to need any explanation.

One great general lesson is doubtless intended to be drawn from Christ's selection of 'bread' as an emblem of himself. He is given to be the great supply of all the wants of men's souls. Whatever our spiritual necessity may be, however starving, famished, weak, and desperate our condition, there is enough in Christ, and to spare.—He is 'bread.'

Rollock remarks, that as soon as the slightest spiritual desire is manifested by anyone, however ignorant and weak, he should be at once directed to Christ. It is what our Lord himself did. As soon as the Jews said, 'Lord, evermore give us this bread,' he cried, 'I am the bread of life.' He never 'quenched the smoking flax.'

[*He that cometh ... hunger ... believeth ... thirst.*] The words 'coming' and 'believing' in this sentence, appear to mean very nearly one and the same thing. To 'come' to Christ is to 'believe' on him, and to 'believe' on him is to 'come' to him.—Both expressions mean that act of the soul whereby, under a sense of its sins and necessity, it applies to Christ, lays hold on Christ, trusts itself to Christ, casts itself on Christ.— 'Coming,' is the soul's movement towards Christ. 'Believing,' is the soul's venture on Christ.—If there is any difference, it is that 'coming' is the first act of the soul when it is taught by the Holy Ghost, and that 'believing' is a continued act or habit which never ends. No man 'comes' who does not believe; and all who come go on believing.

When our Lord says 'shall never hunger,' and 'shall never thirst,' he does not mean that a believer on Christ shall no longer feel any want, or emptiness, or deficiency within him. This would not be correct. The best of believers will often cry, like St Paul, 'O wretched man that I am!' (*Rom.* 7:24). The man who 'hungers and thirsts after righteousness' is blessed (*Matt.* 5:6).— What our Lord does mean is, that faith in Christ shall supply a man's soul with a peace and satisfaction that shall never be entirely taken from him,—that shall endure for ever. The man who eats and drinks material food, shall soon be hungry and thirsty as ever. But the man who comes to Christ by faith, gets hold of something that is an everlasting possession. He shall never die of spiritual famine, and perish for want of soul nourishment. He may have his low feelings at seasons. He may even lose his sense of pardon, and his enjoyment of religion. But once in Christ by faith, he shall never be cast away and starved in hell. He shall never die in his sins.

a. Let us note in this verse how simple are the figures by which our Lord brings his own sufficiency within the reach of man's understanding. He calls himself 'bread.' It was an idea that even the poorest hearer could understand. He that would do good to the poor need never be ashamed of using the simplest and most familiar illustrations.

b. Let us note that faith is a *movement* of the soul. Its first action is 'coming' to Christ. Its subsequent life is a constant daily repetition of its first action. To tell people to 'sit still and wait,' is poor theology. We should bid them arise and come.

c. Let us note that coming to Christ is the true secret of obtaining soul satisfaction and inward peace. Until we take that step our consciences are never easy. We 'hunger and thirst,' and find no relief.

d. Let us note that true believers shall never be altogether cast off and forsaken of God. The man that comes to Christ shall 'never hunger nor thirst.' The text is one among many proofs of the perseverance of the saints.

e. Let us note finally, how simple are the terms of the gospel. It is but coming and believing that Christ asks at our hands. The most ignorant, the most sinful, the most hardened, need not despair. They have but to 'come and believe.'

Luther, quoted by Besser, remarks on this verse: 'These are indeed dear and precious words, which it is not enough for us merely to know. We must turn them to account, and say, Upon these words I will go to sleep at night and get up in the morning; leaning upon them will I sleep and wake, and work and travel. For though everything were to go to ruin, and though father and mother, emperor and pope, princes and lords, all forsook me, though even Moses could not help me, and I had only Christ to look to, yet he will help me. For his words are sure, and he says "Hold fast by me; come thou to me, and thou shalt live." The meaning of these words is, that whoever can believe on that one Man who is called Jesus Christ, shall be satisfied, and cannot suffer either hunger or thirst.'

36.—[*But I said … ye also have seen me, and believe not.*] It is not quite clear to what our Lord refers in this verse, when he says,—'I said.' Some think that he is referring specially to his own words in verse 26: 'Ye seek me, not because ye saw the miracles,' etc. Others think that he refers generally to the testimony he had frequently borne against the unbelief of the Jewish people, in almost every place where he preached.

It seems to me most natural to connect the verse with the saying of the Jews, in verse 30. They had there said, 'What sign showest thou then, that we may see and believe thee?' Why should we not suppose our Lord in this verse to take up that saying, and reply, 'You talk of seeing and believing: I tell you again, and have long told you, that ye have seen me, and yet do not believe'?

The connecting link with the preceding verse, appears to be something of this kind: 'I am quite aware that I speak in vain to many of you of the bread of life and of believing. For I have said often, and now say it again, that many of you have both seen me and my miracles, and yet do not believe. Nevertheless, I am not discouraged. I know, in spite of your unbelief, that some will be saved.'

The unbelief of human nature is painfully exhibited in this verse. Some could even see and hear Christ himself, while he was on earth, and yet remain unbelieving! Surely we have no right to be surprised if we find like unbelief now. Men may actually see Christ with their bodily eyes and have no faith.

37.—[*All that the Father giveth me shall come to me.*] The connection of this verse with the preceding one seems to be this: 'Your unbelief does not move me or surprise me. I foresaw it, and have been aware of it. Nevertheless, your unbelief will not prevent God's purposes taking effect. Some will believe, though you remain unbelieving. Everything that the Father gives me will come unto me in due time: believe, and be saved. In spite of your unbelief, all my sheep shall sooner or later come to me by faith, and be gathered within my fold. I see your unbelief with sorrow, but not with anxiety and surprise. I am prepared for it. I know that you cannot alter God's purposes: and in accordance with those purposes, a people will come to me, though you do not.'

Luther, quoted by Besser, supposes our Lord to say, 'This sermon shall not on your account be of none effect, and remain without fruit. If you will not, another will; if you do not believe, yet another does.'

The English language fails to give the full sense of the Greek in this sentence. The literal meaning of the Greek is, not 'all persons whom the Father giveth shall come,' but 'everything, the whole thing.' It is not a masculine plural, but a neuter singular. The idea is either 'that whole mystical body, the company of my believing people, shall come to me,' or else 'every single part or jot or member of my mystical body shall come to me, and not one be found missing at last.'

We learn from these words the great and deep truth of God's election and appointment to eternal life of a people out of this world. The Father from all eternity has given to the Son a people to be his own peculiar people. The saints are given to Christ by the Father as a flock, which Christ undertakes to save completely, and to present complete at the last day (see

262

John 17:2, 6, 9, 11, 12; and 18:9). However wicked men may abuse this doctrine, it is full of comfort to a humble believer. He did not begin the work of his salvation. He was given to Christ by the Father, by an everlasting covenant.

We learn from these words the great mark of God's elect, whom he has given to Christ. They all come to Christ by faith. It is useless for anyone to boast of his election unless he comes to Christ by faith. Until a man comes humbly to Jesus, and commits his soul to him as a believer, we have no dependable evidence of the man's election.

Beza remarks, 'Faith in Christ is a certain testimony of our election, and consequently of our future glorification.'

Ferus says, 'Cleaving to Christ by faith, thou art sure of thy predestination.'

We learn from these words the irresistible power of God's electing grace. All who are given to Christ shall come to him. No obstacle, no difficulty, no power of the world, the flesh, and the devil, can prevent them. Sooner or later they will break through all, and surmount all. If 'given,' they will 'come.' To ministers the words are full of comfort.

[*Him that cometh to me I will in no wise cast out.*] These words declare Christ's willingness to save everyone that comes to him. There is an infinite readiness in Christ to receive, pardon, justify, and glorify sinners. The expression 'I will in no wise cast out,' implies this. It is a very powerful form of negation. 'So far from casting out the man that comes to me, I will receive him with joy when he comes. I will not refuse him on account of past sins. I will not cast him off again because of present weaknesses and infirmities. I will keep him to the end by my grace. I will confess him before my Father in the judgment day, and glorify him for ever. In short I will do the very opposite of casting him out.'

The distinction between the language of this clause of the text and that of the former clause, should be carefully noticed. They who 'shall come to Christ,' are 'that whole thing' which the Father gives. But it is 'each individual man' that comes, of whom Jesus says, 'I will in no wise cast him out.'

To 'cast out of the synagogue,'—to 'cut off from the congregation of Israel,'—to 'shut out of the camp,' as the leper was shut out (*Lev.* 13:46), were ideas with which all Jews were familiar. Our Lord seems to say, 'I will do the very opposite of all this.'

A. Clarke thinks that the idea is that of a poor person coming to a rich man's house for shelter and relief, who is kindly treated and not 'cast out.' But may we not suppose after all that the latent thought is that of the man fleeing to the city of refuge, according to the law of Moses, who, once admitted, is safe and not 'cast out'? (*Num.* 35:11, 12.)

We learn from these words that the one point we should look to is, 'whether we do really come to Christ.' Our past lives may have been very bad. Our present faith may be very weak. Our repentance and prayers may be very imperfect and poor. Our knowledge of religion may be very scanty. But do we come to Christ? That is the question. If so, the promise belongs to us. Christ will not cast us out. We may remind him boldly of his own word.

We learn from these words, that Christ's offers to sinners are wide, broad, free, unlimited, and unconditional. We must take care that we do not spoil and hamper them by narrow statements. God's election must never be thrust nakedly at unconverted sinners, in preaching the gospel. It is a point with which at present they have nothing to do. No doubt it is true that none will come to Christ but those who are given to him by the Father. But who those are that are so given we cannot tell, and must not attempt to define. All we have to do is to invite everyone, without exception, to come to Christ, and to tell men that everyone who does come to Christ shall be received and saved. To this point we must carefully stick.

Rollock observes how close this glorious promise stands to our Lord's words about God's election and predestination. Election should never be stated nakedly and baldly, without reminding those who hear it of Christ's infinite willingness to receive and save all.

Hutcheson remarks, 'Saints do indeed oftimes complain of casting off; but they are the words of sense and not of faith: they may seem to be cast off when really it is not so.'

38.—[*For I came down … not … mine own will, etc.*] The meaning of this verse appears to be as follows. 'I did not become man and enter this world to do anything of my own independent will and volition, and without reference to the will of my Father. On the contrary, I have come to carry out his will. As God, my will is in entire harmony and unity with my Father's will, because I and my Father are one. As man, I have no other will and desire than to do that which is in entire accordance with the will of him who has sent me to be the Mediator and Friend of sinners.'—What the Father's will about man is, our Lord goes on immediately to state in the two following verses. One part of the Father's will is, that nothing should be lost that he has given to the Son. That 'will' Christ came to carry out and accomplish.—Another part of the Father's will is, that everyone who trusts in Christ, may be saved. That 'will' again Christ came to carry out and accomplish.—The verse before us and the two following are closely connected, and should be looked at as one great thought. It was the Father's 'will' that free salvation by Christ should be brought near and within the reach of everyone, and it was also his 'will' that every believer in Christ should be completely and finally saved. To work out and accomplish this will of his Father was Christ's object in coming into the world.

The expression, 'I came down from heaven,' is a strong proof of the pre-existence of Christ. It could not possibly be said of any prophet or apostle, that he 'came down from heaven.' It is a heavy blow at the Socinian theory that Christ was nothing more than a man.

39.—[*This is the Father's will which hath sent me.*] In this verse and the following, Christ explains fully what was the Father's will concerning the Son's mission into the world. It was that he should receive all and lose none, that anyone might come to him, and that no comer should be lost. It is a cheering and pleasant thought, that free and full salvation, and the final perseverance of believers, should be so expressly declared to be 'the will of the Father.'

[*Of all … given … lose nothing.*] Here again there is the same form of speech as in verse 37. Literally rendered, the sentence would be, 'that of the whole thing which he has given me, I should not lose anything out of it.' The 'losing' must necessarily mean, that 'I should let nothing be taken away by the power of Satan, and allow nothing to come to ruin by its own inherent weakness.' The general sense of the sentence must be, 'that I should allow no member of my mystical body to be lost.'

We have in these words the doctrine of the final perseverance of true believers. It seems hard to imagine stronger words than these to express the doctrine. It is the Father's will that no one whom he has given to Christ should be lost. His will must surely take effect. True believers may err and fail in many things, but they shall never finally be cast away. The will of God the Father, and the power of Christ the Son are both engaged on their side.

We have in these words abundant comfort for all fearful and faint-hearted believers. Let such remember that if they 'come' to Christ by faith, they have been 'given' to Christ by the Father; and if given by the Father to Christ, it is the Father's will that they should never be cast away. Let them lean back on this thought, when cast down and disquieted;—'It is the Father's will that I should not be lost.'

[*Should raise it up again at the last day.*] We have in these words the Father's will that all Christ's members shall have a glorious resurrection. They shall not only not be lost and cast away while they live: they shall be raised again to glory after they die. Christ will not only justify and pardon, keep and sanctify; he will do even more: he will raise them up at the last day to a life of glory. It is the Father's will that he should do so. The bodies of the saints are provided for, no less than their souls.

The idea of some writers, which Bullinger mentions with some favour, that the 'last day' means the day of each believer's death, and the 'raising' his translation in the hour of death to paradise, seems to me utterly destitute of foundation.

The words before us are a strong argument for the 'first resurrection,' as a peculiar privilege of believers. It is said here that believers shall be 'raised again,' as a special honour and mercy conferred upon them. Yet it is no less clearly said in chapter 5, verses 28-29, that 'ALL that are in the graves . . . shall come forth,' both good and bad. It follows, therefore, that there is a resurrection of which saints alone are to be the partakers, distinct from the resurrection of the wicked. What can this be but the first resurrection? (Rev. 20:5.)—It must however in fairness be remembered that resurrection is sometimes spoken of in Scripture as if it was the peculiar privilege of believers, and a thing in which the wicked have no part. In the famous chapter in Corinthians, it is clear that the resurrection of the saints is the only thing in St Paul's mind (1 Cor. 15). That the wicked will be raised again, as well as the righteous, is clearly asserted in several places. But it is sometimes a thing kept in the background.

40.—[This is the will of him that sent me.] These words are repeated in this verse to show that it is no less the Father's will that Christ should receive sinners than that Christ should preserve saints. Both things are alike the purpose and intention of God.

[Every one which seeth the Son, and believeth ... life.] These words mean that 'everyone, without exception, who by faith looks to Christ, and trusts in him for salvation, is allowed by God the Father's appointment to have part in the salvation Christ has provided.' There is no barrier, difficulty, or objection. 'Everyone,' is the expression. No one can say he is excluded.—'Seeing and believing' are the only things required. No one can say that the terms are too hard. Does he see and believe? Then he may have everlasting life.

The expression 'seeth the Son,' in this sentence, must evidently mean more than mere seeing with the bodily eyes. It is the looking with faith at Christ (see John 12:45, where the same Greek word is used). It is such a look as that of the Israelites, who looked at the brazen serpent, and, looking, were healed (see John 3:14, 15, and Num. 21:9). I believe

that this was in our Lord's mind when he spake the words of this verse. Just as every serpent-bitten Israelite might look at the brazen serpent, and, as soon as he looked, was cured, so every sin-stricken man may look to Christ and be saved.

[I will raise him up at the last day.] These words are repeated, I believe, in order to make it sure that a glorious resurrection shall be the portion of everyone that only 'looks' at Christ and believes, as well as of those who enjoy the 'assurance' that they are given to Christ and shall never be cast away. The humblest believer shall be raised again by Christ at the first resurrection, and eternally glorified, just as certainly as the oldest saint in the family of God.

Stier remarks, 'This raising up at the last day, twice emphatically affirmed, points out to us the final goal of salvation, and preserving power; after the attainment of which there is no more danger of perishing, or losing again that eternal life, which is now, the body being raised, consummate.'

Let us mark what abundant comfort there is in this verse for all doubting, trembling sinners, who feel their sins and yet fancy there is no hope for them. Let such observe that it is the will of God the Father, that 'every one' who looks at Christ by faith may have everlasting life. It would be impossible to open a wider door. Let men look and live. The will of God is on their side.

Calvin remarks on this verse, 'The way to obtain salvation is to obey the gospel of Christ. If it is the will of God that those whom he has elected shall be saved, and if in this manner he ratifies and executes his eternal decrees, whoever he be that is not satisfied with Christ, but indulges in curious inquiries about eternal predestination, such a person desires to be saved contrary to the purposes of God. They are madmen who seek their own salvation, or that of others, in the whirlpool of predestination, not keeping the way of salvation which is exhibited to them.'—'To every man, therefore, his faith is a sufficient attestation of the eternal predestination of God.'

JOHN 6:41-51

41 The Jews then murmured at him, because he said, I am the bread which came down from heaven.

42 And they said, Is not this Jesus, the son of Joseph, whose father and mother we know? how is it then that he saith, I came down from heaven?

43 Jesus therefore answered and said unto them, Murmur not among yourselves.

44 No man can come to me, except the Father which hath sent me draw him: and I will raise him up at the last day.

45 It is written in the prophets, And they shall be all taught of God. Every man therefore that hath heard, and hath learned of the Father, cometh unto me.

46 Not that any man hath seen the Father, save he which is of God, he hath seen the Father.

47 Verily, verily, I say unto you, He that believeth on me hath everlasting life.

48 I am that bread of life.

49 Your fathers did eat manna in the wilderness, and are dead.

50 This is the bread which cometh down from heaven, that a man may eat thereof, and not die.

51 I am the living bread which came down from heaven: if any man eat of this bread, he shall live for ever: and the bread that I will give is my flesh, which I will give for the life of the world.

TRUTHS of the weightiest importance follow each other in rapid succession in the chapter we are now reading. There are probably very few parts of the Bible which contain so many 'deep things' as the sixth chapter of St John. Of this the passage before us is a signal example.

We learn, for one thing, from this passage, that *Christ's lowly condition, when he was upon earth, is a stumbling-block to the natural man.* We read that 'the Jews murmured, because Jesus said, I am the bread that came down from heaven. And they said, Is not this Jesus, the son of Joseph, whose father and mother we know? How is it then that he saith, I came down from heaven?'—Had our Lord come as a conquering king, with wealth and honours to bestow on his followers, and mighty armies in his train, they would have been willing enough to receive him. But a poor, and lowly, and suffering Messiah was an offence to them. Their pride refused to believe that such a one was sent from God.

There is nothing that need surprise us in this. It is human nature showing itself in its true colours. We see the same thing in the days of the apostles. Christ crucified was 'unto the Jews a stumbling-block, and to the Greeks foolishness' (1 Cor. 1:23). The cross was an offence to many wherever the gospel was preached.—We may see the same thing in our own times. There are thousands around us who loathe the distinctive doctrines of the gospel on account of their humbling character. They cannot away with the atonement and the sacrifice, and the substitution of Christ. His moral teaching they approve. His example and self-denial they admire. But speak to them of Christ's blood,—of Christ being made sin for us,—of Christ's death being the cornerstone of our hope,—of Christ's poverty being our riches,—and you will find they hate these things with a deadly hatred. Truly the offence of the cross is not yet ceased!

We learn, for another thing, from this passage, *man's natural helplessness and inability to repent or believe.* We find our Lord saying, 'No man can come to me, except the Father which hath sent me draw him.' Until the Father draws the heart of man by his grace, man will not believe.

The solemn truth contained in these words is one that needs careful weighing. It is vain to deny that without the grace of God no one ever can become a true Christian. We are spiritually dead, and have no power to give ourselves life. We need a new principle put in us from above. Facts prove it. Preachers see it. The Tenth Article of our own Church expressly declares it: 'The condition of man after the fall of Adam is such that he cannot turn and prepare himself, by his own natural strength and good works, to faith and calling upon God.' This witness is true.

But after all, of what does this inability of man consist? In what part of our inward nature does this impotence reside? Here is a point on which many mistakes arise. For ever let us remember that the *will* of man is the part of him which is in fault. His inability is not physical, but moral. It would not be true to say that a man has a real wish and desire to come to Christ, but no power to come. It would be far more true to say that a man has no power to come because he has no desire or wish.—It is not true that he would come if he could. It is true that he could come if he would.—The corrupt will,—the secret disinclination,—the want of heart, are the real causes of unbelief. It is here the mischief lies. The power that we want is a new will. It is precisely at this point that we need the 'drawing' of the Father.

These things, no doubt, are deep and mysterious. By truths like these God proves the faith and patience of his people. Can they believe him? Can they wait for a fuller explanation at the last day? What they see not now they shall see hereafter. One thing at any rate is abundantly clear, and that is man's responsibility for his own soul. His inability to come to Christ does not make an end of his accountableness. Both things are equally true. If lost at last, it will prove to have been his own fault. His blood will be on his own head. Christ would have saved him, but he would not be saved. He would not come to Christ, that he might have life.

We learn, lastly, in this passage, that *the salvation of a believer is a present thing.* Our Lord Jesus Christ says, 'Verily, verily, I say unto you, he that believeth on me hath everlasting life.' Life, we should observe, is a present possession. It is not said that he shall have it at last, in the judgment day. It is now, even now, in this world, his property. He hath it the very day that he believes.

The subject is one which it much concerns our peace to understand, and one about which errors abound. How many seem to think that forgiveness and acceptance with God are things which we cannot attain in this life,—that they are things which are to be earned by a long course of repentance and faith and holiness,—things which we may receive at the bar of God at last, but must never pretend to touch while we are in this world! It is a complete mistake to think so. The very moment a sinner believes on Christ he is justified and accepted. There is no condemnation for him. He has peace with God, and that immediately and without delay. His name is in the book of life, however little he may be aware of it. He has a title to heaven, which death and hell and Satan cannot overthrow. Happy are they that know this truth! It is an essential part of the good news of the gospel.

After all, the great point we have to consider is whether we believe. What shall it profit us that Christ has died for sinners, if we do not believe on him? 'He that believeth on the Son hath everlasting life: and he that believeth not the Son shall not see life; but the wrath of God abideth on him' (*John* 3:36).

Notes—John 6:41-51

41.—[*The Jews then murmured at him.*] The verb is here in the imperfect tense. It seems to mean 'the Jews were then murmuring, or beginning to murmur about him.' It was a murmuring that went on among themselves concerning our Lord, and was not openly expressed. 'At him,' would be more literally rendered 'about him.'

I venture to think there is a break, pause, or slight interval implied at this point of the conversation. The speakers called here 'the Jews,' do not appear to be the same who followed our Lord over the lake after being fed with the loaves and fishes, and began the conversation by saying, 'When camest thou hither?' (verse 25). They would rather appear to be the principal people, or leaders, in the synagogue at Capernaum. They had probably heard our Lord's words to the people who had followed him over the lake, and were murmuring at them.—To my own mind, it is by no means clear that there was not at this point a change in the *place* where the conversation was carried on. Up to this point it looks as if the conversation was carried on in the open air. At this point our Lord may have gone into the synagogue, and the rulers of it may have taken up the subject and been murmuring about it when he went in.—I throw out this theory with diffidence. It must at least be conceded that the expressions at verse 25, 'when they had found him at the other side of the sea . . . when camest thou hither?' can hardly be supposed to mean that our Lord was *then* in the synagogue. On the other hand, it is perfectly clear from verse 59, that the latter part of his discourse, at any rate, was spoken 'in the synagogue at Capernaum.' Where, then, I ask, does the slight break come in, which is necessary to reconcile these beginning and ending statements? I reply that it seems to me to come in here,

at this very verse 41. The language, I think, implies a slight pause in time, and a change in the speaker. Stier, I am aware, calls this idea 'highly artificial.' But I cannot see any force in the objection, and I see much difficulty in any other view.

Cyril remarks that a readiness to murmur seemed to be hereditary with the Jews. From the days when they murmured in the wilderness, it was always the same.

[*Because he said, I am the bread ... heaven.*] It does not appear that our Lord had actually used these words. We must therefore suppose that the Jews constructed the saying out of three things that our Lord had said. One was, 'I am the bread of life;'—another, 'I came down from heaven;'—and another, 'The bread of God is he (or it) which cometh down from heaven.'

42.—[*Is not this Jesus, the son of Joseph?*] The word 'this,' in the Greek, has a latent sneer of contempt about it, which our English version cannot fully convey. It is as if they said, 'Is not this fellow,' etc.

The expression 'the son of Joseph,' shows what was the impression that the Jews commonly had about our Lord's birth. They believed him to be the naturally begotten son of Joseph the husband of Mary. The annunciation by the angel Gabriel, the miraculous conception, the miraculous birth of our Lord, are matters of which the Jews apparently had not any knowledge. Throughout the whole of our Lord's ministry we never find them mentioned. For some wise reason a total silence was observed about them until after our Lord's death, resurrection, and ascension. It was not probably till after the death of the Virgin Mary and all her family, that this great and deep subject was allowed to be much brought forward in the church. We can easily see that an unhallowed curiosity might have risen on questions connected with the incarnation, which would only have done harm.

[*Whose father and mother we know.*] These words seem to show that Joseph was still living at this time. They could hardly have been used if Joseph was dead. They also show that Joseph and Mary were known at Capernaum, where this conversation was held. They had either removed there from Nazareth, or else were so connected with Capernaum and such frequent visitors there, that the inhabitants knew them.

[*How is it then that he saith.*] These words would have been more literally rendered, 'How then does this fellow say?' Again, like the beginning of the verse, there is something scornful in the phrase.

[*I came down from heaven.*] The thing that seems to have vexed and angered the Jews was that our Lord should so openly declare his divine origin, by talking of 'coming down from heaven.' They were offended at the idea of one so lowly in dress, and circumstances, and position, taking on himself to say, that he was one who had 'come down from heaven.' Here, as elsewhere, Christ's humiliation was the great stumbling-block. Human nature would not so much object to a conquering Christ,—a Christ with a crown and an army,—a Christ with wealth to shower on all his followers. But a Christ in poverty,—a Christ preaching nothing but heart religion,—a Christ followed by none but poor fishermen and publicans,—a Christ coming to suffer and die and not to reign,—such a Christ was always an offence to many in this world, and always will be.

Rollock remarks with great truth, that with many persons, 'reasoning' (so called) is the grand obstacle to conversion.

43.—[*Jesus ... answered and said.*] This phrase is almost the same as that used in chapter 5, verse 19, when our Lord began what many think was his formal defence of himself before the Sanhedrim. It leads me to think, as I have already said, that there is a slight break at this point of the chapter, and a slight pause, if only of a few hours, in time. Our Lord knew by his divine knowledge that the Jews were murmuring and

saying contemptuous things about him, and he therefore took up their thoughts, and made a reply to them.

[*Murmur not among yourselves.*] This seems a mild hint that they need not waste their time in murmuring. It neither surprised our Lord, nor discouraged him. It is as though he said, 'Your murmuring is only what I am prepared to expect. I know what human nature is. I am not moved by it. Think not that your unbelief will shake my confidence in my divine mission, or prevent my saying what I do. I know that you cannot naturally understand such things as I am speaking of, and I will proceed to tell you why. But cease from these useless murmurings, which neither surprise nor stop me.'

Webster thinks that the idea is the same as that in John 3:7-12: 'I have harder things still to say' (see 5:28).

44.—[*No man can come ... except the Father ... draw him.*] The connection between this verse and the preceding one is not clear. Like many passages in St John's writings, the language is elliptical, and the link must be supplied. But the precise link in the present case is not very evident. I believe it is something of this sort: 'You are murmuring among yourselves because I speak of coming down from heaven; and you are making my apparently low origin an excuse for not believing on me. But all the time the fault is not in my sayings, but in your want of grace, and your unbelief. There is a deeper and more solemn truth, to which you seem totally blind: and that is, man's need of God's grace in order to believe on me. You are never likely to believe until you acknowledge your own corruption, and ask for grace to draw your souls to me. I am aware that it needs something more than argument and reasoning to make anyone believe in me. Your unbelief and murmuring do not surprise me or discourage me. I neither expect to see you nor anyone else believe, until you are drawn by my Father.'—This, or something like it, seems to me the connecting link. One thing at any rate is certain: our Lord did not mean to excuse the unbelief of his hearers: he rather desired to magnify their danger and guilt, and to make them see

270

that faith in him was not so easy an affair as they supposed. It was not knowledge of his origin alone, but the drawing grace of God the Father which they needed. Let them awake to see that, and cry for grace before it was too late.

The general lesson of the sentence, apart from the connection, is one of vast importance. Our Lord lays down the great principle that 'no man whatsoever can come to Christ by faith, and really believe in him, unless God the Father draws him so to come, and inclines his will to believe.' The nature of man since the fall is so corrupt and depraved, that even when Christ is made known and preached to him, he will not come to him and believe in him, without the special grace of God inclining his will and giving him a disposition to come. Moral suasion and advice alone will not bring him. He must be 'drawn.'

This is no doubt a very humbling truth, and one which in every age has called forth the hatred and opposition of man. The favourite notion of man is that he can do what he likes,—repent or not repent, believe or not believe, come to Christ or not come, entirely at his own discretion. In fact man likes to think that his salvation is in his own power. Such notions are flatly contradictory to the text before us. The words of our Lord here are clear and unmistakable, and cannot be explained away.

a. This doctrine of human impotence, whether man likes it or not, is the uniform teaching of the Bible. The natural man is dead, and must be born again, and brought to life (*Eph.* 2:1). He has neither knowledge, nor faith, nor inclination toward Christ, until grace comes into his heart. Man never of himself begins with God. God must first begin with man. And this beginning is just the 'drawing' of the text.

b. It is the doctrine of the Church of England, as shown in the Tenth Article, and of every Protestant confession of faith which dates from the sixteenth and seventeenth centuries.

c. Last, but not least, it is the doctrine of experience. The longer ministers of the gospel live, the more do they find that there is something to be done in every heart which neither preaching, teaching, arguing, exhorting, nor means of grace can do. When all has been done, God must 'draw,' or there is no fruit.—The more the holiest Christians are examined, the more general is their testimony found that without grace they never would have been converted, and that God 'drew' them, or else they never would have come to Christ. And it is a curious fact moreover, that many who profess to deny man's impotence in theory, often confess it in their prayers and praises, almost in spite of themselves. Many people are very low Arminians in print or in the pulpit, but excellent Calvinists on their knees.

When our Lord says, 'No man can come unto me,' we must carefully remember that it is *moral* inability and not *physical* inability that he speaks of. We are not to suppose that any man can have a sincere and hearty wish to come to Christ, and yet be prevented by some mysterious impotence. The impotence lies in man's will. He cannot come because he will not come.—There is an Old Testament sentence which throws much light on the expression before us. It is said of Joseph's brethren, that 'they hated him, and *could not* speak peaceably unto him' (*Gen.* 37:4). Anyone must see at a glance what this 'could not' means. They 'could not' because they would not.

When our Lord says, 'Except the Father draw him,' we must not suppose that the 'drawing' means such a violent drawing as the drawing of a prisoner to a jail, of an ox to the slaughter-house, a drawing in short against a man's will. It is a drawing which the Father effects through the man's own will, by creating a new principle within him. By the unseen agency of the Holy Ghost he works on the man's heart, without the man himself knowing it at the time, inclines him to think, induces him to feel, shows him his sinfulness, and so leads him at length to Christ. Everyone that comes to Christ is so drawn.

Scott remarks, 'The Father as it were cures the fever of the soul; he creates the appetite; he sets the provisions before the sinner; he convinces him that they are wholesome and pleasant, and that he is welcome; and thus the man is drawn to come and eat and live for ever.'

The well-known quotation from Augustine which seems so great a favourite with many commentators on this text, appears to me defective. He argues that God's drawing of men to Christ is so entirely a drawing through man's will, that it is like drawing the sheep by offering it food,—like drawing and alluring a child by offering him nuts.—But there is this wide difference, that both the sheep and the child have a natural taste and inclination for the thing offered. Man, on the contrary, has none at all. God's first act is to give man a will to come to Christ. As the Tenth Article of the Church of England says, we need 'the grace of Christ preventing us, that we may have a good will, and working with us when we have that good will.'

The theory that all members of the church and all baptized people are 'drawn by God,' appears to me a most baseless theory, and practically a most mischievous one. It would reduce the 'drawing' to nothing, and make it a thing which the majority of Christians resist. I believe the drawing is a thing that belongs to none but God's elect, and is a part of the procedure by which their salvation is effected. They are chosen in Christ from all eternity, and then drawn to Christ in time.

There are several very important principles of theology connected with this remarkable sentence, which it may be useful to put down together, before we leave the passage.

a. We must never suppose that the doctrine of this verse takes away man's responsibility and accountableness to God for his soul. On the contrary, the Bible always distinctly declares that if any man is lost, it is his own fault. He 'loses his own soul' (Mark 8:36). If we cannot reconcile God's sovereignty and man's responsibility now, we need not doubt that it will be all plain at the last day.

b. We must not allow the doctrine of this verse to make us limit or narrow the offer of salvation to sinners. On the contrary, we must hold firmly that pardon and peace are to be offered freely through Christ to every man and woman without exception.

We never know who they are that God will draw, and have nothing to do with it. Our duty is to invite all, and leave it to God to choose the vessels of mercy.

c. We must not suppose that we, or anybody else, are drawn, unless we come to Christ by faith. This is the grand mark and evidence of anyone being the subject of the Father's drawing work. If 'drawn' he comes to Christ, believes, and loves. Where there is no faith and love, there may be talk, self-conceit, and high profession. But there is no 'drawing' of the Father.

d. We must always remember that God ordinarily works by means, and specially by such means as he himself has appointed. No doubt he acts as a Sovereign in drawing souls to Christ. We cannot pretend to explain why some are drawn and others are not drawn. Nevertheless, we must carefully maintain the great principle that God ordinarily draws through the instrumentality of his Word. The man that neglects the public preaching and private reading of God's Word, has no right to expect that God will draw him. The thing is possible, but highly improbable.

e. We must never allow ourselves or others to waste time in trying to find out, as a first question in religion, whether we are drawn of God the Father, elect, chosen, and the like. The first and indeed the main question we have to do with is, whether we have come to Christ by faith. If we have, let us take comfort and be thankful. None come to him unless they are drawn.

Augustine remarks: 'If thou dost not desire to err, do not seek to determine whom God draws, and whom he does not draw; nor why he draws one man and not another. But if thou thyself art not drawn by God, pray to him that thou mayest be drawn.'

The words of the Seventeenth Article of the Church of England are weighty and wise: 'We must receive God's promises in such wise as they are generally set forth to us in Holy Scripture: and in our doings, that will of God is to be followed which we have expressly declared unto us in the Word of God.'

Whether the 'drawing' of God the Father is irresistible or not, is a point on which good men differ greatly. My own opinion is decided that it is irresistible. Those whom the Father draws and calls, always 'obey the calling' (see Seventeenth Article of the Church of England). As Rollock truly remarks, there is often a great fight and struggle when the drawing grace of God first begins to work on the soul, and the consequence is great distress and depression. But when grace once begins it always wins the victory at last.

[*I will raise him up at the last day.*] This is the same sentence that we have had twice already, and shall have once again. Whosoever does come to Christ, and has the great mark of faith, shall be raised by Christ to a life of eternal glory at the last day. None come but those who are 'drawn;' but all who do come shall be raised.

45.—[*It is written ... prophets ... taught of God.*] Our Lord here confirms the doctrine of the necessity of divine teaching, by reference to the Scriptures. He had told the Jews nothing but what their own Scriptures taught, and what they ought to have known themselves. It is not quite clear whether our Lord referred to one particular quotation, or to the general testimony of the prophetical Scriptures. The words of Isaiah (54:13) are most like the sentence before us: 'all thy children shall be taught of the LORD.' The Greek of the Septuagint version of that text rather favours the idea that our Lord referred to it. On the whole, however, I incline to the opinion that no one particular text is referred to. It was the general doctrine of the prophets that in the days of the gospel men should have the direct teaching of God.

The words do not mean that under the gospel all mankind, or all members of the professing Christian church, shall be 'taught of God.' It rather means that all who are God's children, and come to Christ under the gospel, shall be taught of God. It is like '[this is] the true light that lighteth every man' (*John* 1:9), where it does not mean that all are lighted, but that such as are lighted are lighted by Christ.

[*Every man ... heard ... learned of the Father, cometh unto me.*] The meaning of this sentence seems to be, 'Every man that comes to me has first heard and learned of the Father.' It is useless to talk of being taught by God, and of God being our Father, if we do not come to Christ for salvation.

Bishop Hooper remarks, 'Many men understand the words, "except the Father draws him," in a wrong sense, as though God did require in a reasonable man no more than in a dead post, and do not mark the words that follow, "every man that hath heard Christ," God draweth with his Word and the Holy Ghost. Man's duty is to hear and learn: this is to say, receive the grace offered, consent unto the promises, and not refuse the God that calleth.'—*Hooper on Ten Commandments.*

46.—[*Not that any man hath seen the Father.*] This sentence seems put in, by way of parenthesis, to prevent mistakes in the minds of our Lord's hearers, both as to the kind of teaching he meant, and the person he intended when he spake of the Father. The Father was the eternal God whom no man had seen nor could see. The teaching was that inward teaching of the heart which the Father gave by his Spirit.

[*He which is of God, he hath seen the Father.*] Our Lord plainly means himself in this verse. It is like John 1:18: 'No man hath seen God at any time; the only begotten Son, which is in the bosom of the Father, he hath declared him.'

I cannot but think that one object our Lord has in view, both here and in chapter 5, verse 37, is to impress on the Jews' minds, that all the appearances of God which are recorded in the Old Testament were appearances not of the first person in the Trinity but of the second. His object in both places, I suspect, was to prepare their minds for the great truth which as yet they were unable to receive,—that, however unbelieving they now were, Christ who was now with them, was that very person who had appeared to Abraham and Isaac and Jacob and Moses.

47.—[*Verily, verily ... He that believeth on me ... life.*] In this verse our Lord returns to the main thread of his discourse, which had been interrupted at verse 40. He now speaks out much more clearly and plainly about himself, dropping all reserve, and revealing himself as the object of faith, openly and without figure. It is one of those great, broad, simple declarations of the gospel way of salvation, which we can never know too well.

He that would have his sins pardoned and his soul saved must go to Christ for it. It is to 'me,' says Christ, that he must apply.—What are the terms held out? He must simply trust, lean back, rest on Christ, and commit his soul to his hand. In a word, he must 'believe.'—What shall such a man get by believing? He 'hath everlasting life.' The very moment he believes, life, and peace with God are his own.—(1) faith, (2) the great object of faith, (3) the present privileges to which faith admits a man, are three subjects which, however often repeated in the gospel, ought never to weary a Christian's ear.

The frequent repetition of this doctrine of 'believing,' is a strong proof of its great necessity and importance, and of man's infinite backwardness to see, understand, and receive it. 'We must believe,—we must believe,' says Rollock, 'is a truth that needs constant repetition.'

48.—[*I am that bread of life.*] Here our Lord distinctly proclaims to the Jews that he himself is that 'bread of life,' that soul-satisfying food, the true bread, the bread of God, of which he had spoken generally in the earlier part of his discourse. He had awakened their curiosity by speaking of that bread as a real thing, and a thing worth their attention. He now unveils the whole truth to them, and tells them plainly, 'I am that bread.'—'If you ask what it is, and where it is, you have only to look at me.'

49.—[*Your fathers did eat manna . . . dead.*] In this verse our Lord points out the inferiority of the manna which the Jews ate in the wilderness to the bread which he himself offered. The manna not only could do nothing for the soul, but was unable to preserve from death those who ate it.

Here, as before, we should observe how our Lord speaks of the miraculous feeding of Israel in the wilderness, as an undoubted historical fact.

Piscator remarks, that our Lord here says emphatically, 'your fathers,' and not 'our fathers.'—He thinks it was intentionally done to remind the Jews how little lasting good their fathers got from the manna, and how unbelieving they were even while they ate of it; for they all died in the wilderness. It was a tacit caution to beware of doing like them.

50.—[*This is the bread ... heaven ... eat ... and not die.*] The object of this verse is to show the superiority of the 'true bread from heaven' to the manna. It is as though our Lord said, 'This bread that cometh down from heaven is bread of such a nature that he that eateth of it shall never die. His soul shall not be hurt by the second death, and his body shall have a glorious resurrection.'

I am not without doubt whether our Lord did not point to himself in speaking the words of this verse: 'This person who now stands before you is that bread which came down from heaven, that anyone eating of it should not die.' But I throw out the conjecture with much diffidence. Lampe seems to favour the idea, saying, 'the pronoun "this" is here demonstrative and pointed to himself.' Trapp and Beza also take this view.

51.—[*I am the living bread ... heaven.*] This sentence is a repetition of the idea that has been already given out in verses 49 and 50. The thought is repeated in order to impress it on the minds of the Jews, and make it impossible for them to misunderstand our Lord's meaning.

We must never be ashamed of repetition in religious teaching.

[*If any man eat of this bread, he shall live for ever.*] The thought here is only an expansion of the one contained in verse 35. There it is said, 'He that cometh to [Christ] shall never hunger.' Here it is, the eater of the bread of life 'shall live for ever.' The meaning is that the soul of the man who feeds on Christ by faith, shall never die and be cast away in hell. There is no condemnation for him. His sins are put away. He shall not be hurt by the second death.

[*The bread ... give is my flesh.*] In these words our Lord goes even further than he has gone yet in explaining the great theme of his discourse. When he speaks of 'my flesh,' I believe he means, 'my body offered up in sacrifice on the cross, as an atonement for man's sins.' It is our Lord's death that is specially meant. It is not merely his human nature, his incarnation, that feeds souls. It is his death as our substitute, bearing our sins and carrying our transgressions.

[*Which I will give for the life of the world.*] These words appear to me to make it certain that our Lord meant 'his body offered in sacrifice as an atonement for sin,' when he said 'my flesh is the bread.'—For he does not say, 'I have given,' or, 'I do give,' but 'I will give.' That use of the future tense seems to me a conclusive proof that 'my flesh' cannot mean only 'my incarnation.' The 'giving' was about to take place, but had not taken place yet. It could only be his death.

When our Lord says, 'I will *give* my flesh,' it appears to me that he can only mean, 'I will give it to die, to suffer, to be offered up on the cross, as a sacrifice for sin.'

When our Lord says, 'I will give my flesh *for the life* of the world,' I believe he means, 'I will give my body to death, on account of, for the sake of, to procure, purchase, and obtain the life of the world.' I will give my death to procure the world's life. My death shall be the ransom, the payment, and the redemption-money, by which eternal life shall be purchased for a world of sinners.'

I hold strongly that the idea of substitution is contained in these words of our Lord, and that the great doctrine of his vicarious death, which is so directly stated elsewhere (*Rom.* 5:6-8) is indirectly implied in this sentence.

When our Lord says, 'I will give my flesh for the life of the world,' I can only see one meaning in the word 'world.' It means all mankind. And the idea contained, I believe, is the same as we have elsewhere: viz., that Christ died for all mankind; not for the elect only, but for all mankind (see *John* 1:29, and 3:16, and my notes on each text). That all the world is not saved is perfectly certain. That many die in unbelief and get no benefit from Christ's death is certain. But that Christ's death was enough for all mankind, and that when he died he made sufficient atonement for all the world, are truths which, both in this text and others like it, appear to my mind incontrovertible.

Let us note, in this verse, what a full and broad offer Christ holds out to sinners: he says, 'If *any man*,' no matter who or what he may have been, 'If any man eat of this bread he shall live for ever.' Happy would it be for many, whose whole hearts are set on eating and drinking, and feasting their poor perishable bodies, if they would only look at these words! It is only those who eat this bread who shall live for ever.

Let us remember how impossible it is for anyone to explain the end of this verse who denies the sacrificial character of Christ's death. Once grant that Christ is only a great teacher and example, and that his death is only a great pattern of self-denial, and what sense or meaning can be got out of the end of this verse? 'I will give my flesh for the life of the world'! I unhesitatingly say that the words are unintelligible nonsense if we receive the teaching of many modern divines about Christ's death, and that nothing can make them intelligible and instructive but the doctrine of Christ's vicarious death, and satisfaction on the cross as our Substitute.

JOHN 6:52-59

52 The Jews therefore strove among themselves, saying, How can this man give us *his* flesh to eat?

53 Then Jesus said unto them, Verily, verily, I say unto you, Except ye eat the flesh of the Son of man, and drink his blood, ye have no life in you.

54 Whoso eateth my flesh, and drinketh my blood, hath eternal life; and I will raise him up at the last day.

55 For my flesh is meat indeed, and my blood is drink indeed.

56 He that eateth my flesh, and drinketh my blood, dwelleth in me, and I in him.

57 As the living Father hath sent me, and I live by the Father: so he that eateth me, even he shall live by me.

58 This is that bread which came down from heaven: not as your fathers did eat manna, and are dead: he that eateth of this bread shall live for ever.

59 These things said he in the synagogue, as he taught in Capernaum.

FEW passages of Scripture have been so painfully wrested and perverted as that which we have now read. The Jews are not the only people who have striven about its meaning. A sense has been put upon it which it was never intended to bear. Fallen man, in interpreting the Bible, has an unhappy aptitude for turning meat into poison. The things that were written for his benefit he often makes an occasion of falling.

Let us first consider carefully, *what these verses do not mean.* The 'eating and drinking' of which Christ speaks do not mean any literal eating and drinking. Above all, the words were not spoken with any reference to the sacrament of the Lord's supper. We may eat the Lord's supper, and yet not eat and drink Christ's body and blood. We may eat and drink Christ's body and blood, and yet not eat the Lord's supper. Let this never be forgotten.

The opinion here expressed may startle some who have not looked closely into the subject. But it is an opinion which is supported by three weighty reasons.—For one thing, a literal 'eating and drinking' of Christ's body and blood would have been an idea utterly revolting to all Jews, and flatly contradictory to an often-repeated precept of their law.—For another thing, to take a literal view of 'eating and drinking,' is to interpose a bodily act between the soul of man and salvation. This is a thing for which there is no precedent in Scripture. The only things without which we cannot be saved are repentance and faith.—Last, but not least, to take a literal view of 'eating and drinking' would involve most blasphemous and profane consequences. It would shut out of heaven the penitent thief. He died long after these words were spoken, without any literal eating and drinking: will any dare to say he had 'no life' in him?—It would admit to heaven thousands of ignorant, godless communicants in the present day. They literally eat and drink, no doubt! But they have no eternal life, and will not be raised to glory at the last day. Let these reasons be carefully pondered.

The plain truth is there is a morbid anxiety in fallen man to put a carnal sense on scriptural expressions, wherever he possibly can. He struggles hard to make religion a matter of forms and ceremonies,—of doing and performing,—of sacraments and ordinances,—of sense and of sight. He secretly dislikes that system of Christianity which makes the state of the heart the principal thing, and labours to keep sacraments and ordinances in the second place. Happy is that Christian who remembers these things, and stands on his guard! Baptism and the Lord's supper, no doubt, are holy sacraments, and mighty blessings when rightly used. But it is worse than useless to drag them in everywhere and to see them everywhere in God's Word.

Let us next consider carefully *what these verses do mean*. The expressions they contain are, no doubt, very remarkable. Let us try to get some clear notion of their meaning.

The 'flesh and blood of the Son of man' mean that sacrifice of his own body which Christ offered up on the cross when he died for sinners. The atonement made by his death, the satisfaction made by his sufferings, as our Substitute, the redemption effected by his enduring the penalty of our sins in his own body on the tree,—this seems to be the true idea that we should set before our minds.

The 'eating and drinking,' without which there is no life in us, mean that reception of Christ's sacrifice which takes place when a man believes on Christ crucified for salvation. It is an inward and spiritual act of the heart, and has nothing to do with the body. Whenever a man, feeling his own guilt and sinfulness, lays hold on Christ, and trusts in the atonement made for him by Christ's death, at once he 'eats the flesh of the Son of man, and drinks his blood.' His soul feeds on Christ's sacrifice, by faith, just as his body would feed on bread. Believing he is said to 'eat.' Believing, he is said to 'drink.' And the special thing that he eats, and drinks, and gets benefit from, is the atonement made for his sins by Christ's death for him on Calvary.

The practical lessons which may be gathered from the whole passage are weighty and important. The point being once settled, that 'the flesh and blood' in these verses mean Christ's atonement, and the 'eating and drinking' mean faith, we may find in these verses great principles of truth, which lie at the very root of Christianity.

We may learn that faith in Christ's atonement is a thing of absolute necessity to salvation. Just as there was no safety for the Israelite in Egypt who did not eat the passover lamb in the night when the first-born were slain, so there is no life for the sinner who does not eat the flesh of Christ and drink his blood.

We may learn that faith in Christ's atonement unites us by the closest possible bonds to our Saviour, and entitles us to the highest privileges. Our souls shall find full satisfaction for all their wants: 'his flesh is meat indeed, and his blood is drink indeed.' All things are secured to us that we can need for time and eternity: 'Whoso eateth my flesh and drinketh my blood hath eternal life, and I will raise him up at the last day.'

Last, but not least, we may learn that faith in Christ's atonement is a personal act, a daily act, and an act that can be felt. No one can eat and drink for us, and no one, in like manner, can believe for us.—We need food every day, and not once a week or once a month; and in like manner, we need to employ faith every day.—We feel benefit when we have eaten and drunk, we feel strengthened, nourished, and refreshed; and, in like manner, if we believe truly, we shall feel the better for it, by sensible hope and peace in our inward man.

Let us take heed that we use these truths, as well as know them. The food of this world, for which so many take thought, will perish in the using, and not feed our souls. He only that eats of 'the bread that came down from heaven' shall live for ever.

Notes—John 6:52-59

52.—[*The Jews therefore strove among themselves.*] This expression shows an increasingly strong feeling among the Jews. When our Lord talked of 'coming down from heaven,' they 'murmured.'—When he speaks of giving his 'flesh to eat,' they 'strove' (it is the word rendered 'ye fight,' in *James* 4:2). In what way the Jews strove it is not very clear to see. We cannot suppose that there were two contending parties,—one favourable to our Lord, and one opposed to him. It probably means that they began to reason and argue among themselves in an angry, violent, and excited manner, such as St Paul forbids when he says, 'The servant of the Lord must not strive' (2 *Tim.* 2:24). The same word is used there as here.

[*How can this man give ... flesh to eat?*] The likeness should be observed between this question and that of Nicodemus (*John* 3:4), and that of the Samaritan woman (*John* 4:11).

There is an implied scornful sense about the expression: 'this man.'

Cyril, in commenting on this verse, points out the unreasonableness and inconsistency of the Jews, above all men, in raising difficulties and denying the possibility of things, because they are hard to explain and preternatural. He summons the Jew to explain the miracles in Egypt, and those in the wilderness, and he concludes, 'There are innumerable things in which if thou inquirest "how" they can be, thou must overthrow the whole Scripture, and despise Moses and the prophets.'

53.—[*Jesus said ... Verily, verily, I say.*] We come now to one of the most solemn and important sayings that ever fell from our Lord's lips. Having brought the Jews step by step up to this point, he now declares to them the highest and most startling doctrine of the gospel.

[*Except ye eat the flesh ... drink his blood ... no life in you.*] When our Lord uses this phrase 'except' at the beginning of a sentence, we generally find something of more than ordinary importance in it. Thus, 'Except a man be born again,'—'Except ye be converted and become as little children,'—'Except ye repent' (*John* 3:3; *Matt.* 18:3; *Luke* 13:3). Here he tells the Jews that they 'have no life,'—no spiritual life, no title to eternal life; that they are in fact dead, legally dead, spiritually dead, and on the way to the second death, if they do not 'eat the flesh and drink the blood' of the Son of man,—that is of himself. In a word, he lays down the principle that eating his flesh and drinking his blood is a thing not only possible but absolutely *necessary* to salvation,—is a thing without which no man can go to heaven.

Considering that the Jewish passover was nigh at hand, and that many of our Lord's hearers were probably on their way to Jerusalem to attend it, it seems highly probable that our Lord desired to direct the minds of those he addressed to himself as the true passover and sacrifice for sin.

The latent idea of the sentence, I firmly believe, is that first passover in the land of Egypt, which was kept on the night when the first-born were slain. The flesh and blood of the lamb slain that night were the means of life, safety, and deliverance to the Israelites. In like manner, I believe, our Lord meant the Jews to understand that his flesh and blood were to be the means of life and deliverance from the wrath to come to sinners. To a Jewish ear therefore there would be nothing so entirely new and strange in the sentence as at first sight may appear to us. The thing that would startle them no doubt would be our Lord's assertion that eating *his* flesh and drinking *his* blood could be the means of life to their souls, as the flesh and the blood of the passover lamb had been to their fathers the salvation of their bodies.

But what did our Lord mean when he spoke of 'eating his flesh and drinking his blood,' as things indispensably necessary to life? This is a point on which wide differences of opinion prevail, have prevailed in every age of the church, and probably will prevail as long as the world stands.

a. Some think that our Lord meant a literal 'eating and drinking' with the mouth of our bodies, and that the 'flesh and blood' mean the bread and wine in the sacrament of the Lord's supper. This is the opinion of almost all the Fathers, though occasional passages may be pointed out in the writings of some, which seem irreconcilable with it. It is the opinion of most Roman Catholic writers, but certainly not of all. It is the opinion of some modern English divines, such as Wordsworth and Burgon.

b. Some think that the 'eating and drinking' here mean the eating and drinking of heart and soul by faith, not of the body, and that the 'flesh and blood' mean Christ's vicarious sacrifice of his body on the cross. They deny entirely that there is any reference whatever to the Lord's supper in the words. They consider that our Lord meant to teach the absolute necessity of feeding by faith on his atonement for sin on the cross. Except a man's soul lays hold by faith on Christ's sacrifice of his body and blood as the only hope of his salvation, he has no title to or part in eternal life. This is the opinion of Luther, Melanchthon, Zwingle, Calvin, Ecolampadius, Brentius, Gualter, Bullinger, Pelican, Beza, Musculus, Flacius, Calovius, Cocceius, Gomarus, Nifanius, Poole, Cartwright, Hammond, Rollock, Hutcheson, Lightfoot, Henry, Burkitt, Whitby, Leigh, Pearce, Lampe, Gill, Tittman, A. Clarke, Barnes, and most modern divines.

Among Romanist writers, this opinion is held by Cardinal Cajetan, Ferus, and Jansenius of Ghent. Even Toletus, one of the ablest Romanist commentators on John, admits that the opinions of writers are not unanimous.

c. Some think that our Lord did not mean any literal eating and drinking, and that he did not refer directly to the Lord's supper when he spake of his flesh and blood. But they do think that our Lord had the sacrament in view and prospect, when he spoke these words, and that he did tacitly refer to that peculiar communion with his flesh and blood, which he afterwards appointed the Lord's supper to be the means of imparting to believing communicants. This is the opinion, *apparently*, of Trapp, Doddridge, Olshausen, Tholuck, Stier, Bengel, Besser, Scott, Alford, and some others.

I decidedly agree with those who hold the second of these opinions. I believe that our Lord, both in this text and all through this chapter, did not either directly or indirectly refer to the Lord's supper; that by his flesh and blood he did not mean the bread and wine; that by eating and drinking he did not mean any bodily act. I believe that by 'flesh and blood' he meant the sacrifice of his own body for us, when he offered it up as our Substitute on Calvary. I believe that by 'eating and drinking,' he meant that communion and participation of the benefit of his sacrifice which faith, and faith only, conveys to the soul. I believe his meaning to be 'Except ye believe on me as the one sacrifice for sin, and by faith receive into your hearts the redemption purchased by my blood, ye have no spiritual life, and will not be saved.' The atonement of Christ, his vicarious death and sacrifice, and faith in it,—these things are the key to the whole passage. I believe this must be kept steadily in view.

It is easy to call the opinion to which I adhere Zwinglian, and low, and irreverent. Hard words are not arguments. It is easier to make such assertions than to prove them. I have already shown that many writers, wholly unconnected with Zwingle or Zwinglianism, maintain the opinion. But I submit that the following reasons are weighty and unanswerable:—

1. To say that our Lord meant the Lord's supper in this text is a most cruel and uncharitable opinion. It cuts off from eternal life all who do not receive the communion. At this rate all who die in infancy and childhood,—all who die of full age without coming to the communion,—the whole body of the Quakers in modern times,—the penitent thief on the

cross,—all, all are lost for ever in hell! Our Lord's words are stringent and exclusive. Such an opinion is too monstrous to be true. In fact, it was to avoid this painful conclusion that many early Christians, in Cyprian's time, held the doctrine of infant communion.

Ferus, the Roman Catholic commentator, who considers the eating and drinking here to be only spiritual, and not to refer to the sacrament, sees this objection clearly and puts it strongly.

2. To say that our Lord meant the Lord's supper in this text opens a wide door to formalism and superstition. Thousands would wish nothing better than to hear, 'He that eateth my flesh and drinketh my blood (that is eats the sacramental bread and drinks the sacramental wine) has eternal life.' Here is precisely what the natural heart of man likes! He likes to go to heaven by formally using ordinances. This is the very way in which millions in the Romish Church have made and are making shipwreck of their souls.

3. To say that our Lord meant the Lord's supper in the text is to make a thing absolutely necessary to salvation which Christ never intended to be so. Our Lord commanded us to use the Lord's supper, but he never said that all who did use it would be saved, and all who did not use it would be lost. How many hundreds repent and are converted on their death-beds, far away from ministers and sacraments, and never receive the Lord's supper! And will anyone dare to say they are all lost? A new heart and an interest in Christ's cleansing blood are the two things needful to salvation. We must have the blood and the Spirit, or we have no life in us. Without them no heaven! But the Scripture never puts between a sinner and salvation an outward ordinance, over which the poor sinner may have no control, and may be unable to receive it without any fault of his own.

Archbishop Cranmer remarks, in his *Defence of the True Doctrine of the Sacrament*,—'The Romanists say that good men eat the body of Christ and drink his blood, only at that time when they received the sacrament: we say that they eat, drink, and feed on Christ continually, so long as they are members of his body.—They say that the body of Christ which is in the sacrament, hath its own proper form and quantity; we say that Christ is there sacramentally and spiritually without form or quantity.—They say that the fathers and prophets of the Old Testament did not eat the body nor drink the blood of Christ: we say that they did eat his body and drink his blood, although he was not yet born or incarnate.'

Ferus says, 'We must take hold of Christ's flesh and blood, not with our hands, but with our faith. He therefore that believes that Christ has given up his body for us, and has shed his blood for the remission of our sins, and through this places all his hope and confidence in Christ crucified, that man really eats the body and blood of Christ.'

Cardinal Cajetan, quoted by Ford, says, 'To eat the flesh of Christ and to drink his blood is faith in the death of Jesus Christ. So that the sense is this: if ye use not the death of the Son of God as meat and drink ye have not the life of the Spirit in you.'

The opinion which many hold, that although our Lord did not directly mean the Lord's supper in this text, he did refer to it indirectly, and had it in view, seems to me very vague and unsatisfactory, and only calculated to confuse our minds. Our Lord is speaking of something which he says is absolutely and indispensably necessary to eternal life. Where is the use of dragging in an ordinance which is not absolutely necessary, and insisting that he had it in view?—The truth of the matter, I believe, lies precisely in the opposite direction. I believe that *afterwards*, when our Lord appointed the Lord's supper, he had in view the doctrine of this text, and used words intended to remind the disciples of the doctrine. But *here* I believe he was speaking of something far higher and greater than the Lord's supper.—When he spoke of the lesser thing, I have no doubt that he intended to refer to the greater, and to turn the disciples' minds back to it. But when he spoke as he did here of the greater thing, I am quite unable to believe that he intended to refer to the lesser.

If our Lord did really refer to the Lord's supper when he spake of eating his flesh and drinking his blood, it seems impossible to understand how Roman Catholics can deny the cup to the laity. 'Drinking Christ's blood' is distinctly said to be as necessary to eternal life as 'eating Christ's body.' Yet the Romish Church will not allow the laity to drink Christ's blood! It is evidently the pressure of this argument which makes some Roman Catholic writers deny that this passage refers to the sacrament. It is a mistake to suppose that they are unanimous on the point.

Rollock starts the question why our Lord did not plainly tell his hearers that by eating and drinking he meant not a bodily but a spiritual act: viz., believing. He replies, that in this as in every case, our Lord did not strive so much to make men understand *words*, as to beget feeling and experimental acquaintance with *things*. When the heart really begins to feel, words are soon understood.

The distinction that Alford and some others draw between the 'flesh' and 'blood' in this text, appears to me very doubtful. They think that 'eating the flesh' refers generally to participation in the benefits of Christ's incarnation and ascension with a human body into heaven; and that 'drinking the blood' refers specially to an interest in the benefits purchased by his death.—I am not satisfied that this is correct. At verse 57, our Lord speaking briefly of the truth just before enunciated, only says, 'He that eateth me, even he shall live by me.' Surely 'eating' there stands for participation in the benefits of Christ's death as well as life!

My own impression is that both 'flesh and blood' are mentioned here by our Lord to make it certain to the Jews that he spoke of his *death*, and of the offering of his whole body in sacrifice on the cross. The body of the sin-offering was just as essential a part of the sacrifice as the blood (see *Lev.* 4:1-12). So also the body of the passover lamb had to be eaten, as well as the blood sprinkled. The 'flesh and blood' are both mentioned here because our Lord had in view the offering of himself as a sin-offering,—and because he would make it

sure that he meant the 'death' of his body to be the life of man's soul. It is not Christ incarnate merely, but Christ crucified as our atonement and sin-offering, that man must feed upon if he would have life.

54.—[*Whoso eateth … drinketh … eternal life.*] This verse is just the converse of the preceding one. As it had been said that without eating and drinking there was no life, so it is now said that he who eats and drinks has life. These words, as I have already remarked, appear to me to make it impossible to interpret the passage of the Lord's supper. Myriads are communicants who have no spiritual life whatever. Everyone, on the other hand, who by faith feeds his soul on Christ's sacrifice for sin, has even now everlasting life. 'He that believeth on him is not condemned.'—'He that believeth on me hath everlasting life' (*John* 3:18; 6:47).

The word 'whoso' would have been more simply and literally rendered 'he that.'

The 'presentness' of a true Christian's privileges should be remarked here again: 'He hath eternal life.'

The Greek word for 'eateth,' in this verse and verse 56, is quite a different word from that used in verse 53. The reason of the difference is not very clear, and no commentator has hitherto explained it. Leigh, Parkhurst, and Schleusner, all agree that the Greek word used in this verse ordinarily denotes the eating of an animal, in contradistinction to that of a man. Leigh observes that the word 'noteth a continuance of eating, as brute beasts will eat all day, and some part of the night.' I venture to suggest that the word is purposely used, in order to show that our Lord meant the habit of continually feeding on him all day long by faith. He did not mean the occasional eating of material food in an ordinance.

The word is only used in this and verses 56, 57, and 58, and in Matthew 24:38, and John 13:18.

[*I will raise him up at the last day.*] These words are a fourth time repeated, and purposely, in my judgment, to show who they are of whom Christ is speaking. He is not speaking of all who receive the Lord's supper, but of those persons who are 'given to him by the Father,'—'who see the Son and believe on him,'—who 'are drawn by the Father and come to Christ' (John 6:39, 40, 44). These are the same persons who eat his flesh and drink his blood by faith. To them belongs the privilege of a part in that first and glorious resurrection, when Christ shall call his people from the grave at his second coming.

55.—[*For my flesh is meat indeed, and my blood is drink indeed.*] The word 'indeed' here would be more literally rendered 'truly;' and the word 'meat' answers to our word 'food.' The meaning is, 'My flesh is more truly food, and my blood is more truly drink than any other food and drink can be. It is food and drink in the highest, fullest, noblest sense,—food and drink for the soul, food and drink that satisfies, food and drink that endures to everlasting life' (see verse 35).

Rollock remarks that the best way to understand this verse is to make trial of Christ, and to feed on him by faith. We shall soon discover how true the words are.

Ferus suggests that there may be a latent reference here to the forbidden fruit which Satan promised should be 'meat and drink indeed' to Adam and Eve. *This* stands out in contrast to *that* food. By eating the food Satan held out, came sin and death; by eating the food Christ holds out, comes life and heaven.

56.—[*He that eateth my flesh, and drinketh my blood.*] These words are precisely the same as those at the beginning of verse 54; and there is no reason why 'whoso' there, should not have been 'he that,' as here. In the one case, the man who eats and drinks Christ's flesh and blood is said to possess eternal life, and in the other, to be intimately joined to Christ. But it is the same person.

[*Dwelleth in me, and I in him.*] This expression is meant to convey to our minds the close and intimate union that there is between Christ and a true Christian. Such a man is said to dwell, or abide in Christ, and Christ to dwell, or abide in him. Christ is the house, or home or hiding-place, within which the believer's soul, as it were, resides; and Christ dwells in the believer's

heart by his Spirit, comforting, nourishing, and strengthening him. (See 1 John 3:24, and 4:15, 16. See also John 15:4, where 'Abide in me, and I in you,' might have been equally well rendered, 'Dwell in me, and I in you.')

Just as 'food and drink' received into a man's body become part of the man's self, and are incorporated into his system, and add to his health, comfort, and strength,— so when a man by faith feeds his soul on Christ's sacrifice for his sins, Christ becomes as it were part of himself, and he becomes part of Christ. In a word, there is as intimate a union between Christ and the believer's soul as there is between a man's food and a man's body.

57.—[*As the living Father, etc.*] This verse explains the intimate union between Christ and the true believer, by a far higher and more mysterious figure than that of the union of our food and our body. The illustration used is drawn from that unspeakable and inexplicable union which exists between the two first persons in the Trinity,—God the Father and God the Son.—It is as though our Lord said, 'Just as the Father sent me into the world to be born of a woman and take the manhood into God, and yet though I am among you as man I live in the closest union and communion with God,—even so the man that by faith feeds his soul on my sacrifice for sin, shall live in the closest union and communion with me.'—In a word, the union between Christ and the true Christian is as real and true and close and inseparable as the union between God the Father and God the Son.—While the Son was in the world, the carnal eye discerned little or nothing of his union with the Father. Yet it was a true thing and existed. Just so the carnal eye may see little or nothing of the union between Christ and the man who feeds by faith on Christ. Yet it is a real true union.—Just as the Son, though equal to the Father as touching his Godhead, does live in an ineffable and inscrutable way through and by the Father, the Son never being without the Father nor the Father without the Son,—so in like manner the man that feeds on Christ enjoys spiritual life only through and by Christ. Is not this

St Paul's thought: 'I live: yet not I, but Christ liveth in me.'—'To me to live is Christ' (*Gal.* 2:20; *Phil.* 1:21).

Whether our Lord is here speaking of his human nature or of his divine nature, is not quite clear. I incline to think, with Cyril and Chrysostom, that it is the divine nature.

Rollock remarks, that we have three living ones spoken of here. 1. The living Father. 2. The living Son. 3. The living believer. As we are sure of the life of the Father, so we may be sure of the life of the believer. The three lives are linked together.

Hutcheson remarks, 'Christ's living by the Father is not only a pledge of our life, but our life holds also some proportion or similitude to his. For as he hath life communicated by eternal generation, so by regeneration we are made partakers of the divine nature.'

Winer remarks that the Greek preposition rendered 'by,' in this verse, means literally 'on account of;' and that the sentence means, strictly and properly, 'I live owing to the Father:' that is, 'I live because the Father lives.' Schleusner and Parkhurst say much the same.

The 'living Father' is a remarkable phrase. It is like the 'living God' (*John* 6:69; *Acts* 14:15; *Rom.* 9:26; 2 *Cor.* 3:3; 6:16; 1 *Thess.* 1:9; 1 *Tim.* 6:17). It must mean the Father who is the source of life: who hath 'life in himself' (*John* 5:26).

58.—[*This is that bread, etc.*] Here our Lord sums up the whole discourse. He reverts to the saying with which the Jews had begun, about the fathers eating manna in the wilderness, and repeats the main points he would have his hearers carry away. These points were as follows:— 1. That he himself was the true bread which had come down from heaven, to feed the world by the sacrifice of himself. 2. That they must not cling to the idea that their fathers had ever eaten this true bread, for they all died in the wilderness, and their souls received no benefit from the manna. 3. And that those, on the contrary, who would eat of the bread he had come down to give, should live for ever, have everlasting life, and their souls never die.—It is as though he said, 'This sacrifice of myself is the true bread from heaven, of which I spoke at the beginning. The eaters of this bread are in far better circumstances than your fathers when they ate manna in the wilderness. Your fathers died in spite of the manna, and beside that received from it no spiritual benefit whatever. He, on the contrary, who by faith eats the bread of my sacrifice for sin, shall have everlasting life, and his soul shall never die.'—All the expressions in the verse, we should remark, have been used frequently in the discourse, and now all are grouped together, and presented in one view.

59.—[*These things said ... synagogue ... Capernaum.*] This verse is not sufficiently noticed, I venture to think. I ask anyone to compare it with the beginning of the discourse in this chapter, at verse 25: 'When they had found him on the other side of the sea, they said,' etc. Are we to suppose that they found him in the synagogue? I cannot think it. To me it seems that there must have been a slight break or pause in the discourse. It began at the landing-place, or outside the city. It was resumed, after a short interval of a few hours perhaps, in the synagogue. And, as I have said before, the break appears to me to be at verse 41.

Both the discourse of this chapter, and that of the preceding one, have this point in common, that they seem to have been delivered before formal assemblies of Jews.

In concluding the notes on this very important passage, I take occasion to express my entire dissent from the common opinion held by many, that the sixth chapter of John was intended to teach the true doctrine of the Lord's supper, as the third was intended to teach about baptism.—My own opinion is flatly contrary. I hold that in neither chapter are the sacraments referred to at all. I believe that the third chapter was intended to counteract erroneous views about baptism, by teaching the far higher truth of spiritual regeneration; and I believe that the sixth chapter was intended to counteract erroneous views about the Lord's supper, by teaching the far higher truth of the necessity of feeding on Christ's sacrifice by faith.—In fact the true antidote to wrong views of baptism and the Lord's supper, is a right understanding of the third and sixth chapters of St John's Gospel, and the whole of St John's first epistle. Writing, as St John did, the last of all the inspired writers, I believe he was divinely inspired to record things which the church of Christ needed most to know. And I regard it as a most striking fact, that while he altogether omits to describe the institution of the Lord's supper, and says little or nothing about baptism in the Gospel, he dwells at the same time most strongly on these two mighty truths, which he foresaw were in danger of being forgotten: viz., the new birth, and faith in the atonement.—Surely it is possible to honour baptism and the Lord's supper, without thrusting them in everywhere in our interpretation of Scripture.

JOHN 6:60-65

60 Many therefore of his disciples, when they had heard *this*, said, This is an hard saying; who can hear it?

61 When Jesus knew in himself that his disciples murmured at it, he said unto them, Doth this offend you?

62 *What* and if ye shall see the Son of man ascend up where he was before?

63 It is the spirit that quickeneth; the flesh profiteth nothing: the words that I speak unto you, *they* are spirit, and *they* are life.

64 But there are some of you that believe not. For Jesus knew from the beginning who they were that believed not, and who should betray him.

65 And he said, Therefore said I unto you, that no man can come unto me, except it were given unto him of my Father.

WE learn from these verses, that *some of Christ's sayings seem hard to flesh and blood.* We are told that 'many' who had followed our Lord for a season, were offended when he spoke of 'eating his flesh and drinking his blood.' They murmured and said, 'This is an hard saying; who can hear it?'

Murmurs and complaints of this kind are very common. It must never surprise us to hear them. They have been, they are, they will be as long as the world stands. To some Christ's sayings appear hard to understand. To others, as in the present case, they appear hard to believe, and harder still to obey. It is just one of the many ways in which the natural corruption of man shows itself. So long as the heart is naturally proud, worldly, unbelieving, and fond of self-indulgence, if not of sin, so long there will never be wanting people who will say of Christian doctrines and precepts, 'These are hard sayings; who can hear them?'

Humility is the frame of mind which we should labour and pray for, if we would not be offended. If we find any of Christ's sayings hard to understand, we should humbly remember our present ignorance, and believe that we shall know more by and by. If we find any of his sayings difficult to obey, we should humbly recollect that he will never require of us impossibilities, and that what he bids us do, he will give us grace to perform.

We learn, secondly, from these verses, that *we must beware of putting a carnal meaning on spiritual words*. We read that our Lord said to the murmuring Jews who stumbled at the idea of eating his flesh and drinking his blood, 'It is the spirit that quickeneth; the flesh profiteth nothing: the words that I speak unto you, they are spirit, and they are life.'

It is useless to deny that this verse is full of difficulties. It contains expressions 'hard to be understood.' It is far more easy to have a general impression of the meaning of the whole sentence, than to explain it word by word. Some things nevertheless we can see clearly and grasp firmly. Let us consider what they are.

Our Lord says, 'It is the spirit that quickeneth.' By this he means that it is the Holy Ghost who is the special author of spiritual life in man's soul. By his agency it is first imparted, and afterwards sustained and kept up. If the Jews thought he meant that man could have spiritual life by bodily eating or drinking they were greatly mistaken.

Our Lord says, 'The flesh profiteth nothing.' By this he means that neither his flesh nor any other flesh, literally eaten, can do good to the soul. Spiritual benefit is not to be had through the mouth, but through the heart. The soul is not a material thing, and cannot therefore be nourished by material food.

Our Lord says, 'The words that I speak unto you, they are spirit, and they are life.' By this he signifies that his words and teachings, applied to the heart by the Holy Ghost, are the true means of producing spiritual influence and conveying spiritual life. By words thoughts are begotten and aroused. By words mind and conscience are stirred. And Christ's words especially are spirit-stirring and life-giving.

The principle contained in this verse, however faintly we may grasp its full meaning, deserves peculiar attention in these times. There is a tendency in many minds to attach an excessive importance to the outward and visible, or 'doing' part of religion. They seem to think that the sum and substance of Christianity consists in baptism and the supper of the Lord, in public ceremonies and forms, in appeals to the eye and ear, and bodily excitement. Surely they forget that it is 'the spirit that quickeneth,' and that the 'flesh profiteth nothing.' It is not so much by noisy public demonstrations as by the still quiet work of the Holy Ghost on hearts that God's cause prospers. It is Christ's words entering into consciences which 'are spirit and life.'

We learn, lastly, from these verses, that *Christ has a perfect knowledge of the hearts of men.* We read that 'he knew from the beginning who they were that believed not, and who should betray him.'

Sentences like this are found so frequently in the Gospels that we are apt to underrate their importance. Yet there are few truths which we shall find it so good for our souls to remember as that which is contained in the sentence before us. The Saviour with whom we have to do is one who knows all things!

What light this throws on the marvellous patience of the Lord Jesus in the days of his earthly ministry! He knew the sorrow and humiliation before him, and the manner of his death. He knew the unbelief and treachery of some who professed to be his familiar friends. But 'for the joy that was set before him' he endured it all (*Heb.* 12:2).

What light this throws on the folly of hypocrisy and false profession in religion! Let those who are guilty of it recollect that they cannot deceive Christ. He sees them, knows them, and will expose them at the last day, except they repent. Whatever we are as Christians, and however weak, let us be real, true, and sincere.

Finally, what light this throws on the daily pilgrimage of all true Christians! Let them take comfort in the thought that their Master knows them. However much unknown and misunderstood by the world, their Master knows their hearts, and will comfort them at the last day. Happy is he who, in spite of many infirmities, can say with Peter: 'Lord, thou knowest all things; thou knowest that I love thee' (*John* 21:17).

Notes—John 6:60-65

60.—[*Many therefore of his disciples.*] It is plain that these were not true believers. Many who followed our Lord about, and were called his 'disciples,' had no real grace in their hearts, and followed him from carnal motives. We must expect to see the same thing in every age. Not all who come to church, nor all who profess to admire and follow popular preachers, are real Christians. This is far too much forgotten.

[*This is an hard saying.*] This does not mean 'hard' in the sense of being 'difficult to understand.' It is not so much 'hard to the comprehension,' as 'hard to the feelings.' Parkhurst defines it as 'shocking to the mind.' It is the same word that is used in the parable of the talents: 'Thou art an hard man' (*Matt.* 25:24) and in the Epistle of Jude: 'the hard speeches which ungodly sinners have spoken against him' (*Jude* 15).

Some think that the 'hard saying' means the whole discourse. My own opinion is that it refers specially to our Lord's concluding words about eating his flesh and drinking his blood.

[*Who can hear it?*] The 'hearing' here is evidently the hearing so as to believe, receive, and obey. 'Who can believe, receive, and obey such a saying as this?' (See *John* 5:24; 8:43; 10:3, 16, 27; 18:37; *1 John* 4:6.)

61.—[*Jesus knew in himself.*] This means, that he knew by that divine knowledge through which he always 'knew what was in man' (*John* 2:25).

[*His disciples murmured at it.*] This would be more literally rendered 'His disciples are murmuring about this.' He spoke at the very moment of their murmuring.

[*Doth this offend you?*] This means, 'Is this saying of mine a stumbling-block to you? Is the doctrine of eating my flesh and drinking my blood, too humbling a doctrine for your hearts to receive?'

62.—[*What and if ye shall see the Son of man ascend?*] This means, 'What will ye think and say of my ascension into heaven?' What will your feelings be, if you behold this body of mine going up to that heaven from whence I came down? Will you not be much more offended?' (See *John* 3:12.)

The first thing, we must remember, that the Jews 'murmured' about, was our Lord's saying that he 'came down from heaven.' The second thing was, his saying that he would 'give them his flesh to eat.' Both times our Lord's human body was the subject.—Here our Lord asks them what they would think if they saw that same body 'ascending up' into heaven. Even then, after his ascension, they would have to 'eat his flesh, and drink his blood,' if they desired eternal life. What would they think of that? Would they not find it even more difficult to receive and believe?

[*Where he was before.*] This is an expression which no Socinian can explain. It is a clear assertion of the 'pre-existence' of Christ.

Some think, as Olshausen and Tholuck, that our Lord only means generally, 'If you are offended and unbelieving, even now, while I am with you, how much more will ye be, when I go away!' But this is a frigid and unsatisfactory interpretation.

It is fair to say that Stier thinks, with Chrysostom, Cyril, Theophylact, and others, that our Lord did not mean that his ascension would be a greater difficulty to his disciples, but that, on the contrary, it would remove their doubts and weaken the offence which they now felt. Hutcheson and Alford seem to agree with this. But I cannot see it. Stier thinks our Lord implied, 'Then, after my ascension, it will be disclosed to you, how, and in what way, my human corporeity, become heavenly and glorified, may be given to be eaten, and to be drunk' (compare *John* 8:28).

63.—[*It is the spirit, etc.*] This text is, perhaps, one of the most difficult in the Gospel of St John. It is easy to slur it over, and be satisfied with a vague impression that it means 'We are to put a spiritual sense on our Lord's words.' That, no doubt, is a true idea. But when we come to a close examination of the words which compose the verse, I think no one can be satisfied with such a loose interpretation of Scripture. That our Lord's words 'are to be taken spiritually,' may be very true. But to say so, is not to explain the verse.

What is meant by the expression, 'It is the spirit that quickeneth'?

a. Some think that 'the spirit' here means, 'the divine nature of Christ' (as *Rom.* 1:4; *1 Pet.* 3:18), in contradistinction to his human nature, here called his 'flesh' (see *1 Cor.* 15:45). They consider our Lord to mean, 'It is my divine nature, as God, which is the means of communicating spiritual benefit to men. My human nature, as flesh, could of itself, do no good to souls. It is not, therefore, any carnal eating of my flesh that could be of use to you, and I did not mean any such eating.'

This is the opinion of Cyril, Cartwright, Poole, Bishop Hall, Trapp, Toletus, Rollock, Hutcheson, Leigh, Burkitt, Quesnel, Burgon, and Wordsworth.

b. Some think that, 'the spirit' here means 'the Holy Spirit,' the third person of the Trinity. They consider our Lord to mean, 'It is the Holy Spirit who alone can convey spiritual life to the soul of man. The mere eating of flesh, whether my flesh or any other flesh, cannot do good to the inner man. When, therefore, I spoke of "eating my flesh," I did not mean the

bodily act of eating any literal flesh, but a very different kind of eating, and a very different sort of flesh.' This is the opinion of Zwingle, Melanchthon, Calvin, Bucer, Ecolampadius, Pellican, Flacius, Bullinger, Cocceius, Diodati, Piscator, Musculus, Baxter, Lampe, Henry, Scott, Stier, Besser, Alford.

c. Some think that 'the spirit' here means, 'the spiritual doctrine, or sense,' as opposed to 'the letter,' or literal sense of scriptural language (*2 Cor.* 3:6). They consider the sentence to mean, 'It is the spiritual sense of my words, and not the literal, which is quickening, or life-giving to the soul. When I spoke of "my flesh," I did not mean my flesh literally, but my flesh in a spiritual sense. My flesh literally could be of no use to anyone.' This seems to be the opinion of Chrysostom, Theophylact, Euthymius, Brentius, Beza, Ferus, Cornelius à Lapide, Schoettgen, Pearce, Parkhurst, A. Clarke, Faber, Barnes, Webster. But it is not easy to make out clearly, in every instance, what is the precise meaning put on the words, 'the spirit,' by the interpreters who take this third view. There are not a few shades of variety in their opinions.

I must acknowledge that I find it difficult to give a decided opinion on the comparative merits of these three views of the expression before us. There is something to be said for each of the three. On the whole, I think the second and third are more satisfactory than the first; and I incline to prefer the second to the third. But I say this with much hesitation.

Rollock, who holds strongly that 'the spirit' means Christ's divine nature, maintains that 'the flesh' means the whole human nature of Christ. He thinks that the meaning of 'the flesh profiteth nothing' is, that all the works of our Lord's body, whether in life or death,—his fulfilling the law, his sufferings on the cross,—derive their whole efficacy from the union of the two natures. 'It is the divine nature that is life-giving. The human nature, alone and separate from the divine, is useless and unprofitable.' He holds, therefore, that to eat the human nature of Christ alone (i.e., his flesh) could do us no good; as, unless we could eat his divine nature also, it would be unprofitable. He concludes, therefore, that the only eating of Christ that can be useful to the soul, must of necessity be the spiritual eating of faith, and not any carnal eating of the Lord's supper. Hutcheson agrees with this view.

The expression, 'The words that I speak unto you, they are spirit, and they are life,' is just as difficult as the former part of the text. The word 'spirit,' here, at any rate, cannot mean the divine nature of Christ. If it were so taken, the sentence would be unmeaning.—The word 'spirit' must either mean the 'Holy Spirit,' or 'the spiritual sense,' as opposed to the letter. The sentence then might be paraphrased in either of the following ways:— 1. 'The words that I speak to you, received into your hearts and believed, are the Spirit's influence, the ministration of the Spirit, and the Spirit's means of giving you life.' This is Rollock's view. Or else 2. 'The words that I speak unto you are to be taken in a spiritual sense; or, are spiritual words: and, taken in that sense, are life-giving to the soul.'—This is Augustine's view.

I must honestly confess that neither of these explanations is quite satisfactory; but they are the nearest approach I can see to a satisfactory interpretation. The sentence is evidently a concise elliptical one, and it seems impossible to convey it in English, without a paraphrase.

Alford paraphrases the sentence thus: 'The words that I have spoken, viz., the words "my flesh and blood," are spirit and life: spirit, not flesh only; living food, not carnal and perishable.' I venture to think that this explanation is not more precise or satisfactory than either of those I have suggested.

The expression 'The words that I speak unto you,' must probably be confined to the words our Lord had spoken about eating his flesh and drinking his blood, and not referred to the whole discourse.

After all, however difficult and elliptical the sentence before us may be, there is a truth which throws light on it, with which every true Christian must be familiar. It is the words of Christ brought home to the hearts of men by the Spirit, which are the great agents employed in quickening and giving spiritual life to men. The Spirit impresses Christ's words on a man's conscience. These words become the parent of thoughts and convictions in the man's mind. From these thoughts spring all the man's spiritual life. The soul is not benefited by bodily actions, such as eating or drinking, but by spiritual impressions, which the Holy Spirit alone can produce. In producing these spiritual impressions the Spirit specially employs the agency of Christ's 'words,' and hence comes the great principle, that 'his words are spirit and life.'

64.—[*There are some of you that believe not.*] The connection of this sentence with the preceding verses seems to be this: 'The true account of your murmuring and thinking my sayings "hard" is your want of faith. You do not really believe me to be the Messiah, though you have followed me and professed yourselves my disciples. And not really believing in me, you are offended at the idea of eating my flesh and drinking my blood.'

[*Jesus knew from the beginning who ... believed not.*] This is one of the many places which declare our Lord's divine knowledge of all hearts and characters. He was never deceived by crowds and apparent popularity, as his ministers often are. When it says 'from the beginning,' it probably means 'from the beginning of his ministry, and from the time when the unbelieving "many" before him first professed to be his disciples.' Of course our Lord, as God, knew all things 'from the beginning' of the world. But it does not seem necessary to suppose that this is meant here.

Rollock remarks our Lord's example of patient teaching and preaching to all without exception, though he knew that many did not and would not believe. He points out what a pattern it is to ministers. Christ knew exactly who would believe. Ministers do not know.

[*Who should betray him.*] We should not fail to notice in this expression our Lord's marvellous patience in allowing one whom he knew to be about to betray him to be one of his apostles. It was doubtless meant to teach us that false profession must be expected everywhere, and must not surprise us. How much we ought to tolerate and put up with, if our Lord tolerated Judas near him! The pain and sorrow which the foreknowledge of the conduct of Judas must have caused to our Lord's heart, is a circumstance in our Lord's sufferings which ought not to be forgotten.

65.—[*And he said, Therefore said I, etc., etc.*] The connection of this verse seems to be as follows: 'There are some of you that believe not, and that is the reason why I said to you that no man can come to me unless the Father gives him grace to come, and draws his heart to me. The Father has not given you grace, and drawn you to me, and therefore you do not believe.'

JOHN 6:66-71

66 From that *time* many of his disciples went back, and walked no more with him.

67 Then said Jesus unto the twelve, Will ye also go away?

68 Then Simon Peter answered him, Lord, to whom shall we go? thou hast the words of eternal life.

69 And we believe and are sure that thou art that Christ, the Son of the living God.

70 Jesus answered them, Have not I chosen you twelve, and one of you is a devil?

71 He spake of Judas Iscariot, *the son* of Simon: for he it was that should betray him, being one of the twelve.

THESE verses form a sorrowful conclusion to the famous discourse of Christ which occupies the greater part of the sixth chapter. They supply a melancholy proof of the hardness and corruption of man's heart. Even when the Son of God was the preacher many seem to have heard in vain.

Let us mark, in this passage, *what an old sin backsliding is*. We read that when our Lord had explained what he meant by 'eating and drinking his flesh and blood,' 'From that time many . . . went back, and walked no more with him.'

The true grace of God no doubt is an everlasting possession. From this men never fall away entirely, when they have once received it. 'The foundation of God standeth sure.' My sheep 'shall never perish' (2 *Tim.* 2:19; *John* 10:28). But there is counterfeit grace and unreal religion in the church, wherever there is true; and from counterfeit grace thousands may and do fall away. Like the stony-ground hearers, in the parable of the sower, many 'have no root in themselves, and so in time of temptation fall away.' All is not gold that glitters.

All blossoms do not come to fruit. All are not Israel which are called Israel. Men may have feelings, desires, convictions, resolutions, hopes, joys, sorrows in religion, and yet never have the grace of God. They may run well for a season, and bid fair to reach heaven, and yet break down entirely after a time, go back to the world, and end like Demas, Judas Iscariot, and Lot's wife.

It must never surprise us to see and hear of such cases in our own days. If it happened in our Lord's time, and under our Lord's teaching, much more may we expect it to happen now. Above all, it must never shake our faith and discourage us in our course. On the contrary, we must make up our minds that there will be backsliders in the church as long as the world stands. The sneering infidel, who defends his unbelief by pointing at them, must find some better argument than their example. He forgets that there will always be counterfeit coin where there is true money.

Let us mark, secondly, in this passage, *the noble declaration of faith which the Apostle Peter made*. Our Lord had said to the twelve, when many went back, 'Will ye also go away?' At once Peter replied, with characteristic zeal and fervour, 'Lord, to whom shall we go? thou hast the words of eternal life. And we believe and are sure that thou art that Christ, the Son of the living God.'

The confession contained in these words is a very remarkable one. Living in a professedly Christian land, and surrounded by Christian privileges, we can hardly form an adequate idea of its real value. For a humble Jew to say of one whom scribes and Pharisees and Sadducees agreed in rejecting, 'Thou hast the words of eternal life; thou art the Christ,' was an act of mighty faith. No wonder that our Lord said, in another place, 'Blessed art thou, Simon Bar-jona: for flesh and blood hath not revealed it unto thee, but my Father which is in heaven' (*Matt.* 16:17).

But the question with which Peter begins is just as remarkable as his confession. 'To whom shall we go?' said the noble-hearted apostle. 'Whom shall we follow? To what teacher shall we betake ourselves? Where shall we find any guide to heaven to compare with thee? What shall we gain by forsaking thee? What scribe, what Pharisee, what Sadducee, what priest, what rabbi can show us such words of eternal life as thou showest?'

The question is one which every true Christian may boldly ask, when urged and tempted to give up his religion and go back to the world. It is easy for those who hate religion to pick holes in our conduct, to make objections to our doctrines, to find fault with our practices. It may be hard sometimes to give them any answer. But after all, 'to whom shall we go,' if we give up our religion? Where shall we find such peace, and hope, and solid comfort as in serving Christ, however poorly we serve him? Can we better ourselves by turning our back on Christ, and going back to our old ways? We cannot. Then let us hold on our way and persevere.

Let us mark, lastly, in this passage, *what little benefit some men get from religious privileges*. We read that our Lord said, 'Have not I chosen you twelve, and one of you is a devil?' And it goes on, 'He spake of Judas Iscariot, the son of Simon.'

If ever there was a man who had great privileges and opportunities, that man was Judas Iscariot. A chosen disciple, a constant companion of Christ, a witness of his miracles, a hearer of his sermons, a commissioned preacher of his kingdom, a fellow and friend of Peter, James, and John,—it would be impossible to imagine a more favourable position for a man's soul. Yet if anyone ever fell hopelessly into hell, and made shipwreck at last for eternity, that man was Judas Iscariot. The character of that man must have been black indeed, of whom our Lord could say, he is 'a devil.'

Let us settle it firmly in our minds, that the possession of religious privileges alone is not enough to save our souls. It is neither place, nor light, nor company, nor opportunities, but grace that man needs to make him a Christian. With grace we may serve God in the most difficult position,—like Daniel in Babylon, Obadiah in Ahab's court, and the saints in Nero's household. Without grace we may live in the full sunshine of Christ's countenance, and yet, like Judas, be miserably cast away. Then let us never rest till we have grace reigning in our souls. Grace is to be had for the asking. There is One sitting at the right hand of God who has said, 'Ask, and it shall be given you' (*Matt.* 7:7). The Lord Jesus is more willing to give grace than man is to seek it. If men have it not, it is because they do not ask it.

Notes—John 6:66-71

66.—[*From that time.*] It is doubtful whether the Greek words here might not have been better translated, 'Upon this,'— 'After this conversation.'

[*Many of his disciples.*] This expression shows that the number of persons who followed our Lord about, and professed themselves his disciples, must have been large.

[*Went back.*] This is a metaphorical expression, signifying 'retreat, desertion, forsaking a position once occupied.' It is the same that is rendered in the account of the Jews coming to take our Lord in the garden, 'they went backward, and fell to the ground' (*John* 18:6).

[*Walked no more with him.*] The simplest view of this expression is that these deserters from our Lord walked no longer in his company as he went about teaching, as they had done, but returned to their own homes. No minister of the gospel should feel surprised if the same thing happens to him.

Not a few of these very 'disciples' probably had been forward in wishing to make our Lord a 'king,' the day before. Such is popularity: here today and gone tomorrow!

67.—[*Then said Jesus unto the twelve, Will ye also go away?*] We cannot suppose that our Lord asked this as if he did not know what the apostles were going to do. We may be sure that he who 'knew from the beginning who they were that believed not' (v. 64), knew the hearts of his apostles. The question was evidently asked to prove his chosen followers, and to draw forth from them an expression of feeling (see *John* 6:6).

The word 'will' here, would be more accurately rendered, 'Do you wish?' 'Have you a will?'

We should note that this is the first time

St John speaks of 'the twelve.' We know, from the other Gospels, that 'the twelve' were employed in distributing the loaves and fishes to the five thousand (*Luke* 9:12, 16).

68.—[*Then Simon Peter answered him.*] The fervour and impetuosity of Peter's character, come out here as in other places in the Gospels. He is the first to speak, and to speak for his brethren as well as himself. Only the night before this very scene, he had been the first, in the storm on the lake to say, 'Lord, if it be thou, bid me come unto thee on the water' (*Matt.* 14:28). And here, in like manner, he is the first to profess loudly his determination not to go away, and his faith in Christ.

[*To whom shall we go?*] This question is a strong burst of feeling. 'To what teacher, to what master, to what leader shall we go, if we leave thee? Where are we to find anyone like thee? What could we gain by leaving thee?' The question was one which might well be asked, when we remember the state of the Jewish nation, and the universal prevalence of Pharisaism or Sadduceeism. But this is not all. It may always be asked by true Christian men, when tempted to give up Christ's service. True Christianity undoubtedly has its cross. It entails trial and persecution. But to whom shall we go, if we give up Christ? Will infidelity, deism, Socinianism, Romanism, formalism, rationalism, or worldliness give us anything better? There is but one answer! They cannot.

[*Thou hast the words of eternal life.*] This would be more literally rendered, 'Thou hast words of eternal life.' 'Thou possessest instruction about everlasting life, such as we can hear nowhere else, and such as we find soul-comforting and edifying. The sayings that fall continually from thy lips, about eternal life, are such as we cannot leave.' Our Lord's expression should be remembered. 'I have given unto them *the words* which thou gavest me' (*John* 17:8).

69.—[*And we believe and are sure.*] This would be more literally rendered, 'We have believed and have known.' Moreover, the 'we' is emphatic.—'Whatever others may please to think, however many may go away and forsake thee, after following thee for a little, it is not so with us. We have believed and known, and do believe and know.'

[*Thou art that Christ, the Son of the living God.*] This might equally well have been rendered, 'Thou art the Christ.' The sentence is a noble confession, when we remember the time in which it was made, and the universal unbelief of the leaders of the Jewish nation. We may remember that it is precisely the same confession that is recorded to have been made by Peter, after which our Lord said to him, 'Blessed art thou, Simon Bar-jona: for flesh and blood hath not revealed it unto thee, but my Father which is in heaven' (*Matt.* 16:17).

We must not, however, misunderstand the extent of Peter's confession. He declared his faith that our Lord was the anointed Messiah, the Son of the living God. The Messiahship and divinity of Christ were the points on which he and the other apostles laid firm hold. But the sacrifice and death of Christ, and his substitution for us on the cross, were not things which he either saw or understood at present (see *Matt.* 16:22, 23).

a. We should notice that a man's heart may be right towards God, while he remains very ignorant of some great doctrines of the Christian faith. It certainly was so with Peter and the apostles, at this time.

b. We should also notice that there is nothing man is so backward to see as the sacrifice of the death of Christ, the substitution, and the atonement. It is possible to be right about Christ's divinity and Messiahship, and yet be in the dark about his death.

c. We should notice how ignorant Christians often are of the state of others' souls. Peter never suspected any one of the

twelve to be a false apostle. It is a fearful proof that Judas must have been, in all outward demeanour and profession, just like the rest of the apostles.

70.—[*Have not I chosen you twelve?*] I do not think that the 'choosing' here spoken of, means anything more than selection for office. The word is evidently used in this simple sense, in Luke 6:13: 'Of them, he chose twelve, whom also he named apostles.' Acts 6:5: 'They chose Stephen, a man full of faith.' Acts 15:22: 'It pleased the apostles,—to send chosen men of their own company to Antioch.' I say confidently that in each one of these cases the Greek word rendered 'chosen,' the very same word that is used here, can mean nothing more than 'chosen or selected for an office.' This I believe, with Poole, Henry, and Hutcheson, is the meaning here.

I disagree with Alford's remark, that 'the selection of the twelve was the consequence of the giving of them to him by the Father,' and that Christ's 'selecting, and the Father's giving, and the Father's giving and drawing, do not exclude final falling away.'—This remark is built on the gratuitous assumption that Christ's 'choosing,' here spoken of, is the same as that 'choosing unto salvation' which is the special privilege of believers. Of that 'choosing unto salvation,' our Lord speaks in another place, where he carefully draws the distinction between the true disciples and the false: 'I speak not of you all: I know whom I have chosen' (*John* 13:18). Of that choosing unto salvation Judas was not a partaker. Of the other choosing unto office, as in the verse before us, undoubtedly he was a partaker.

Burgon, and many others, agree with Alford, and dwell on the expression before us as an apparent proof that men 'chosen to salvation' may fall away. But their reasoning appears to me inconclusive.

Even Quesnel, the Romanist commentator, remarks, 'The being duly called to the ecclesiastical office is not sufficient, if a man live not suitably to that holy vocation.' Toletus, the Spanish Jesuit, says much the same.

[*One of you is a devil.*] This is a singularly strong expression, and gives an awfully vivid impression of the wickedness of Judas. Of course, he was not literally and really 'a devil,' but a man. The meaning is, 'One out of your number is so completely under the influence of the devil, such a servant of the devil, that he deserves to be called nothing less than a devil.' Our Lord, in another place, says of the wicked Jews, 'Ye are of your father the devil' (*John* 8:44). So St Paul says to Elymas, 'Thou child of the devil' (*Acts* 13:10). When we read at a later period, 'The devil having now put into the heart of Judas Iscariot . . . to betray him' (*John* 13:2), it must mean the final working out of a wicked purpose, which under the influence of the devil Judas had long had in his heart.

Let us note that even now Judas is called 'a devil,' long before our Lord's betrayal and crucifixion. This helps to show that he never was a faithful disciple, even from the first.

Let us note that the only other expression of our Lord that at all approaches the one before us in strength, is the one which on another occasion our Lord applies to his zealous apostle Peter: 'Get thee behind me, Satan' (*Matt.* 16:23). While we condemn the wickedness of Judas, let us not forget that even a true-hearted apostle may so far err and be mistaken that he needs to be sharply rebuked and called 'Satan.' A thoroughly bad man is 'a devil'; but even a good man may need to be called 'Satan!'

Rollock observes that Jesus never used so strong an expression about his open enemies who went about to slay him. It was a hypocrite and a false apostle whom he called 'a devil.' Nothing is so wicked as false profession.

71.—[*He spake of Judas Iscariot, the son of Simon.*] The word 'Iscariot,' according to some, means 'a man of Kerioth.' Kerioth was a town of Judah (*Josh.* 15:25).— According to others, it means 'a man of Issachar.'—According to Lampe, and others, it is a Syriac word, meaning 'the bearer of the purse.'—We are told that he 'had the bag' (*John* 13:29).

It is remarkable that St John four times in his Gospel calls Judas 'the son of Simon.' We do not exactly know why, unless it is that Simon was a person well known by name, or that St John wished to make it quite clear that Judas Iscariot was not St Jude, the faithful apostle and cousin of Christ, by naming his father. There is no proof whatever that Judas was the son of 'Simon the Canaanite,' the apostle; though it is somewhat curious that in the list of apostles given by Matthew and Mark, Simon and Judas Iscariot are named in close juxtaposition (*Matt.* 10:4; *Mark* 3:18-19).

[*He it was that should betray him.*] This would be more literally rendered, 'He was about to betray him.' The expression seems to imply that to betray such a master as Christ was so eminently a work of the devil that the betrayer ought to be spoken of as 'a devil.'

The frequency of our Lord's warnings and hints addressed to Judas Iscariot is very remarkable. Rollock observes what an awful proof it is of the hardness of the heart that a man so warned should not be conscience-stricken and repent.

END OF VOLUME 1